British Business Policy:
A Casebook

By the same editors

John M. Stopford (*with L. T. Wells Jr*)
Managing the Multinational Enterprise

Derek F. Channon
The Strategy and Structure of British Enterprise
British Banking Strategy and the International Challenge
The Service Industries: Strategy, Structure and Financial Performance
Multinational Strategic Planning (with Michael Jalland)

BRITISH BUSINESS POLICY: A CASEBOOK

JOHN M. STOPFORD, DEREK F. CHANNON

and

DAVID NORBURN

M

Selection and Preface © John M. Stopford,
Derek F. Channon and David Norburn 1975

Copyright in the individual chapters is shown at the opening of each

All rights reserved. No part of this publication may be reproduced or transmitted, in any form or by any means, without permission

First edition 1975
Reprinted 1979

Published by
THE MACMILLAN PRESS LTD

London and Basingstoke
Associated companies in Delhi
Dublin Hong Kong Johannesburg Lagos
Melbourne New York Singapore Tokyo

Printed in Great Britain by
Unwin Brothers Limited
The Gresham Press
Old Woking, Surrey
A member of the Staples Printing Group

ISBN 0 333 17718 5 (paperback)

The paperback edition of this book is sold subject to the condition that it shall not, by way of trade or otherwise, be lent, resold, hired out, or otherwise circulated without the publisher's prior consent, in any form of binding or cover other than that in which it is published and without a similar condition including this condition being imposed on the subsequent purchaser

This book is sold subject to the
standard conditions of the
Net Book Agreement

Contents

Preface		vii
Acknowledgements		ix
1	Tizer Limited (A) J. M. STOPFORD and P. EDMONDS	1
2	Tizer Limited (B) J. M. STOPFORD	15
3	Weiss Konstruktion GmbH D. F. CHANNON	23
4	The European Automobile Industry D. F. CHANNON	28
5	The Air Inclusive Tour Holiday Industry D. L. WRIGHT	47
6	Thomson Holiday Holdings (A) D. L. WRIGHT and J. M. STOPFORD	56
7	Thomson Holiday Holdings (B) J. M. STOPFORD	71
8	Croydon Chemicals Company Ltd J. M. STOPFORD	87
9	Big Buy Supermarkets (A) D. F. CHANNON and B. CROWE	104
10	Big Buy Supermarkets (C) D. F. CHANNON and B. CROWE	121
11	Makepiece Company E. P. LEARNED, adapted by J. M. STOPFORD	134
12	Barry McKenzie J. M. STOPFORD and P. EDMONDS	136
13	Michael Parsons S. D. THOMAS	145
14	Crown Company E. P. LEARNED, adapted by S. D. THOMAS	150
15	Burton Group Limited D. JONES and D. F. CHANNON	152
16	Reed International Limited A. MESULACH, J. LEHRER and S. WOOD	172
17	Norcros Limited D. F. CHANNON	191
18	Lonrho D. ROBINSON and D. F. CHANNON	208
19	Slater Walker Securities (A) D. F. CHANNON	228
20	Slater Walker Securities (B) D. F. CHANNON	250

Preface

This book deals with the problems of general managers as they face decisions about the future of their firms. Because there is no general theory of the firm that provides a standard frame of reference for resolving all the issues of general management, the book is in the form of a series of case studies. By observing the experience of others, one can learn about the judgements that a successful manager must make, and create an analytical perspective for the appropriate framework for decision in each situation.

The general management perspective gained from the exercise of judgement is important not only for those who aspire to be general managers, but also for those who work in specialist capacities and who need to understand the decisions and pressures in other parts of the firm. Such a perspective is also important to outside advisers, such as consultants, financial analysts and bankers. In the modern mixed economy in Britain, civil servants are increasingly involved directly in business; they too need a general management perspective.

The cases are all current and reflect the industrial and organisational issues of the 1970s. Most of them describe British firms. The book thus goes some way towards filling the long felt need for reducing the reliance in British business schools on United States materials. We have carefully chosen cases that together provide the basis for a complete introductory course in Business Policy, General Management or Corporate Strategy for students at many levels.

A wide variety both of industries and of types of firm is portrayed. There are manufacturing firms in electronics, textiles, chemicals, paper, printing, cars, construction and soft drinks. The service sector is represented by firms in retailing, package holidays, and financial services. The strategies of these firms range from concentration on a narrow product line to conglomerates, spanning many industries. Some of the firms are small, some medium-sized, and some are multi-million pound giants. Although most of the firms are operating primarily in Britain, a few have expanded abroad and are clearly numbered among the so-called multinational corporations. The primary focus is on the management of change in firms as a whole, but a few cases highlight the personal situations and influences of individual managers. All but two of the cases are based on actual situations. In a few instances however the names have been disguised at the firms' request. The two exceptions, the Makepiece and the Crown cases, are adaptations of cases originally written at the Harvard Business School. While it is generally important for the purposes of learning about management to work with actual events, the two situations described apply just as much to contemporary British management as they did to United States management in the past. In writing and selecting the cases, we have avoided labelling them in terms of the specific issues raised. It is just as important to learn how to recognise a problem as it is to resolve one. The variety of issues in the cases is no more than a means to the end of extending the students' range of skills and understanding of general management.

We have taught these cases on a wide variety of courses at the London and Manchester Business Schools, including the M.Sc. and M.B.A. Programmes, the middle and senior level executive programmes and short specialist courses. Many of these cases have also been taught in other universities, polytechnics, colleges of further education, in-house company programmes, both in Britain and abroad. They have been tested in the classroom and polished in the light of the reactions from both students and practitioners.

All but one of the cases are published here for the first time. They have all, with four exceptions, been written solely or jointly, by one of us. In writing some of these cases we have been ably assisted by Michael Balfe, Bruce Crowe, Peter Edmonds, David Jones, Joe Lehrer, Steve Wood, David Robinson, and David Wright. We are especially grateful for the major contributions made by Avi Mesulach in writing the Reed International case; Denis Thomas in the Michael Parsons case; David Wright in developing large portions of the cases in the holiday business; and Edmund P. Learned in the original versions of the Crown and Makepiece cases.

The encouragement of our colleagues and the partial financial support generously provided by the administrations of both the London and Manchester Business Schools is gratefully acknowledged. Our thanks go especially to the many managers whose firms are described. Their active encouragement provided the spur for us to undertake the work, and their willingness to allow others to learn from their own experience made this book possible.

John Stopford
Derek Channon
David Norburn

April 1975

Acknowledgements

We are grateful to the following for permission to reproduce copyright material: Extel Statistical Services Ltd, 37/45 Paul Street, London EC2A 4PB, for exhibits in Chapters 2, 18 and 19; the *Financial Times* for excerpts in Chapter 7; the *Guardian* for excerpts in Chapter 17 and the map in Chapter 18; Bernard Hollowood for the cartoon in Chapter 7; Moodies Services Ltd for the exhibit in Chapter 17; *The Times* and *Sunday Times* for excerpts in Chapter 7.

1 Tizer Limited (A)*

In the spring of 1972 Mr P. Quinn described to the casewriter his move from Polyfoil Ltd, an aluminium foil manufacturer, to Tizer Ltd, the soft drinks manufacturer. Mr Quinn had been the general manager of Polyfoil Ltd, a subsidiary of Alcan Ltd, until February 1970, when he assumed the position of managing director of Tizer Ltd. Mr Quinn was reviewing both his evaluation of Tizer prior to joining the company, and his subsequent approach to the task of returning the company to a position of profitability.

THE SOFT DRINKS INDUSTRY

In 1970 the total value of the British soft drinks market was in excess of £200 millions. From 1963 through to 1969, the value of this soft drinks market had been increasing at a rate of 9.1 per cent per annum. Within the soft drinks business, there were three major product areas,

1. Concentrated soft drinks—squashes—need to be diluted before drinking
2. Mixers—soft drinks and fruit juices—generally to be added to spirits and alcoholic drinks
3. Carbonated soft drinks—e.g. lemonade, Coca-Cola.

By 1968 concentrated soft drinks represented 54 per cent of the total market, and unconcentrated soft drinks 46 per cent. The market for concentrated soft drinks had grown faster than that for unconcentrated soft drinks (from 1963 production of unconcentrated soft drinks had grown at 4 per cent per annum).

There were two main types of carbonated soft drinks

1. Branded products—e.g. Schweppes, Coca-Cola, Pepsi, etc. Products being sold under a manufacturer's or brand name.
2. Commodity products—e.g. lemonade, limeade, dandelion and burdock, etc. These products were not sold under a brand name, and this had resulted in fierce price competition between local drink manufacturers, with resultant narrow profit margins.

Immediately after the war, there were some 2000 companies manufacturing soft drinks. By 1969 this number had been reduced to between 500 and 600, due to intense competition. Many of the companies that went out of business were small regional companies serving local markets who had not the resources to withstand competition from the major manufacturers. Within the concentrated soft drinks market in 1968, there were four major companies controlling 55 per cent of the market: Schweppes, Beechams, Reckitt and Colman, and Unilever. For the unconcentrated soft drinks market, the major market shareholders were Corona (20 per cent), Schweppes (10 per cent), Coca-Cola (8 per cent), Pepsi-Cola (7 per cent), CWS (6 per cent), Whites (5 per cent) and Tizer (3-4 per cent). Most of the major companies retailed their products on a national basis. With their large financial resources, they were in a position to invest in the latest high-speed bottling plants, as well as in advertising and promotion. In the retail chains and supermarkets, this gave them a significant advantage against the local manufacturers in competing for shelf space.

Sales of soft drinks had traditionally been made through local 'corner shop' retail outlets. However, during the 1960s the pattern of demand had significantly changed with the advent of supermarkets, chain and self-service stores. National chain stores and supermarkets were able to buy in bulk from the major soft drinks manufacturers to the disadvantage of the small local manufacturers. The small local manufacturer had difficulty in serving the national chains, and also in competing in price with the major soft drinks manufacturers on bulk ordering. Off-licences had also been a traditional

---

* Copyright © London Business School 1972

retail outlet for the soft drinks manufacturers. Acquisition by brewing companies of soft drinks manufacturers had, however, resulted in many of the off-licences being tied to the brewers' products. Thus the opportunities for small manufacturers to gain access to the high volume retail outlets (with the consequent lowering of distribution costs) had been limited.

Immediately prior to 1970 there had also been significant changes in the type of packaging used for the products. Supermarkets and chain stores did not want returnable bottle sales. The result was an expansion in the use of cans, plastic cup drinks, and one-trip bottles: can production of soft drinks increased from 300 million units in 1967 to 450 million units in 1970; and sales of soft drinks in one-trip bottles increased from 180 million units in 1968 to 363 million units in 1970. Furthermore, the use of newer materials in packaging led to changes in the package design and in the advertising carried on the packages.

TIZER LIMITED (Pre-1970)

Tizer Ltd was founded in 1933 as a manufacturer of soft drinks. Over the years the company grew and established itself as a major manufacturer of carbonated soft drinks sold in returnable bottles. By the early 1960s Tizer was operating twenty-one depots spread across the country. These regional depots combined both production and regional sales departments in all but one of the depots.

In 1969 Tizer's major products were still the carbonated soft drinks sold under the trade names of Tizer and Jusoda. These products were sold in three different sizes of returnable bottle, i.e. 6 oz., 25 oz., and 40 oz. The company also manufactured a line of concentrated cordials under the trade name of Nectose, in order to enter the fast-expanding concentrated soft drinks market. A franchise agreement had recently been made with the American Royal Crown Cola Company to permit Tizer to enter the cola market, which represented over 20 per cent of the UK carbonated soft drinks market. Tizer did not produce soft drinks in cans or paper cups and nearly all sales of carbonated drinks were in returnable bottles. The company had invested approximately £1 million in bottles and boxes.

Exhibit 1 (see end of case study) identifies the organisational structure of the company as of 1969. The company operated on a regional basis. Each depot/branch operated within an assigned geographic territory. Each branch manager was in charge of a production facility, a storage facility, a group of van drivers/salesmen, a fleet of vehicles and an administrative staff. Most of the managers were men who had originally been van drivers/salesmen, and had risen through the ranks to assume their current positions.

Because no single branch manufactured a full product line, it was necessary to 'trunk' products by lorry from one branch to another to try to maintain adequate supplies at each branch. Trunking became very critical each summer at the height of the seasonal demand, to prevent stockouts and loss of sales. The production equipment at the branches was, in many cases, quite old and of a design incompatible with modern bottling equipment. Therefore the branches were dependent on the head office engineering department for parts and major servicing overhauls.

The company as a whole owned a fleet of 560 vehicles in varying states of repair and these were assigned to particular branches. The vehicles were used for trunking as well as for the supplying of retail outlets. Selling was undertaken at each branch by a team of van drivers/salesmen who sold direct to retail outlets. Tizer had traditionally sold to the small retail outlets and each driver had his own route and accounts to which he sold. Sales were made to the retailers either on a direct cash transaction or a credit sale basis, by the van driver/salesman. The tasks of the salesman included loading the vehicle, making rounds, cashing in his takings at the branch on completion of the rounds, checking the remaining stocks on the lorry as well as off-loading empties collected on the round. The van drivers/salesmen were paid commission on sales; different products had different commission rates which could be adjusted depending on whether any particular product was being promoted.

The operating performance of the company deteriorated through the 1960s. Whilst sales turnover had remained nearly constant at £3 million per annum since 1961, profitability fell from 1963 onwards. In 1969 profit after tax fell drastically from £133,355 to £29,986 (see Exhibit 2). At this stage, representatives of an institutional shareholder intervened and insisted that a new managing director be found from outside the company. The services of a management selection consultant were engaged, and in February 1970 Mr P. Quinn became managing director of Tizer Ltd.

QUINN'S EVALUATION OF TIZER LIMITED

Many people ask what makes a person leave the security and prospects of a well-paid job with one of the world's biggest industrial groups to take on such a hot seat. The answer is simple: I saw in Tizer a very challenging situation; a situation with some good assets that could provide the foundation of a long-term recovery. When I was at Alcan, I had already successfully turned round a subsidiary in a similar position.

Prior to my applying for the position, I had made a detailed study of available (1968) financial reports so that I could make up my mind whether the company could be turned around. People who fail in such turnaround situations are liable to carry the tag with them through their careers.

My accounting qualification helped me to analyse some of the more fundamental problems. I felt that a staff of 1375 people should be producing more than £3 million sales. Sundry debts had been allowed to increase from £212,206 in 1967 to £288,933 in 1968 in a period of declining sales. The company also had a very high level of liquid assets, which could have been invested elsewhere to reduce the operating costs. The level of depreciation of the fixed assets at approximately 66 per cent suggested that much of the equipment was fairly old; even without knowing Tizer's method of depreciation. Why were some of the liquid assets not being invested in equipment to spur sales? In the reserves and surplus, six reserves were being held, as against the three one would expect to find, i.e. capital, revenue, profit and loss. The number of reserves suggested either little financial faith in the business or a lack of planning. Dividend and sales promotion expenses should be deducted out of current profitability not past profit. (Exhibits 3 and 4 provide financial details for 1967 and 1968.)

Looking at the fixed assets, there were no indications of the true value of the assets; however, I assumed that if the plant and equipment was not worth as much as stated, then the property was worth more. Hence the net worth of the company was probably reasonably represented. Even so half the net worth of the company was in property and the return on assets was down to 4 per cent. The company was making no use of debt and all these factors indicated that the company's assets were lying 'fallow' whilst the plant was running down. The money should have been in working capital, transport and bottling equipment. There was, moreover, no shortage of assets with which to turn the company around.

Some of the comments in the Chairman's Report (Exhibit 5) raised serious questions in my mind, for example: 'I am reluctant to forecast trading prospects for 1969, because the soft drinks industry is so susceptible to variations in the weather.... The company experienced difficult personnel relations in distribution.'

I looked at the problems in general management terms, because I felt that my general management experience with Alcan would be relevant. There were similarities between Polyfoil and Tizer; the biggest common point was in marketing. Foil is sold to the consumer through the grocery trade, which has its own methods of buying. You sell it with consumer advertising and consumer promotional support. Tizer products are largely sold through the grocery and food trades to the same buyers with a similar marketing approach. Tizer products are, of course, also sold through other retail outlets.

In both cases, the products are being sold in literally millions of units at very low prices; this demands a certain frame of mind. A man who is used to selling huge capital items valued at hundreds of thousands of pounds cannot think in terms of the other end of the scale where you are selling millions of items at pennies a time. The total over the year may be the same, but it demands a different approach to business.

From an external analysis, I considered Tizer to have a major strength in the market awareness of the Tizer name; however, from a marketing angle, I was aware that the real growth areas were in non-returnable bottles, cans, squashes, and the multiple stores. Tizer was not pursuing any of these areas.

I feel that managers often make mistakes in changing companies. They move to companies involved in an unfamiliar business and then they find that, although the general management skills and responsibilities are the same, they cannot be applied in quite the same way. You have got to know something about the business you are in before dealing with the general management responsibilities of creating policies, creating a management structure, setting up budgets, and controlling performance against those budgets.

Parts of the job were, of course, new to me. Tizer as a public company had 4,000 shareholders, and this clearly meant involvement in financial public relations work with the shareholders. There was an obvious need to convince the shareholders that Tizer was worth sticking with. The public relations work would also have to be designed to have a secondary appeal to the trade. There was undoubtedly a lot of thought in the trade two years ago that Tizer was a dead company, and that there wasn't any point in continuing to buy from Tizer because it was going out of existence. It would be necessary to create more confidence in the company so that buyers would feel the company was going to stay in business, and that it would be worth supporting.

Another new area was in terms of labour relations. Almost 100 per cent of Tizer employees were members of unions and the unions were fairly militant. Tizer, in the year before I joined, had had a very sorry record of strikes and industrial strife, particularly within the sales organisation. My involvement in Alcan in labour relations had been at second hand.

IMMEDIATE ACTIONS

On arrival at Tizer, I felt as chief executive that I had four priority tasks to be discharged. They were

(a) to define the true nature of the company's business

(b) to create a company strategy and plan

(c) to build a strong team of people

(d) to set up and measure performance objectives to achieve that plan.

Ideally these tasks are sequential. However, in practice, you have to deal with them concurrently at times.

To define the true nature of the company's business for a marketing orientated company like Tizer really means starting at the marketing end. What are your markets, who are your customers, and what are they buying from you? If you assume that they are buying satisfactions from you rather than physical products, what are these satisfactions? Although it sounds good to say that one starts off with the market and the consumer, I think basically that you are trying to compare and so you initially require a basis for comparison. Very often one must contrast the most and the least successful firms in your business. What are the successful firms doing that is giving them success, and what are the unsuccessful firms doing that is causing problems? What is successful about Coke or Corona on the one hand, and unsuccessful about our small local competitors?

Tizer as a company lined up much more with the local competitors. It was, in effect, a series of twenty or so branches, all of which were small local operators rather than a cohesive national company operating in a similar manner to Coke or Corona. Coke seemed to have identified with the satisfaction area of soft drinks; what sells Coke is not that it is a better soft drink, but the whole aura around the product. Corona, in contrast, does not have the same image, but its strength lies in a much greater national identity, an efficient network, central objectives and standard operating methods—in other words, a rational, national approach to the business.

Having made these external comparisons, one can identify why people are buying your product and which people should be buying your product. Then it is possible to define the type of sales and marketing organisation required to reach this market, and the people required to manage that organisation. When making such comparisons and evaluations, it is impossible to be totally objective; you are bound to apply your own personal standards to some extent. The difference between success and lack of success is presumably whether your personal standards happen to be successful standards. There's a lot of timing and luck involved in business success—being in the right place at the right time—and if you are in tune with current market needs, you are far more likely to be successful than if you are out of tune. Tizer's method of doing business through regional production plants selling to small local retail outlets was very much out of tune with the needs of the seventies.

When determining the true nature of the company's business, it is important to evaluate your own management team. If you are to be successful you have to have the right team as soon as possible. This process of evaluation is in many ways judgemental. There are, of course, practical aspects like the setting of objectives and assessing performance against those objectives. If you agree an objective with a manager and it is not attained then there is cause for anxiety. If the pattern is repeated then you have to replace him. However, an evaluation of this nature presents two problems

1. Information systems tend to be based on accounting, and not all operations can be transplanted into accounting terms.
2. The higher the management level, the longer the time span required to evaluate a manager against objectives.

The major measure to me was a man's ability to get results, to get things done. If they failed to achieve results due to an inability to cope with elementary techniques of management, they had to be suspect. Clearly another point to consider is the ability of the management to function as a team. If, as was certainly the case with Tizer, there is obvious evidence of conflict among the board members, then changes have to be made.

My evaluation of the existing management team included branch managers. One of my first priorities was to visit all the branches and branch managers and see them personally two or three times so that I would have some personal knowledge of some fifty or sixty people in the company. My personal evaluation only went as far as branch managers, because beyond that level there would be just too many people to know, and also because there is a very strong case for saying that the branch manager is the critical level of management. Our first real line manager ought to be the supervisor, but they have not, in the past, been given a lot of management responsibilities. In fact, they can only basically influence sales level, which, although very important, is not necessarily a management function.

Whilst evaluating the branch managers, I also had the opportunity to appraise the physical assets of the company. There were obviously some very fundamental changes needed in the physical assets, but it would have been a waste of effort to try to do too much internally until we were satisfied that we had a position in the market. Relocation of the physical assets of the company could not be considered until we had determined where our market was.

The evaluation of the company's financial position was another major area. Again you cannot accurately evaluate whether your financial resources are adequate for the job until you know, at least, in outline, what your commitments are going to be. However, one has got to have some criteria for assessment before looking at the details. If you are in a heavy industrial situation, you may require £1 of capital for £1 of sales. Now, the lighter your business becomes, the less capital you need per £1 of sales, so that when you finally get down to retailing, you can do your turnover with a minus capital. Companies like Tesco realised years ago that they could do turnover with a minus capital, and therefore the more branches they opened the more money came in.

Looked at in this way, Tizer's turnover of £3 million was not enough from a company that had a net worth of £2½ million. On general principles, in this business, £2½ million net worth of company should support at least £5 million, and possibly as much as £10 million turnover. When I realised that 50 per cent of Tizer's net worth was in property, I felt immediately that for a trading company far too much of the company's net worth was in property. However, this did not mean that if the company were to run short of cash for trading, there would be property available for conversion into cash.

Having made these evaluations of the company, marketing emerged as the one critical area to the development of a strategy. As a consumer product manufacturer, it was essential to have a lot of market information and a strong marketing team. I brought in a consulting group to provide me with the market information which I did not have the time, nor the company the skills, to obtain. If you know what the market is for each product, you can then determine how to sell it, how to produce it, and how to finance that production.

The determination of the objectives for the company inevitably, I suppose, comes back to financial terms. One definition I had was 'Profit is not the name of the game, but it is the score'. Thus we were not in business to make a profit, but it was merely telling us how well we were doing in our business. The influence of shareholders in determining a financial objective is clearly that, in order to keep them happy, you have to provide dividend income and sheer capital growth. To do so, you have to ensure that the objectives established are adequate for them. However, the financial objective set to meet shareholders' needs must also be a realistic target for the company to reach.

Clearly, when I came to the company, there were in a situation that did not satisfy the shareholders, and it was also clear that it was going to take some time. My initial assessment was that it would take three years, not necessarily to satisfy our shareholders, but at least to make them feel that we would substantiate a promise.

To determine the shareholders' opinion in Tizer's case, I spoke to half a dozen major shareholders who held 35-40 per cent of the total shareholding. From these people I got a reading of what the opinion of that major body was, although obviously I could not solicit the opinion of 4,000 individual shareholders.

Having identified their expectations, there was then the question of determining how far one could meet their needs without it proving detrimental to the ongoing business. With a known difficult position to be negotiated over the next two or three years, the more money that could be available internally the better. However, the responsibility to the shareholders, the need to keep them and try to give them confidence in the company's future, all pointed to payment of a dividend. If we had not had to worry about shareholders, we could have made investments with long-term paybacks; instead we had to think of short-term returns. We might have spent £3-400,000 on advertising as an investment for the future. It would, however, have been a risk investment, and one can only assume that, had the shareholders been asked to choose, they would not have chosen that sort of risk. The same approach applies in terms of fixed assets. With our very dilapidated vehicle fleet, we had to adopt a policy of replacing it progressively over a 3-4 year period, even though we had the cash to do it straight away.

All the shareholder and business constraints are finally accommodated in the routine function of budgeting, in order to arrive at one financial objective. The budgetary system should be flexible enough for the budgets to be adjusted to the various activities that are going on which were not originally allowed for, and at the same time still produce an acceptable end result, bearing in mind the total work to be done. The final figure came about by massaging the figures from a 'top-down' and 'bottom-up' budgetary process until they finally agreed. Basically, the function of budgeting is an allocation of resources, and you allocate resources to achieve what you feel is the optimum result within the external circumstances. The allocation of resources has to be fitted in to a time framework, and in my view the chronic sickness of the company meant taking a fairly long view of this. Really we had to say what we wanted to achieve in 3-5 years' time. How do we set about it? What is the shortest time period in which we can achieve a satisfactory result? How do we achieve it? Within this sort of framework, you can start setting up short term objectives. Even if you do know what your end objectives are going to be in detail, you still tend to come back to the fact that in the early stages you have got to have a budget of some sort. Part of the art of management is stretching people to do more than they think they can produce, and a budgetary system allows you to state objectives that are going to stretch them.

The above outlines much of the process by which I set about returning Tizer to a position of profitability.

EXHIBIT 1   Tizer Limited.   Organisational Chart

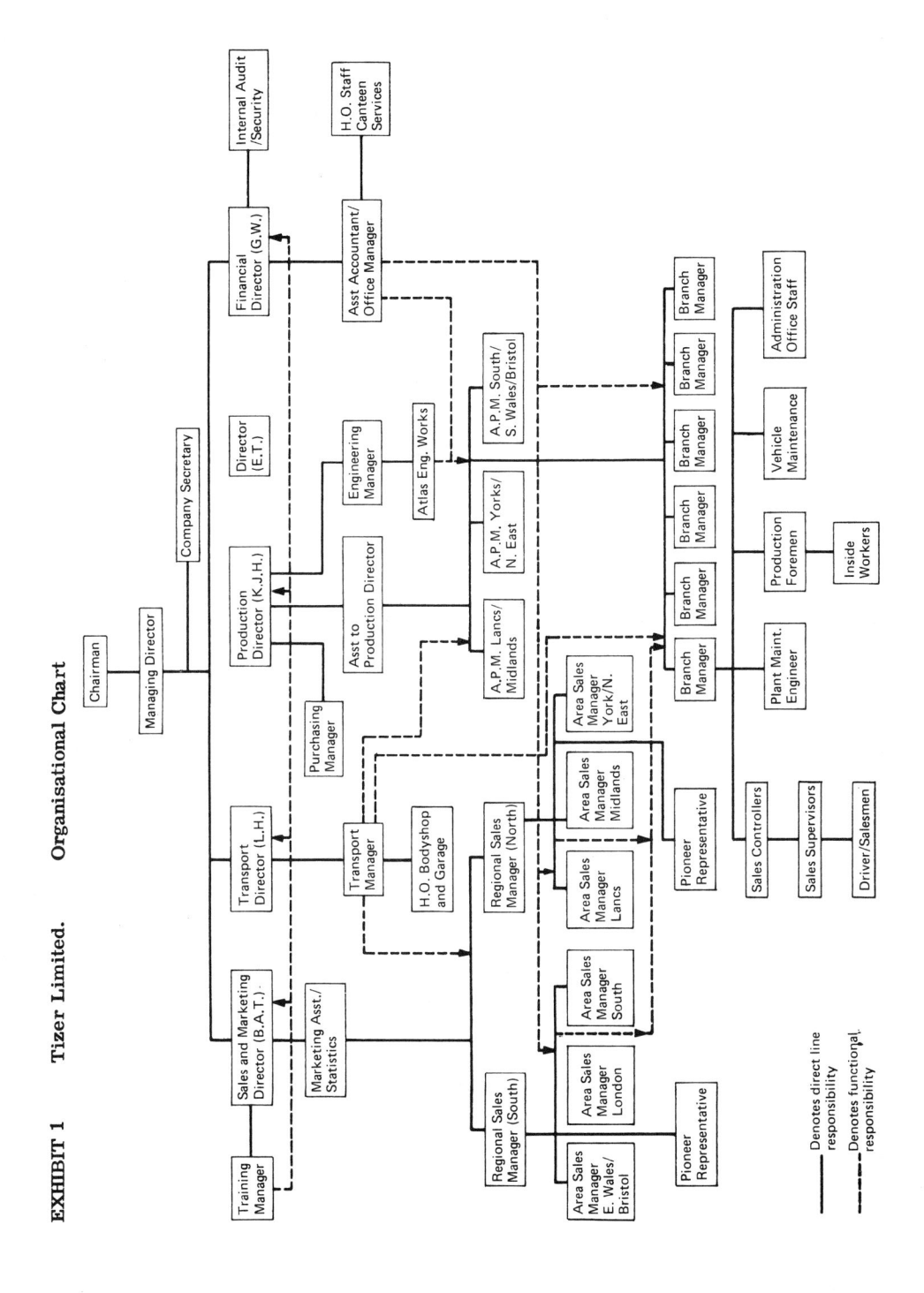

EXHIBIT 2   Tizer Limited.

Excerpts from Extel card (up-dated to 26.5.70)

MINERAL WATER AND CORDIAL MANUFACTURERS

Co. was formed to acquire following businesses engaged in manufacture and distribution of mineral waters, botanic beers, cordials, non-alcoholic wines and vinegar. Co. has an agreement with Royal Crown Cola Co. of Columbus Georgia, to bottle and sell Royal Crown Cola in Great Britain.

SUB. COS: Hampshire Mineral Water Co. Ltd, (Mineral Water Manufacturers); Our Boys Mineral Water Co. Ltd, and Rider Wilsons Table Waters Ltd (ceased to trade during 1969); Hills Chapman Ltd (property Co.).

DIRECTORS: F. Hindle (Chairman); P. Quinn, (Managing Director); L. Hilton, E. Taylor, B. A. Taylor, G. Wilkinson, K. J. Hammer, MBE, E. D.

DIRECTORS' INTERESTS in Ord. shares of Co. at 31.12.69: Beneficial 15,941: as trustees 850,000.

CONSOLIDATED PROFIT AND LOSS ACCOUNT

Year ended 31 Dec	Turnover* £000	Divs & Int. recd £	Net profit before tax £	Total tax £	Net profit after tax £
1960	a	27,065	494,542	231,139	263,403
1961	a	33,104	619,571	303,381	316,190
1962	a	30,048	480,596	219,405	261,191
1963	a	31,853	598,160	293,561	304,599
1964	a	36,727	567,471	246,646	320,825
1965	a	47,047	438,588	134,967	303,621
1966	a	45,194	443,760	171,421	272,339
1967	a	41,682	361,112	157,551	203,561
1968	2,984	41,810	231,840	98,485	133,355
1969	2,949	47,657	60,111	30,125	29,986

Year ended 31 Dec	% on ordinary, less tax		Retained profit for year £	Depn £	Av. no employees
	Earned	Paid			
1960	43.0	Int 7½ Fin 17½ Bon 2½	94,966	87,747	a
1961	51.6	Int 7½ Fin 17½ Bon 2½	147,753	92,585	a
1962	42.6	Int 7½ Fin 17½ Bon 2½	92,753	98,398	a
1963	49.7	Int 7½ Fin 17½ Bon 7½	105,537	136,135	a
1964	54.3	Int 7½ Fin 17½ Bon 17½	69,262	131,304	a
1964	j39.5				
1965	30.4	Int 7½ Fin 17½ Bon 2½	e28,621	131,746	a
1966	27.2	Int 7½ Fin 17½ Bon 2½	M 2,661	133,304	a
1967	20.4	Int 7½ Fin 17½	M46,439	122,093	a
1968	13.3	Int 7½ Fin 7½	M16,645	102,609	kl, 360
1969	3.0	Int Nil Fin 7½	M45,014	92,181	kl, 360

* Excluding purchase tax. (a) Not disclosed. (e) Dividends deducted gross (Income Tax retained £30,937). (j) Estimated earnings after allowing for Corporation Tax at 40%. (k) Remuneration £1,038,000 in 1968, and £1,126,000 in 1969. (M) Minus

8

LONDON PRICES OF 5/- ORDINARY SHARES

Cal. Year	1961	1962	1963	1964	1965	1966	1967	1968	1969	*1970
Highest	26/6	25/6	29/9	27/9	27/9	24/10	26/7	24/3	21/9	11/9
Lowest	20/4	20/-	20/3	21/4	22/-	14/3	16/1	17/1	6/9	8/3

*To 18 May

NET ASSET VALUE (BOOK VALUE), excluding intangibles, at B/s. date per 5/- Ord. share: 1969 11/-

FINANCE ACT, 1965. So far as is known Co. is not a close company within provisions of Act.

LAND AND BUILDINGS. Value of land and Building is substantially in excess of book value and valuations made since 31.12.69 indicate that this excess could be in region of £500,000 in open market, but as major part is used for trading Co. it is opinion of Directors that current open market value is not of great significance in context of these accounts.

CHAIRMAN'S STATEMENT. Trading results are disappointing as Directors had hoped to achieve an increased turnover. Failure of this, and a fall in Group's total gross sales value by £35,000 can be specifically attributed to a number of factors among which were (a) a policy of rationalisation of manufacturing, by closure or reduction to distribution points of certain units, particularly closure of their branch in Glasgow due to an increasing non-profitability which had applied for some years in spite of changes in management, whilst certain smaller branches in the NorthEast and in South Wales were closed or consolidated for same reason; (b) inability during exceptional weather in June and July (when they were able to trade at full production for first time for some years) to recoup general fall during poor winter months at beginning of year, and (c) a price increase granted by Ministry in August last which for a time met sales resistance in certain areas. In addition, account must be taken of increasing encroachment into family soft drink market of American brands of Cola products.

Fall in profit however overtook amount lost in turnover due to persistent rises in labour, materials and in operating and marketing costs during year which had to be absorbed by Co. Both turnover and profit suffered from labour unrest whilst changed regulations in SET alone cost Co. £20,000. An additional charge for packaging costs was sustained despite reduction in volume, although to a minor extent this was offset by increased deposit charge on 40 oz. size bottle. An outstanding item of expense was substantial increase in cost of transport aggravated by new regulations imposed by Road Transport Act, 1968. Return to profitability depends upon ability to contain or pass on these extra costs.

Board have given continual attention to product innovations and, in view of reduction of number of trips of returnable bottle, to extension of marketing operations including that of use of non-returnable bottle. During latter part of 1969 a pilot operation in this type of outlet was started and in present year sales into multiple stores and supermarkets are being extended. It is as yet too early to forecast success and profitability of these operations in a highly competitive market.

As American branded Cola accounts for approx. 25% of carbonated drinks sold in UK decision was taken during latter part of 1969 to enter competition in this field. Co. subsequently negotiated franchise agreement to bottle and market in Great Britain Royal Crown Cola, and Co. has now commenced to produce this Cola. Last year, he referred to a proposed development of a new major production unit. In view of large capital commitment required by this project Co. is now considering this matter again before proceeding.

N.B. At the time of Quinn's taking over, liquidation of the company would have realised 13s. 6d. per share. (Casewriter's notes.)

Source: Extel Statistical Services Ltd

EXHIBIT 3 Consolidated Balance Sheet as at 31 December 1968

1967 £		£	£
	SHARE CAPITAL OF TIZER LIMITED		
£1,500,000	*Authorised* 6,000,000 Ordinary shares of 5/- each	£1,500,000	
£1,000,000	*Issued* 4,000,000 Ordinary Shares of 5/- each, fully paid		£1,000,000
	RESERVES		
12,201	Capital	26,652	
1,000,000	Revenue	1,000,000	
75,000	Dividend equalisation	75,000	
40,000	Sales promotion	25,000	
60,000	Taxation equalisation	60,000	
167,325	Profit and loss account	170,673	
1,354,526			1,357,325
£2,354,526	TOTAL CAPITAL AND RESERVES		£2,357,325

1967 £		£	£
	FIXED ASSETS (See note)		
886,580	Land and Buildings		823,153
547,828	Plant, machinery and motor vehicles		530,849
1,434,408			1,354,002
	CURRENT ASSETS		
409,711	Stock in Trade	361,631	
240,309	Sundry debtors & amounts prepaid	323,481	
232,174	British Government and other securities (Market value £228,894— 1967 £221,552)	232,174	
475,000	Municipal and other deposits	475,000	
241,446	Cash at Bankers and in hand	179,832	
1,598,640		1,572,118	
	Deduct: **CURRENT LIABILITIES**		
247,048	Sundry creditors and amounts accrued	293,583	
157,894	Current taxation	155,592	
175,000	Provision for final dividend (Gross) now recommended	75,000	
579,942		524,175	
1,018,698	NET CURRENT ASSETS		1,047,943
2,453,106			2,401,945

		1968	1967
	Deduct: DEFERRED LIABILITY		
157,170	Corporation Tax due 1st January 1970		103,210
2,295,936			2,298,735
58,590	Add: GOODWILL at cost less amounts written off including net premiums on shares acquired in subsidiary companies		58,590
£2,354,526	TOTAL NET ASSETS		£2,357,325

NOTE ON ACCOUNTS

1. FIXED ASSETS

	1968	1967
LAND AND BUILDINGS	£	£
At Cost 1 January 1968	684,020	650,370
At Valuation	369,418	369,418
	1,053,438	1,019,788
Additions during the year at cost	13,424	44,059
Less: Disposal during the year	69,195	10,409
	997,667	1,053,438
Cumulative depreciation	174,514	166,858
At net book value 31 December 1968	£823,153	£886,580
Freehold	740,003	800,338
Leasehold	83,150	86,242
	£823,153	£886,580
PLANT, MACHINERY AND MOTOR VEHICLES	1,613,937	1,607,275
Additions during the year at cost	92,672	61,820
Less: Disposal during the year	167,150	55,156
	1,539,459	1,613,939
Cumulative depreciation	1,008,610	1,066,111
At net book value 31 December 1968	£530,849	£547,828

Source: Annual Report

EXHIBIT 4   Consolidated Profit and Loss Account
Year ended 31 December 1968

1967 £			£
468,549	Trading Profit of the year		308,249
—	Add: Profit arising on change of stocktaking basis		18,291
1,966	Profit on sale of properties		8,433
470,515			334,973
	Add: Investment income		
9,540	Investments	10,067	
32,142	Cash on deposit	31,743	
41,682			41,810
512,197			376,783
	Deduct:		
122,093	Depreciation of Fixed assets	102,609	
2,818	Loses on sales of fixed assets	5,139	
25,520	Directors' remuneration	27,790	
1,506	Other miscellaneous charges	6,111	
151,937			141,649
360,260	Profit of the year subject to taxation		235,134
152,443	Deduct: Taxation on profit of year		96,786
207,817	Profit of the year after taxation		138,348
174,508	Add: Balance brought forward from previous year		167,325
35,000	Add: Transfer from sales promotion reserve		15,000
417,325			320,673
	Deduct: Share dividends:		
75,000	Interim 7½% (Gross) already paid	75,000	
175,000	Final 7½% (Gross) now recommended	75,000	
250,000			150,000
£167,325	Balance carried forward to next year		£170,673

Source: Annual Report

EXHIBIT 5   Chairman's Review

To the Shareholders.

Dear Sir or Madam,

I beg to submit this Review with the Accounts and Directors' Report of your Company for the year ending 31st December, 1968. Following on the Companies Act 1967 the published Accounts for the year with the accompanying notes and Directors' Report are set out to give more information than in previous years.

First I wish to refer to the death in December of Mr. Pickup, the founder of the business and until 1962 Chairman of the Company, since when he remained on the Board and maintained an active interest in its affairs until just before he died. He combined a long experience of every aspect of the mineral water trade with a shrewd appraisal of its commercial and manufacturing problems which enabled him to enlarge a small business into its present-day position. I personally regret the passing of a respected colleague and life-long friend.

The trading results of the year have proved most disappointing, particularly as the general price increase introduced last May was expected to absorb a greater part of the ever rising costs than had been the case in the previous year, but this was dependent on volume turnover being at the least maintained. In the event this volume was not achieved and a substantial fall in the trading profit has resulted.

The fall in business can be attributed to several factors. The main reason being the weather conditions prevailing in a summer reported to be the wettest since 1931, particularly in the South. Two increases in purchase tax during the year together with a general increase in price necessitated by increased costs caused our selling prices to be uplifted by 15% which resulted in resistance to sales. In addition the Company experienced difficult personnel relations in distribution. These factors collectively diminished the impact of an increased marketing effort mounted by our sales organisation during the year.

As mentioned briefly in the Directors' Report the trading profit was further depleted by a higher level of replacement bottles necessitated by a very severe fall in the average number of journeys per bottle. This may have been affected by a slowing down in replacements by the same number of consumers, such as happens in cold or wet summer weather, leading to both slow turnover and increased wastage. Your Directors have taken steps to mitigate this problem which is causing concern to the carbonate soft drinks industry at large who rely upon the returnable bottle to keep down packaging costs, but these measures are not expected to become effective until 1970.

I am reluctant to forecast the trading prospects for 1969 because experience has shown how susceptible the soft drinks industry is to variations in weather, especially in the peak summer months, whilst the particularly bad weather in the early months of this year has resulted in a reduction of sales against target.

Your Board are naturally continuing their policy of strengthening the sales organisation. The Company's main product still remains a firm favourite and, commencing in 1969, the use of our nationally known registered trade mark 'Tizer' is to be developed so that advantage is gained from a more extensive consumer exposure to this name. Consideration is particularly being given to product innovation in order to strengthen the Company's competitiveness in a changing market situation, whilst a feasibility study is also being carried out into an alternative method of selling by pre-ordering.

Your Directors are pursuing a policy of concentrating production into fewer manufacturing plants in the future with a view to reducing overall production costs and a new major unit is already in the process of being developed.

Resulting from these activities the Board are confident that long-term development of sales and profitability will materialise.

Your Directors have decided to recommend the payment of a Final Dividend of $7\frac{1}{2}$% less tax making 15% less tax for the year.

Following the resignation of Mr. Williams and the death of Mr. Pickup, Mr. G. Wilkinson and Mr. K. J. Hanmer, M.B.E., E.D., have been appointed to the Board of the Company and the Annual General Meeting will be asked to confirm these appointments. Mr. Wilkinson joined the Company early in 1968 as Financial Controller to implement the Touche, Ross, Bailey, Smart & Co. report and has taken full charge of the accounting and financial matters of the Company. Mr. Hanmer joined the Company in May 1968 having previously managed a major Soft Drinks manufactory abroad.

I regret to have to report the death earlier this year of our Secretary, Mr. W. E. Speake, who had held the position for some 19 years.

In closing this Review I would particularly like to thank all those employees who have made special efforts in a difficult trading period.

FRANK HINDLE,
Chairman.

Source: Annual Report

2 Tizer Limited (B)*

This case reviews the developments in Tizer Ltd between the time when Mr Quinn became Managing Director in 1970 and the sale of the company to A. G. Barr of Glasgow on 7 December 1972.

MR QUINN'S ADMINISTRATION

Once he had assumed office, Mr Quinn moved quickly to cure the problems he had identified in his preliminary audit of the company (described in Tizer Limited (A)).

His overall goal was to establish Tizer as a strong national soft drinks manufacturer and distributor. He believed that a growth target of 20 per cent per annum for sales was achievable. He also believed that within four years Tizer ought to be making at least 15 per cent pre-tax return on investment.

As a first step towards realising these goals, Mr Quinn assembled a new younger team of top managers. New directors of finance and sales were appointed by the summer of 1970, as were new managers of marketing and transport. Together with existing personnel in operations, engineering, personnel and administration, they constituted what Mr Quinn considered a well-balanced group with the skills and experience necessary to create the desired growth.

The changes instituted on the marketing side were described by Mr Sproat, the new sales manager, as follows.[1]

> Everything we have done in the last eighteen months has been aimed at getting Tizer firmly positioned in the branded section of the market and out of the commodity area where local bottlers are still cutting each other to pieces in trade price wars without making any serious attempt at expanding the total market.
>
> We aim to restore Tizer to its rightful position as one of the leading branded soft drinks, and then to do likewise with our Jusoda range and with Royal Crown Cola.
>
> So we had taken the first step. We knew where we wanted to go. But how to get there? We identified our major weaknesses as:
>
> — an old-fashioned image
> — a declining market share
> — inadequate channels of distribution through which we sold our products.
>
> These problems are closely interrelated but they also need specific attention and remedies.
>
> Firstly, we tackled the old-fashioned image. We commissioned depth research to find out what the consumer really thought of Tizer. Most of them—and Tizer is as well known by soft drink consumers as Coca-Cola—thought of Tizer with affection but as rather dull. So we commissioned Conran Design to prepare for us a completely new corporate identity which shows Tizer's public face to the consumer. Conran have done a superb job, and we now have an image which is vivid, contemporary and alive, but which still suggests a product with a long and honourable history.
>
> And this is not just to be seen on our products. The new identity covers vehicles, stationery, factory signs, salesmen's uniforms—every area in which the consumer or trade customers come into contact with us.
>
> We were also faced with a very serious decline in market share, much of which can be traced to our failure to keep abreast of changes in packaging and containers. Many of us—and particularly in recent months those of us who claim to be socially aware—are fulsome in their praise of returnable bottles. Unfortunately, consumers at large do not seem to share this enthusiasm and are buying their drinks increasingly in non-returnable bottles and cans.

---

* Copyright © John M. Stopford 1973
[1] Presentation to the Northern Stock Exchange, October 1971.

In the middle of last year we introduced a range of non-returnable bottles, including Tizer itself. Sales of these are increasing steadily. In April of this year, we brought out Tizer in ring-pull cans. Sales of Tizer cans have been sufficiently encouraging to allow us to consider an early introduction of other canned drinks.

Our third major problem was our failure to keep pace with the changing pattern of retail distribution. Here in the north we have a sentimental attachment to the corner shop, immortalised in Coronation Street. Corner shops still exist and in large numbers. My belief is that they always will. But self-service stores, supermarkets and even hypermarkets are each year taking an increasing share of total food and confectionery purchasing, and Tizer has simply not been sufficiently aware of these changes. Such outlets require non-returnable containers, as previously stated, and these have recently been added to our range.

But really curing these problems is a long term task: a task which must be carried through by managers with professional marketing and selling skills and a broad and vigorous outlook. Frankly there were not sufficient people of this style in the company when Peter Quinn arrived. But today we now have a compact, but effective marketing department, including a marketing manager and two brand managers. Their role is simply defined: development and implementation of effective marketing policies to achieve our objective sales and profit.

The particular concerns are brand and product marketing strategies which include such items as advertising and promotion—both above and below the line—market research and evaluation, packaging design and product innovation. In short they are concerned with the use of resources and the coordination of policies and activities which are aimed at satisfying the needs of our customers—but at a profit.

While the marketing department was and is working so hard to get our product range right in every way, we also had to begin the job of ensuring that Tizer products are available in all those outlets and places where the consumer now shops or enjoys his leisure.

So I recruited a team of key account salesmen, all men experienced in negotiating at top level with major multiple organisations. They have been presenting Tizer to such organisations for some time now and you can now see Tizer products on the shelves of renowned retailers like Sainsbury and Tesco, or you can buy Tizer from new-style discounters like Kwik-Save and Woolco.

We are well represented in multiple off-licence groups and the confectionery/news chains which are rapidly gaining strength throughout the country. And in the vital 'on-premise' area we are at this time conducting a major sales compaign to have our products available in all types of catering and leisure outlets—licensed or unlicensed.

Also, we have created a mobile sales development team whose job is to go into districts where we have sales problems or to open up areas where we hope eventually to establish branches. This is the sort of organisation which is common in the field of fast-moving consumer goods, but which did not exist in Tizer until only a few months ago.

We are also working hard to improve the sales effectiveness of our 300-strong driver sales force by better on-job training, more attractive promotional activity and better merchandising aids.

Our aim in 1971 has been to reinforce our traditional business in terms of products, whilst developing new products and getting into new channels of distribution.

In relation to reinforcing our traditional business we initiated substantial media campaigns this year. We ran a major TV compaign throughout the north of England from May to September.[2] We used children's comics for a campaign aimed specifically at our younger customers. We redesigned the labels on our entire range. We engaged in promotional activity specifically aimed at our corner-shop customers. And we undertook special below the line activity to strengthen our grip on multiple retailing. This package has served to increase the awareness of trade and consumers alike of the new Tizer.

We have also done much in the new product area, particularly in terms of products suited for modern distributive channels. As previously stated we introduced NRBs and cans. We supported the can introduction in the south of England with cinema commercials shown throughout the south and the south-west. We also

---

[2]Tizer did not advertise during the period when the new image was being developed.

brought to the market, Quencher—a range of still drinks in four flavours, in cartons—which have been a great success.

And of course we have obtained the franchise for Royal Crown Cola, an American cola of international repute, which will greatly help us in our drive on catering outlets.

For the future, we have plans to attack the huge squash market much more vigorously. I have mentioned other flavours of cans. There are other products under detailed consideration. We are moving into the export field.

In distributive terms, we must consolidate our position as a leading supplier of carbonated drinks to multiple organisations. We have detailed plans aimed at achieving this. We are currently examining the possibility of private label packing of carbonates. And we are alert to all developments in competitive products packaging and labelling.

The production and distribution functions were put under the control of Mr Hanmer, assistant managing director. Mr Hanmer had joined Tizer in 1968 after twenty years in the Far East and was the oldest of the executive directors. He described the changes instituted as follows:[1]

As the beginning of 1970 the company operated twenty-one factories throughout the country from Newcastle in the north to Southampton in the south and Swansea in the west.

From each one of these factories sales were achieved through a total of approximately 350 van salesmen selling in the main to retail outlets. The sales vehicles had open bodies which exposed the products to the elements and many of the vehicles would very shortly have commanded a high price in the vintage car market.

Each factory had its own bottling line or lines supplying its own sales needs, and production was carried out very much on a make-today, sell tomorrow basis, which resulted in very poor productivity figures, underutilization of labour, wastage of raw materials and poor quality control. Also because of the intermingling of sales and production functions, we had poor stock control.

The bottling equipment in use was to a large extent designed and fabricated in Tizer's own engineering workshops, and although probably very adequate in the 1930s, had been out of date for more than a decade. As this equipment grew older, so the expenditure on maintenance and replacement of worn parts made ever-increasing drains on company profits.

Managers of undoubted and unquestionable loyalty to the company had, in the main, been promoted from their original jobs as van salesmen and, not having had adequate training in production techniques or budgetary control, were unable to run their factories so as to produce the best financial results.

The management structure was such that factory managers found themselves in a split command situation: they were responsible to a sales director and a production director simultaneously. This frequently resulted in a confused situation ultimately leading to inefficiency in both functions, and a top-heavy and disgruntled workforce.

In summary, we had to deal with low productivity, over capacity, out-of-date equipment and poor organisation. Therefore we set out to rationalise the total operation to increase productivity, and create an effective sales organisation in order to increase sales, and achieve an increased turnover with a smaller total workforce.

To achieve the objectives, the following actions have been, or are being, taken. Production has ceased at ten production units and is being concentrated still further so that we shall enter 1972 with six production units for carbonated products and one production unit for squashes, supplying twenty-three depots throughout the country.

All production units have been or will be equipped with plant and machinery which will not require the services of the previous central engineering workshop, which has been disbanded. In fact, one of the production units will be fitted with high speed machinery of continental manufacture, which will make use of the very latest production and mechanical handling techniques. The remaining production units will operate against centrally-planned production programmes in order to

---

[3]Northern Stock Exchange presentation, October 1971.

achieve maximum rationalisation and productivity. The closure of production units has brought, and will bring about, further reductions in the total workforce.

The transport fleet will be supplemented with a primary distribution fleet of heavy-load carrying vehicles with trailers to supply goods from production units to sales depots, and the retail sales vans replaced with up-to-date covered vehicles so that non-returnable cardboard containers can readily be carried.

Our management structure has been reorganised so that managers are directly responsible to regional managers, who in turn are directly responsible to the operations director. We are also setting up a central laboratory for routine quality control and flavour research and development.

With an eye to the future, we have this year recruited graduates as management trainees, some of whom are currently doing a six-months stint as driver/salesmen.

We believe that our van selling force will be our primary means of increasing sales turnover for some time to come—and this is the reason why we are re-equipping our sales force with new vehicles, new uniforms, a planned programme of sales promotions, ranging from incentives for the individual salesman to retailer and consumer promotion schemes. But we are nevertheless investigating other means of supplying retailers and have already two tele-sales depots operating in the south of England on a pilot scheme basis.

By the end of 1970 the start of these activities had produced a small loss, and had had no appreciable effect on turnover. By the end of 1971 a large loss had been recorded, but turnover had increased by almost 20 per cent. Exhibits 1 and 2 provide the relevant financial information.

Time, however, had run out for Mr Quinn. On 6 December Armour Trust Ltd offered for the whole of Tizer equity at an underwritten value of £2,300,000. The offer was satisfied by an issue of ordinary shares and partly convertible unsecured loan stock, which provided the Tizer shareholders with an offer equivalent to 55 pence/share, at the date of issue. Tizer's institutional shareholders, including Slater Walker, accepted the offer immediately. Only a small group of shareholders considered that Tizer would be better off as an independent company, but they were unable to muster enough votes.

ARMOUR TRUST'S ADMINISTRATION

Armour Trust was a financial holding company with close links to the Slater Walker empire. At the time Tizer was purchased, Armour was active in the fields of property development, consumer finance, and television retailing.

In the offer document Mr Quinn and his board, after consultation with their advisers, forecast a pre-tax loss for the year to 31 December 1971, of about £90,000, before charging extraordinary losses of £27,000. In the event the disclosed losses totalled £244,000, before charging extraordinary losses of £140,000.

The management of Armour attempted to stem these losses mainly by selling off property and closing sales branches. They were, in effect, reversing Quinn's policies of national expansion and instituting policies designed to make Tizer once more a collection of regional bottlers.

The Armour Trust administration lasted only for one year and one day. Under an agreement dated 7 December 1972, A.G. Barr & Company Limited acquired the whole of the issued capital of Tizer with effect from 3 December 1972. The transaction was for cash. Armour Trust received £2,000,000 on 8 December and £500,000 on 12 April 1973.

In the statement to shareholders, Armour Trust attributed the problems of Tizer to a lack of effective control systems. They stated

> Your Board instituted new financial and operational controls within Tizer, which inevitably required a number of months to produce tangible improvements. In the opinion of your Board these new controls were proving effective and Tizer was on the recovery path but, due to the poor summer of 1972, the results of Tizer for the period to 2 December 1972 were dissappointing.
>
> In November 1972 your Board was approached by Barr who wished to purchase Tizer and thereby create the largest group exclusively engaged in the soft drinks trade in the United Kingdom. Your Board considered that such a merger would be likely to lead to the faster development of Tizer and the better safeguard of the future of its employees. Furthermore, your Board considered that although

the rationalisation programme which was being implemented would have led Tizer in due course to a good level of profitability, the proceeds of sale could be more profitably utilised in other directions. The offer from Barr was, therefore, accepted.

EXHIBIT 1   Tizer Limited (B)

Income Statement

(£'000s)

	1969	1970	1971	1972 (to 2 Dec)
Turnover	2,949	2,978	3,551	3,266
Trading profit (loss)	143	68	(104) (est)	(13)
Add				
Surplus on sale of branches	9	13	See Note 2	See Note 3
Investment income	48	46	20 (est)	—
	200	127	(84) (est)	(13)
Deduct				
Depreciation	92	105	110	116
Other	39	49	50	68
	131	154	160	184
Profit/(loss) before tax and extraordinary items	69	(27)	(244)	(197)
Extraordinary items	—	—	(340)	111

1. At 31 December 1970, the value of plant, machinery and motor vehicles was reduced by £165,551 to allow for items which, in the opinion of the directors and in view of the plans for rationalisation of production in 1971, had little or no further useful life. This amount, together with a terminal loss on reorganisation of £95,160, was charged to reserves in the 1970 accounts.

2. Extraordinary expenditure (less income) charged in the consolidated profit and loss account in the year ended 31 December 1971, but not charged above, was as follows:

Costs incurred on closure of branches and withdrawal of certain production facilities	£ 97,912
Stock written off on cessation of Royal Crown Cola franchise	23,700
Expenses in connection with the acquisition of Tizer by Armour	15,250
Surplus arising from sales of investments and properties (net)	(13,217)
Costs of redesigning Tizer's 'logo'	16,992
	140,637
Provision for Tizer redevelopment costs	199,000
	£339,637

3. Extraordinary income (less expenditure) charged in the consolidated profit and loss account in the year ended 2 December 1972 but not charged above, was as follows:

Surpluses on sale of properties	£149,000
Costs incurred in closure of branches and withdrawal of production facilities	(50,491)
Other income (being £28,388 less expenditure of £15,791)	12,597
	£111,330

Sources: For 1969 and 1970, Tizer Limited Annual Reports
For 1971 and 1972, Armour Trust Records

EXHIBIT 2   Tizer Limited (B)

Consolidated balance sheets

(£000s)

	1969	1970	1971	1972 (2 Dec)
FIXED ASSETS				
Land and buildings	805	1,321	1,242	1,043
Plant, machinery and motor vehicles	551	419	505	618
Goodwill	59	—	—	—
	1,415	1,740	1,747	1,661
CURRENT ASSETS				
Stocks	406	495	575	797
Debtors	300	336	315	417
Investments	677	422	221	—
Cash	36	12	10	4
Amount owing by Armour	—	—	—	271
	1,420	1,265	1,122	1,489
CURRENT LIABILITIES				
Creditors	302	350	684	608
Bank Overdraft	—	57	—	477
Taxation	99	5	3	—
Dividend (Gross)	75	25	—	—
Amount owing to fellow subsidiary	—	—	—	10
Provision for branch closures	—	—	—	159
	477	436	687	1,253
NET CURRENT ASSETS	943	829	435	236
Deferred taxation	94	—	—	—
NET TANGIBLE ASSETS	2,264	2,569	2,182	1,897

Notes: 1. Totals do not match because of rounding errors.

2. Buildings stated (except for 1969) at 1970 open market valuation.

3. Stocks have been valued at the lower of cost and net realisable value or, for certain returnable cases, at cost less provision for deterioration. The value of manufactured stocks includes an appropriate addition for production overheads.

4. At 31 December 1971, following the acquisition of Tizer by Armour, provision of £199,000 was made to meet expected future expenditure and losses expected to be incurred over the following two years arising from the closure and relocation of certain of Tizer's branches. The amount of £159,083 shown above represents the balance of this provision after charging expenditure in the period to 2 December 1972.

5. Capital expenditure authorised at 2 December 1972, but not provided for above amounted to £45,000, of which £39,000 had been contracted for.

6. At 2 December 1972, there were unrealised surpluses of £390,863 arising from the revaluation of properties in 1970. No provision has been made for the potential liability to tax on the chargable gains which may arise is such surpluses were realised by the sale of the freehold and leasehold properties at the values stated above.

7. There are losses for taxation purposes amounting to approximately £900,000, which are available for set-off against taxable trading profits arising in future to relieve the liability to taxation thereon.

Sources: 1969 figures from Annual Report
1970 and 1972 figures from Shareholder Offer Documents
1971 figures from Armour Trust

3 Weiss Konstruktion GmbH*

Kurt Schleiffer, twenty-seven, recently appointed personal assistant to Gunther Weiss, chief executive and owner of the private company Weiss Konstruktion, was considering what recommendations he ought to make to Mr Weiss on how the company could best develop the potential for its patented system of constructing 'Microbore' pipelines in the United States. Mr Schleiffer, a graduate of a well known European business school, had elected to join a small company after graduating, and had been attracted to Weiss by promises of an interesting and challenging job, and by the exciting growth prospects he believed lay ahead for the company.

THE WEISS 'MICROBORE' SYSTEM

These growth prospects centred upon the company's 'Microbore' pipeline system, which had been conceived, developed and patented by Mr Weiss. Weiss Konstruktion, started by Mr Wilhelm Weiss in Koblenz, was originally engaged in construction engineering, including a substantial business in pipework installation for the chemical industry of the Ruhr. In 1967, after the death of his father, Mr Gunther Weiss, an electrical engineer, had left his job as a technical manager for a large German electrical products manufacturer to take over the family business. In 1968 the company made heavy losses as the result of taking on a number of unprofitable fixed-price contracts and faced severe liquidity problems. Recent financial performance is shown below:

DM (000s)	1968	1969	1970	1971	1972
Turnover	17737.1	11470.6	9744.2	9113.4	12665.8
Earnings before tax (after interest)	(1344.6)	647.4†	323.7	390.1	1294.8
Earnings after tax	(1269.9)	639.1	323.7	365.2	780.2
Capital employed	6474.0	5353.5	3469.4	3676.9	4125.1

† Extraordinary figure due to late settlement of 2 major contracts

Source: company records

Mr Weiss decided that he would get out of conventional contracting and attempt to apply his technical skills to develop medium and high technology products, which could be profitably exploited in the construction industry.

The first such product Mr Weiss had developed was a new system for building small, underground pipelines suitable for carrying gas, water under pressure, a number of chemicals, and which could also be used to carry utility service cables, such as telephone and electrical supplies. Unlike the conventional system of laying such pipelines, which normally involved digging a trench, laying the pipeline and then refilling the trench, the method developed by Mr Weiss allowed pipes to be installed without trenching, thereby minimising traffic disruption and environmental damage.

The system involved first sinking a vertical shaft down to the level at which the pipeline was to be installed. Then, utilising concepts used in the oil industry, Mr Weiss had developed a method of rotary horizontal drilling. A rotary table, connected to a mobile engine at ground level above the shaft was mounted precisely by means of a datum laser at the foot of the shaft. A patented drilling bit slid through the rotary table attached to a drill pipe made up in 5 metre lengths and assembled at the bottom of the shaft. As the table was rotated by the engine this in turn rotated the drill pipe and bit. While the bit was drilling, fluid was pumped down the rotating pipe from a tank on the surface, emerging through the bit to keep it cool, and returning, carrying with it the drill cuttings. These cuttings were separated out by means of a series of

---

* Copyright © Manchester Business School 1973

sieves before the fluid was recirculated to the main tank. The sieves were periodically cleared and the waste hauled away from the site. The pipeline was bored by applying pressure on the drill bit, which was capable of handling most ground conditions. As drilling proceeded, new 5 metre lengths of the drill pipe were added. Exhibit 1 shows a schematic diagram of the process.

When the required length had been drilled, usually to connect with a second vertical shaft sunk at the end of the pipeline, the bit and drill pipe were removed and replaced with the pipeline itself. This was made up of 5 metre sections of patented design, such that the pipe could be weld jointed to ensure no liquid or gaseous leakage up to moderate pressures. The pipe was then rigidly set in position by pumping liquid cement through the pipe followed by drilling fluid, the two liquids being separated by a polyurethane foam 'pig'. When the cement reached the end of the pipe it returned along the outside, filling the annulus and the surrounding earth to provide a rigid fixing. The drilling fluid was then pumped out, the pipeline cleaned and inspected by insertion of a clearing 'pig' attached to a small diameter closed-circuit TV camera. The line was then ready for use. Using this method, Mr Weiss considered it was possible to drill pipelines of up to 40 cm diameter for up to 200 m or, for smaller diameter pipes of up to 22 cm, nearly 700 m. Longer distances could be drilled by means of sinking further vertical shafts to connect additional lengths of pipeline.

THE MARKET FOR THE 'MICROBORE' SYSTEM

Mr Weiss believed that the system he had developed was especially suitable for installing underground pipelines and utility services in urban areas or under major highway systems. The system had set out to be directly competitive with open trench installations which were labour intensive and caused extreme traffic disruption. In the 'Microbore' system, the labour force consisted of only a three-man drilling team and ground disturbance was limited to the sinking of a few vertical shafts, which could be located so as to minimise urban or traffic disruption. Under these conditions the system was considered to be directly competitive in price without including allowances for traffic inconvenience. It was also quicker to complete because drilling was little affected by prevailing surface weather conditions, which tended to restrict trenching in winter. When Weiss had announced the system in 1970, city authorities in West Germany had expressed great interest and a number had placed experimental contracts.

In order to exploit the potential of 'Microbore' and to avoid what he perceived to be the pitfalls of construction contracting, Mr Weiss decided to franchise his system to a series of local contractors throughout West Germany. The country was divided into a series of fourteen geographic areas, including West Berlin. Exclusive franchises were signed with ten construction firms to cover twelve of the fourteen areas by the end of 1972. At first the novelty and skills required to operate the 'Microbore' system had deterred large contractors and the early franchises had been allocated to smaller specialist firms. The rapid success of these companies, however, together with increased interest by local authorities, had led to a number of major contractors seeking franchises. By the end of 1972 over 80 per cent of West Germany was covered by the franchise system, and over 70 km of pipelines had been laid. Further, more urban authorities were beginning to specify 'Microbore' installations after the success of initial trials.

The role of Weiss Konstruktion in the franchise operation meant that the company was not itself directly involved in contracting. The franchisees paid Weiss a royalty for every five-metre section of pipe laid. In addition, Weiss supplied the patented drillbits, which were manufactured by an engineering company to a Weiss specification. The pipe sections were also supplied exclusively from Weiss. They too were made up by three outside tube manufacturers, who also machined the patented sealing system on each 5 m length. The non-consumable elements of the system—the rotary table and drill fluid tanks, screens and pumps—were made up by Weiss principally by assembling components from other manufacturers, and were sold to franchisees as capital equipment. Drilling fluid was also made up by the company and supplied direct to the contractors. The principal source for profits for Weiss came on the sales of pipe sections, and although the sealing system was patented it was not considered difficult for any reasonable engineering workshop to duplicate it. Royalty payments were relatively low and the sales of drill bits, fluid and capital equipment, although profitable, were very small.

EXHIBIT 1   Weiss Microbore pipelaying system

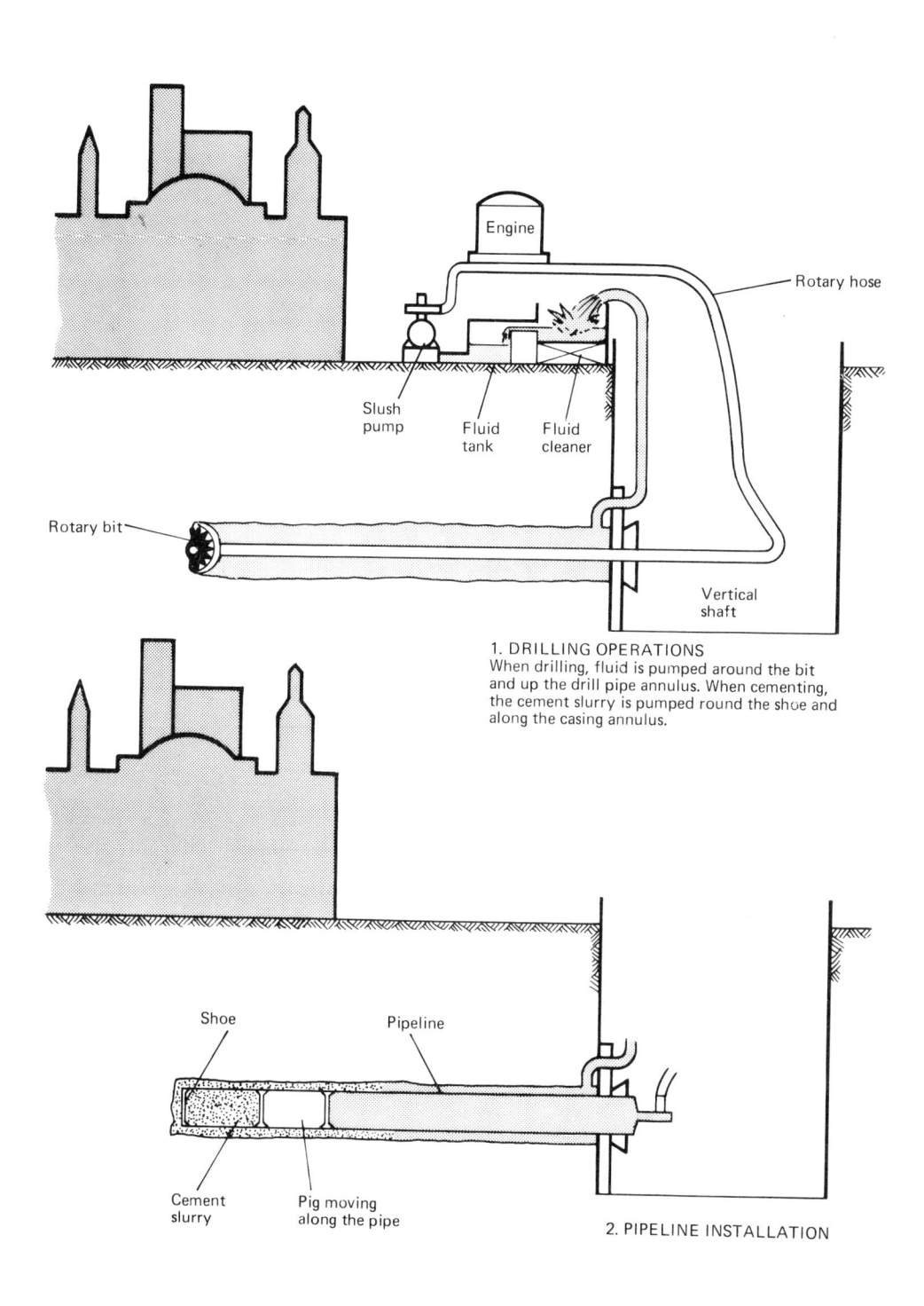

1. DRILLING OPERATIONS
When drilling, fluid is pumped around the bit and up the drill pipe annulus. When cementing, the cement slurry is pumped round the shoe and along the casing annulus.

2. PIPELINE INSTALLATION

INTERNATIONAL PROSPECTS

In addition to a large potential market for 'Microbore' in West Germany, Mr Weiss believed similar opportunities existed in other countries, especially where there was substantial urbanisation and environmental issues were important. His system had attracted substantial attention in the German press and technical magazines, and this had led to the receipt of many enquiries from other European countries. As a result, in early 1973 Mr Weiss had assigned responsibility for international activities to Karl Reiner, who was successful in rapidly concluding franchise deals with a few contractors in France, Belgium, Holland and Great Britain. Drill bits, capital equipment and drilling fluid were to be supplied direct from Germany, but Mr Reiner had made arrangements for local tube makers to supply the lengths of pipe. The setting up of these franchises meant that Weiss's limited management capacity was heavily committed and enquiries from other countries apart from Japan and the United States were allowed to lapse.
In April 1973 Weiss Konstruktion had signed an exclusive licence deal with Sumitomo Construction of Japan. This gave the Japanese company exclusive rights to 'Microbore' technology in Japan, including the rights to manufacture pipes, drill bits, capital equipment, and drilling fluid, and to sublicence other construction companies for installation work, in return for a capital fee of DM 1 million, and standard royalty payments on a pipe length basis.

THE MANAGEMENT TEAM

Although Mr Weiss had been responsible for developing the technology of 'Microbore', its practical application was the work of two drilling engineers, Karl Reiner and Johann Kindelberger, both of whom had former experience as 'roustabouts',[1] and then as assistant drillers in the oil industry. These men, together with Mr Weiss, a finance director and the newly appointed Kurt Schleiffer, made up the management team. Reiner and Kindelberger were responsible for maintaining contacts with contractors and training their specialist drilling crews. They could also be called out as troubleshooters when a contractor got into difficulties.

PROSPECTS IN THE UNITED STATES MARKET

Mr. Weiss believed that the most important market possibilities lay in the United States. An American magazine, which had reprinted translations of German articles on 'Microbore', had generated nearly 2,000 enquiries about the system, expecially from the heavily populated East and West Coast regions. These enquiries had included requests from a number of major US utility suppliers, including Bell Telephone and the Tennessee Valley Authority; from urban authorities such as Boston, Cleveland and New York state highway authorities; from chemical companies, such as Du Pont; and from oil and natural gas distributors, such as Sun Oil and Texaco. Many enquiries had also come from pipeline construction concerns, who were interested in taking a licence for 'Microbore'.
    One such enquiry had come from the small Texas based oil well company, Gulf Wildcat Inc., of Houston, Texas. This company was known to Mr Reiner from his time in the oil industry around the Gulf of Mexico. In March 1973 he had therefore travelled to Houston to supervise the experimental 'Microbore' installation in downtown Dallas by Gulf Wildcat utilising components and drilling equipment flown out from Germany.
    When Mr Reiner returned to Koblenz, he advised Mr Weiss that Gulf Wildcat were anxious to take a licence for the 'Microbore' system. In addition, a number of other drilling contractors known to Gulf had visited the site in Dallas and had been equally impressed. Mr Reiner considered it would be relatively easy to find companies who might wish to accept a licence agreement in the United States. Mr Reiner was also confident that the system could be franchised in Western Europe, although he had not systematically explored this possibility.
    Mr. Weiss was somewhat unsure as to how he should handle the development of the American market. He believed the United States could in the long term represent a much larger market than West Germany, and therefore felt that Weiss Konstruktion

---

[1] Roustabouts were production labourers in oil well construction. Oil well drilling was usually supervised by technically-trained drilling engineers.

should consider establishing a direct presence there in order to control any franchise arrangements set up. Against this was the fact that the licensee arrangement would provide a capital sum immediately which could aid development in Europe, the shortage of available management, and uncertainties about the strength of the company's position and the exact size and nature of the American market. A direct presence would also raise questions of who should manage such an operation, legal and fiscal arrangements, the appointment of equipment suppliers, as well as establishment, supervision and training franchises. In view of his uncertainties, Mr Weiss asked Mr Schleiffer to analyse the problem and make recommendations as to the best way to exploit what appeared to be a significant opportunity. At the same time he had no wish to dampen Mr Reiner's enthusiasm for his contacts in the USA, fully recognising that practical considerations would be essential to the company irrespective of the course of action chosen.

4 The European Automobile Industry*

In 1969 Western Europe overtook the United States as the largest automobile manufacturing centre in the world. In the two decades of the 1950s and 1960s Western Europe's car production boomed and average annual growth rates of between 7 and 8 per cent were consistently recorded as the industry moved to fulfil the pent-up demand of Europeans who, with rising affluence, were able to afford their first cars. As a result of this rapid growth, the automobile industry was a major employer in most of the developed nations of Europe, was a leading exporter and earner of hard currency, and as such a key component in many national economies. Its success or failure, therefore, could be expected to have a significant impact on the level of employment, the balance of payments and the economic welfare of many nations.

By the early 1970s, however, the industry was under increasing pressure from rapid inflation, increased competition, labour problems and political and social forces directed against the private car. These forces were expected to have a different impact on specific countries and companies with interests in the industry, but in the main they were the cause of considerable apprehension in many board rooms around Europe.

Then, at the end of 1973, the industry was subjected to a new bombshell in the form of the energy crisis. Following a resumption of fighting in the Middle East the developed world was hit first by an oil embargo imposed by the main Arab oil-producing countries, and, when this was eventually lifted, to massive hikes in crude oil prices. Western Europe was especially badly hit by the energy crisis being almost totally dependent on imported oil and by the end of 1974 most European countries were running massive oil deficits on their balance of payments. Further, as the effect of high energy prices worked their way through the economy they brought a rapid increase in domestic inflation rates and growing signs of worldwide recession.

The crisis hit the carmakers particularly hard. By the end of 1974 petrol prices had more than doubled throughout much of Europe and petrol economy had suddenly become a prime factor once again in car purchase decisions. Sales of large cars slumped drastically by some 50 per cent while economy and diesel models increased their penetration. Nevertheless overall sales showed declines of between 20 and 30 per cent in most European markets as general recession developed. Further, rapid inflation in material and labour costs was also depressing sales as car prices increased faster than disposable income.

By the end of 1974, as the impact of the new crisis worked out, the industry had begun to plan for serious recession, production was being cut back as vast stockpiles of unsold cars accumulated, labour layoffs and short-time working became a regular feature, and heavy losses appeared inevitable. The first real casualties had developed with Citroen being acquired by Peugeot and Volvo acquiring Daf. British Leyland, with severe liquidity problems, were forced to turn to the government for rescue, while the small specialist sports car producer, Aston Martin, went into voluntary liquidation. Rumours were also rife of serious impending financial problems for a host of other manufacturers as inadequate profits led to severe liquidity problems in the face of massive wage and stock inflation. Further, the future seemed highly uncertain, and new planning on product policy, future investment, and even survival added to the already serious problems of the European producers.

To provide a better understanding of the future risks and opportunities the changing forces and trends seemed likely to create for the automobile manufacturers, this note discusses the following topics: (1) the structure of the industry; (2) the development of the European car market and the position in the early 1970s; (3) trends in economic and technical development and government policy; (4) the responses of the car makers.

THE STRUCTURE OF THE EUROPEAN MOTOR INDUSTRY

By 1974 the Western European automobile industry had been reduced to just over twenty manufacturers and of these over half were small specialist producers. The

---

* © Manchester Business School 1974

EXHIBIT 1   Car production by major manufacturers by country 1970

('000s of units)

	USA			W. Germany			Italy		France			UK	Holland	Sweden	
	GM	Ford	Chrysler	VW	BMW	D. Benz	Fiat	Alfa-Romeo	Renault	Citroen[1]	Peugeot	BLMC	Daf	Saab	Volvo
USA	2,979	1,976	1,263	—	—	—	—	—	—	—	—	—	—	—	—
Germany	808	409	—	1,718	161	280	12	—	—	—	—	—	—	—	—
Italy	—	—	—	—	—	—	1,537	105	—	—	—	51	—	—	—
France	—	—	352	—	—	—	—	—	931	416	505	—	—	—	—
UK	168	500	173	—	—	—	—	—	—	—	—	800	—	—	—
Japan	19*	220*	246*	—	—	—	—	—	—	—	—	—	—	—	—
Sweden	—	—	—	—	—	—	—	—	—	—	—	—	—	74	204
Belgium	177	234	—	80	—	—	—	—	110	26	20	35	—	—	17
Spain	—	—	39	—	—	—	290*	—	87*	28	—	25*	—	—	—
Canada	223	409	239	—	—	—	—	—	10	—	—	—	—	—	—
Australia	156	87	57	—	—	—	—	—	—	—	—	30	—	—	—
S. Africa	28	30	17	21	—	—	—	—	—	—	—	18	—	—	—
Brazil	48	53	11	201	—	17	—	—	—	—	—	—	—	—	—
Mexico	27	35	—	30	—	—	—	—	—	—	—	—	—	—	—
Argentina	24	21	11	—	—	—	46	—	21	15	21	—	—	—	—
Other	—	37	—	—	—	—	144	—	17	—	—	50	70	—	—
TOTAL	4,657	4,011	2,408	2,050	161	297	2,029	105	1,176	485	546	1,009	70	74	221

[1] Fiat acquired a large stake in Citroen in 1969.   * Part-owned

Source: J. Ensor, *The Motor Industry* (Longman, 1971)

principal manufacturers in Europe are shown in Exhibit 1. These manufacturers could be divided into three main categories; (1) the European subsidiaries of the big three US producers; (2) the European volume producers; (3) the smaller specialist manufacturers which did not produce a full model range.

The American Subsidiary Companies

In 1974 the three major US manufacturers, General Motors, Ford and Chrysler, all had well-established subsidiary operations in Western Europe. Ford and General Motors had both formed their first European subsidiaries well before the Second World War, in Great Britain and West Germany. Chrysler had become established somewhat later by acquiring smaller manufacturers in the United Kingdom, Spain and France.

In total the European subsidiaries of the major US producers held over 30 per cent of the European automobile market in 1972, with Ford taking 13 per cent, General Motors' subsidiaries, Opel and Vauxhall, 11 per cent and Chrysler's subsidiaries, Chrysler U.K. and Simca, 7 per cent.

The General Motors and Ford subsidiaries were considered to be the leaders in marketing and production techniques in Europe. They were generally more profitable than the European volume producers, although they had not succeeded in expanding their market share and had indeed lost ground since the mid 1960s. In contrast, Chrysler had expanded its market share, primarily by improving its distribution system.

The American companies' approach was different from that of the European volume producers in several respects. First, they produced only a limited range of basic models, which were concentrated almost entirely in the volume sectors of the market, except the smallest A/B segment. The range of these basic models was significantly extended by making them available with a wide choice of body, power train and trim options. For example, General Motors' Opel subsidiary produced six basic models which were available in forty-three different derivatives, while Ford's German subsidiary produced fifty-six derivatives from four basic models. This policy was, however, being urgently reviewed as a result of the energy crisis and both Ford and General Motors had plans to introduce new small car models in the mid 1970s.

Secondly, the American companies believed that the European car buyer was principally interested in good value for money. As a consequence, their models were simply engineered and provided the maximum space at minimum cost, with styling taking precedence over expensive engineering features, such as front-wheel drive, rotary engines or pneumatic suspension. Finally, a policy of fairly rapid design changes was adopted at least for the cheaper models, which tended to be replaced every three or four years to encourage buyers to trade in.

Because of their relatively small model range and the use of production techniques derived from their present parent companies, Ford and Opel in particular enjoyed greater productivity than any of the other European manufacturers save Volkswagen.

General Motors

The largest American manufacturer had two principal subsidiaries in Europe, Opel in Germany and Vauxhall in Great Britain. Until the early 1970s, General Motors had maintained a policy of open competition between its European subsidiaries and as a consequence little cooperation had taken place between Opel and Vauxhall on model policy, interchangeability of parts and the like.

General Motors' German subsidiary, Opel, very small producers immediately after the Second World War, had expanded rapidly in the post-war period. In 1972 the company overtook Volkswagen as the largest supplier in Germany, and was the most profitable small car producer in Europe. Its production had increased steadily and exports had been developed in Europe and North America, where Opel cars were sold through the Buick division of General Motors. The company had its major production facilities near Frankfurt, where capacity was being expanded to 1.1 million units. In addition, Opel operated an assembly plant at Antwerp for assembling Opels for the US market and Vauxhalls and Opels for local markets. Smaller assembly plants were located in Switzerland and Denmark. Opel produced a model line of six cars in 1972, covering all areas of the market with the exception of the mini car and luxury segments. Nevertheless G.M. planned to re-enter the small car market, first by introducing a model in the UK based on the successful Opel Kadett; and in 1976 with a true mini car, probably from Opel but possibly built in Spain.

In contrast, the performance of General Motors British subsidiary, Vauxhall, had been poor. Although production capacity at the company's two plants, at Luton and Liverpool, was over 450,000 vehicles, production was only 250,000 in 1972. Vauxhall produced a model range of three cars in twenty-three derivatives, spanning similar segments of the market to Opel. In addition, the UK was General Motors' main manufacturing site for commercial vehicles in Europe, concentrating mainly on light vans and medium trucks, sold under the Bedford name.

Ford of Europe

In 1967 Ford formed a European management group to co-ordinate the activities of its main European operations in Britain and Germany. Until 1967 the two subsidiaries had been independent with the British subsidiary notably more successful. With the formation of the European management company, a policy of an identical model range in Britain and Germany was introduced in both main production centres.

By 1972 Ford had three major plants on the European continent, two in Germany, at Cologne and Saarlouis, and one in Belgium at Genk, together with two in Britain at Dagenham and Liverpool. The German operations had been expanded more rapidly in recent years, following a reallocation of export markets in favour of the German subsidiary and by 1972 production capacity was about equal in both countries, with a combined total of 1.2 million units. In addition, Ford manufactured a range of vans and trucks, principally in the UK, and tractors in the UK and Belgium.

Ford which had steadily moved out of the A/B market segment as its Cortina/Taunus range became bigger, planned in 1974 to come back strongly with a revamped Escort bottom-of-the-line model and prototypes of an even smaller model front-wheel drive car, code-named Bobcat, similar to the Fiat 127 or Renault 5, were under test. Production of this car was anticipated to start in 1976 from Ford's new plant at Valencia in Spain and Saarlouis.

Chrysler

The smallest and least profitable of the American manufacturers had been late to enter the European market. During the 1960s Chrysler, therefore, acquired three small and relatively weak European companies; Rootes in England, Simca in France and Barreiros in Spain.

Originally Chrysler had intended to build different model lines in each country using common components. However, financial difficulties of the parent company had forced its European policy to become more like that of Ford. It was intended to produce individual models in either France or Britain, but not in both, with engines and transmissions being shared between the two subsidiaries. In addition, Chrysler had integrated its European distribution system. Total Chrysler European production was 600,000 units, about the same number as Ford or Opel built in one country.

Chrysler, with no subcompact car of its own to market in the US, was especially hard hit by the swing to smaller models as a result of the energy crisis. In Europe both the Spanish and British subsidiaries were in some difficulties by the end of 1974 as a result of labour problems and falling sales. The company's French subsidiary Simca had performed best, due in large part to its small car range.

The European Volume Producers

In 1973 there were four major European volume producers, one from each of the main car-producing nations; France, Germany, Italy and Great Britain. These four companies, Renault, Volkswagen, Fiat and British Leyland Motors, had evolved as the main national car producers in their respective countries, and together accounted for some 50 per cent of the total European market. In 1974 the enforced merger of Peugeot and Citroen effectively created a fifth major, although this company was not yet operating as an integrated concern. The largest of these companies was Volkswagen, which was the biggest motor manufacturer in terms of sales outside the United States, although it was second to Fiat in unit production and market share in Europe. Renault, which had rapidly expanded its European market share in recent years, was approaching Volkswagen's European sales, while the fourth contender, British Leyland, held the smallest market share of the volume producers and had lost ground since its formation in 1968. The formation of Peugeot/Citroen created the third largest European producer in volume terms, and the new privately-owned company was actually larger than the state-owned Renault.

The European producers held special positions in their respective home countries and had effectively become national champions. This relationship was reinforced in the case of Renault, which was owned by the French State. Volkswagen was also partly state-owned, and following its search for liquidity British Leyland seemed destined to become largely nationalised during 1975.

In contrast to the American subsidiary companies, the European producers placed more emphasis on superior engineering in model design. More stress was placed on road-holding, compactness and performance than on exterior styling. As a result, European cars tended to be more expensive to produce than the American-inspired designs and often incorporated features such as front-wheel drive and hydraulic suspension. By producing cars with advanced engineering the European manufacturers aimed to maintain the model life of their cars and the average age of their models in 1973 was about eight years. Further, when new models were introduced older models were not necessarily terminated; thus Renault, after the 1972 introduction of its new small car, the R5, maintained production of its R4 and R6 models, which also competed in the A/B market segment. In recent years, to meet competition from the American subsidiaries, some new models had been introduced, such as the British Leyland Marina, which were along more conventional lines and designed to appeal to consumers more interested in value for money, as distinct from advanced engineering.

As well as maintaining a long model life, the European producers made their models available with far fewer options than the American manufacturers, preferring instead to produce a wider range of vehicles. British Leyland, for example, although the smallest of the European volume producers, manufactured over 20 different models with little interchangeability of parts between them.

Volkswagen

Volkswagen was in 1973 the second largest manufacturer in Europe, producing some 2.5 million vehicles in the company's production plants in Germany and abroad. The majority of this production was exported to other countries and only some 700,000 vehicles were sold domestically.

In 1945 at least 60 per cent of the company's main production facilities at Wolfsburg had been destroyed and limited production of a few thousand vehicles was undertaken by the British Army. Between 1948 and 1972 the company expanded rapidly as the Volkswagen Beetle successfully exploited both German and overseas markets, especially in North America. Until 1961, Volkswagen produced only the Beetle, but during the 1960s a number of new models were developed to extend market coverage. In addition, Auto Union and NSU were acquired and the company formed a joint venture with Porsche to produce a mid-engined sports car.

By 1974 Volkswagen and its subsidiaries were completing a thorough facelift of its European model line in the face of falling sales of the traditional Beetle. In addition, the company had developed overseas manufacturing facilities in Brazil, Argentina, South Africa and Belgium. As a result, Volkswagen competed in every segment of the market, although the company was still heavily dependent on the Beetle. This model still accounted for the majority of sales, but had began to lose ground in recent years in many of Volkswagen's most important markets, especially the United States and the German domestic market. Nevertheless, the high volume of Beetle production had enabled Volkswagen to extensively automate its production facilities and so achieve low manufacturing costs. Recognising the problems associated with the Beetle, Volkswagen had spent extensively in recent years to introduce a completely new-model range of cars. These, based largely on Audi design, were being introduced in 1973-4 and included a new small car, the Golf, to compete against the R5 and Fiat 127, as well as the new medium and sports coupé models, the Passat and the Sirocco. Despite the relative success of the new model range, however, Volkswagen sales in 1974 were some 30 per cent down on 1973 and heavy losses were incurred due to lower volume, inflation and the high cost of the new model programme. By the end of 1974 the company was forced to introduce large-scale labour layoffs, and Chief Executive Rudolf Leiding had resigned.

Volkswagen was also a large producer of commercial vehicles, specialising in the light end of the truck market.

Renault

Renault, the largest French auto manufacturer, produced some 1.1 million units in 1971, of which over 660,000 were for export. Renault, which was state-owned, had been the main force behind the export drive of the French motor industry and had expanded its capacity by nearly 70 per cent between 1968 and 1972. Profits were not considered to be of primary concern at Renault, where the main objective as a state corporation was to spread jobs and technology throughout the state, as well as contributing significantly to overseas earnings by exports.

After an abortive attempt to develop sales in the United States, which failed due to product deficiencies and an inadequate sales and servicing organisation, the company had turned to Europe for its main export markets. To support its export efforts, Renault had substantially broadened its model line in the late 1960s and the early 1970s and by 1973 produced eight models, covering all the main volume segments of the market. Renault was especially strong in smaller cars, where it produced three models in each of the A/B and C segments. Some of these models were of recent origin, but the remainder had been introduced during the early 1960s and were still being continued.

In 1966 Renault entered into a major association with the smaller, family-owned, Peugeot company. Although a full merger between the state- and privately-owned companies was not possible, research and development were shared, as were many components, and joint ventures were formed to produce engines and transmission assemblies. The heads of the two companies also met monthly to discuss strategy and co-operation.

Peugeot/Citroen

Largely as a result of the energy crisis the merger was announced in June 1974 between Peugeot and Citroen, the two leading private French auto producers. In 1974, Citroen, barely profitable in recent years, was stretching its financial resources to the limit with plant expansions and the introduction of two new models. The move, coming only one year after the termination of an abortive link with Fiat, was made possible by the Michelin family, who owned some 35 per cent of Citroen, striking a deal with the Peugeot family who still dominated Peugeot.

The new company produced Europe's third largest car manufacturer by volume after Fiat and Volkswagen. The two companies' model ranges were, however, dramatically different, Peugeot producing a balanced model line from its small 104 to its large 504 model, each fitting into an established market segment at the top end of the price and quality range. Citroen, in contrast, had produced significantly advanced engineering models such as the D series, the GS and SM-but spasmodically, without an apparent consistent strategy. At the bottom of its range was the aged 2CV.

In the short run it appeared the merger would produce little save an immediate saving of the Citroen financial position. The two companies had been fierce rivals for the French market and their model ranges, although different in philosophy, competed strongly against each other. In the long term the merger would only make sense if rationalisation of the model ranges took place.

Citroen and Peugeot both manufactured commercial vehicles in substantial quantity and production had expanded in the late 1960s and early 1970s.

Fiat

The dominant Italian motor manufacturer, Fiat, held over 60 per cent of the Italian market, a position of dominance not repeated in any other European national market. The company was still run by the Agnelli family and had grown rapidly to become the largest non-US auto maker in the post-war period, with overall production reaching over 2 million units, by 1970. Since then, the company's position had slipped back as the result of serious industrial unrest. Like Renault, Fiat had concentrated its export marketing efforts in Europe and had an extensive product line of fourteen different models, serving all segments of the market. The depth of the Fiat model range made it unique in Europe and each model was usually available in a wide range of variants. A great deal of attention however, was paid to ensuring the greatest complementarity of parts throughout the entire model range, thus ensuring economy in production.

Because of the primary demand nature of the Italian market, Fiat was especially strong in the production of small cars and had four models in the A/B segment, including the recently-introduced Fiat 126, 127 and 128 models. The company had traditionally been weak in the luxury segments of the market and had acquired the bankrupt Lancia company, which it had begun to revamp into a manufacturer of luxury saloon cars. In addition, Fiat had joined with Ferrari to produce the Dino sports car.

Fiat had been active in selling its know-how and design skills overseas in the new automobile-producing nations, such as Spain and Eastern Europe. In addition, Fiat had linked with the French Citroen company, which had resulted in a joint sales operation in various countries and was expected to pay off in terms of new model policy in the future.

Italy, particularly hard hit by the energy crisis coupled with rampant domestic inflation, serious labour relations problems and weak government, had forced Fiat to undertake major compromises with its work force in order to maintain the company's survival in the face of recession.

In addition to automobiles and trucks, Fiat was the most diversified and vertically integrated of the European producers, with interests in steel, machine tools, automotive components, aircraft, tractors, marine engines, nuclear plant, locomotives and railway rolling stock.

British Leyland Motors

The last independent British volume producer, BLMC, was formed in 1968 as the result of a merger between British Motor Holdings, which already incorporated the Austin, Morris and Jaguar companies, and Leyland Motors, which included Standard Triumph and Rover.

As a result of the merger and the continuation of many of the models of previously independent companies, British Leyland had the most extensive model range—some twenty-six cars—of all the European producers. Many of these models were relatively old, however, and their components were not integrated. With that and a comparatively small production output and an under-developed distribution system, British Leyland tended to be a relatively weak competitor in the European market. The company's share of the British market, however, remained high, although it had declined markedly since the mid 1960s in the face of increased competition from imports. Since 1968, the company had been rationalising its model policy, modernising its production facilities and building a European distribution system. By 1975 BLMC had hoped to be selling over 500,000 units in continental Europe, but the energy crisis and a weak financial position was forcing the company to drastically rethink its plans. Should a trend to small cars develop, the company could offer its mini range, which although over ten years old still sold well, and it had high hopes for its recently-introduced Allegro model in the 1100-1300 cc class.

Poor labour relations coupled with deficiencies in model line and production efficiency had resulted in low profits. Thus in 1974 with high inflation causing severe liquidity problems, BLMC had been forced to seek government help to provide essential working capital. This help was only granted in return for a measure of public ownership and British Leyland was thus likely to join Renault as a state-controlled corporation during 1975.

In addition to its extensive automobile range, British Leyland was the largest European manufacturer of commercial vehicles, with a range extending from light vans to heavy trucks and buses. The company also produced tractors and earth-moving equipment.

The Specialist Producers

In 1973 there were still some fifteen specialist manufacturers operating in the European market. These manufacturers did not produce a full model line and tended to avoid competing with the large volume producers in the mass market segments. A few, such as Daf, Citroen and Saab, did produce small cars, however, but in relatively low volume and these companies had tended to link with other specialist manufacturers in distribution, to provide adequate market coverage and a sufficient turnover for their dealers.

Most of the volume specialist producers, such as Volvo, BMW, Mercedes and Alfa Romeo, tended to concentrate on the luxury car segments, where they had established a prestige image that made it difficult for the volume producers to dislodge them. As a result, these companies had been able to expand their volume and achieve relatively high profitability during the 1960s. These firms had, however, been hit hard by the energy crisis as fuel economy became a more significant buying feature.

In addition to the volume specialist producers, there were a number of very small producers of high-quality sports cars, such as Maserati, Ferrari, Aston Martin, Jensen and Lotus, which had produced road cars based on experience gained from racing. Rising costs and limited production had caused these manufacturers increasing difficulty during the 1960s and many of them had therefore forged links with volume producers, in order to remain viable. The energy crisis posed these firms a further threat as car buyers sought fuel economy, and at the end of 1974 Aston Martin was forced into liquidation in the face of falling sales and severe liquidity problems.

THE DEVELOPMENT OF THE EUROPEAN AUTOMOBILE INDUSTRY

During the 1950s and 1960s the demand for automobiles in the main industrialised countries of Western Europe grew rapidly, as shown in Exhibit 2. As a result of rising *per capita* income and a growing population, most of whom had never owned a car, the number of automobiles in use expanded, especially in Germany, France and Italy, which together with the United Kingdom were the main car manufacturing centres in Europe.

EXHIBIT 2 New car registrations and unit production by country 1950-73

('000s of units)

	West Germany		France		Italy		UK	
	New Production	Registrations	New Production	Registrations	New Production	Registrations	New Production	Registrations
1950	216.1	160.0	257.3	198.5	99.9	80.0	522.5	134.4
1955	705.4	376.7	553.3	452.0	230.8	161.6	897.6	511.4
1960	1816.8	970.3	1175.3	638.6	595.9	381.4	1352.7	820.1
1965	2733.7	1517.6	1423.4	1057.1	1103.9	886.3	1722.0	1148.7
1970	3527.9	2107.1	2458.0	1296.2	1719.7	1364.6	1641.0	1126.8
1973	3649.9	2031.0	3202.4	1745.8	1823.3	1449.1	1747.3	1661.6

Source: Society of Motor Manufacturers and Traders, and industry estimates

Initially, individual countries of Western Europe developed as local national markets and in the major car-producing countries these local markets were dominated by indigenous manufacturers, which grew rapidly with rising consumer demand. In addition, export sales were sought, especially by British and German manufacturers, with the primary overseas markets tending to be North and South America in the case of German car makers, and North America and the former Empire territories in the case of the British.

In the late 1950s, the principal nations of Europe divided themselves into two major trading blocks, the European Economic Community (EEC), comprising France, Germany, Italy, Holland, Belgium and Luxembourg; and the European Free Trade Area, comprising Great Britain, the Scandinavian countries, Eire and Austria. As a result of these major political moves and subsequent reductions in tariffs between the members of the trading blocs, the automobile manufacturers increasingly came to enter one another's markets, especially within the EEC. As the car manufacturers from the main car-producing nations built up their distribution networks across Europe, the shares of the car makers in their own national markets gradually declined (see Exhibit 3).

THE EUROPEAN MARKET IN 1973

By 1973 the principal car-making companies in Western Europe could look forward to a home market of some 9 million vehicles per annum, principally within the EEC, where the removal of tariff barriers had meant a growing homogeneity in what was once, a brief decade before, a series of largely isolated national markets.

This market could be further subdivided into a series of seven main segments. Exhibit 4 shows the models produced in each of these segments. The larger of these, which were mainly served by the volume producers, were the mini (A/B), small (C), family (C/D), and full-sized (D) markets. The remaining segments, large (E), luxury (F) and sports (G) were much smaller in volume; and although a number of the volume producers had models in these segments, they were also the main market for the smaller, specialist car producers.

The European subsidiaries of the US companies, with the exception of Chrysler, did not compete in the A/B market, which they considered to be relatively unprofitable. The main contestants in this market segment, British Leyland, Fiat and Renault, were relatively unprofitable. The British Leyland Mini, first introduced in 1959, was initially aimed at meeting the need for a small, cheap, first-purchase car. During the 1960s

EXHIBIT 3 Market share in EEC by major manufacturers
(%)

	Fiat 1964	Fiat 1968	Fiat 1971	VW 1964	VW 1968	VW 1971	Ford 1964	Ford 1968	Ford 1971	GM 1964	GM 1968	GM 1971	Renault 1964	Renault 1968	Renault 1971	BLMC 1964[1]	BLMC 1968	BLMC 1971
Belgium/Lux.	7.6	11.3	8.8	7.1	12.9	11.2	18.8	13.5	14.0	14.6	12.6	9.7	8.7	8.3	10.3	2.6	5.0	3.1
France	2.5	6.6	5.2	0.8	1.9	2.6	3.8	3.1	4.9	2.9	3.7	2.6	25.7	27.7	29.3	1.0	2.3	1.7
Germany	5.0	7.7	7.9	29.8	31.9	28.9	15.0	13.4	14.6	26.2	19.6	18.8	2.7	6.1	7.1	0.1	0.7	0.7
Italy	73.8	74.5	64.3	3.5	4.8	4.8	2.2	1.2	3.3	3.2	2.7	3.4	0.7	1.8	3.5	0.1	4.5	4.2
Netherlands	10.1	12.7	11.0	14.5	16.6	9.1	16.4	13.0	11.6	16.9	14.9	15.6	6.6	6.4	7.8	3.5	5.5	3.6
Total EEC	20.5	25.6	21.6	13.1	13.9	13.9	9.1	7.2	9.4	12.9	9.9	10.1	9.5	11.2	12.1	0.7	2.8	2.2
UK	0.9	1.3	2.8	2.2	1.4	4.7	25.7	27.3	18.8*	11.4	13.2	11.4	0.7	1.0	3.2	37.0	40.6	40.2
Denmark	8.4	8.5	7.7	15.8	14.5	14.3	16.3	14.8	13.1*	18.4	11.6	13.4	4.7	4.5	4.1	8.9	22.6	15.2
Ireland	3.2	9.9	11.2	10.2	10.4	11.4	31.0	27.3	18.8*	8.0	14.5	10.7	0.5	3.5	7.1	36.7	28.6	24.4
Total enlarged EEC (9)	N/A	20.3	17.8	N/A	11.6	12.2	N/A	11.6	11.3	N/A	10.7	10.5	N/A	9.0	10.3	N/A	10.7	9.3

[1] BMC only
* Seriously affected by strike in the UK

Source: INSEAD and British Leyland

EXHIBIT 4   Product ranges of the European car manufacturers by market sector 1974

		BLMC	Ford	GM	Chrysler	Fiat/Lancia	VW/Audi	Datsun	Mercedes	Renault	Peugeot/Citroen	Toyota	Volvo	Saab	BMW	Alfa	Mazda
MINI	A/B	Mini Clubman			Imp	850 126 127		100/ Cherry		R4 R6 R5	104 Dyane Ami 8 2 cv						
SMALL	C	1300 Marina Allegro	Escort	Viva Firenza Kadett	Avenger 1100*	128	1200 1300 1302 Golf Scirocco	120/ Sunny		R12	204 GS	Corolla				Alfasud	1000 1300 818
FAMILY	C/D	Maxi Toledo 1500 Dolomite	Cortina Taunus 12/15M	Ascona Magnum	Hunter Sceptre 1301* 1501*	124 132 Lancia Beta	1500/1600 1600 Passat Audi 80	160/ Bluebird 180SSS 200L		R16	304	Carina		96 95		Guilia Alfetta	616 929 RX2 RX3
FULL-SIZE	D	1800/ 2200 B Series	Capri	Victor Ventora Rekord Manta	160/180 Alpine/ Rapier	124/ Coupe 125 Lancia Fulvia	411	240KGT 260C		R15/17	404 504	Corona Celica		99		2000	RX4
LARGE	E	Rover 2200/ 3500 Triumph 2000/ 2500	Consul Granada	Commo-dore		Lancia 2000	Audi 100 RO 80		220 230 240D		D/DS/ Pallas	Crown	144 145 164 244 245		2002 520 525		
LUXURY	F	XJ/Sov Limousine	Granada/ Ghia			130			250 280 350 450 600		SM				2500 3.0 3.3		
SPORTS	G	Midget MGB Spitfire Triumph/ TR6 Stag E Type	Mustang II	GT		DINO	914	260Z	450SL/ SLC							Montreal 2000GTV Spider	

* Simca

these consumers had begun trading up with growing affluence, and in many markets a decline had occurred in A/B car demand (see Exhibit 5). In Italy alone, A/B cars had remained as the leading market segment. In the early 1970s, a new wave of competition began in the A/B market with the introduction of major new models by Renault, Peugeot and Fiat and one still to be launched, by Volkswagen. These new entries were made to challenge the supremacy of the British Leyland Mini, and to tap what the manufacturers considered might be an important new market in urban transport and second cars.

EXHIBIT 5   Segmentation of the main European car markets 1965-70
%

	UK 1965	1970	W. Germany 1965	1970	Italy 1965	1970	France 1965	1970	Total 1965	1970
A/B	14.2	11.5	6.3	7.7	64.1	44.7	27.5	25.7	21.9	20.0
C	38.1	41.7	37.0	35.2	17.4	26.9	30.7	22.2	32.2	32.0
C/D	18.6	19.4	17.1	14.5	2.7	10.9	14.8	27.4	14.9	17.5
D	14.9	13.7	28.9	31.1	11.2	10.4	18.8	17.3	21.3	20.1
E	10.4	9.3	8.3	8.1	3.2	4.1	7.3	6.3	7.3	7.6
F	2.0	2.2	1.7	2.6	0.1	0.5	0.3	0.4	1.3	1.5
G	1.8	2.2	0.7	0.8	1.3	2.5	0.6	0.7	1.0	1.3

Source: INSEAD

By 1973 the main volume market had become the C, C/D and D segments, which catered for the family and fleet operator purchasers. In these segments competition between all the volume producers had become intense. The differing philosophies of the American and European producers had led to a proliferation of choice for consumers. In recent years several European manufacturers had added new models, which attempted to compete with the American subsidiaries in offering more conventionally engineered cars and a value-for-money concept, while at the same time maintaining their traditional, more sophisticated engineering models. British Leyland, for example, actually offered three model lines, a Morris line with conventional engineering, to compete for price-conscious consumers and the important fleet market, the Austin line, with more advanced engineering, including transverse engine and front-wheel drive, and the Triumph line of more luxuriously finished speciality cars. Most manufacturers, and especially the American subsidiaries, had introduced a proliferation of options and derivatives available for their basic models. For example, Ford offered its Cortina/Taunus model in Germany, with forty-six derivatives, compared with only eighteen derivatives for its 1965 model.

The E and F market segments were the main areas where the specialist companies, especially Volvo, BMW, Alfa Romeo and Mercedes, experienced considerable growth and high profitability in recent years, as the market for executive cars had previously been relatively small and on the European mainland dominated by Mercedes and Citroen, with Volvo established in Scandinavia and Jaguar and Rover, both still independent, successful in Britain. By 1973 new entrants, including BMW, Alfa Romeo, Fiat, through its acquisition of Lancia, and Volkswagen, by the acquisition of Audi, had successfully invaded the market. In addition, companies like Triumph and Peugeot, builders of expensive small cars, had expanded their lines upwards, and after several unsuccessful attempts the American subsidiary companies were also making new efforts to tap the luxury market.

The sports car market was a small segment, which could be roughly divided between the small, relatively cheap, specialist cars, principally built by volume manufacturers, and very expensive luxury machines, built by the famous racing marque companies. The market had shown relatively little expansion and was threatened by the introduction of safety requirements. Unlike the specialist manufacturers serving the executive market, many of the famous sports car manufacturers had experienced difficulty due to rapidly increasing costs and very limited production. By 1973 companies such as Porsche, Ferrari, Maserati, Matra, Alpine and Lotus had been forced to forge links with volume manufacturers to remain viable. As a result, several of the volume producers had attempted to develop new market segments by the introduction of high-performance sport saloon cars, incorporating the expertise of the specialist sports car and racing designers. Ford had introduced its Capri to tap the market for a small sporty car, similar to its successful Mustang in the United States, Fiat the Dino, incorporating a Ferrari engine, Citroen the SM, a joint development with Maserati, and Volkswagen the mid-engined VW-Porsche.

THE IMPACT OF THE OIL CRISIS

By the end of 1974 the trends of the European market toward larger average engine sizes and to a lesser extent larger body shells had been dramatically reversed. The success of unilateral price increases by the oil-producing countries seemed to indicate that Western Europe might face a decade during which oil prices would increase steadily. This was in sharp contrast to the experience of the 1960s when reduced transport costs and competition between producers had led to low oil prices. Further, there were signs that at least some European governments were taking steps to reduce their balance of payments deficits by reducing oil consumption by introducing either formal rationing or rapid price increases.

As a result, petrol consumption in most European countries was down some 10 per cent by the end of 1974 as motorists used their cars less for commuting or began to switch to smaller cars. Sales of small cars had held to about their 1973 levels in most European markets, while large car sales and especially those of the cheaper models such as the Ford Granada range, had slumped by some 50 per cent. Further, predictions for 1975 were extremely gloomy, with a market of around 7.5 million vehicles compared with 9.3 million in 1973, or only some 60 per cent of industry working capacity. Beyond 1975, industry leaders were highly uncertain about the future, but most did not anticipate any return to a growth position until the late 1970s. The slump could not have come at a worse time, as many companies had capacity increases nearing completion or new model launches in hand.

Some motor producers were already rethinking product policy plans. While Renault, British Leyland and Fiat had traditionally been strong in this segment Volkswagen was increasing its range of economical cars with the introduction of the 1100-1300 cc Golf, and plans were advanced for an even smaller 900 cc model. Further, the American big two, Ford and General Motors, planned to move into the small car market, while Peugeot and Alfa Romeo, traditionally specialist producers of expensive medium-size cars, had recently introduced small cars in the 1100-1300 cc class.

PRESSURES ON THE AUTOMOBILE INDUSTRY

Despite the large size of the European domestic market and the fact that Europe was the largest car manufacturing centre in the world, as the 1970s evolved it seemed likely that a number of significant new pressures would make an impact on the industry. These pressures were principally the following:

1. A declining growth rate for cars in Europe;
2. The threat of increased competition from Japan and other emerging automobile manufacturing nations;
3. Industrial unrest;
4. Social pressure against the car;
5. Cost inflation.

A Declining Growth Rate for Cars in Europe

In 1972 the car market in Great Britain expanded by almost 40 per cent over 1971, while in France an improvement of 14 per cent was recorded. These two, however, provided the only two bright spots in an otherwise bleak year for the European car markets, as market growth elsewhere began to slow and, in the case of West Germany, showed a marginal decline. Further, few experts believed that the enormous expansion of the

British market was anything more than a temporary aberration, caused by several years of tight credit controls, which had been relaxed to release pent-up demand. Industry leaders were somewhat divided as to the impact of the oil crisis on future demand. M. Pierre Dreyfus, head of the French Renault Company, expected the drastic recession in the industry to persist for at least two years. His pessimism was shared by Signor Giovanni Agnelli, President of Fiat, and Mr John Barber, Managing Director of British Leyland. All agreed, however, that the high growth of the 1960s would not be repeated.

The Threat of New Competition

The Japanese automobile industry had shown phenomenal growth during the 1960s. From a total production of less than 200,000 vehicles in 1960, Japan's motor manufacturers built 5.8 million vehicles in 1971, 3.7 million of which were automobiles.

As a result of this increase in output, the Japanese manufacturers were proving a serious threat to European manufacturers in world markets, in particular in Asia, Australia, Southern Africa and North America. By 1972 Japanese cars dominated the automobile market in Asia, and over one million vehicles were sold in the United States and Canada.

However, restrictions placed on imports by the US government, together with a decline in their domestic market, had forced the Japanese manufacturers to increase their efforts to sell cars in Western Europe. In 1969 the Japanese exported 90,000 cars to Europe and by 1972 this had risen to a total of 242,000.

Initially the Japanese had concentrated their efforts on the fringe markets of Europe, such as Norway, Greece, Portugal and Switzerland, where there was little or no indigenous manufacture. In 1972, however, a more concerted effort was made to enter the major European markets, as shown in Exhibit 6. In Britain, sales doubled and Datsun overtook Volkswagen, the third largest importer. Toyota, still somewhat smaller than Datsun, tripled its British sales. On a smaller scale, rapid growth took place in Germany and France, where sales doubled over 1971.

EXHIBIT 6 Japanese car sales in Western Europe 1969-72

	Sales ('000 units)		Increase (%)	Total Market (million units)	Share (%)
	1969	1972		1972*	
UK	4	43	975	1.65	3
Switzerland	5	42	740	0.25	16
Netherlands	6	40	567	0.45	9
Belgium	13	32	147	0.32	10
Finland	15	18	20	0.1	17
Austria	0.3	16	—	0.2	8
Portugal	3	16	433	0.07	22
Norway	6	12	100	0.08	16
W. Germany	2	7	250	2.05	0.4
Denmark	3	6.5	116	0.1	6.5
Sweden	0.5	5	2,000	0.22	2
France	6	5	(17)	1.6	0.3
Italy	—	0.8	—	1.5	0.1
TOTAL	63.5	242.0	281	8.6	3

* Estimated

Source: Financial Times and INSEAD

The manufacturing costs of the main Japanese producers were the lowest in the world, due to a combination of American-style production methods, coupled with European wage rates and highly efficient shipping, using special-purpose car freighters. As a result, the landed cost of Japanese cars in Europe was still lower than that of any equivalent European automobiles.

While the Japanese cars were not advanced in engineering concepts, their well-proved arrangement of front engine and rear-wheel drive meant that they had proved extremely reliable and manufacturing costs remained low. The cars, even small ones, were therefore fitted with a wide range of factory-fitted extras, such as headrests, self-seeking radios, additional lamps and the like, which were expensive options on the more basically equipped European cars. By the end of 1974, Datsun in particular was making rapid progress in Europe with its highly successful small-car Cherry and Sunny ranges, and Honda was attacking with its even smaller 600 cc Civic model. In the UK Datsun was outselling Chrysler and Vauxhall.

To preserve foreign exchange, many developing nations offered considerable incentives to manufacturers to establish local manufacturing plants. When such plants were erected they usually started as assembly operations, but frequently became manufacturing facilities as demands were made for higher percentages of locally produced components. These fledgling industries were usually protected by high tariff barriers, but as production capacity grew and became more economic such local operations often began to seek export markets.

In the post-war period, automobile manufacturing had developed in South Africa, India, Iran and Turkey. In addition, in recent years there had been a very rapid development of car manufacturing and assembly in the less developed nations of Western Europe, especially in Spain and Yugoslavia and in Eastern Europe. By the use of advantageous fiscal measures the Belgian government, too, had encouraged rapid development of automobile manufacturing and assembly during the 1960s.

It was also anticipated that the Western European car makers could well expect a challenge from Eastern Europe to develop during the 1970s. Having been re-equipped with Western transfer lines, machine tools and, in some cases, with actual Western auto designs, the Eastern Bloc countries were expanding production rapidly. It was expected that these countries might well seek to sell part of this production in export markets, especially Western Europe.

Industrial Unrest

The automobile industry had experienced significant problems of labour unrest, which from time to time erupted into damaging strikes, often terminated by inflationary wage settlements. The British industry, in particular, had experienced severe industrial relations problems throughout the 1960s and early 1970s, and had a far worse record of working days lost through strike action than any other European car-producing country except Italy. Partly as a result of this serious disruption in production, British manufacturers had lost market share, almost consistently, during the five years prior to 1972.

There were signs, however, that the more peaceful atmosphere in other European car plants was changing. In France, where a severe national strike created a political crisis in 1968, a further serious strike affected the new Renault plant at Le Mans in 1971. In Italy the 1970s had begun with an even worse industrial relations record than the British. High absenteeism and frequent wildcat strikes had erupted in the car plants of Northern Italy. The state-owned Alfa Romeo company was the target of ugly strikes and riots in 1971, which prevented the company from achieving any increase in production over the 1969 level. The Fiat company lost 36 million man-hours through strikes and absenteeism in 1971 and 1972, with the result that total output had been unable to expand for three to four years.

In West Germany labour relations had been remarkably good, due mainly to the large annual wage increases granted during the boom years of the 1960s. However, with the rising value of the DM, German labour rates were the highest in Europe and the effect on the competitiveness of car production was expected to be felt, especially in export markets. As a result of declining profitability it seemed likely that harder industrial bargaining would take place as the manufacturers became less generous in their wage settlements. Already a major confrontation had occurred in 1971 with a strike by metalworkers, which had paralysed the industry of southern Germany. The recession was also seriously affecting the position in northern Germany, and Volkswagen in particular was trying to cut its domestic work force substantially.

Some labour experts believed that financial motivation was by no means the most significant reason for the poor industrial relations record of the industry; but rather that the boredom, repetitiveness and frustration of assembly line production led to a psychological readiness to strike or go absent.

Social Pressures Against the Car

Despite the oil crisis and the unexpected setback it presented to the automobile industry there were significant social pressures emerging against the private car due to congestion, pollution and questions of safety.

In Western Europe, Germany, Britain and the Netherlands were already heavily congested, as were northern Italy and parts of France. Britain were perhaps worst off due to a lack of alternative means of transport which carried a high proportion of freight elsewhere in Europe. In addition, Britain had a poorly developed inter-urban motorway system by comparison with its neighbours. As a result of congestion, therefore, there was growing social and political pressure to legislate against the use of private cars, especially in urban areas where pollution was an additional problem, in favour of public transport systems. The oil crisis, however, had forced some rethinking of pollution controls because of the decreased engine efficiency caused by anti-pollution devices.

With regard to safety, the most stringent regulations had been introduced in the United States, where as a result it was anticipated that cars would become heavier, slower, less manoeuvreable and substantially more expensive. Those European manufacturers with large export sales to the United States were being forced to redesign their models to meet the new American regulations. Volvo, for example, in 1974 had introduced a redesigned model range to incorporate many additional safety features and this range was also being sold in Western Europe to prevent the necessity of offering two uneconomical ranges for different markets. While other manufacturers were expected to follow the example of Volvo, safety engineering in Europe was moving in somewhat different directions compared with the USA due to differences in road systems, the type of accidents and the size and design differences between European and US automobiles. However, the effect of the fuel crisis and the growing worldwide recession, resulting in lower automobile usage and road accidents, had led some manufacturers to postpone plans for increased safety as they battled for economic survival.

Cost Inflation

The most important processes in automobile manufacture were in metal-processing, finishing and assembly. Economies of scale existed in metal pressings for car bodies; by the use of mechanical handling and high-speed presses it was possible to achieve up to an annual production of approximately 1 million units per year in a single plant, although because die-life was limited the effective optimum level of production was only about 400,000 units. Another key process was the machining of engine-block castings in transfer lines, where the optimum production units were 300,000 to 400,000 units. Other important components such as transmission systems and rear axles could also be produced more economically in quantity. Assembly, on the other hand, was a labour-intensive process with an optimum scale of only 125,000 to 250,000 units, although some manufacturers had attempted to reduce labour content by increased automation. The savings achieved by producing several models in one plant were considerably less than a multiplicity of scale economies for single utilisation. A further cost factor of increasing importance was the cost of marketing, distribution and service, where the development of an effective Europe-wide dealer network was estimated to require a production volume of at least 1 million units.

In the early 1970s inflation in Western Europe was a serious problem in all the major car producing countries. Further, the impact of oil price rises had resulted in a sharp increase in inflation, with only Germany enjoying a rate of less than 10 per cent in 1974. Because of increased labour and raw material costs, the price of new cars produced in Europe had risen by an average of about 25 per cent between 1969 and 1972. The accelerating pace of inflation was apparent in that in 1974 alone price rises throughout Europe had been on average between 20 and 30 per cent. In future, while inflation was expected to continue at a high rate, the additional cost of safety and anti-pollution features was expected to add anything up to 30 per cent to the price of new cars, depending on the timing and extent of new regulations. Over-capacity leading to severe competition meant very low profit margins. As a result severe liquidity pressures were emerging on the car makers in the face of inflation in raw material and finished goods stocks, and the high cost of new model investment programmes.

For the average consumer, the costs of motoring were rising at an alarming rate. In addition to the increased cost of purchasing, car repairs and insurance were also rising rapidly, while petrol prices had virtually doubled in 1974 alone. At the same time, used car prices had not kept pace with the rising cost of new cars, and, therefore, depreciation had increased rapidly during the early years of a car's life. This was expected to continue as replacement became a greater factor in car purchase; rates of depreciation in the United States were still approximately double those in Europe. Some experts considered that almost every cost connected with motoring was rising by a minimum of 15 per cent a year and there were signs of the inflationary spiral increasing in the near future.

EFFECTS OF PRESSURES ON THE AUTOMOBILE INDUSTRY

The primary effects of all these pressures on the European motor industry were twofold:

1. increased concentration;
2. a narrowing of industry profit margins.

Increased Concentration

Since the Second World War, there had been a substantial contraction in the number of independent automobile producers, primarily by acquisition. In Europe, only the Ford and General Motors subsidiaries had grown entirely by internal growth, although even Ford had acquired certain of its supplying companies. In France, Citroen had acquired Panhard in 1965 and Berliet in 1967, before being forced to link with Peugeot in 1974; in Italy, Fiat acquired Lancia and Autobianca; in Germany, Volkswagen had absorbed Auto Union and NSU; in Britain, the formation of British Leyland had effectively reduced the British-owned automakers to one; and in 1974 Volvo had acquired Daf.

In addition to these outright mergers there had been a proliferation of less complete links, such as trade investments, joint ventures and intercompany agreements on assembly, component supply, research and development, and component manufacturing; Volkswagen and Daimler Benz had an agreement on research. These less formal arrangements were, perhaps, developing as a substitute for transnational mergers, of which there had been remarkably few. It was anticipated that any such linkage between the major manufacturers would be difficult, since they would prove politically very sensitive.

Nevertheless, the percentage of output by the major companies had increased considerably, and this trend was expected to continue. In addition, where there was scope for further national mergers, it was considered that economic pressures might well ensure these took place at an accelerating rate during the 1970s.

Narrowing of Profit Margins

During the 1960s and early 1970s there had been a gradual reduction in the level of profitability achieved by the major manufacturers, as shown in Exhibit 7. Despite rapidly rising costs, the intensity of competition was such that no manufacturer was able to pass on all cost increases without incurring rapid and lasting erosion of market share. For example, General Motors' Opel subsidiary was forced to rescind a proposed price increase in France, caused by upward valuation of the DM and devaluation of the franc. Sales dropped dramatically because of the increased prices, with the result that Opel were again forced to reduce their prices.

Each company tried to recapture increased costs by raising prices on specific models, or in specific markets at a time when it would do least harm. Some were prepared to maintain low prices in an effort to improve market share. For example, Volkswagen in Britain had deliberately held down the price of some of its models in order to improve penetration after the revaluation of the DM. Similarly Renault, supported by the French Government, had deliberately forgone short-term profitability, in order to substantially improve capacity and overall market share, while Fiat priced aggressively in France and Germany where it, too, wished to build up market share.

As a result of reduced profitability, the volume producers had been forced to increase their borrowing in order to maintain investment in production equipment, new models and improved distribution. Only the specialist car producers successfully exploiting the luxury markets, such as Volvo, BMW, Peugeot, had been able to show significant profit improvements in the early 1970s.

EXHIBIT 7   Return on investment for the leading automobile producers 1968-73

	1968	1969	1970	1971	1972	1973
General Motors	12.3	11.5	4.3	10.6	11.8	11.8
Ford	7.0	5.9	5.2	6.3	7.5	7.0
Chrysler	6.6	1.9	(0.2)	1.7	4.0	4.2
Volkswagen	7.8	6.0	4.5	1.3	1.7	1.5
Fiat	3.4	1.2	0.4	1.0	1.0	0.0
Renault	0.5	2.9	0.1	(2.2)	0.9	0.7
British Leyland	3.1	2.7	0.1	2.0	2.9	2.8
Daimler Benz	6.8	5.4	5.4	8.0	5.3	4.5
Volvo	3.8	4.0	2.8	2.0	2.5	3.0
Peugeot	2.7	3.7	8.8	2.7	4.3	4.0
Citroen	0.3	0.0	(35.8)	0.3	1.7	3.1
BMW	n.a	6.4	4.0	3.1	7.2	6.0

The effects of the oil crisis were threatening profitability and especially the liquidity of all manufacturers. As inflation increased, the sheer cost of maintaining stocks, with prices rising 20 per cent or more, was stretching even the major manufacturers to the limit. Already by the end of 1974 severe warnings had been issued by top management at Renault and Fiat of future problems unless urgent government action were taken to curb inflation; and BLMC had been forced to seek direct government aid. In addition, the move toward smaller cars was also expected to reduce profitability since margins on small vehicles were traditionally low.

RESPONSES OF THE AUTOMOBILE INDUSTRY

In responding to the threats and opportunities posed by the forces acting on the motor industry, the major companies had acted in one or more of the following ways:

1. Increased investment in research;
2. Changes in work procedures and wage systems;
3. Increased product choice;
4. Increased integration;
5. Growth overseas;
6. Diversification;

Increased Investment in Research

To meet legislation, both actual and anticipated, on safety and pollution, the car makers in Europe and the USA were spending substantially more on research and development. Mercedes and Volvo had both built experimental safety vehicles, which incorporated features such as hydraulic bumpers, rigid passenger compartments, skid-resistant braking systems, and the like. Rover, too, had consciously designed its cars to meet increasing needs of passenger safety. The energy crisis was also resulting in a rapid search for improvements in fuel economy. Already poor fuel consumption had dramatically reversed the industry's interest in rotary engines as a solution to pollution.

The rising costs of servicing were being met by the development of electronic diagnosis systems. Volkswagen, in 1972, had introduced its first models with built-in wiring which measured the efficiency of various key items, so that when the car was serviced it could be plugged into a computer for instant diagnosis.

Changes in Work Procedures and Wage Systems

To combat increasing industrial unrest, a variety of new methods were being attempted. At BLMC, new wage payment methods were being introduced to replace piecework payment by a standard daywork system. In addition, the company had located new production in less developed areas such as Merseyside and Scotland, where more adequate supplies of labour were available. Non-indigenous Algerian labour was heavily used by Renault, while in Germany Turkish, Yugoslav and Italian workers manned many of the assembly lines. By the use of workers from areas of high unemployment or relatively poor countries, the manufacturers hoped, not always with success, that the economic incentives of assembly line work would outweigh its obvious disadvantages.

The potentially most encouraging developments, however, had appeared in Sweden, where an alternative to assembly line operations was being tested as a method of reducing labour turnover, absenteeism and worker dissatisfaction. Both the Volvo and Saab companies had installed experimental lines, which relied on a batch production system. Under this system workers were divided into groups at specific work stations, where they assembled a complete major component in batches. The workers were free to determine their own pace of work and to rotate jobs between the group. Apart from improved social contact, they had the satisfaction of producing a complete sub-assembly.

Increased Product Choice

There was a growing tendency, especially on the part of the American subsidiary companies, to develop models for specialised market niches, either by the development of complete new models or by the use of an extensive range of options which effectively permitted consumers to personalise their vehicles. Ford had introduced its Capri model, successfully using both these strategies. The car, developed simultaneously in Germany and Britain, was aimed at a new market niche for a small sporty saloon car, similar to that established by Ford in the USA with its Mustang. The size of this niche would probably have been too small in any one country to justify the extensive investment in such a model. However, by introducing such a speciality car on a Europe-wide basis, Ford had captured a large share of a new high-growth market segment. In addition, the company offered the Capri in twenty-six option packs, with three engine options and a variety of interior and exterior trim options to further broaden its appeal. Other manufacturers, such as Renault and Opel, had since followed Ford into this market segment, with the Renault 17 and the Opel Manta.

The European manufacturers still offered fewer options and variants than the American manufacturers, but most had extended their model range by the introduction of new cars aimed at meeting specific consumer needs. Renault had successfully developed a series of cars, such as the Renault 16, which combined the advantages of saloon models with those of the estate car. Speciality car producers, such as BMW and Reliant, had also opened a new niche for fastback estate cars, selling in the luxury class.

Increased Integration

To combat rising costs and take advantage of the growing homogeneity of the European market, manufacturers were actively integrating their marketing, development and manufacturing facilities, increasing interchangeability of parts or forming joint agreements with others to undertake joint development or use common components.

The American manufacturers, and Ford in particular, had led in integrating production and marketing facilities. In 1968, Ford had created a European management organisation which had been responsible for integrating the model range of its British and German subsidiaries and strategically distributing its new investment on a Europe-wide basis. Chrysler had also formed a similar management organisation in 1971 and intended to concentrate production of specific models at each of its European plants, using as many common components as possible. General Motors, slower than the others, was in the process of more closely linking its Opel and Vauxhall operations.

Growth Overseas

The motor manufacturers were increasing their degree of international activity. British Leyland, for example, had acquired Innocenti, its Italian assembler; and was substantially expanding its assembly operations in Belgium. Cash problems had, however, forced BLMC to curtail some of its plans for expansion, and it had been forced to close down much of its operations in Australia. Other manufacturers had made similar moves; Ford and General Motors had begun to exploit the developing markets in Spain, while Fiat had entered Spain and Eastern Europe and was already the most international of the European manufacturers. Many of the American and European manufacturers had established production or assembly operations in Belgium, where GM, Ford, VW, Renault, Citroen, Peugeot, British Leyland and Volvo had all set up facilities.

Apart from transnational investment within Europe, however, the leading manufacturers were also actively expanding in the newly-developing markets around the world. In this, the Europeans followed the major American manufacturers, which were still expanding their international operations. By 1973 General Motors had established substantial assembly or manufacturing facilities in ten countries, Ford in twelve and Chrysler in nine. Most active amongst the European makers were VW in South America, British Leyland in the former British Empire territories, and Fiat in a variety of developing countries. As a result of this activity, every few weeks a new assembly operation, often set up by dealers of the major motor companies, came into operation, and export sales of CKD vehicles were expanding much faster than sales of fully assembled cars.

Diversification Away From Automobiles

As a result of low profitability, over-capacity and the energy crisis, several of the leading manufacturers were seriously contemplating reducing their dependence on the automobile industry. Volvo and Daimler Benz amongst the specialist manufacturers were engaged in a wide range of engineering products in 1974, and had been noticeably less affected by auto industry cycles. Amongst the volume manufacturers Fiat and Peugeot were most diversified, although automobiles still represented the largest single component of sales. In addition, Renault announced that it was seriously planning to extend non-automotive interests.

5 Air Inclusive Tour Holiday Industry*

(up to February 1970)

On Monday 5 July 1841 the first inclusive tour (IT) available to the public set out from Leicester railway station. Five hundred and seventy men and women travelled to Loughborough, a distance of eleven miles, to take part in a temperance meeting and gala: the price of the day's excursion was one shilling, half the normal fare, and included tea with lavish helpings of ham. The organiser was a Mr Thomas Cook, then aged thirty-three.

Twenty-six years later he invented a device upon which much of the success of the IT holiday industry was based, the hotel coupon. It conferred upon its bearer the right to demand lodging and meals at any hotel named within the scheme. Thomas Cook was the first to recognise that although those who had never left their own country before, who were unacquainted with foreign tongues, and who wished to visit other lands and to see with their own eyes the historic places and sights about which they had read, were glad to join a personally conducted tour to the continent, there were many persons imbued with the English love of independence and isolation. They preferred to travel either alone or else in company with their family or personal friends, to stop at the place which pleased them as long as they desired, to select their own route and to feel themselves free to follow the impulse of the moment. For these clients Cook negotiated with the hoteliers an arrangement whereby he undertook to guarantee payment for certain rooms and meals if the hotelier agreed to lodge and entertain clients provided by Cook himself. So successful was this scheme that by the 1890s 1,200 hotels in various parts of the globe accepted the coupons, and that in these the traveller was 'free from all doubts and anxieties about the length of his bill and the accuracy of its items'.

It was not, however, until after the Second World War that the air inclusive tour holiday industry began to develop. Although Cooks had organised holidays to Nice using chartered aircraft as early as 1938, it was the ready availability of considerable numbers of war-surplus aircraft in the late 1940s which enabled the air IT holiday to 'take off'. In addition, a number of islands in the Mediterranean, formerly unknown to the ordinary tourist, had been equipped with military runways by the US Air Force.

One of the first IT companies to start business was Horizon Holidays founded by Vladimir Raitz. The company was set up in 1949, and in its first year of operation carried 300 holidaymakers in Dakotas from London to a holiday camp in Calvi, Corsica. The all-inclusive price for the holiday was £32.10s. Another company that began operations in the early 1950s was Whitehall Travel which organised air IT holidays for civil servants. Universal Sky Tours, founded in 1954 by Captain Langton, a former pilot, had grown to be the second largest firm in the air IT industry in the mid 1960s (the largest was Lunn-Poly). In 1965 Sky Tours had sold a total of 75,600 holidays during the summer season to Spain, Italy and Yugoslavia.

Other companies, such as Global, had different origins. Initially established shortly after the war as retail travel agents, they soon saw the opportunity of creating and selling their own ITs. Global began in 1951 selling IT holidays by coach to Oberammagau and Rome. In 1956 Global set up a subsidiary company, Overland, also offering European holidays by coach, but priced at 25 per cent below those sold by Global itself. This was achieved by using larger coaches and more modest hotels. Overland was immediately successful; 25,000 holidays were sold in the first three weeks. Not until 1960 did the companies first use air transport: Global flew direct from London to resorts in Spain and Italy, and Overland used air transport to cross the Channel. In the winter season of 1961-2 Global offered sunshine holidays at resorts in the Mediterranean for the first time.

THE GROWTH OF COMPETITION

The decade of the 1960s was a period of rapid growth and many changes in the air IT industry. In 1962 an estimated 0.6 million UK residents went on air IT holidays

---

* Copyright © London Business School 1972

abroad out of a total of 2.5 million going overseas on holiday. By 1969 the figures were 1.7 million and 4.35 million respectively, as Exhibit 1 below shows.

EXHIBIT 1 UK residents returning to the UK from foreign holidays*

(thousands)

	All routes	By air		By sea	
	Total	Total	IT	Total	IT
1962	2,495	1,235	591	1,260	521
1963	2,793	1,368	675	1,425	537
1964	3,146	1,671	903	1,475	570
1965	3,521	1,828	1,148	1,693	609
1966	3,953	2,096	1,373	1,857	549
1967	3,986	2,172	1,448	1,814	496
1968	3,846	2,204	1,507	1,642	391
1969 (estimate)	4,350	2,500	1,700	1,850	400

* Excludes Irish Republic

Source: International Passenger Survey, Board of Trade

In the early years of the decade a substantial proportion of those going on air ITs travelled on scheduled services. Charter services, however, rapidly took over the lion's share of the market. The IT companies organised these charters in response to the increasing level of competition; substantial savings were possible through high utilisation and high load factors on chartered aircraft. The overall growth and destination of charters are shown in Exhibit 2.

EXHIBIT 2 Passengers by air from the UK on **inclusive tour holidays by charter services***

(thousands)

	Summer			Winter	
	Total	Spain	Italy	Total	Spain
1962	291	78	55		
1962/3				—	—
1963	404	113	75		
1963/4				7	2
1964	568	195	103		
1964/5				22	9
1965	724	251	137		
1965/6				36	13
1966	1,172	413	210		
1966/7				42	13
1967	1,320	582	206		
1967/8				92	44
1968	1,463	815	183		
1968/9				164	85
1969 (estimate)	1,800	1,100	200		

* Excludes North or South America, the Far East, Australasia and Africa south of the Sahara. IT holidays by scheduled services are not included.

Source: Transport Development Unit from data provided by Civil Aviation Department, Board of Trade

The rapid growth of the industry and the high profits being made by the successful operators stimulated the formation of many new IT companies. The UK Travel Trade Directory of 1965 reported that there were 377 companies creating and operating tours to seventy-four countries. The competition forced prices down, only to reveal ever greater numbers of holidaymakers keen to take their first foreign holidays on the beaches of the Mediterranean.

In Europe too there was dramatic growth. The Swedish government, for example, took the view that inclusive tour holidays were a socially desirable form of recreation, and that IT companies should be permitted the maximum possible freedom to sell as many holidays as possible. By 1968 the figure for air ITs was 387,000 or 5.0 per thousand head of population as compared with 2.7 per thousand head in Great Britain. In Germany the total sales of air ITs by 1968 was 862,000. One of the leading department stores in the country, Neckermann and Reisen, increased their sales from 18,000 holidays in 1963 to 220,000 in 1968 with an anticipated 380,000 in 1970. This growth throughout Europe led to intense competition for the best facilities, especially hotels, at the most popular Mediterranean resorts. The proportion of the populations in European countries travelling abroad by air IT charter is indicated in Exhibit 3.

EXHIBIT 3   Air inclusive tours from the leading European countries

	1968 Air ITs (thousands)	1966 Estim. Pop. (millions)	Air ITs per thousand
Great Britain	1,518	54.8	2.7
Germany	862	59.6	1.4
Denmark	484	4.7	10.3
Sweden	387	7.8	5.0
Spain	239	31.9	0.7
Holland	224	12.5	1.8
France	203	49.4	0.4
Italy	111	51.9	0.2
Switzerland	67	6.0	1.1
Finland	63	4.6	1.4
Belgium	60	9.5	0.6
Austria	45	7.3	0.6
Norway	45	3.8	1.2

Source: Transport Development Unit

AIRCRAFT AND HOTELS

Since the most costly components of the air IT holiday were the aircraft seat and the hotel bed, every attempt was made to reduce these costs to a minimum. An analysis of the figures of a leading IT company in 1966 showed the following:

	£	%
Average holiday price	48.4	100
Hotel cost (inc. transfers)	18.3	38
Aircraft cost	16.5	34
Overheads	4.8	10
Agents' commission	3.9	8
Profit	4.9	10

The traditional method of securing aircraft seats in the early 1960s was the series charter: the tour operator contracted with an airline for a series of flights, say twenty-five on a once-weekly basis, to a specified destination. By the middle of the decade, the larger IT companies with access to substantial funds had gone over to time charters. Under this arrangement the aircraft was leased from the airline for a guaranteed minimum utilisation of, say, 1900 hours per annum, at a specified hourly rate. Should the tour operator be able to use the aircraft for more than the specified minimum, the hourly rate dropped substantially. In 1970 the going rate for a Boeing 737 with seating capacity for 124 passengers was of the order of £400 per hour for the first 1900 hours, £290 per hour thereafter, and perhaps a special mid-week winter rate of £250 per hour. This represented therefore a minimum financial commitment of £750,000, but if fully utilised meant a reduction in aircraft cost of about 15 per cent compared with the series charter. (The terms of payment were usually an initial deposit of 5-10 per cent, and thereafter monthly payments in advance, calculated on the planned utilisation.)

A number of large IT companies recognised that aircraft costs could be reduced still further by entering into medium/long-term (5-10 years) time charter arrangements with an airline. This transferred a part of the commercial risk normally carried by the airline to the IT company. In return the airline was naturally willing to reduce its prices, especially as aircraft became more and more expensive. For example, as of February 1970, Clarksons had a long-term time charter contract with Autair and Global had a similar arrangement with Caledonian.

The final step in aircraft seat cost reduction was the vertical integration of IT company and airline. Two of the largest IT companies had taken this step: Thomson Travel Holdings, the holding company for Sky Tours, Gaytours, and Riviera Holidays, owned Britannia Airways; and Monarch Airways was owned by Cosmos.

Changes in the methods of acquisition of hotel beds also occurred. Throughout the 1960s, particularly in the second half of the decade, there was a shortage of beds in the most popular resorts. Not only were British companies in competition with each other, but also they competed directly with the Scandinavians and the Germans. The IT companies further discovered that British holidaymakers did not take kindly to being accommodated in a hotel dominated by fellow guests of a different nationality—different social habits led to friction and ill-feeling.

The original method of obtaining beds was to have an annual contract with the hotelier and to renew that contract each year. The growing competition for beds led to rapid increases in prices and consequent uncertainty for the IT companies—a problem exacerbated by the fact that they had to print their summer season brochures before the contracts for that season had been negotiated with the hoteliers. Furthermore, no IT company could be confident that the beds it had used one year would be available the following year: the hoteliers were in a strong position to negotiate last-minute contracts with competing IT companies.

As a result, the practice of contracting with a hotelier for a block of beds in his hotel for 7-10 years became increasingly common. The normal contract had three particular features: first, an initial deposit was required, usually amounting to between 10 and 20 per cent of the total value of the contract (sometimes it was as high as 50 per cent), to be repaid over the length of the contract; second, the negotiated rate per bed at night increased by an agreed fixed percentage every year to allow for inflation; third, the IT company had to give a guarantee that there would be an agreed level of occupancy of the beds, averaged over the whole summer season, below which a financial penalty was incurred. For the 1970 summer season the going rate for a two-star hotel bed in Benidorm or Mallorca, for example, was approximately £1.30 per night, rising at 4 per cent per annum over a seven-year contract, and an initial deposit of £250 per bed.

A third method of obtaining beds also developed in the late 1960s. This was the long-term (15-25 years) turnkey lease, in which the IT company took over a complete hotel, fully equipped and furnished, and was entirely responsible for providing the management. Usually a deposit was required amounting to perhaps three years' rent in advance. This scheme guaranteed beds for years ahead, and allowed total control over the quality of service provided. There were, however, some problems. Local hoteliers resented a hotel leased and managed by an IT company, because the company tended to favour its own hotel, especially in lean years. In addition, local hoteliers usually ran their own hotels as family businesses, thereby reducing overheads significantly. Furthermore, they usually arranged their financial accounts so as to attract the minimum tax liability, a practice which the foreign hotelier could not adopt if he wanted to maintain his good name with the local and national authorities.

Whether the hotel was locally managed or managed by a foreign IT company, it had to pay its way, and make a reasonable profit within the holiday season. The great majority of hotels in the Mediterranean resorts only operated within the summer months, usually between 26 and 32 weeks of the year. During this time, they had to earn sufficient to cover all fixed costs throughout the year. As a result, the marginal costs of operating during the winter were less than half of the 'normal' summer costs. Some hoteliers were content to charge less than marginal cost during the winter because the hotel staff could then be offered full-time employment throughout the year.

INTEGRATION AND THE ENTRY OF 'BIG BUSINESS'

One result of these changes in the methods of acquiring aircraft seats and hotel beds during the 1960s was an increased demand for funds. These demands were beyond the resources of many companies. Unless a company was prepared to see its market share decline, there appeared to be no alternative but to look for assistance outside its own resources. At the same time, a number of large organisations saw the small or medium-sized IT company as an excellent route into the profitable air IT industry. The shipping companies, whose business was steadily being eroded by the boom in air travel, were among the most active in this respect.

One shipping company made a study in the late 1960s to determine how best to enter the industry. The study concluded that, in order to be competitive and to survive, it was necessary to operate on a substantial scale. This meant catering for the mass holiday market, and this in turn meant setting up a new company. The cost of entry was estimated at £4-5 million: approximately half of this sum was required to obtain aircraft at the most competitive rates on time charters; £1 million was needed to secure hotel beds; the balance was divided between initial launching costs and setting up an efficient central organisation.

Most companies decided to buy existing tour operators rather than start up a new venture. In 1965 Thomson Industrial Holdings, part of the Thomson Organisation, bought three IT companies, Universal Sky Tours, Riviera Holidays and Gaytours. Also in 1965 Shipping and Industrial Holdings acquired Clarksons, which at that time specialised only in short tours to Europe. In 1966 Air Holdings increased its investment in the IT industry by purchasing Lyons; it already owned Whitehall Travel and Leroy, both acquired in 1964. During 1967 Fortes bought Millbanke and in 1968 followed up with Hickie Borman and Swans. In 1969 Swans was split up into two components: Swan Tours, which was sold to the Diner's Club; and W. F. and R. K. Swan, which was retained by Fortes.

By 1969 more than 50 per cent of all air IT holidays from the UK were sold by only eight companies. The twenty-one members of the Tour Operators' Study Group (TOSG), which had been formed in 1968 by the leading IT companies to act as a forum for discussion on matters of mutual interest, accounted for over 85 per cent of the business. The combined turnover of the twenty-one members and thirty-six other tour operators totalled £106 million in 1969: profits before tax totalled £1.6 million.

Certain IT companies, however, wished to retain their independence. They opted out of the low-priced market, and instead they either offered a specialised product or catered for a different segment of the market. The largest of the independents was Horizon Holidays, which successfully attempted to cultivate an upper-class image (the up-market). Horizon operated on a national scale and offered departures from several regional airports. Some independents concentrated on particular countries: Yugotours on Yugoslavia; Balkan Holidays on Bulgaria (with the backing of the Bulgarian Ministry of Trade); and Exchange Travel on Malta, Gibraltar, and Cyprus. Another type of specialist was the Travel Club. Founded by Harry Chandler in 1936, the Travel Club sold only 11,000 holidays in 1969 but was considered to be one of the most profitable IT companies in the industry (in terms of profit as a percentage of average holiday price). Chandler recognised that he could not afford time charters nor big block bookings of hotel accommodation. Competition with Thomsons and Clarksons in the mass market was impossible. He deliberately aimed for the up-market and offered a highly personalised service. Almost all his customers first heard of the Club by word of mouth; there was no advertising nor use of travel agents. Nonetheless, the Club sold holidays in Spain, Italy, Switzerland and Yugoslavia at good hotels in both the well-known resorts and in the off-beat corners of Europe.

PRICE REGULATION OF ITs

Under a UK government regulation, loosely known as Provision 1, the price of air inclusive tours was partially controlled. It was government policy not to restrict the volume of air IT traffic, but to prohibit all IT companies from selling any holiday at a price less than the scheduled service economy class fare to the same destination. This policy was enforced by the Board of Trade through the Air Transport Licensing Board (ATLB) to whom all airlines were required to submit applications for any flight to and from the UK and to specify both the purpose of the flight and the fare to be charged. Until about 1965 this regulation did not pose any problem for the IT companies. Later on, as the Edwards Committee report made clear, the situation changed.

EXHIBIT 4   Extract from the Report of the Committee of Enquiry into Civil Air Transport

(Chairman: Sir Ronald Edwards)

Presented May 1969

Provision 1 of the Price Regulation of Inclusive Tours

706   For the most part the adoption of Provision 1 has not, in the past, been a major problem for tour operators: they have been able to develop the inclusive tour business to destinations in Spain and Italy without being hampered unduly by the price regulation imposed by the ATLB. In the recent past, however, developments have occurred which have caused the tour promoters to complain vigorously that Provision 1 has become a serious problem in the conduct of their business. These developments in the inclusive tour market are: (a) the introduction of tours to more distant destinations; (b) the attempt to develop new tour traffic at low prices during the winter period, and (c) the introduction of short duration tours. In addition, special problems in tour pricing arose in 1967 as a result of devaluation. IATA fares were increased but there was no justification, in the view of tour promoters, for a corresponding increase in IT prices.

707   We have taken evidence from tour operators and other travel agents, from scheduled and non-scheduled airlines and other people interested in this subject, and we fully recognise that significant problems do arise.

708   The following simplified examples of the operating costs of scheduled and chartered services will illustrate the nature of these problems which derive essentially from three factors: (a) a charter flight may contain more seats on the aircraft; (b) the load factor is likely to be significantly higher; (c) some of the indirect costs would be lower for the charter operation.

709   Considering first only (a) and (b) above, let us assume that the same aircraft costs per hour will be achieved in both types of operation and that for the charter operation about 10 per cent more seats are fitted in the aircraft. When the resulting direct costs per seat mile are converted to a cost per passenger mile, at load factors of 60 per cent for scheduled and 85 per cent for IT charter operations, the aircraft operating costs of charter operations are seen to be less than two thirds of those of scheduled operations. Ignoring other indirect cost advantages which may be enjoyed by the charter operator and which may be quite substantial, normal scheduled fares of, say, 8d. a mile short-haul and 6½d. a mile long-haul would correspond to charter seat prices of about 5d. and 4d.

710   Thus the differences of 3d. and 2½d. per mile available for hotel and meal costs in an inclusive tour sold at the price equal to the return scheduled fare would, on this basis, yield about £20 for a stage length of 800 miles and about £80 on a route of 4,000 miles. The first figure is inadequate to cover summer season hotel costs for two weeks, whereas for the long trip a tour operator could provide hotel accommodation at substantially less than the amount available. Hence on these long routes Provision 1 is bound to be a major problem for the tour promoter. The 4,000 mile case used in the foregoing example is, of course, a very long route, but the problem which arises on this route will also occur on shorter routes, and it is for the reasons just described that the ATLB with the agreement of the Board of Trade made exceptions to the application of Provision 1 on tours operated to places like Rhodes (1,700 miles).

711   Even on quite short routes the tour operator faces a problem with Provision 1 during the winter period when cheaper charter rates are available, cheaper hotel rates can be negotiated, and the applicable fares on scheduled services tend to be higher (summer excursion fares are not available). In such circumstances a tour operator who wanted to organise a winter holiday at a low promotional price found that Provision 1 prevented this.

            *   *   *   *

In order to resolve the problem, the government began to relax Provision 1 after April 1968. For the winter season of 1968-9, the minimum price allowed for an air IT holiday of eight days' duration was reduced to 50 per cent of the normal tourist class round-trip fare available on the route in question. This applied to almost all destinations in Europe. In April 1969 this relaxation of Provision 1 was extended to the winter of 1969-70. For the summer season of 1970 the prices of eight-day and twelve-day holidays were relaxed to 80 per cent and 90 per cent respectively of the relevant fare during the 'shoulder periods'—1 April to 15 June and 16 September to 15 October. Significantly, the Board of Trade stated that for holidays of four days or less, the 'control price would be determined on merit by the ATLB'.

The reasons for some form of price control of IT holidays were set out by the ATLB in November 1968.

1. To prevent price cutting leading to deterioration in holidays through entry of less scrupulous operators.
2. To prevent pressure on tour operators' margins leading to the collapse of companies.
3. To prevent pressure on charter prices leading to financial difficulties for airlines or jeopardising operating standards.
4. To avoid such a disparity in price between IT traffic and scheduled traffic that diversion to charter becomes a reality making it difficult for airlines to maintain scheduled services.

There was no doubt that both (1) and (2) above had taken place on a few occasions resulting both in serious inconvenience and in financial loss to many holidaymakers. In 1965 a number of tour operators had gone bankrupt, the most notable of which was Fiesta Holidays (the company was later the subject of a Board of Trade enquiry and one of the directors was prosecuted). Fiesta's collapse led to the establishment of a Common Fund by the Association of British Travel Agents (ABTA). Under this scheme all members of ABTA contributed to the Fund a certain sum every year related to their turnover. In the event of a member (who might be either a travel agent or a tour operator) going bankrupt, the Fund was available to rescue holidaymakers who were stranded abroad, and to compensate those who had paid for, but not yet taken, their holidays.

The Common Fund was the butt of much criticism by both travel agents and tour operators. Many companies objected to the principle of paying for the errors of judgement or unscrupulousness of others. There was disagreement as to whether travel agents should be responsible for the failures of tour operators and vice versa. Perhaps most important, it was recognised that the sum available in the Fund (at 30.6.68 it stood at approximately £60,000) would be insufficient to finance a series of small failures or the failure of even one medium-sized operator.

Matters were brought to a head by the collapse of another tour operator, Wrights, in the summer of 1969. The company had built up an excellent reputation in Tunisia but collapsed due to lack of liquidity through trying to expand too rapidly. The Fund was only just adequate to pay the necessary compensation. This situation led TOSG to serious consideration of a new proposal. The idea under discussion in the early months of 1970 was that the members of TOSG should each put up a bond to the value of 5 per cent of their turnover. Initially it was proposed that the bond should be put up by the parent company of a tour operator (for example, by Great Universal Stores for Global), or by an insurance company or by a merchant bank. In the event of the collapse of a bonded tour operator, the bond would be cashed and the operators's liabilities met. No other tour operator would bear any financial loss. TOSG believed that such a scheme was preferable to price regulation by the ATLB.

Neither in Germany nor in Scandinavia were tour operators subject to an equivalent of Provision 1. They were therefore able to price their holidays below those of the UK firms, especially in the winter and over long-haul routes. Further, both the Germans and the Scandinavians had developed the practice of selling IT holidays at give-away prices at airports a few hours before the departure of the aircraft if there were any seats available (for example, £5 for two weeks in Corsica). For the tour operator the scheme produced additional revenue which he would otherwise have had to forgo; it also reduced the likelihood of the operator failing to reach any guaranteed level of occupancy at his hotels and thereby incurring financial penalties. For the holidaymaker, it provided the chance of an incredibly cheap holiday, provided he was prepared to risk whether he got a holiday at all, and also where he went.

In the UK the ATLB saw Provision 1 primarily as a means to protect the scheduled airlines, and also the independent (charter) airlines. TOSG argued that, in this respect too, Provision 1 was undesirable, if not counter-productive. Vladimir Raitz of Horizon Holidays quoted the cases of Palma in Mallorca and Dubrovnik in Yugoslavia as examples of a number of airports first used by Horizon as charter destinations, and subsequently used by BEA as destinations for their scheduled flights. It was true, however, that in Europe SAS and Iberian Airlines had had to abandon their scheduled services between Mallorca and Scandinavia as a result of competition from charter services.

SELLING IT HOLIDAYS

A distinctive feature of the air IT holiday industry in the UK was the high proportion of holidays sold through general retail travel agents (in February 1970 there were approximately 2,750 throughout the UK with a total of 4,000 offices). A survey by the Economist Intelligence Unit (EIU) in 1968 estimated this proportion as 83 per cent, as against 77 per cent for airline seats and 68 per cent for sea passages. The sale of IT holidays by travel agents represented the most profitable part of their business since they normally received a commission of 10 per cent on each sale and occasionally an overriding commission of an additional $2\frac{1}{2}$ per cent. As a result, any attempt by the IT companies to bypass the travel agent, by selling direct to the public or using some other outlet, met with strong resistance.

The travel agents were in a powerful position. Since many IT companies marketed almost identical holidays, and 'brand loyalty' was low, the agents had great influence on whose holidays were sold. They could effectively 'black' any IT company they chose without seriously affecting their volume of business. Furthermore, all the largest travel agents (25 per cent were responsible for 78 per cent of business in 1968) were closely linked through ABTA and could, in theory, if they so wished, act together against any individual IT company. This was unlikely, but the threat remained.

For the IT companies, who operated on load factors of 85-90 per cent, and for whom each additional sale after breakeven represented almost pure profit, the maximisation of outlets was increasingly important. The EIU survey suggested that the number of outlets could be increased by the use of supermarkets, banks, mail order houses, etc. In Germany the most successful IT company, Neckermann and Reisen, was a large chain of department stores which had a mail order list of $4\frac{1}{2}$ million people. By aggressive pricing the company had gained over 25 per cent of the German IT market. In Germany and in Holland the banks were making serious attempts to enter the travel industry. In Australia the sale of holidays through women's journals was highly successful, an indication, perhaps, of the power of the female in choosing the family holiday.

In the UK a number of IT companies had attempted either to bypass or to supplement the general travel agent, usually without success. Most companies included in their brochure a booking coupon but, despite the fact that the IT holiday had become a relatively standardised product, very few members of the public chose to use this method of purchase. In 1969 two new schemes were initiated, one by Clarksons in conjunction with the *Daily Mirror,* and the other by the *Readers' Digest.* Neither appeared to be particularly successful. Another small independent IT company, Key Tours, planned to sell 25,000 holidays in 1970 in conjunction with a company in the consumer goods field, Provident Clothing and Supply, which had a field sales force of 13,000 agents. These agents made personal calls on householders and the idea was to sell holidays direct to the consumer.

Another strategy open to the IT companies was the acquisition of a chain of independent travel agents. Vertical integration had not proceeded far in this direction, possibly because of the threat of boycott from other travel agents should an IT company make a serious move towards such a policy. None the less Horizon Holidays had acquired a dozen or so agents, strategically sited in the most important cities; Lunn-Poly, who were estimated to have sold nearly 100,000 holidays in 1969, owned about sixty agents; and Thomas Cook, who had 155 offices throughout the UK, were attempting to market both their own IT holidays and holidays in association with BEA (Silver Wing). Global was moving in the direction, not of acquiring independent agents, but of giving them maximum support, including training facilities to encourage the subsequent promotion of Global Holidays. The EIU survey found that little capital was normally required to set up an agency and that staff costs accounted for between 60 and 65 per cent of the total running costs. Significantly, the EIU study revealed that provincial and country town agents were generally very profitable: 75 per cent showed profits in excess of 20 per cent of total revenue (total value of ticket sales less remissions to carriers and tour operators); 40 per cent of suburban agents showed profits in excess of 20 per cent of total revenue, but city shopping centre agents showed small profits.

6 Thomson Holiday Holdings (A)*

In February 1970 Thomson Holiday Holdings (THH) was facing a serious situation. Profits had been steadily declining since 1965. Bookings for the 1970 summer season were marginally down on those for 1969, indicating a further and possibly substantial deterioration in profits. Five months previously, in September 1969, a new managing director, Bryan Llewellyn, had been appointed, the fifth in two and a half years. Llewellyn knew that he could do very little to improve the situation in the current year (1970), because the various holiday programmes had been finalised some months before his appointment. His problem was to decide on the best policies for THH in 1971 and through the remainder of the decade.[1]

DEVELOPMENT OF THH

In 1964 the Thomson Organisation (see Exhibit 1) had decided to expand its activities and diversify out of newspapers and advertising. It was decided to go into the travel business and that entry would be through the acquisition of existing companies, rather than the creation of new enterprises. A new subsidiary, Thomson Industrial Holdings (TIH), was set up in February 1965 to handle any such acquisitions.

EXHIBIT 1   Thomson Organisation
             Group financial statistics
             (£000s)

	1968*	1969
NET ASSETS/FUNDS EMPLOYED	56,403	62,148
TURNOVER		
Newspapers	48,018	51,826
Magazines, books and exhibitions	18,377	19,260
Travel companies	12,400	15,217
Other activities	8,461	9,131
Total	87,256	95,434
TRADING PROFIT		
Newspapers	6,413	6,130
Magazines, books and exhibitions	1,322	1,604
Travel companies	822	1,301
Other activities	(172)	1
Total	8,385	9,036

* 1968 figures exclude Scottish Television, whose sales were £2.64 million and trading profit £471,000 up to 23 July 1968—the date on which Thomsons relinquished control.

Source: Annual reports

---

[1] Certain names and figures have been disguised and some events have been described in only summary form by the author.

* Copyright © London Business School 1972

During 1965 and the early part of 1966 TIH bought three inclusive tour (IT) holiday companies. The largest of these, and the second largest company in the air IT industry, was Universal Sky Tours, trading under the brand name of Sky Tours. The company had been founded by Captain Langton, a former pilot, and owned its own airline, Britannia Airways, which at that time operated six Britannia 102 aircraft. Universal Sky Tours also owned another subsidiary, Voyagers, which was a general retail travel agency holding an International Air Transport Association (IATA) licence (an essential asset for any successful travel agent).

The second company bought by TIH was Riviera Holidays. Riviera had been set up in 1959 by Aubrey Morris, a taxi driver from the East End of London. The company had initially been called Taxi Flights and organised holidays by rail to the Italian Riviera. However, in 1962 Riviera started to fly out of Southend with Channel Airways. The company then flourished, specialising in low-priced holidays, and in 1965 sold 28,000 holidays to the popular resorts in Spain and Italy.

Gaytours was the third and smallest of the companies acquired by TIH. Like Riviera, the company had a strong, almost exclusive regional bias. It had been founded in the 1950s by Norman Corkhill, and operated out of Manchester, selling holidays in the low-priced market. Together with Gaytours, TIH acquired Planet Holidays, a general travel agency in Manchester, also with an IATA licence. Corkhill had bought Planet Holidays both for the IATA licence, and to act as a base for a new brand of package holiday, called Luxitours, designed to appeal to the more affluent market in the North.

TIH appointed one director to the board of each of the three IT companies. Each company was initially allowed to operate independently of the other two and almost independently of Thomson House, the head office of the Thomson Organisation. Langton, Morris and Corkhill were, however, three forceful men who had created successful companies and who jealously cherished their complete independence. Late in 1966 Langton left Sky Tours. In January 1967 THH was established, as a subsidiary of TIH, in an attempt to coordinate the activities of the three travel companies. Britannia Airways remained under the direct control of TIH (see Exhibit 2). Aubrey Morris was appointed as the first managing director of THH, with Norman Corkhill as the deputy managing director.

EXHIBIT 2   Simplified Company Organisation Charts

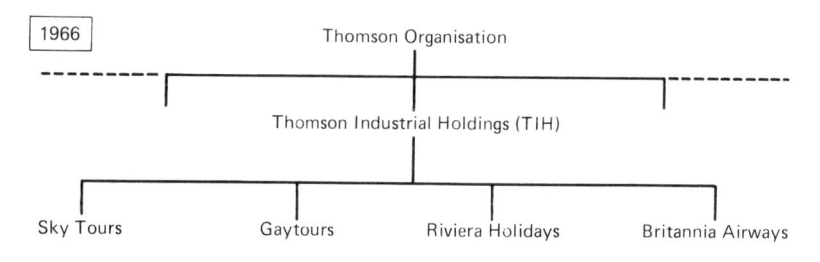

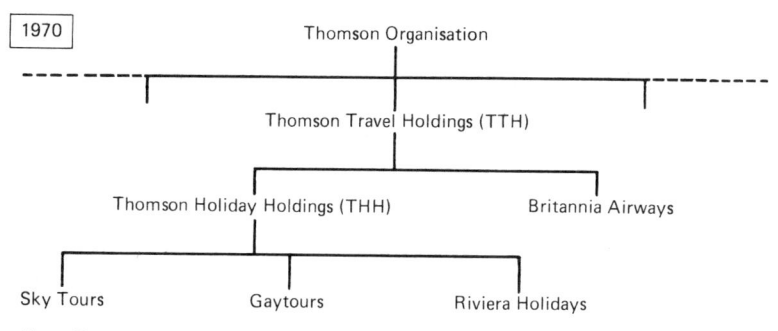

1966

```
                    Thomson Organisation
                            |
              Thomson Industrial Holdings (TIH)
                            |
   ┌────────────┬───────────┴──────────┬──────────────────┐
Sky Tours    Gaytours          Riviera Holidays      Britannia Airways
```

1970

```
                    Thomson Organisation
                            |
              Thomson Travel Holdings (TTH)
                            |
              ┌─────────────┴─────────────┐
   Thomson Holiday Holdings (THH)      Britannia Airways
              |
   ┌──────────┼──────────┐
Sky Tours  Gaytours  Riviera Holidays
```

Note: Travel agencies and hotel companies have been omitted.

Source: Company records

In July 1967 TIH became Thomson Travel Holdings (TTH). To the board of directors of TTH was appointed an outsider to the Thomson Organisation, Hilary Scott, who had been an accountant. It was felt that Scott could provide the professional management expertise required by the rapid expansion of THH. Unfortunately Scott and Morris clashed constantly. In March 1968 Morris resigned. Corkhill took over for an interregnum of three weeks, and in April 1968 Scott was appointed managing director. However, this arrangement also proved unsatisfactory. In September 1968 another new man, Alan Todd, an economist, was brought in as managing director and Scott became chairman.

In 1969 the difficulties at board level came to a head. Between January and April three of the THH directors left to set up a new venture, 4S Travel. In June Alan Todd resigned and three months later he left: prior to his departure, Hilary Scott had also taken another appointment. Finally, in September, with the morale of THH and its subsidiary companies at a low ebb, Bryan Llewellyn took charge. Formerly the marketing director of Thomson Regional Newspapers, he had had no previous experience in the travel industry.

MANAGEMENT ORGANISATION

By the time Llewellyn was appointed managing director, THH was largely organised on functional lines. Reporting to him were seven directors.

Title (Name)	Responsibilities
Finance and Administration (Ken Hollingdale)	Finance and administration, including data processing
Marketing (Peter Finch)	Marketing, field sales, reservations (telephone bookings) and passenger relations
Operations (Riddy Williams)	Aircraft scheduling and movements; also reservations (confirmation, cheques and tickets)
Continental (Norman Lewis)	Negotiation of all hotel contracts and leases; also resort representatives
Overseas division (Norman Corkhill)	Management of all hotels on lease and other operations overseas
Development and Special Projects (Lionel Steinberg)	Development of new types of holiday and special projects, e.g. holidays to Mexico for the World Cup
Northern Operations (Vincent Cobb)	All activities of THH in the North of England

In the three years since early 1967 the management functions of the three IT companies had gradually become more centralised, especially those of Sky Tours and Riviera. These two companies still, however, retained a degree of autonomy, in particular their brand names and their own holidays. The brand managers of Sky Tours and Riviera were responsible (to the marketing director of THH) for the various holiday programmes of each brand and for all advertising including brochures. The holiday prices were determined jointly by the brand managers, the marketing director and the managing director of THH, the latter making the final decision.

Gaytours in Manchester, however, still retained a considerable degree of independence from THH in London. Under Vincent Cobb who, in addition to being northern operations director, was also general manager of Gaytours/Luxitours, there were individual managers responsible for sales, reservations, operations and accounts. These managers were not responsible to the relevant functional departments in London.

MARKETING AND PRODUCT POLICY

Product policies of the THH companies

Sky Tours was by far the largest company within THH, selling its products on a national scale. Lionel Steinberg, who had been personal assistant to Captain Langton—the founder of Sky Tours—in 1965, stated that 'Sky Tours had a reputation of giving good value for money and was the mass market leader'. The company concentrated its efforts on summer sunshine holidays in the Mediterranean resorts. An attempt had been made to create a winter sunshine programme in the 1964/5 and 1965/6 seasons, but the prices were not sufficiently attractive to make the programme a success. Another attempt was made in 1967/8 (after constant pressure had finally persuaded the Board of Trade to relax Provision 1 in respect of winter holidays—see 'Price Regulation' below), this time with sufficient response to justify its continuation, although at less than a tenth of the scale of the summer programme (see Exhibit 3).

EXHIBIT 3   Sales of Holidays by Thomson Holiday Companies 1964-9

(thousands of holidays)

Year	Sky Tours Summer	Sky Tours Winter	Riviera	Gaytours	Luxitours	Universal Coach Tours	Sky Tours Minitours
1964	59		11	11	—	—	—
64-5		1					
1965	76		24	12	—	—	—
65-6		2					
1966	105		39	16	2	—	—
66-7		—					
1967	136		48	17	4	6	—
67-8		7					
1968	146		38	16	8	—	—
68-9		10					
1969	155		35	18	11	—	1

Note: Not included are the figures for the 1968-9 winter sunshine programmes of Riviera, Gaytours and Luxitours.

Source: Company records

In the 1965 summer season, Sky Tours sold holidays to three countries only—Spain, Italy and Yugoslavia. The company offered a choice of thirteen different resorts, seven of these in Spain; four departure airports—London (Luton), Manchester, Glasgow, and Newcastle; a summer season from mid-April to the end of October (with prices at four levels depending on the time of year) and three lengths of holiday—11, 12 and 15 days. By 1970 the range of products had expanded substantially: there was a choice of eleven countries, nineteen resorts, and seven departure airports. The season lasted from mid-March to the first week in November, and there were four lengths of holidays —8, 11, 12 and 15 days (see Exhibit 4).

Riviera Holidays expanded successfully until 1968, when they suffered a sharp reverse. Up to and including the 1967 summer season, Riviera had always flown with Channel Airways out of Southend. However, during that year Aubrey Morris, the managing director of THH, fell out with Channel Airways. He decided to contract with another airline, British Eagle, for the 1968 season, because it was offering very attractive rates from London Heathrow. The results were disastrous. This was due in part to the fact that although Riviera was a well-known brand in the counties east of London, and flew from the local airport, it was little known elsewhere; in part it was due to the devaluation of sterling in 1967; and lastly to the military coup in Greece, which seriously affected a new programme of 9,000 holidays travelling by air to Italy and thence by sea to Greece.

Because Riviera could not fill all the aircraft contracted from British Eagle, certain flights had to be cancelled. Holidaymakers who had already booked on these flights were transferred to Britannia Airways flying out of Luton. By the end of the 1968 season, approximately half of Riviera's 38,000 holidaymakers had flown with Britannia. This represented a windfall for that airline, because at the height of the 1967 summer season, it had found itself with substantial spare capacity available. In the 1969 season all Riviera's business was carried by Britannia. However, there was a further decline in the number of holidays sold; a total of 35,000 out of a planned capacity of 48,500. In the winter of 1968/9 Riviera attempted to market a Mediterranean sunshine programme, but only 282 holidays were sold. The success of the 1969/

EXHIBIT 4   Sky Tours Product Range

	Length of season	Barrier[1] periods	Departure Airports	Countries	Resorts[2]	Length of Holidays (days)
1965	11/4-31/10	7	4	3	13	11, 12 & 15
1966	2/4-31/10	7	4	3	12	11, 12 & 15
1967	18/3-31/10	7	4	3	13	11, 12 & 15
1968	29/3-9/11	7	7	6	18	8, 11, 12 & 15
1969	29/3-26/10	8	7	9	18	8, 11, 12 & 15
1970	14/3-5/11	8	7	11	19	8, 11, 12 & 15

Notes: [1] Barrier periods—see below for one type of holiday.

[2] Resorts—a resort is defined as an area having its own airport.

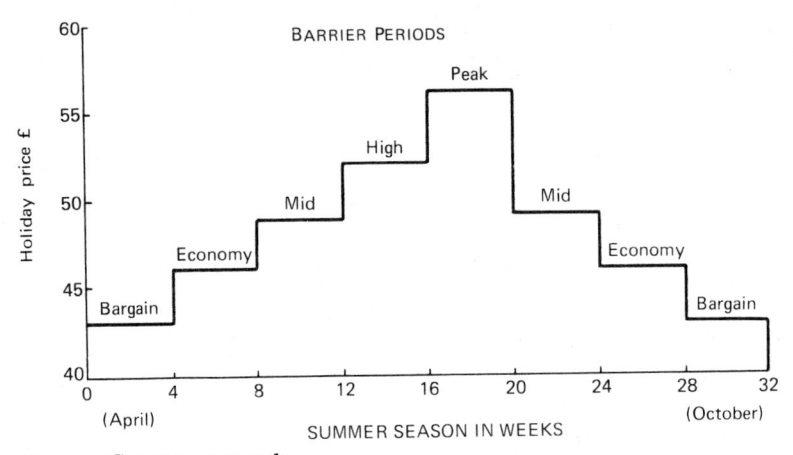

BARRIER PERIODS

(chart: Holiday price £ vs Summer season in weeks, from 0 (April) to 32 (October); stepped pattern — Bargain (~43), Economy (~46), Mid (~49), High (~53), Peak (~57), Mid, Economy, Bargain)

Source: Company records

70 winter programme hardly looked more promising, with bookings for less than 1000 holidays.

In the North of England, Gaytours and Luxitours showed steady and profitable expansion. Gaytours was in the same low-priced mass market as Sky Tours and in the summer season of 1969 sold 18,000 holidays; planned capacity for the 1970 season was 26,500. Luxitours, selling a more expensive holiday, had grown from an initial 2,000 sales in 1966 to 11,000 in 1969 and a planned 17,000 in 1970. In the winter of 1968/9 the two brands independently launched a winter sunshine programme, but sales were disappointing—together only just over 1,000 holidays. However, they persisted and in 1969/70 it appeared that sales might be twice those of the previous season.

In an attempt to make the best of all the resources of the travel companies, especially hotels and aircraft, THH tried to introduce a number of different types of holidays. Universal Coach Tours was launched in 1965, but sold only 6,000 holidays out of a planned 20,000; the following year's programme was abandoned. A separate company, Mediterranean Cruise Ships, was established in 1968 to break into the air-cruise business (flying to a port in the Mediterranean and boarding a 'luxury' floating hotel for a fortnight's cruise). This project was also abandoned, this time before any sales were made; no further plans were under consideration although the company still existed in February 1970. In the summer season of 1969 Sky Tours Minitours was introduced to sell short stay special holidays in Europe. For example, there were 3-4 days' visits to flower displays and religious festivals. The winter season of 1969/70 saw the introduction of Sky Tours Royal, selling holidays to the Caribbean and travelling on scheduled airlines. It appeared in February 1970 that less than 500 sales would be made. For the 1970 summer season, two further new programmes were put on the market: Villapartments (by air to your own villa at a Mediterranean resort); and Club Mediterranné (cheap holidays for young people). With the latter, THH simply acted as agents to handle the UK sales of the French company of that name.

EXHIBIT 5 Price trends in Selected Sky Tours and Clarksons Hotels (1965-1970)

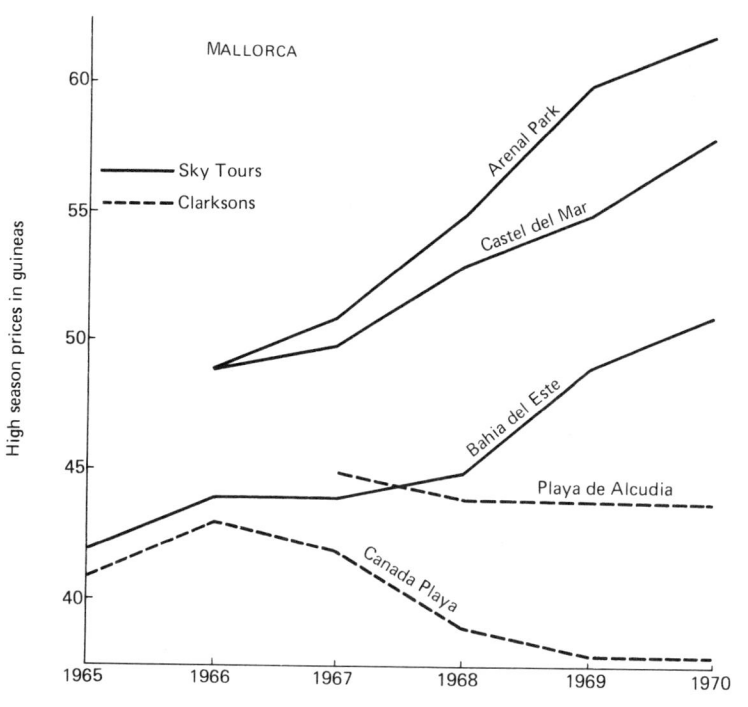

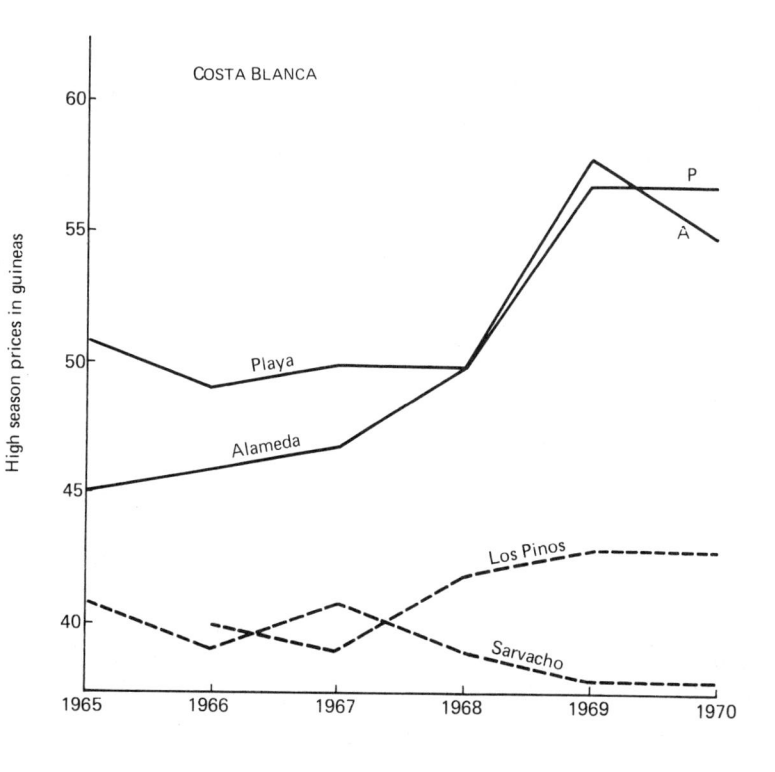

Notes on Exhibit 5

Hotel	IT company	No. of days holiday	Flight	Hotel facilities
MALLORCA				
Arenal Park	Sky Tours	15	Midweek: Day	PB
Castel del Mar	Sky Tours	15	Midweek: Day	PB & B
Bahia del Este	Sky Tours	12	Midweek: Night	—
Playa de Alcudia	Clarksons	15	Midweek: Night	Pb, B & SV
Canada Playa	Clarksons	12	Midweek: Night	PS
COSTA BLANCA				
Playa	Sky Tours	15	Weekend: Day	PS
Alameda	Sky Tours	15	Weekend: Day	—
Los Pinos	Clarksons	15	Midweek: Night	PS
Sarvacho	Clarksons	12	Midweek: Night	PS

Notes: 1. Key to hotel facilities: PB - Private Bathroom
PS - Private Shower
B - Balcony
SV - Sea View

2. Supplements for the more popular flight times were approximately similar for both companies:

Midweek:	Night	0
Midweek:	Day	1 guinea
Weekend:	Night	2 guineas
Weekend:	Day	4 guineas

3. All hotels are approximately of the same standard, i.e. 2-3 star.

Source: Company records

Pricing

In a report written in the early part of 1967 Brian Navin, an economist from the Thomson Organisation, wrote, 'The bewildering variety of brochures, with different resorts, hotels and lengths of holiday offered, result in an imperfect market from which the consumer has a baffling range of choices facing him. Except within broad price bands, he cannot assess value for money. Marginal changes in prices by individual operators are therefore unlikely to result in vastly increased sales.'

He went on to say, 'Prices are partly determined by the degree of competition and partly by the required return on investment. However, it is not absolutely necessary to match exactly competitors' prices. On the other hand, it is dangerous to charge grossly higher prices than our competitors for a similar holiday. Therefore a flexible pricing policy might be used rather than a flat percentage mark-up on costs.'

When Bryan Llewellyn took over as managing director in September 1969, he put in hand an analysis of THH's pricing policy and that of his competitors, Clarksons in particular (see Exhibit 5). In 1965 and 1966 the whole question of pricing had been left very much in the hands of the individual companies. In 1967 pressure was applied from Thomson House to do something about the falling profits of THH. Aubrey Morris decided that there was no alternative but to increase prices for the 1968 season. (As stated above, although the programmes of the individual IT companies were decided jointly by a panel of three, the managing and marketing directors of THH and the general manager (later brand manager) of each IT company, prices were the final decision of the managing director of THH. They were decided more on the basis of return on investment than on the prices of the competitors.) The prices for the 1969 and 1970 seasons were further increased because of the continued fall in profits. The results turned out to be opposite to those intended. Bookings for the 1970 season indicated a fall compared to 1969 season, and it was feared that total sales might only just exceed 200,000 holidays.

The analysis of THH pricing policy ordered by Llewellyn showed the following picture for the years 1965-69, and an estimate for 1970.

	THH sales (Summer season) (thousands)	Total Market (Summer season) (thousands)	THH as % of total	THH average net Price £
1965	112	724	15.4	44.9
1966	162	1,172	13.8	44.5
1967	211	1,320	15.9	44.6
1968	208	1,463	14.2	45.8
1969	219	1,800 (estimate)	12.2	47.8
1970	210 (estimate)	2,200 (estimate)	9.5	49.7

A new method of calculating the prices went some way towards introducing a flexible market-oriented policy. The example shown below indicates the basic procedure.

EXHIBIT 6   Sample Price Calculation

Route   London-Palma
Aircraft   Boeing 737/200
Capacity   124 seats (@ 90% load factor = 111 passengers)
Block time[1] 4 hours 15 minutes
Season   32 weeks summer
Holiday   14 nights

Cost per passenger at 90% load factor

	£
Aircraft	14.60
Aircraft catering	.40
Hotel	19.00
Transfers	.50
Sub-total	34.50
Overheads and profit[2]	9.00
Travel agents' commission	4.80
Total	48.30

Notes: 1. Block time represented the aggregate time from 'chocks off' to 'chocks on' in both directions, i.e. it included both flying time and time spent taxiing.

2. The figure of £9.00 for 'overheads and profit' was notionally split £6.00 and £3.00 respectively. It was included as a standard figure in the cost sheet for every holiday.

Seasonal price variations

Season	No. of weeks	Price—£
Peak	6	56
High	3	52
Mid	(4 + 3)	49
Economy	(4 + 4)	46
Bargain	(4 + 4)	43

Selling and Advertising

Five months after THH was formed in January 1967, Peter Finch, a marketing supervisor from Thomson House, was appointed to the new post of marketing director. Previously, responsibility for marketing and selling had been in the hands of the general manager of each company. Late in 1968 an additional new post was created, that of general sales manager. This was the idea of Peter Finch, who believed that direct liaison with 'the trade' (i.e. the travel agents) was vital to obtain maximum sales. Twelve representatives were appointed to cover the country for Sky Tours and Riviera and nominally for Gaytours/Luxitours. In practice the latter company resented any attempt to control from London, and initially did not cooperate.

Following the traditional practice of the travel business, THH had virtually no direct retail outlets. Approximately 85 per cent of all IT holidays were sold through independent general travel agents. The balance was sold either direct through postal applications—every brochure had a booking coupon—or through branch offices in major cities such as London, Manchester, Glasgow, Cardiff, and Newcastle; these offices sold only THH holidays and acted as the local reservation office for general travel agents in the area. THH also owned three general travel agents, one each in London, Blackpool and Manchester, which retailed THH holidays in addition to those of other IT companies.

The prime selling vehicle of all the IT companies was undoubtedly the brochure. By 1970 these had become lavishly produced items, vast quantities of which were printed. THH had a brochure for each brand with a different one for each season and type of holiday. Sky Tours, for example, for the 1970 summer season had four brochures going out under its brand name—Winter Sunshine 1969/70, Royal 1969/70, Summer Sunshine 1970 and Minitours 1970. In addition, the summer brochure was printed separately for the four main regions—London and the Midlands, South England, Wales and the South-West, and North England and Scotland. In 1969 the THH companies spent a total of over £250,000 on the printing of brochures alone. In 1970, the figure was

EXHIBIT 7   Advertising expenditure of major IT companies 1966-9

(£000s)

	THOMSON HOLIDAYS				CLARKSONS	HORIZON	GLOBAL
	Sky Tours	Riviera	Gaytours	Luxi Tours			
1966							
Press	37.9	21.6	4.6	2.5	34.1	66.3	81.8
TV	9.6	—	9.9	—	6.0	10.0	—
Total	47.5	21.6	14.5	2.5	40.2	76.3	81.8
1967							
Press	74.9	24.4	11.0	4.7	65.8	72.8	48.2
TV	50.2	1.7	18.6	3.7	31.4	31.9	9.4
Total	125.0	26.1	29.6	8.4	97.1	104.7	57.6
1968							
Press	78.1	1.8	7.3	5.3	43.5	23.7	15.2
TV	82.2	19.0	8.7	4.0	105.1	49.9	43.4
Total	160.3	20.8	16.0	9.3	148.6	73.6	58.6
1969							
Press	129.1	70.0	12.2	9.6	150.9	50.6	26.4
TV	105.6	—	9.3	5.7	53.9	60.7	47.4
Total	234.7	70.0	21.5	15.3	204.8	111.3	73.8

Source: Company records

£340,000: of this, the Sky Tours Summer Sunshine brochure cost £210,000 for a run of 2,000,000 and Riviera Summer Sunshine £47,000 for 350,000. Luxitours alone spent £30,000 on brochures for its summer and winter programmes. In addition to these costs, there were heavy distribution expenses amounting to almost as much as the cost of the brochures themselves.

Exhibit 7 shows the large sums all the major IT companies spent on advertising in the press and TV to back up the brochures and point of sale material. In 1969 the THH companies spent over £335,000 in this way and were likely to reach £390,000 in 1970.

Marketing and future product policy

When Llewellyn was appointed managing director of THH in September 1969, the suggestion was made that the reason he had been selected was because of his experience in marketing. It was indicated that he should concentrate his effort in THH in that direction.

The operations manager Roger Lambert, a former general manager of Riviera Holidays, who had been with that company since 1959, commented, 'Up to and including the 1970 season, there just was no real marketing policy—it was all very *ad hoc*. We were only concerned with the next season. Little thought was given as to the direction the company should take and where the markets lay.' Brian Gurnett, who in September 1969 was offered the new appointment of group marketing manager, reporting to Peter Finch, put it more succinctly: 'Our marketing policy had been very simple: double or quits. If a particular programme sold well, we doubled it the following year; if badly, we dropped it.'

The first task of Brian Gurnett was to make a detailed study of future market opportunities. The purpose of the study was to identify particular segments of the market on which THH might profitably concentrate and to make recommendations on future product policy. In fact the study made many recommendations, among them that THH should penetrate new markets—the middle-class 'executive' B/C1 group, the new C2 entrant, and the family with young children; that new products should be developed— short duration holidays, children's facilities, off-peak attractions, and holidays to medium-haul destinations.

The study examined in particular the characteristics of foreign holidaymakers, especially those on air ITs.

Social class	All UK adults	Foreign holidaymakers All types	Air ITs
	(Percentage in each social class)		
AB	14	29	23
C1	22	33	35
C2	34	26	31
DE	30	12	11
	100	100	100

As anticipated, those going on foreign holidays tended to be of higher social class than the UK population in general. However, the foreign air IT holidaymaker was more concentrated in the C1 and C2 classes. Additional data showed that new IT holidaymakers tended to be more concentrated in the C2 group and confirmed IT holidaymakers in the C1 group. There were indications that brands based on segmentation by class were more likely to have long-term stability, with a natural flow of new entrants who could be persuaded to remain loyal, than brands segmented by age group. It was believed that membership of social class type groupings did not change much during the course of an individual's life (unlike age!). Further data indicated that in the period to 1975 there would be a rapid increase in the number of upper and middle class executives and in the proportion of national disposable income controlled by them.

The study showed that there was a significant difference between those families with children who took holidays in the United Kingdom and those taking holidays abroad.

Possession of children	UK holidaymakers	Foreign holidaymakers		
	Total	Total	Confirmed IT	New IT
	(Percentage with children in specified age ranges)			
Ages 0-4 only	14	7	4	5
Ages 5-15 only	22	19	15	20
Both ages	11	5	1	4
Nil	53	69	80	71
	100	100	100	100

Since it was also known that the child-rearing age groups of the population would be expanding over the next few years, the study recommended that increasing attention be given to catering for children.

Other conclusions were that the increase in the length of holidays of the working population would encourage the development of second holidays and longer holidays; that there was an increasing level of expenditure on leisure; that the demand for foreign holidays by region of residence did not seem likely to change substantially, but growth in the longer distance holidays would be mainly in the South East.

PRICE REGULATION

Llewellyn believed that there was a good chance that the trend away from price regulation of air IT holidays by the government would continue. The latest directive allowed a further relaxation in the prices of 8-day and 12-day holidays, and significantly the Board of Trade had stated that for holidays of four days or less 'control prices would be determined on their merits by the Air Transport Licensing Board (ATLB).'. He felt that within the next few years, given sufficient pressure from IT companies, price restrictions on short-duration holidays, long-range holidays, and winter holidays would be almost entirely lifted.

FINANCE

The financial results of THH in the years from 1966-9 clearly indicated the gravity of the situation facing Llewellyn (see Exhibit 8). Although the net revenue (i.e. the gross revenue less travel agents' commission) of the IT companies had increased from £8.4 million in 1966 to £11.5 million in 1969, net profit had fallen from £696,000 to £236,000. Bookings for the 1970 summer programme indicated that sales would be similar to those of 1969, if not lower. Despite, therefore, the increase in holiday prices, net revenue for 1970 was unlikely to exceed £12 million at best.

EXHIBIT 8   Statement of revenue and costs of THH

(£000s)

	1966	1967	1968	1969
REVENUE (Net of agents' commission)	8,430	10,045	10,277	11,530
COSTS				
Aircraft charters	2,337	2,273	3,398	3,773
Hotels and transfers	4,582	6,192	5,181	5,668
Overheads	855	1,166	1,451	1,805
OPERATING PROFIT	656	414	253	284
INTEREST RECEIVABLE (Payable)	40	46	18	(48)
NET PROFIT BEFORE TAX	696	460	235	236

Source: Company records

Costs on the other hand seemed likely to be significantly higher than those of 1969. Hotel costs were up by 10 per cent and aircraft charges by even more. Overhead costs were also likely to show a substantial further increase. In 1966 the cost of overheads represented 10 per cent of the average net price per Sky Tours passenger, this being divided between the costs of promotion, e.g. advertising (3½ per cent), and the costs of administration (6½ per cent). By 1969 the figure for total overheads had risen to more than 15 per cent. In 1970 with more money being spent on advertising and more on central administration, in particular on sophisticated data processing facilities, the figure would be even higher.

AIRCRAFT AND HOTELS

Aircraft

Not until the 1969 summer season did all three IT companies contract exclusively with Britannia Airways for their aircraft requirements. Britannia, however, maintained itself at arm's length from THH and charged the market rate for use of its aircraft. In addition, Britannia was perfectly free to obtain business outside the THH companies, and succeeded in doing so on an increasing scale. In 1969 over 40 per cent of the company's revenue came from outside charter contracts.

After the takeover of Britannia Airways by the Thomson Organisation in 1965, detailed studies were carried out to decide on jet procurement. The studies showed that the Boeing 737 offered considerable economic advantages for the type of business provided by the IT companies and an order for four 737s was signed in 1966. As at 1969 the company operated five 737s and four Britannia 102s. For the 1970 season there would be an additional three 737s.

The rates charged by Britannia Airways to the IT companies were as follows for 1970 for the Boeing 737s on time charter.

Up to 1900 hours	£390 per hour
Over 1900 hours	£280 per hour
Mid-week flying in winter	£250 per hour

The second four 737s acquired by Britannia were on long-term leases of twelve years at an average annual rate per aircraft of £271,000: this worked out at a more expensive rate than that for the first four 737s, which had been bought from Boeing with the assistance of a large loan from the US Export-Import Bank. The direct operating costs of the 737s were estimated to be approximately £150 per hour excluding depreciation or leasing charge and landing and handling charges.

Aircraft utilisation of Britannia's jet fleet was not as high as that for Autair who carried a large proportion of Clarksons' traffic, or for BUA who carried both the Horizon group and the Fortes group—Hickie Borman, Milbanke and Swans (Hellenic)—another major complex of IT companies. Figures from the *Business Monitor* put out by the Board of Trade showed that whereas Britannia's average annual utilisation of the Boeing 737s was 2470 hours in the twelve months from 1.7.68 to 30.6.69, the figure for Autair with the BAC 1-11s was 2780 hours, and for BUA, also with BAC 1-11s, 2785 hours. It was noticeable that Britannia's utilisation of aircraft in the first and fourth quarters of the year was the main reason for the overall lower utilisation over the full year.

THH management recognised that higher utilisation of Britannia's aircraft could be achieved. This could be done by concentration of passengers into fewer aircraft, with increased weekday, night and off-season flying, and fewer departure/destination points. However, it was appreciated that from a demand point of view, to take all these actions would be suicidal for THH. It would also utilise only three or four Boeing 737s.

Hotels

THH obtained hotel beds in three different ways. The first was the annual renewable contract with a hotelier, the second the medium-term contract (7-10 years) for a block of beds in an hotel, and the third the turn-key lease of a complete hotel for a long period (15-25 years). In the third scheme THH was usually entirely responsible for the hotel management.

Over the years since 1965 there had been three related developments. First, it came to be recognised that the negotiation of hotel contracts and leases could best be carried out by the three IT companies working together, i.e. through THH, rather than individually. (It was not until the 1968 summer season that Sky Tours' and Riviera's hotel contracting was integrated, and Gaytours'/Luxitours' the year after.) Secondly, as the competition for beds mounted, THH moved away from annual renewable contracts to the medium-term block bookings. By the summer season of 1969 over 50 per cent of the beds used by THH were secured on medium-term contracts and by the 1970 season the figure was about 75 per cent (see Exhibit 9). Thirdly, the number of hotels at which holiday accommodation was offered declined and the number of beds in each hotel more than proportionately increased. In 1965 Sky Tours used 93 hotels in the 13 resorts at which holidays were offered. By 1968 this had risen to 148 in 18 resorts, but by 1970, with the rapid increase in medium-term contracts for larger blocks of beds, the figure was down to 96 in 19 resorts.

EXHIBIT 9   Number of beds by type of contract/lease

Contract/lease	1969 Number	%	1970 Number	%
Annual renewable contract	9,153	38.6	4,617	19.8
Medium-term block booking	13,090	55.1	17,040	73.3
Long-term lease	1,486	6.3	1,601	6.9
TOTAL	23,729	100.0	23,258	100.0

Source: Company records

Although THH was the first group of IT companies to lease an entire hotel for a long period—Mellieha Bay Hotel in 1966—less than 7 per cent of THH's beds were provided in this way by 1970. It required both substantial commitment and, probably more important, management expertise in an area with which the Thomson Organisation was unfamiliar. Hotels on lease were normally owned by a consortium in which a subsidiary of the Thomson Organisation or TTH had a share, occasionally a controlling interest. The Mellieha Bay Hotel, for example, was owned by Beaufort Investments in which TTH had a 49.14 per cent share. It was leased back to Mellieha Bay Hotel Ltd, a wholly owned subsidiary of TTH, which was responsible for the management.

Occasionally a hotel came into the hands of THH by default. In order to secure beds on a medium-term contract, large deposits were paid to the hotelier by the IT company. In a few instances with THH, the hotelier had subsequently proved to be incompetent or unfortunate, and had been on the verge of total financial collapse and bankruptcy. One of the only ways, therefore, for THH to secure the return of the balance of its deposit was to make an offer to take over the hotel.

EXHIBIT 10   Sales of Clarksons holidays

Year	Summer Sunshine	Winter Sunshine	Short Tours	Lakes and Mountains	Winter Snowjet
	(thousands of holidays)				
1964	1		21	—	
1965	6		39	—	
1966	15		64	—	
1967	50		74	—	
1967-8		8			—
1968	103		75	—	
1968-9		17			2
1969 (est.)	190		90	5	

Source: Company records

With the trend towards medium-term and long-term leases, the requirement for deposits had increased enormously. By the end of 1970, it was expected that deposits made to hoteliers as prepayments for future hotel accommodation or as finance for construction of new hotels (in return for which hoteliers granted preferred allocation rights) would exceed £3.5 millions. UK exchange control regulations would have made such a sum both costly and difficult to obtain, were it not for the fact that through the world-wide activities of the Thomson Organisation, THH had access to funds outside the UK.

COMPETITORS

Clarksons

By 1969 Clarksons Holidays had become the market leaders in terms of numbers of holidays sold (see Exhibit 10). They appeared to have achieved this by aggressive pricing, and by concentrating their resources in well-defined areas. An examination of their 1970 Summer Sunshine programme showed the following:

	Clarksons	*Sky Tours*
Departure airports	6	7
Destination countries	6	11
Destination resorts	19	19
Destination hotels	145	96
Barrier periods	7	8
Length of season	1/3–30/11	14/3–5/11
Length of holidays	11, 12 & 15 days	8, 11, 12 & 15 days

Up to 1969 Clarksons had flown from only London and Manchester; it was not until the 1970 season that they had chosen to fly from Newcastle, Bristol, Cardiff and Teesside. However, it appeared that they were planning an enormous increase in sales since they had applied for a total of 495,000 charter seats in 1970 from the ATLB compared with the 285,000 seats granted in 1969. Detailed examination of their 1966-70 brochures showed too that they had many departures both during the mid-week and during the night hours. Common departure times were 22.00 hours on Monday, Wednesday and Friday, returning at 04.00 hours at the end of the holiday.

Unlike Thomsons, Clarksons had not got involved in the ownership and operation of hotels, but had rather concentrated on block bookings of beds on seven-year contracts, leaving the day-to-day management to experienced local hoteliers.

A recent development of some interest was Clarksons' link-up with the newly formed Mirror Club. The *Daily Mirror* in 1969 had set up a holiday club for its readers, and for only 50p provided a programme of overseas holidays vetted by experts. All the holidays were arranged in conjunction with Clarksons.

Horizon

Horizon was unique amongst the largest IT companies in having successfully resisted all attempts to take it over. It was also unique in deliberately aiming at the 'up-market' on a large scale with holidays noticeably higher priced than those offered by Clarksons and Thomsons. As Lionel Steinberg put it, 'Horizon offered a more expensive, more discriminating package with more departure airports, more resorts and smaller hotel allocations.'

In 1970 it was estimated that the Horizon group might sell about 200,000 holidays. The group consisted primarily of Horizon Holidays, operating out of London (Gatwick), Manchester, Newcastle, Bristol, and Cardiff: Horizon Midlands out of Birmingham and Castle Donnington: Horizon Holidays (Scotland) out of Glasgow, and 4S Travel operating on a national scale. It was rumoured that Horizon Holidays (Ireland) was in the process of formation to operate out of Dublin.

Horizon made explicit appeal to specific groups within the total holiday market. They specialised in providing holidays for families with small children at hotels with facilities such as children's playgrounds, nurses and children's menus; in holidays for young people, mainly in their twenties, such as Horizon's Club 18-30, where hotels or apartment blocks were taken over in their entirety for Club members, in order that they should not feel frustrated in their noise-making and other activities by people outside their age group.

Another feature of Horizon Holidays was that they sold 25 per cent of their holidays direct through a dozen or so well-sited retail outlets owned by Horizon and situated in the most important cities in the UK.

Global

Global was the sixth amongst the largest IT companies in air-charter holidays in 1969. However, this understated its position overall, since Overland, another brand name used by the Global organisation, sold a substantial number of package holidays using surface transport, e.g. by rail to resorts in Spain and Italy with accommodation in hotels, or by coach to a port in the Mediterranean for a holiday cruise in the sun. Global itself offered holidays by coach to Europe: either circular tours to a number of countries and resorts, or direct to one resort.

Global's Summer Sunshine programme of 1969 had offered a large number of provincial departure airports, eleven in all, including Belfast and Dublin. There was a choice of six countries and a total of sixteen resorts. Global also offered holidays to appeal to special interest groups. For example there were the winter and summer sunshine programmes for golfers; there were programmes to Israel and 'Lands of the Bible.' In general it could be said that Overland was designed to appeal to the less affluent 'down-market' and Global to the 'up-market'. Global had also made a determined effort to obtain business from the independent foreign holiday market by using the scheduled airlines and offering great flexibility in constructing a 'package' to suit individual taste.

7 Thomson Holiday Holdings (B)*

This case provides a sketch of developments in Thomsons and the air inclusive tour industry between the end of 1970 and October 1972. The story is thus carried forward from where the Thomson Holiday Holdings (A) case leaves off.

Bryan Llewellyn's first two years of running the travel arm of the Thomson Organisation proved to have been filled with changes occurring much faster than might have been expected when he first took office. Not only did the pace of expansion accelerate in the industry generally, but also government regulations changed substantially to alter the nature of that expansion. Some of the major operators in the industry suffered appalling losses and everyone experienced reduced margins. Within Thomsons itself, major changes also occurred. The managerial structure was altered: the Sunair Lunn-Poly group was acquired to add further brand names and a chain of retail outlets; and the original marketing policy of maintaining a proliferation of brands was abandoned in favour of bringing most of them under the umbrella of the Skytours name, and later the Thomson name.

By October 1972 it had become clear that the optimistic growth projections rampant among the industry's planners a year earlier were irrelevant. Answers to many pressing questions had to be found if any of the major operators were to continue to grow profitably.

ORGANISATIONAL CHANGES

At the end of September, after a series of adjustments, Thomson Travel Holdings (TTH) consisted of four operating subsidiaries together with a central unit concerned with planning and systems development. The originally separate tour operating companies had been merged into a single company, Thomson Holidays Ltd (THL). Britannia Airways Ltd (BAL) remained a separate company operating a fleet of eleven aircraft. Thomson Overseas Developments Ltd (TODL) had been formed to manage the group's hotel and other resort interests. The fourth subsidiary, Leycester Holdings (LH), had been created to control the group's retail outlets after the acquisition of Lunn-Poly and Camkin Travel in mid-1972. Bryan Llewellyn had been promoted to become managing director and chief executive of TTH.

The board of TTH had twelve members as follows:

Managing Director and Chief Executive*		(Bryan Llewellyn)
Thomson Holidays Ltd:	Chairman	(Norman Corkhill)
(THL)	Managing Director*	(Francis Higgins)
Britannia Airways Ltd	Chairman	(Lord Thomas)
(BAL)	Managing Director*	(John Sauvage)
	Financial Controller	(B. Mucclestone)
Thomson Overseas Developments Ltd		
(TODL)	Managing Director*	(Vincent Cobb)
Leycester Holdings	Chairman*	(John Camkin)
(LH)	Managing Director*	(Nick Redfern)
	Director	(Ronald Jenkins)
Planning Director		(Sergio Viggiani)

Six men, indicated above by an asterisk, formed the executive committee of TTH which had considerable decision-making powers. There was also a planning committee

---

* Copyright © J. M. Stopford 1972

with equivalent powers and a membership identical to that of the executive committee, except for the addition of Mr Viggiani, the planning director. To discharge their numerous tasks, both committees met monthly.

Thomson Holidays Ltd, the largest of the four subsidiaries, was organised into seven functional departments. Exhibit 1 provides details of those functions.

EXHIBIT 1   Management organisation of Thomson Holidays Limited

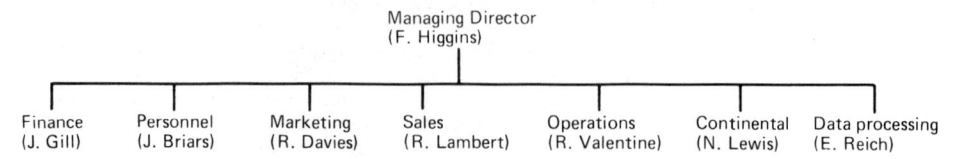

```
                        Managing Director
                            (F. Higgins)
    ┌──────┬──────────┬──────────┬────┴─────┬────────────┬──────────┬──────────────┐
 Finance  Personnel  Marketing   Sales    Operations   Continental  Data processing
 (J. Gill) (J. Briars) (R. Davies) (R. Lambert) (R. Valentine) (N. Lewis) (E. Reich)
```

Further descriptions of responsibilities:

Finance:	i/c finance, also company secretary
Personnel:	i/c personnel, training and administration
Marketing:	i/c programme design, brochures, research and development of new programmes
Sales:	i/c telephone sales and field sales force
Operations:	i/c programme control
Continental:	i/c hotel contracting
Data processing:	i/c computer operations and client services such as processing of booking forms and issue of tickets

Source: Company Records

Considerable turmoil in personal assignments accompanied the series of reorganisations leading to this structure of TTH. Men were promoted or moved from one subsidiary to another. While some men were recruited from outside to fill new positions, others resigned. A press release, dated 25 September 1972, reported many of these moves.

> Nicholas Redfern joins the board of Thomson Travel Holdings Ltd, to become Managing Director of Leycester Holdings Ltd, the newly formed fourth subsidiary of Thomson Travel Holdings Ltd, which will control the operation of the group's 56 retail outlets. Ronald Jenkins, Director and General Manager of Lunn-Poly will join him on the Board.
>
> Brian Gurnett moves to Britannia Airways as Marketing Director and leaves the Board of Thomson Holidays Ltd.
>
> Within Thomson Holidays, the following Board appointments have been made: Roger Davies becomes Marketing Director, Roger Lambert becomes Sales Director and John Gill has been appointed Financial Director.
>
> Two new Board appointments have been created: Erich Reich becomes Data Processing Director, and Roy Valentine is appointed Programme Control Director.
>
> Elis Evans has accepted an appointment as Managing Director of Pearl and Dean and will be leaving Thomson Holidays Ltd at the end of this month. Lionel Steinberg has signified his wish to be released of his directorship of Thomson Holidays Ltd and will be leaving at the end of this year.

ACQUISITIONS

During 1972 Thomsons made two acquisitions, one minor and the other of great significance. The minor one was John Camkin Travel, a firm owning eight retail travel agencies. The major one was Sunair and Lunn-Poly.

Describing negotiations for the purchase, *The Times* reported on 4 August:

> Thomson Holidays, which is Britain's second largest tour operating company, confirmed last night that talks are in progress for the acquisition of the Sunair Lunn-Poly business from Trafalgar House Investments. If the deal goes through, Thomsons will be running neck and neck with Clarksons, hitherto the undisputed

market leader in terms of size. Neither Thomsons nor Trafalgar House was prepared to discuss the financial aspects.

Lunn-Poly, before its merger with Sunair, was sold to Cunard early in 1971 for an estimated figure of £300,000. Like Thos Cook and Son, Lunn-Poly was originally part of the government-owned Transport Holding Co., which bought it in 1968 for a sum believed to be close to £1m. It was subsequently described by Transport Holding Co. as a 'disastrous investment'. The combined Sunair Lunn-Poly company's estimated turnover for 1972 is around £20m. It was sold with Cunard to Trafalgar House Investments in August last year. Shortly after the acquisition, Mr Nigel Broakes, Trafalgar's chairman, described the group's brief exposure to the travel industry as having 'given us some surprises concerning inadequate margins and unrealistic pricing policies'.

Earlier this year, THL was a strong contender for Lunn-Poly's former sister company Thos Cook and Son. After Cooks went to a rival consortium headed by the Midland Bank, it was rumoured for some time in the travel industry that THL was anxious to divest itself of Lunn-Poly.

Sunair Lunn-Poly carries about 400,000 passengers a year. If the talks are successful, the acquisition will bring Thomson Holidays' passenger total close to one million. It would also take Thomsons into new areas of the tourist industry, particularly winter sports, where Lunn-Poly have traditionally been strong. For while Thomsons offer winter sun holidays to Jamaica, for instance, or special interest winter holidays to Moscow for example, they have not previously developed into the ski resorts.

The deal which would include Sunair Lunn-Poly's 48 retail travel agencies could affect air charter arrangements with British European Airways. BEA through its own charter subsidiary, BEA Airtours, has a contract with Lunn-Poly which expires in April next year. After this date, Lunn-Poly's business could well be diverted to Britannia, the independent charter airline owned by the Thomson Organisation. BEA yesterday announced the signing of a £1.6m contract for holiday charter flights with Global Tours for next summer. However, it says that this is not intended as a replacement for the possible loss of Sunair Lunn-Poly's business.

After negotiations had been successfully completed, *The Times* made a further report on 8 August:

> Agreement has been reached for Thomson Holidays to acquire control of Sunair Lunn-Poly from Trafalgar House Investments. Mr Victor Matthews, managing director of Trafalgar House yesterday declined to name the price but commented, 'There are no substantial sums involved.'
>
> The price would be based on a formula related to Sunair's performance for the year ending in September. Mr Matthews expected there would be a loss. He added that if the company had continued under THL's control, he personally would have liked to have seen its inclusive tour prices raised by at least 20 per cent next year.

Mr Llewellyn, as reported in the *Financial Times* on 16 August 1972, outlined the reasons for acquiring Sunair and Lunn-Poly as follows:

> Sunair [he said] had accommodation capacity needed for steady expansion, although some would be dropped soon. Sunair was also a strong operator out of Gatwick, an airport where Thomson was seeking a larger market share. Lunn-Poly's winter sports interests was another welcome acquisition. Another big incentive to the merger was Sunair/Lunn-Poly's group of 50 travel agents. These would be grouped with Thomson's existing retail outlets under a separate management from Thomson Holidays.
>
> [Mr Llewellyn added that] Thomson was also concerned about Sunair and Lunn-Poly falling into the hands of 'some other large interests outside the package tour business.' Additional new competition within tour operating would not be a good thing.
>
> It looks as though we are entering some semblance of a period of stability within the industry, in which prices can be allowed to reach realistic levels and proper attention can be given by all to the quality of holidays. A new company with ambitions in the industry might have meant that 1973 would see yet once again an operator going for market share at the expense of price and the public's satisfaction.

EXPANSION OF THE BUSINESS

After a slight decline in 1970, the number of holidays sold increased dramatically during 1971 and advance sales for the 1972 summer season indicated a continuing upward trend. The winter holiday business grew even faster. Exhibit 2 provides a breakdown of sales by brand.

EXHIBIT 2   Sales of Holidays by Thomson Holiday Companies (1968-early 1972)

(thousands of holidays)

Year	Sky Tours	Riviera	Gaytours	Luxitours	Breakaway (Minitours)	Total
SUMMER SEASON						
1968	146 (170)	38 (50)	16 (?)	8 (?)	—	208
1969	155 (177)	35 (49)	18 (?)	11 (?)	1 (2)	220
1970	142 (213)	24 (42)	23 (27)	13 (17)	5 (6)	207
1971	324* (291)	—	* (33)	* (20)	8 (25)	332
1972	246† (472)	—	—	—	—	
WINTER SEASON						
1968/9	10 (14)	—	1 (?)			11
1969/70	13 (21)	1 (2)	1 (1)	1 (1)	—	16
1970/1	36 (40)	—	3 (4)	—	—	39
1971/2	109 (123)	—	—	—	—	109

Note: Figures in brackets indicate number of holidays offered for sale, i.e. final capacity. (?) indicates number unknown.

   * Sky Tours, Gaytours and Luxitours all offered their own holiday brands. Combined final capacity was 344,000 of which 324,000 were sold.

   † Number of holidays sold as at 17.12.71. All other brands discontinued.

Source: Company Records

    Over the period 1965-71 Spain continued to be the most important location of Thomson's holidays. Efforts to develop sales in other countries, notably Italy, were, however, beginning to show results (see Exhibit 3)

    At the same time, Thomsons changed the mix of types of booking contract with the hotels. These changes were in response to changes in both the economics of running hotels and increased competition of tour operators based in other northern European countries. The trend was markedly in favour of medium-tern block bookings, as Exhibit 4 below shows.

    During the same period Thomsons had reversed earlier policies and began to buy their own hotels. They owned outright or on long lease, ten hotels at the end of 1972 and were expected to increase that number substantially by 1977.

    As the volume of business expanded, Britannia Airways increased the size of its fleet. By the end of 1970 all the very old Britannia aircraft had been sold and a fleet of eight Boeing 737s acquired. A ninth 737 and two 707s were added a year later. Exhibit 5 shows the utilisation, by quarter, of the fleet and indicates the enormous seasonal variations in use. The efforts of Thomsons to extend the length of the summer season and to build up a winter season are reflected in the changed utilisation figures over the period 1968-71. (Note that Britannia sells some of its capacity—both

EXHIBIT 3 Location of Sky Tours Holidays sold

(thousands of holidays)

Year	Spain	Italy	All other countries	Total†
SUMMER SEASON				
1965	60	16	—	76
1966	80	21	5	106
1967	99	24	13	136
1968	127	16	3	146
1969	131	14	10	155
1970	117	12	13	142
1971	271	31	23	324
WINTER SEASON				
1965/6	15	—	—	15
1966/7	—	—	—	NIL
1967/8	7	—	*	7
1968/9	10	—	—	10
1969/70	11	—	2	13
1970/1	34	*	1	36
1971/2	83	4	22	109

† figures do not necessarily add up due to rounding errors
* less than 1,000

Source: Company Records

EXHIBIT 4 Number of beds 1969-71, by type of contract

Type of contract	1969	%	1970	%	1971	%
Annual renewable contract	9,153	38.6	4,617	19.8	5,606	20.8
Medium-term block booking	13,090	55.1	17,040	73.3	18,905	70.2
Long-term lease	1,486	6.3	1,601	6.9	2,412	9.0
TOTAL	23,729	100.0	23,258	100.0	26,923	100.0

Source: Company Records

for cargo and passengers—to users outside TTH.) Comparative figures for Autair/Court and part of BEA's scheduled-service fleet are also provided in Exhibit 5.

It is of interest to note that Court Line, which has a five-year agreement with Clarkson's Holidays, announced in August 1972 a decision to buy two Lockheed Tristars with an option on a third. These aircraft cost approximately £10 million each. During the same week Mr Llewellyn announced that Britannia Airways would add two more Boeing 737s to its fleet in 1973. He added that no purchases of wide-bodied jets were likely before 1975.

A further development of Thomson's business occurred when the company announced in August 1972 its entry into the cruise market. After several years of research and negotiation with shipping lines, Thomson decided to use the former transatlantic liner, S.S. *Ithaca,* for Mediterranean cruises in 1973. Operated by the Ulysses line, the ship was expected to complete its refitting at Bilbao before February 1973.

EXHIBIT 5 Aircraft utilisation by three selected airlines

Airline and aircraft		1968 1st	2nd	3rd	4th	1969 1st	2nd	3rd	4th	1970 1st	2nd	3rd	4th	1971 1st	2nd	3rd	4th	1972 1st
BRITANNIA																		
Britannia	No:	7	9	9	7	7	7	6	4	4	4	4	4	—	—	—	—	—
	Util:	203	556	848	273	265	387	659	159	54	413	454	92	—	—	—	—	—
Boeing 737	No:	—	—	2	2	2	5	5	5	6	8	8	8	8	8	8	8	9
	Util:	—	—	909	409	315	839	1,091	432	399	712	1,017	416	422	850	1,039	587	586
Boeing 707	No:	—	—	—	—	—	—	—	—	—	—	—	—	—	1	1	2	2
	Util:	—	—	—	—	—	—	—	—	—	—	—	—	—	821	1,246	468	565
AUTAIR/COURT																		
BAC 1-11 (300–400)	No:	2	3	3	4	5	5	5	2	1	1	1	1	—	—	—	—	—
	Util:	72	826	1,040	454	439	848	1,148	620	352	461	913	321	402	—	—	—	—
BAC 1-11 (500)	No:	—	—	—	—	—	—	—	2	5	7	7	6	7	10	10	8	10
	Util:	—	—	—	—	—	—	—	232	350	800	1,019	458	357	770	1,112	669	555
BEA																		
Trident 1C	No:	22	22	21	21	22	21	21	21	21	21	21	21	21	21	21	20	21
	Util:	463	599	657	463	410	625	661	527	556	641	683	549	491	593	622	466	417
Trident 3B	No:	—	—	—	—	—	—	—	—	—	—	—	—	2	7	9	13	15
	Util:	—	—	—	—	—	—	—	—	—	—	—	—	306	498	536	471	549

Notes: 1. The figures for the Trident 1C and Trident 3B are given as examples of aircraft utilisation on BEA's scheduled services.
2. No: This gives the number of aircraft in service at the end of each quarter.
3. Util: This is the average utilisation per aircraft for each quarter, expressed in flying hours.

Source: *Business Monitor*, Civil Aviation series CA5

Warning signals that the growth in demand for air IT holidays would not continue unabated appeared early in the 1972 summer season. Overall demand did not simply level off; it declined. Some early indications were that the decline was greatest in the low-price end of the market.

PRICING

When the pound was let loose to float or sink on world markets, all the tour operators faced the problem of how to minimise their losses. Their immediate reaction was to try collectively to raise prices by equal percentages. An article in the *Financial Times* on 5 July 1972 commented on the failure of the initial TOSG meeting and on some of the wider issues.

> Around tea-time to-day men from 22 of Britain's biggest package tour companies will meet in the Edwardian elegance of the Café Royal at London's Piccadilly Circus. The groups they represent carry more than three-quarters of the inclusive tour customers that the U.K. send abroad—approaching 3m. people at the last count. They meet knowing that the travel industry is about to enter its busiest period. In a week or two the schools will break up for the long summer holiday and parents will start packing the suntan cream and the travel pills.
> At the top of the agenda will be the question of the floating pound. A week ago the same companies agreed to differ on the level of any surcharge that might be necessary on package tours as the pound wobbled downwards. One by one they have since applied additional charges to their customers averaging around the 5 per cent mark. It begins to look inevitable that some among them at least will be looking for a further 2 per cent by the end of this week. Another decision to agree to disagree is likely from the operators when they hold the second part of their talks tomorrow.
> However, the immediate problems of the floating pound may prove to be simply a straw in the wind—perhaps even, as has been unkindly suggested, the straw that breaks the camel's back. The companies meeting today (they are Apal, Arrowsmith, Blue Cars, British Caledonian, Clarksons, Cooks, Cosmos, Global, Horizon, F. W. Ingham, Leroy, Lord Brothers, Lunn Poly, Milbanke, Panorama, Sunair, Swans, Thomson Sky Tours, Travel Club, Wallace Arnold, Whitehall, Wings and Yugotours), are well aware that the last year or so has seen the basis upon which package tourism has grown in Britain changed somewhat.
> Assorted factors have contributed to this, and the problem of the pound is simply the last in a long line. Broadly speaking, the companies have found that (a) size gave them greater management problems than they had anticipated; (b) continued growth could not be taken for granted, and (c) inflation (and now effective devaluation) plays havoc with long-term pricing policies.
> The effects of the first two problems have been seen already. Clarksons lost its £2.7m. last year in a dramatic demonstration of both. Thomson Skytours, the No. 2 in air tours, camouflages its figures by mixing a charter airline and a package company under one umbrella, but is reportedly breaking even after a difficult year or so. Cosmos, the Lichenstein-based Swiss-backed group, is normally more than discreet about profit levels but admits it will break even or make a slight loss on the activities of the past year.
> It is intriguing that the companies which have managed best in trying circumstances seem to be the Horizons, Wings and Panoramas of this world. It is arguable that this is not necessarily due to the quality of the management, however impressive Horizon's dynamic duo, Messrs Vladimir Raitz and Len Coven, may be. It is to some extent due to the way in which the bottom has fallen out of down market growth. These companies aim heavily at the middle market, white-collar executive. He seems to have suffered less in the economic doldrums than the skilled artisan and general office worker who make up the bread and butter business of the biggest groups.
> It seems clear that the bigger companies were simply not equipped to deal with the puff going out of this side of the business. And it was while they were adapting themselves to the new facts of marketing life that the problems of the pound began to make things much worse.
> Pointing out the alleged folly of the tour operators in not buying either their currencies of their beds forward is a relatively easy task now that everyone can see which way the exchange cat has jumped. However, the game is rather more

complex and sophisticated than at first appears. The operator relies on currency being available forward, then he has to decide which currencies to head for (buying drachmas forward, for example, may not have been wise. In the past, too, the peseta has gone down with the pound).

One or two operators did bet against the peseta and escuedo and have come out of it with wry grins if not smiles. Others have done deals in the past which, in currency terms, have worked in their favour. Thomson, for example, fixed its beds in Jamaica and Jugoslavia in dollars. When the dollar wandered down the exchange lists Thomson emerged with a profit. Now it is virtually back to square one again.

What has really trapped the operators this time is the fact that the currency crisis has come at the very worst part of the year. With the summer rush about to start there is no time at all to reorganise bills. That is why they have mostly become involved in the messy and embarrassing business of collecting surcharges at the airports or in the resorts.

But why have these surcharges been so important? The effect of a revaluation of the peseta against the pound on hotel bills is obvious. It will directly add around £1.50 at present rates to the average two-week holiday. Less apparent are the implications of airline charges. Late last week the charter airlines—they include Court, Britannia, Dan Air, BEA Airtours, Monarch and Laker—had their own meeting and decided on a 50p surcharge for passengers. This had been expected. The shock was that the charge was 50p per seat, not 50p per client carried.

The implications of this are considerable. Package tour flights rarely fly full, although this is the ideal for which all companies strive. Something in excess of 90 per cent is considered a very good performance. Assuming 85 per cent, this means that on a flight with a theoretical 100 seats, there are 15 50p's to be paid for seats which have not been used. To this must be added the fact that we are now in mid-season. At the end of the summer rush, charter flights will be flying out empty to pick up the last of the returning holidaymakers. That empty leg still qualifies for the 50p surcharge. With these and various other factors one medium sized operator reckoned it would cost him 86p per passenger to pay the 50p that the airline demanded.

Already several tour operators have been talking in terms of a 10-15 per cent rise in package tour prices for the summer 1973 season. The rapid rise in costs since then means that the range will almost certainly be around 15-20 per cent. This means that the £50 holiday this year could be £60 next. 'But,' said one of them, 'we would obviously price it at £59.50.'

The tour companies argue that even a rise to that level will not have the bad effect on sales that one might normally expect. 'We reckon that inflation will be recognised and that people will expect to pay more. And remember, what with VAT and other things the holiday in Britain is not going to rise by much less. We shall still be competitive. Anyway, the consumer does not necessarily see it the way that you and I do: £9 on a £45 holiday does not sound as bad as 20 per cent.'

In spite of all that, most of the tour operators to whom I have spoken during the past few days feel that 1973 will be a cautious year as far as planning for growth is concerned. The theory of how the consumer will take a substantial rise in holiday costs is one thing; the practice might prove quite another.

One of their minor problems at the moment is that the brochures for next summer are to a large extent in the final stages of preparation. For some operators it would be extremely difficult and very expensive to reprice some of the tours in the brochure. This means that many of those glossy offerings will have errata slips inside their covers saying that the prices are wrong. Inevitably this will mean the end of brochures priced page by page. In future, the catalogues will be like those in so many other businesses—page after glossy page with lots of facts but no prices. These will be on separate sheets, printed at the last moment and easily detached and replaced by other, higher, figures.

But that is not the only change the industry faces. There are big moves afoot for radical changes in marketing techniques. Here the perpetually sensitive relationships between the tour operators and the retail agents are at stake, and no operator will risk his neck by spelling out what the future holds. However, in private they will happily chat away about computer bookings, sales via supermarkets and differential pricing policies.

The thin end of the wedge could come when the Midland/THF/AA consortium really makes its weight felt as the new owner of Thos Cook. Sales via banking halls and AA offices may be just the start of major alterations in travel marketing techniques.

Whether the new Civil Aviation Authority will allow the much demanded changes in pricing policy remains to be seen. The bigger companies are keen to introduce a system similar to that already used by the supermarkets. At its most extreme you would pay £70 for a holiday if you wanted to guarantee your room and resort six months ahead—but £10, say, if you were prepared to turn up at the airport and take what was on offer. In between there would be a sliding scale. A week or so before a tour was due to leave the unsold seats, like unsold jam, would be going cheap. At the moment it is against the regulations, but it is widely in use in Scandinavia.

The big question remaining is whether or not all the members of this industry can survive the pressures and the changes through which they are currently passing. There does not seem much doubt that the current exchange crises will cost most of them money, at almost whatever level the surcharge is placed, because the operators will be constantly jumping to keep up with yesterday's situation.

Holidays are not in danger—the bonding scheme and the fact that most operators are part of substantial groups to a large extent buffers the customer against dramatic collapse. But it may well be that the backers of the present tour operating houses will decide that this is one business from which they would prefer to take a rest.

Later in July, the *Financial Times* reported that price increases of up to 20 per cent were expected for 1973. Tour operators were, however, having difficulty in adjusting their brochures to the new rates. The report continued

> Clarksons, Blue Sky, Horizon Midland and the Castle Group, are going ahead with brochure prices based on pre-flotation exchange rates. Thomson, Horizon, Cosmos and Global, among others, are re-vamping their holiday offers with prices based on current rates.
>
> If the pound rate against the peseta stays at its present level the first three will have to surcharge. If the peseta weakens the other would be morally obliged to refund.
>
> Yesterday, at the annual meeting of Clarksons' parent company, Shipping Industrial Holdings, the holiday company managing director, Mr John Straw, said that price rises of 10 to 15 per cent 'will come in with our 1973 brochure which goes out in the early autumn.' Holidays in Britain would also cost more, partly because of VAT, he added.
>
> Clarksons, according to Mr Straw, was looking for an increase of about 7 per cent overall. Operations were going very well. After last year's loss of £2.7m. he thought a provision of £1.6m. for this year 'should be enough.'
>
> Around 5 per cent of the 15 to 20 per cent price rise that is anticipated throughout the tour industry will be due to the effective devaluation of the pound. The rest is caused by inflation and by the tour operators reacting to a situation in which many of them are making losses.

By the end of August Mr Higgins, managing director of Thomson Holidays, had announced average price increases of 9 per cent. Other operators had announced increases of differing amounts. For example, Olympic Holidays stated that its Greek holidays would cost no more than 7 per cent more in 1973 than in 1972. Some commentators expected, however, that prices would eventually rise faster than these announcements suggested. They expected that, by the end of 1974, prices could rise by up to 50 per cent above those prevailing at the beginning of 1972.

Late in October a sharp fall in the value of sterling produced an agreement among TOSG members for further increases in the price of winter IT holidays. *The Times,* on 31 October, commented

> The cost of winter package tour holidays is likely to rise by up to 4 per cent within the next few days. Prices went up between 4 and 6 per cent following the floating of the pound on June 23.
>
> The fresh increases will come in the form of surcharges on holidays now being booked or booked but not yet taken.
>
> An emergency meeting of the Tour Operators' Study Group, whose members carry about 90 per cent of all package tour holidaymakers, will be held tomorrow evening to discuss the surcharges.
>
> Mr Harry Chandler, TOSG chairman, said: 'The downward float of the pound is a very worrying thing. It is obvious that since we fixed the last surcharge on

winter holidays the pound has sunk from about 6 per cent to between 9 and 10 per cent. The surcharges fixed then are obviously not applicable now.'

Mr Chandler said that the surcharge by most tour operators was likely to be less than 4 per cent, it was hoped it would be possible to get members to apply the same rate of increase, although this would be difficult to achieve, mainly because of competition within their ranks.

He added that it was difficult to foresee from when the surcharges would apply, since accounting procedures varied. However, some surcharges might be asked on departures taking place this weekend, although it was unlikely that any holidaymakers would be asked to pay extra for holidays they had already taken.

Mr Chandler, who owns The Travel Club, a tour operator based in Upminster, Essex, said future surcharges would not be ruled out while the pound fluctuated on foreign exchange markets.

But, he added, if the pound were to improve over the next few months the surcharge would come off. 'It does work both ways,' he said.

PRICE REGULATION

To complicate matters further, the industry had to adjust to significant changes in the government's regulation of prices. The application of Provision 1 had been relaxed since the summer season of 1970. For example, for the 1971 summer season, 16 June to 30 September, minimum prices for 11- and 12-day holidays were to be 90 per cent of those for 15-day holidays, and for 8-day holidays 50 per cent of those for 15-day holidays, for both weekend and mid-week travel.

The greatest change, however, took place in the price regulation of winter holidays. In 1970-71, Thomson Holidays appealed against a ruling of the ATLB that the prices at which they wishes to sell 3-4 night 'winter sun' holidays in resorts such as Mallorca were too low. The Department of Trade and Industry upheld the appeal. For the following winter of 1971-2 the minimum price of tours of seven nights or less in countries such as Spain and Italy was reduced to a notional £1.

This change helped to stimulate the growth of short winter holidays to such an extent that certain tour operators feared that traffic was being diverted from the traditional summer holiday abroad to a short winter holiday in the sun, plus a summer holiday in Britain or Northern Europe. The marginal costing of the short winter holiday was therefore being seriously questioned. Other changes, especially with respect to the licensing of tour operators and the price controls on general charter operations, were expected before the end of the year.

ADVERTISING AND PROMOTION

A series of mistakes and a growing band of disgruntled holidaymakers tarnished the reputation of the industry. Adverse comment in the press increased, and a number of court cases were found in favour of the plaintiffs. The following abridged article by the Insight Consumer Unit of the *Sunday Times*, appearing on 29 October 1972, was typical.

> This week the great 1973 holiday race gets under way. The tour operators launch their big promotional efforts for next summer, and the bookings start flooding in. The stakes are enormous. Some $3\frac{1}{2}$ million people will take a package tour next summer, paying anything from £20 to more than £200 each. But it means trying to keep happy the equivalent to the total populations of Birmingham, Manchester, Liverpool, Leeds, Coventry and Wolverhampton.
>
> The large majority will undoubtedly find the holidays excellent value. But the flow of reports in recent years of unfinished hotels, badly delayed flights, and fines under the Trade Descriptions Act for misleading brochures, indicate that the industry has serious problems.
>
> The operators claim, optimistically, that 99 per cent of holidaymakers are satisfied. But even this would mean 35,000 dissatisfied customers—equivalent to the population of a country town like Salisbury. And, unlike a faulty television set or washing machine which can be mended or replaced, a holiday, once ruined, can never be regained.
>
> True, some of the last-minute problems are unavoidable. But our investigation suggests something more disturbing: that the seeds of discontent for thousands of

holidaymakers next summer have already been sown. We have found:
- Astonishing ignorance among many travel agents about the holidays they sell.
- Inadequate and unclear brochures.
- That holidaymakers are nearly always forced to sign away important legal rights.
- That the industry is so competitive that clients are suffering in a cost-cutting war.

Dominating the package business is the Mediterranean holiday. Resorts have mushroomed in the past decade into sun factories. In just 10 of them the seven tour operators which carry 70 per cent of Britain's package tourists (Clarksons, Thomson, Horizon, Cosmos, Sunair, Global, 4-S) use between them no fewer than 224 hotels. Of these, 57 are shared by two or more companies.

Anyone planning to visit a resort he doesn't already know has a daunting task finding the best value holiday—as illustrated by our investigation of one typical resort, Lido di Jesolo, near Venice. We concentrated our attention on three hotels: the Aquileia (used by Clarksons, Global, Horizon); the Eden (Clarksons, Cosmos, Sunair); and the Cesare Augustus (Global, Horizon, Sunair).

Armed with next summer's brochures, our reporter set out to compare their descriptions with the reality. His report:

'Lido di Jesolo is a narrow ribbon of modern hotels sprawling along the Adriatic coast for the best part of eight miles. Cosmos describes it romantically as a former "playground for the wealthy Doges of nearby Venice." Unhappily for the Cosmos copywriter, the last of the Doges abdicated in 1797, when there was nothing there but marsh and scrub.

The town is totally dependent on the holiday industry and has about as much charm as a well-planned factory estate. It does, however, have a fine sandy beach. Of the three hotels only the Cesare Augustus fully measured up to the expectations aroused by the brochures. Even then the Sunair brochure wrongly places the hotel "in the middle of Lido di Jesolo" when it stands at the western end of the town.

At the Hotel Eden the "armchairs in zingy colours" (Cosmos) turned out to be in very plain and un-zingy shades of dark green, sober red and tan. The hotel occupies a corner site on "sophisticated Piazza Mazzini" (Clarksons)—"a pretty square of gardens, outdoor cafes, shopping arcades, everything" (Cosmos). In fact, the square is one of the rowdiest places in the resort. One of the town's busiest bars, equipped with jumbo-sized juke box, shares the hotel building's ground floor, together with the Stork night club.

One of the most disturbing aspects of brochure writing is the way the less attractive features of hotels or resorts are overlooked. Horizon's brochure accurately describes the Hotel Aquileia as "the attractive and well-designed Aquileia, situated only 200 yards from its own private section of beach." What it forgets to mention is that somewhat closer than the beach is one of the town's noisiest cross-roads; hotel residents have a close-up view of the traffic pouring up and down two busy dual carriageways.'

Most tourists cannot, of course, examine a resort's hotels before choosing a holiday. And, apart from brochures, the main source of information about the choice available is the travel agent. We visited eight in central London, posing as potential customers, to see how good and impartial their advice is, again concentrating on the same three Lido di Jesolo hotels.

No agent seemed to know that there was a choice of operators for these hotels; more seriously, none even tried to find out through the simple expedient of comparing the brochures. None, for example, pointed out that a couple going to the Cesare Agustus for a fortnight in high season with Sunair would pay £36 less than a couple going to the same hotel with Global.

Five of the eight agents told us that generally Horizon offered the best value for money. Horizon's brochure was given such a hard sell in the Haymarket office of Wakefield Fortune that the salesman even denied that other operators used Lido di Jesolo. Anyway, he said (quite wrongly), no other brochures were out yet.

Advice from agents varied considerably. At T. Llewellyn Davies in Trafalgar Square, we were urged to book with Clarksons: 'They're all the same, so you might as well go for the cheapest.' The same agency told us that both the Aquileia and the Eden have sea views and are 'very quiet'—which is untrue on all counts.

At the Lunn-Poly agency in the Grand Arcade, Trafalgar Square, we were handed a copy of 'The Camkin Report'—Lunn-Poly's own 44-page comparative survey of tour operators. Thomson Holidays comes out of the report particularly well, although other firms also get some bouquets. Was Lunn-Poly in any way connected with the big tour operators? we asked—'No. The report is quite impartial,' we were told. In fact, the Lunn-Poly/Camkin chain of around 60 travel agencies is part of the Thomson Organisation, as is Thomson Holidays (and the *Sunday Times*). The booklet itself makes no mention of this.

At another Lunn-Poly agency, in Regent Street, the connection with Thomson was mentioned; indeed impartiality here was taken to the extent of recommending Horizon.

Only once did we find some really helpful information about Lido di Jesolo. At Pontin's, Oxford Circus, a salesgirl told us: 'Don't go to the Eden whatever you do. There's a road like a motorway right outside it and it faces a square that's full of fire engines and police cars and heavy lorries that keep you awake half the night.'

She knew, 'because I went there last year and we were double-booked, four to a room. There were people shouting outside and the food was atrocious.' She claimed that Clarksons had been offering the same holiday for £10 less—'and their clients were getting better service. So you should go for the cheapest holiday.'

Perhaps the most impartial holiday guide is a little-known book which circulates among travel agents. It is called the Agents' Hotel Gazetteer for the Resorts of Europe (£7.50 Continental Hotel Gazetteers).

To anyone dazzled by the brochures' sunbaked landscapes, golden sand, shimmering seas and tranquil fishing villages, the Gazetteer's descriptions can come like a cold douche. 'A most beautiful prison....Visitors most unwelcome' is how it describes the San Dominico Palace in Taormina, Sicily. Or: 'A good imitation of a multistorey car park' (Hotel Bonavida, El Arenal, Majorca); 'Mausoleum-type hotel.... Almost sepulchral' (Summer Palace Thermae, Rhodes); 'Straddling Dirty Dick's rather noisy snack-bar' (New York Hotel, Corfu)....

The Gazetteer, produced by two businessmen who became disenchanted with their former jobs in the travel industry, can now be found on the shelves of some 2,000 travel agents throughout the country. As there are about 4,000 agencies altogether, the would-be client has, alas, only a 50-50 chance of being granted access to it—unless of course he reckons £7.50 a reasonable insurance premium and buys the book himself.

It could be worth it, if only to unravel the descriptions of hotels and resorts in the brochures of the seven companies which dominate the market. We have found they contain some amazing discrepancies....

The tour operators' excuses for brochure inaccuracies are hard to accept in view of the fact that detailed information of the kind contained in the Gazetteer is available to them. Most, if not all, the major holiday firms have detailed 'confidential' questionnaires filed away at their head offices and containing fundamental facts about their product which never reach the public.

While space restrictions obviously rule out their inclusion in the brochures (the most detailed of the ones we have managed to see runs to 15 pages) it is a pity that such facts are not made available to clients through travel agents.

Not surprisingly, there are many price differences among the seven companies. Most variations are within £3 to £5 per person for ostensibly the same package, but we found four more dramatic examples. The difference between the cheapest and most expensive two-week high-season holiday for a couple in Magaluf, Majorca, was £18; in Malgrat £20; in Lido di Jesolo £36; and in Hammamet, Tunisia, a staggering £43. Despite the price differences, the holidays are basically the same—the same hotels, the same food, the same facilities.

But there is another facet to the cost question that cannot be so readily spotted by a comparison of basic prices in the brochures—without exception, the tourist will have to pay more for his holiday than the basic advertised cost. Airport taxes, over-flying surcharges and devaluation surcharge (mandatory) and accommodation supplements (optional) can increase the bill dramatically.

The peripheral differences between virtually identical holidays can be important. These are some of the points to look out for:

● **Length of Holiday:** Beware the tag '15-day' holiday, 4S, for example, shows a 15-day holiday at Benidorm, leaving Gatwick at 10.45 pm on Sundays, and returning at 8.10 am on Sundays a fortnight later. Even counting the four-hour, each-way journey as part of the holiday, this is only 13 days 9 hours 25 minutes. A slight delay on one flight could mean that under 13 days are actually spent in Benidorm.

Cosmos and Clarksons also use this kind of '15-day' terminology, though Thomson, Sunair, Global and Horizon say either '14-day' or 'two-week'.

● **Supplements:** These vary widely. At the Hotel Albatros in Porec, Yugoslavia, for instance, Thomson clients are charged 5p a night per head for a sea view from their room whereas those travelling with 4S are invited to pay 15p each a night for presumably the same view.

● **Departure times:** These can be misleading. What might look like a reasonable flight (9 am from Gatwick) could in fact turn out to be quite the opposite even for the Londoner living in, say, Hampstead who wants to make his own way to the airport. With check-in time generally one hour before departure on charter flights, we estimate he would have to get up at 5.30 am to catch a taxi at 6.30 am to Victoria for the 7.06 am train to Gatwick.

● **Different airports:** All the companies we looked at offer holidays from several provincial airports, though programmes vary widely and are more limited than from Gatwick or Luton. For instance, 4S offers a choice of four provincial departures as well as Gatwick for its Hotel Albatros holiday in Porec; Thomson offers only one (Glasgow).

● **Different aircraft:** Although the brochures abound with pictures of Boeings, Tri-Stars and BAC 1-11s, the package-deal client should not be surprised if the comfort in these planes is somewhat less than on scheduled flights. The BAC 1-11 seats 96 on BEA scheduled flights, for instance, but on package tours can seat 119—in which case they often have non-reclinable seats.

Some of the most serious pitfalls, however, lurk in the small print of the booking conditions. Generally Cosmos offers the least restrictive terms while Clarksons vies with 4S for the toughest.

The only company we have come across which avoids these legal traps is the Travel Club of Upminster, a small firm which quite simply has no booking conditions—and consequently leaves the client's rights intact.

One clause common to all seven major operators incorporates all the conditions of sub-contractors (such as foreign bus companies, hotels and airlines) into the main contract. It is doubtful if this is binding because (except for Clarksons) the client has no chance to study them before the main contract is made.

Exemptions of liability and special terms are extremely varied but important points emerge. Clarksons manages to cram so many caveats into its persuasive, chatty text that many legal come-backs seem to have been neatly removed—despite its emphasis on the word 'guaranteed' on the cover. Prices can be raised, itineraries changed and hotels substituted.

4S also maintains 'absolute discretion' to change and substitute hotels, and the client indemnifies the company for the cost of cables and telephone calls, no matter who makes a mistake or changes the booking. This company also carries a swingeing total exclusion of liability for injury and disaster whether caused by defects in vehicles, hotels, etc. *caused by their fault or anyone else's fault* (our italics). This is capped by a real gem: 4S is not to be held liable for any misrepresentations.

This clause is in fact open to challenge under Section 3 of the Misrepresentation Act, 1967, which gives courts the power to declare any such attempt to avoid liability invalid.

Horizon also makes a hopeful attempt to avoid liability by declaring that it is only the agent (and not the principal) for all hotel and transport arrangements. If the courts uphold this legal side-step, it means that a disappointed customer is left only with the thin chance of taking costly legal action in a foreign court.

But things are looking brighter for the holiday client. In a succession of recent cases operators have been declared 'reckless' under the Trade Descriptions Act and heavily fined (£5,000 in the case of Sunair). Other fines have ranged from £50 on Thomson (for lacking 'enormous private swimming pool illuminated at night') to £150 on Horizon ('our own private sandy beach nearby') and £200 on Travis ('kindergarten on the doorstep'). Twelve days ago Swan Tours had to pay £125 damages for, among other things, promising a yodeller who did not match up to expectations.

One major reason why tour companies have run into difficulties is that they have been locked in a vicious price war. And, while they can fairly boast that holidays are, in real terms, much cheaper than ever before, the result is that the risks of things going wrong are higher than they need be.

To break even, the operator must have his aircraft and hotel accommodation 88 per cent full as an average throughout the season. Since cancellations can easily run to 10 per cent, there is a tendency for operators to overbook to ensure a profitable load.

Aircraft schedules are often drawn up so tightly that a delay of a few hours for weather or a slight technical hitch may mean that flights will run late for days afterwards.

Other faults we have already described—such as over-optimistic brochures, and cramped aircraft—also stem from the over-riding financial objective of keeping costs down and volume up.

Even then, profits cannot be guaranteed. Clarksons recently announced that it would make a loss this year of 'well over' the £2.7 million it lost in 1971. And Sunair Lunn-Poly, which has just been taken over by Thomson, was, in the words of one senior executive, 'building up to a crescendo of mess'. The administration had 'collapsed completely'.

Financial stringency within the companies does not, however, seem to have affected the lavish treatment they give to travel agents. 'Incentive schemes' range from free flights and free holidays for travel agents to 'educational' facility trips abroad that in some cases, according to one disenchanted member of the Association of British Travel Agents, are nothing but 'boozy jollies'. All are designed to promote the benefits of booking with the host company, and are additional to the 10 per cent commission they give agents.

Most of the seven companies we studied have special incentives for the individual agency staff, varying in generosity from Horizon's holiday scheme (two free holidays up to £70 value based on 150 bookings) to a straightforward £1 per head gift for every booking over 50 through the summer season.

The whole question may be considered at ABTA's annual convention, which begins next Saturday in Vienna. Belatedly, ABTA has realised that its code of conduct needs urgent revision. A working party is now redrafting the code, which should take effect next spring.

But even if ABTA does start growing some teeth, this would still be no substitute for improved service from the tour operators themselves. Above all, they must close the gulf between the expectations created by brochures and by travel agents, and the disappointing reality of many holidays. This may mean higher prices: security and a better service will cost money. But the typical customer is buying blind a product which may form the most expensive single item in his annual budget. Is honesty and reliability too much to expect from the tour operators in return?

In spite of such reporting, the industry was pressing ahead with its advertising campaign for the 1973 summer season. Thomsons was planning to use newspaper advertising extensively, together with TV, a short film shown in the interval in cinemas, and its normal brochures. Exhibit 6 reproduces the text of a typical Thomson newspaper advertisement, which included a picture of a hostess and child.

CLARKSONS

The crashing losses recorded by Clarksons hung like a sword of Damocles over the industry. One could joke about the problem, as did *The Times* (see Hollowood cartoon).

'Let's stick to Majorca and Clarkson's. There aren't many package tour people who can offer the same loss per head per booking.'

EXHIBIT 6 **Thomson Holiday Holdings**
Advertisement in *The Times*
21 October 1972

"You didn't know you had an Auntie Sandra in Majorca, did you?"

As you can see, when Thomson take you on holiday we don't just take care of the big things. We can very often take care of the little ones, too.

At any hotel listed in the Thomson Summer Sun brochure as having a baby patroller, you can leave them playing, paddling or having their meals together under the careful supervision of some of the nicest 'aunties' they could wish to meet.

Or leave them sleeping safe and sound at night under the same watchful eye while you wine, dine or trip the light fantastic.

But Thomson not only take care of you when you're at your holiday hotel. We've even taken the hard work out of getting there. By flying from airports near you. By providing coaches and special British Rail concession fares from wherever you live. Even advising you about airport parking costs.

So wherever you go, to Europe's beaches, Europe's Lakes, Mountains and Fjords or on a Thomson Mediterranean Cruise, you know you're going to be free to enjoy yourself.

The Thomson brochures at your local travel agent will give you all the details.

Thomson Holidays

We take care...you're free to enjoy yourself

One could also use Clarksons as an example of the likely fate awaiting other major operators.

In addition to compounding Clarksons' operating problems, the increasing losses resulted in a postponement of American Express's plans to increase their existing equity stake in the business. *The Times,* on 14 October 1972, reported

> The £6.52m deal whereby American Express had the right to acquire up to a 49 per cent stake in Clarksons Holidays has been postponed, because of a worse-than-expected loss position of the holiday company. Clarksons is Britain's biggest package tour operator.
>
> The postponement was announced yesterday by Shipping Industrial Holdings, Clarksons' parent company, together with the interim profit statement for SIH for the six months to June 30. The Stock Exchange reacted to the news by marking the SIH share price down from 255p to 175p, wiping £12.9m off the group's market capitalization.
>
> In their statement the SIH directors, headed by Mr Jocelyn Hambro, reported that this year's losses at Clarksons are 'likely to be much worse' than the £2.7m deficit incurred in 1971. This compares with the previous expectation of a £1.5m loss at Clarksons during 1972, a prediction given by Mr Hambro at the end of June in his SIH annual review.
>
> The results of the holiday company were a major disappointment, the board add and in the circumstances—and at the suggestion of SIH—it has been agreed with American Express that the negotiations over Clarksons require 'more time for mutual consideration'.
>
> An SIH spokesman refused to disclose the extent of Clarksons' losses, but the statement does admit that the £1.5m provision made in the 1971 accounts for this year's expected losses was 'underestimated'. Because of this the SIH directors are deferring consideration of any interim dividend payment until February or March of next year.
>
> The problems facing Clarksons and the other inclusive tour operators were set out in the 1971 SIH report. Prices listed in package holiday brochures are established up to 18 months ahead of the actual holiday. The key factors on which the prices are based are the capacity of aircraft, hotels and ships and the capacity load factor on the one hand, and the cost of bookings, prices paid for aircraft, hotels and ships and administration costs on the other.
>
> With the trend towards larger aircraft accurate forecasts of the expected load factor are crucial for profit margins. As the SIH directors pointed out, the holiday selling price, once set, cannot be changed without incurring very large costs.
>
> In the current year much work has been done on improving all aspects of Clarksons' business, and while the directors stress that this does not imply that the task is complete, bookings for the latter part of 1972 show that the company has retained its share of the market.
>
> Under the original agreement with American Express, the United States company was to take a 19 per cent interest in Clarksons for £1.58m and subscribe for an unsecured loan stock, dated 1972-78 and guaranteed by SIH, which was convertible into a further 16 per cent of Clarksons' equity for £1.92m. In addition American Express had an option to take another 14 per cent of the capital for £3.02m before December, 1978.
>
> These terms would have meant an immediate cash injection of £3.5m into Clarksons. As the deal has now been shelved, arrangements for immediate working capital are at present being completed with the company's bankers.
>
> Excluding Clarksons, the SIH interim results shows a slight upturn in pre-tax profits from £2,161,000 to £2,175,000. No breakdown is given, but it is stated that the major divisions, ship-broking, ship-owning and insurance, traded satisfactory.
>
> Ship-broking profits fell because of continued low freight rates but the insurance broking and underwriting divisions together managed a slight improvement.

The policies that Clarksons developed to cure their ailments would directly affect the success of their competitors' policies. Thomsons, as Clarksons closest rivals, were likely to be the most critically affected.

8   Croydon Chemicals Company Ltd*

In the summer of 1969, Mr Hartley, the executive chairman of Croydon Chemicals, was reviewing Croydon's acquisition programme. During the mid-1960s it had become clear that Croydon had outgrown the strategy which had served so well since the firm had been founded in 1936. At the same time, however, prices in Croydon's major markets fell so sharply that a fight for survival became management's major preoccupation. Nevertheless, while the company was struggling to re-establish its profitability, various studies were conducted and actions taken to throw off some of the shackles of the past.

The case describes the company and the developments between 1966 and 1969 that had led to the decision to become acquisitive.

PRODUCT LINES

The original product had been a line of leather finishes. Research started during the Second World War and continued afterwards had resulted in new products, all of which were made at the company's single works near Manchester. The success of these new products was such that, by 1967, leather finishes accounted for only 2 per cent of Croydon's turnover. Croydon was by then active in the following five major product areas.

1. *Plasticisers and stabilisers*   A wide variety of phthalate and epoxy plasticisers and stabilisers were made. These chemicals were used by manufacturers of PVC plastics to impart flexibility to their products and to stabilise them against deterioration through light and heat. In 1967 Croydon gained about half its total sales from this product group, and had a UK market share of about 30 per cent.

2. *Polyurethane intermediates*   These were produced for the polyurethane foam industry as intermediates in the manufacture of flexible and rigid polyurethane foams which were widely used in upholstery in the motor and furniture industries, and for insulation and packaging. A number of urethane chemicals for non-foam applications such as elastomers and lacquers were under active development. In 1967 this group contributed almost 20 per cent of company sales and represented a market share of 35-45 per cent.

3. *Surfactants*   These materials form the base of various domestic and industrial cleaners and detergents. They are also used for large numbers of specialised purposes in the manufacture of agricultural chemicals, cosmetics, silicones and textiles. This group sold only small amounts to the manufacturers of household washing powders. Instead, the company concentrated on specialised uses, though they did have some sales to manufacturers of liquid household cleansers, such as washing-up liquids. For this reason, overall market share figures were not meaningful for this product group. Nevertheless, Croydon believed that they had a significant share of those areas where they did compete.

4. *Herbicides*   Since 1961 Croydon had manufactured a chlorinated herbicide, known as Nopalad, which was largely sold overseas. The company also sold an intermediate chlorinated compound to other UK herbicide manufacturers. Sales of herbicides represented less than 5 per cent of total Croydon sales in 1967. Although the share of the total herbicide market was very small, Croydon was one of only three producers and had a substantial share of its specialised segment.

5. *Products for leather*   Croydon manufactured a range of pigment finishes, fat liquors, wetting agents and impregnants, as well as a number of products for the fur

---

[1] See Croydon Chemicals Company Ltd (IMEDE, 1962) for a description of the early years of the company. Both there and in the present study the company's name and all other names have been disguised: company and industry figures have been modified by a constant multiplier.

* Copyright © London Business School 1973

industry. In 1967 these accounted for less than 2 per cent of total Croydon sales, representing a market share of about 5 per cent.

THE NATURE OF THE BUSINESS

With sales of less than £13 million in 1969, and with approximately 1000 employees, Croydon was a small company in an industry dominated by giants such as Drake International, ECE, and UK Chemicals. As Exhibit 1 shows, much of the business involved buying raw materials from Croydon's customers and competitors. Mr Hartley explained the competitive position of the company.

> We went into the plasticiser business when it was a relatively new field. Only a few of the large chemical firms, like Todd, had entered the market before us. Because the market grew so fast and we were so small, we could expand without any serious competition. The same was the case for the early years of our other major products.
>
> Things are different now. The technology has matured, and the growth market has slowed. We have become an important manufacturer of undifferentiated products competing directly with the industry giants. Our strength lies in the flexibility of our production and marketing, our speed of response and our ability to manufacture a product tailored to a client's specific needs. Also many of our customers are in competition with our competitors and want an independent source of products.
>
> Even these strengths, however, do not make our position in the industry secure, as the recent price squeeze proved. The key economic factor of our business is not turnover, but the value added in manufacture at Croydon; that is the difference between raw material costs and our sales revenue. Ordinarily 70 per cent of our sales revenue is raw material costs, so we only have a 30 per cent margin to work on. In 1964-5 the orderly marketing of our major products broke down and for some time we had vicious price cutting. Meanwhile, the cost of raw materials held firm, so that our profitability was seriously affected (see Exhibits 2 and 3 for summarised financial data). It took us about three years to recover to a reasonable level of profitability.
>
> One solution might have been to increase the number of operations we performed on the raw materials in order to increase the added value. Our sale in 1962 of 20 per cent of the equity to Drake International did not, however, provide nearly enough capital. Although it is a gross oversimplification, the problems may be explained as follows: for our plasticiser business, integration backward would have meant moving into base chemicals and/or petrochemicals, integration forward into setting up a plastics plant. Neither option was feasible, given our skills and financial resources. For our other products it would have meant moving into the finished product market. We did not have the necessary expertise or aptitude to enter into consumer marketing; besides, we did not really want to do so.
>
> In 1964, when the latent problems became actual ones, there was no real possibility of increasing the proportion of our sales in the high value-added areas of leather chemicals and herbicides. In leather chemicals we were losing money because of low volume of output (much less than plant capacity) and the large research and development staff needed in that area. Leather chemicals are really a relic of our origins, and could not be the solution for us. Herbicides and agricultural chemicals did not offer expansion opportunities because of the competition of large companies with superior expertise in that area. Thus, to regain our profitability, we had to concentrate our efforts on our existing major products. A measure of our success in this endeavour is the fact that our tonnage output more than doubled between 1964 an d 1969. Yet, because of the fundamental problems in this part of the industry, our sales and profits increased much more slowly.

STRATEGY RE-EXAMINED

During the period of recovery from 1964, it became increasingly apparent that a fresh look at the company's strategy was needed. Mr Harley explained

> Although we regained our profitability by 1967, it was clear to us that Croydon retained as insecure and metastable a position in the industry as before. In 1966

the board had asked me to write a report on how the future prospects of the company might be improved. Either Croydon could sell out to a larger company, or additional funds, to help finance a continuing independent role, could be raised by a public share issue.

A summary of the report is contained in Exhibit 4. The table of contents of the full report is also shown in Exhibit 4 to indicate the scope of the analysis.

In order fully to understand the argument in the report, two important issues require some elaboration. These issues are discussed in the following two sections.

THE RELATIONSHIP WITH DRAKE

In 1962 Croydon had sold 20 per cent of its equity to Drake International. For Drake, the sale provided an outlet for many of its products; for Croydon, the sale provided badly needed cash. This money allowed Dr Waldner, the founder of Croydon, to retain control without having to make a public share issue.

Drake treated its 20 per cent holding primarily as a portfolio investment and restricted its relationship with Croydon to arm's-length transactions. Drake did not, for example, nominate any directors, though it could very well have insisted on at least one seat on the board. In terms of its day-to-day management Croydon remained an independent private company. There was, however, one limitation to this independence.

In practical terms Croydon, or more specifically the Waldner family, could not sell out, raise further equity or acquire other firms by means of issuing more shares without first offering Drake equal terms on a share-for-share basis. For so long as Croydon's management remained content with the then existing ownership arrangements, this limitation to their independence was of no consequence. The events of 1964 and the following years, however, led Mr Hartley and his colleagues to conclude that the limitation had to be removed.

In his report, Mr Hartley examined the implications of a continuing independent role for the relationships with Drake. He argued

> An evaluation of the likelihood for Croydon's success in an independent role is not complete without stressing the continuing development of our relationship with Drake. The conclusions which have been drawn in relation to the vendor's agreement and the need for arm's-length operation must not detract from our duty to give to Drake's equity holding as much meaning as is possible within the limitations which appear inescapable. The interdependence between the two companies based on the wide range of 10-year raw material agreements into which we have entered goes some way towards justifying Drake's investment of substantial funds in Croydon. I believe, however, that deliberate policy, and well-conceived channels of communications, could lead to a number of new and mutually profitable arm's-length transactions which would provide increasing justification for Drake's maintenance of equity in Croydon. Some of the areas we might explore are further rationalisation of United Kingdom manufacture and research in urethane chemicals, more cooperation in the field of additives for plastics, and a fresh look at some of the fruits of Drake research which do not involve heavy investment in petroleum-based chemistry. This area is one in which I believe we have missed past opportunities, but this should not preclude a decision to examine it anew.

SELL-OUT POSSIBILITIES

The consultants drew up a list of criteria (shown in Exhibit 5) for potential acquirers of Croydon. In applying these criteria to specific companies, the consultants were given several important guidelines. First, the existing raw material commitments to Drake were in no way to be undermined by potential acquirers. Second, by agreement with Drake, Drake was not to be considered as a candidate, because that would be incompatible with the expressed wish of the Waldner family to protect, as much as possible, the separate identity of the company. Third, at Drake's request, no sale was to be considered to any petroleum company or large chemical company, whose primary long-term motive in buying Croydon could be the acquisition of an outlet for petroleum-based raw materials.

From the initial list of potential acquirers, three US firms were contacted. All three showed considerable interest in the proposal. In one case, however, discussions were terminated by Croydon because of a clear difference in management philosophy. The second firm decided not to pursue the matter further because Croydon would not fit well with their overall European strategy. The third firm remained extremely interested until the discussions were promptly halted by Croydon's decision to accept Mr Hartley's recommendations and thus seek to retain an independent role.

An important consideration in reaching this decision was the risk that, by selling out, the employees would be demoralised. Mr Hartley considered that even though this risk was present in all decisions to sell, it was particularly high for Croydon, because the company had evolved a very 'personal' style of management, and had made, during the period of its growth, unusually heavy demands on many of its employees.

CREATING AN INDEPENDENT ROLE

The heart of the report on Croydon as an independent company was a six-year forecast prepared by Mr Hartley late in 1967. Exhibit 6 summarises the forecast judged to be the most likely situation; other equally detailed forecasts based on alternative assumptions were also prepared. Fundamental to the forecast was the expectation that the added value of Croydon's existing products would decline, and that new products were needed to offset the erosion in margins.

Several targets were set. A return on shareholders' funds of 12 per cent after tax was considered a reasonable and attainable objective. By 1973 the volume of sales of new products was expected to be £2 million per year, provided that an investment of £$\frac{1}{2}$ million of new capital was added to those funds already available for such a programme of expansion.

Several partially related development projects were to be the source of new products. These projects were selected in accordance with a modified product strategy. Previously, Croydon had emphasised one-step conversions of petrochemicals. Although demand for these conversions was expected to grow, new work was to concentrate on more specialised chemicals. In particular, the new projects were aimed (a) to seek a measure of integration in specific fields by manufacturing non-petroleum based chemicals used in Croydon's existing processes, and (b) to move nearer the ultimate consumer by upgrading some of the materials already produced.

Mr Hartley considered that his forecast was conservative in the early years, and optimistic in the later years when the expected returns on the new products might well not be achieved. Even so, he did not feel justified at that stage in making a more pessimistic forecast. As it stood, Croydon's shareholders would be better off for at least five years if the company was sold outright—at a minimum expected price of £6 million—rather than performing as forecasted. Only in the long-term might the shareholders gain more by remaining independent.

Before any serious work could be started on developing a new strategy, several issues had to be resolved. These were the preconditions for success contained in Exhibit 4. The relationship with Drake was amicably renegotiated on the lines suggested by Mr Hartley. In addition, a Drake nominee was invited to sit on the Croydon board.

To provide the financing needed, the company made a public issue in the autumn of 1968. One million shares were offered at a minimum price of £1.60 per share.[*] Of these shares, 680,000 were offered by existing shareholders, the remainder being shares authorised but not previously issued. Croydon obtained a price of £1.87 per share. 'We were very lucky,' Mr Hartley commented, 'to hit the top of the market, but it put an additional pressure on us to justify the rating we were given.'

MANAGEMENT DEVELOPMENT

The other two preconditions involved changes in management thinking and practice. To understand the implications of these changes, a review of developments before 1968 is needed.

---

[2] The company had changed its authorised capital from 1 million shares of £1 each to 4 million shares of 25 pence each in September 1968.

Originally, Dr Waldner had dominated the management of his company. In the mid-fifties he began to step back from an executive role, handing over many decisions to Messrs Hartley and Swift. These two men became joint managing directors, with Mr Hartley responsible for the commercial functions and Mr Swift for the technical functions. Later on, Mr Hartley became deputy chairman, at which time, Mr Ashton took over the commercial functions. The three formed a triumvirate, in which Mr Hartley was the 'crown prince'. His colleagues agreed that Mr Hartley's gradual emergence as the general manager replacing Mr Waldner was the best recipe for a smooth evolution in management. The full list of directors is shown in Exhibit 7, together with their qualifications and job titles in 1967 and 1968.

Mr Hartley had joined the company as a trainee in 1947, when he left the army. He went to evening classes in commerce at the Manchester College of Technology. Later on with the moral support of Dr Waldner and the financial support of a BIM scholarship, he went to Harvard. On his return to Croydon, armed with an MBA, he soon emerged as the 'leader of the loyal opposition to Waldner's regime'. He considered himself to be a democratic leader; his colleagues, used to debating with him, shared this view, and on many issues supported Mr Hartley wholeheartedly.

Mr Swift joined Croydon's technical staff in 1952 and had become a board member in 1957. He was described by his colleagues as an outstanding chemical engineer and a particularly hard worker. His speciality—the planning and design of chemical process equipment and plant—had been of enormous value to the company over the years.

Mr Ashton joined as a trainee at the same time as Mr Hartley and became a board member in 1962. He was described by his colleagues as a very able businessman and negotiator. He was also regarded as a doer rather than a planner, and he put great store in experience rather than qualifications such as degrees. He described the current vogue for further education (and management education) as 'the green stamp society—one spends one's life collecting diplomas rather than actually doing anything'.

These three men had been among the seven managers who reported directly to Dr Waldner. As they emerged as the senior members of the cabinet, they assumed more responsibilities than those reflected in their titles. Dr Waldner had been unwilling to hurt anyone and had not wished to signal any losses of prestige. Consequently, over the years, there was some ambiguity in the responsibilities of each manager. For so long as Croydon continued with its original strategy, ambiguity in responsibility caused few problems; each manager knew the others well enough informally to sort out difficulties as they arose.

There were some weaknesses in the structure, revealed by the task of implementing the new strategy of independence. Symptomatic of the weaknesses was the fact that, although there was a six-year forecasting system, no long-term plans for product development had been formulated. There were also problems of inadequate delegation of responsibility, fragmentation of effort and control of R & D. Most of these weaknessess were, however, considered relatively minor and not worth much attention until after the future course of the company had been mapped out in detail.

Nevertheless, over the course of a few months after Mr Hartley's recommendations had been accepted, a number of changes occurred. The effect of these changes was to clarify the relationships among the senior mangers. Mr Hartley described them.

First, I, as chief executive, began to devote more of my time to pursuing acquisition and major growth opportunities. I was also responsible for finance and personnel functions and for overall company performance. Second, all other functional and operating responsibilities continued to be delegated to two broad management-orientated executives, Mr Swift and Mr Ashton. Mr Swift used his technical skills as technical managing director and Mr Ashton his business skills as commercial managing director. Third, Mr Reddington, reporting to Mr Ashton, had become responsible for licensing, purchases, and for our small overseas companies. Fourth, Mr Bowman, reporting to Mr Swift, continued as research director. Fifth, a corporate development committee was established to develop company objectives *inter alia* by defining acquisition criteria and evaluating potential acquisitions. Sixth, an executive committee of three was established. Mr Swift, Mr Ashton and I became responsible for major operating decisions, and gave attention to integrating the activities of the two main functional groups.

There were uncomfortable aspects of these changes for some of the men concerned. Differences in status, previously disguised, were underlined. Even by those who lost most by the reorganisation, the changes were accepted as an integral part of the package needed to make the new strategy work. Mr Ashton, who had earlier been the strongest proponent of the sell-out, welcomed the decision to go it alone. 'We had worked to build a company for Dr Waldner', he stated, 'and in the process had developed our own emotional investment in its future. It was a great challenge to devise and implement a feasible strategy as an independent unit.'

SEARCH FOR ACQUISITIONS

Once Croydon had become a public company with stated growth aspirations, management attention shifted to the problems of making the corporate development committee work effectively. There was a need to gain a larger technical and sales base. Furthermore, after one unsuccessful attempt at an opportunistic acquisition, there was a clear need for more precise definitions of objectives, needed resources and suitable candidates for acquisiton.

In February 1969, after several months of work, the corporate development committee agreed on a set of overall objectives and a philosphy of growth. The core of the philosophy was summarised in a committee minute.

(i) To be an independent and growing group of well-managed and competitive chemical companies in different markets. Each company will retain its separate identity but will gain new strength for growth and greater resistance to being acquired by being linked to a holdings-type board. The board will be strong in both general and financial management, and will not be dominated by any one of the constituent companies.

(ii) Croydon's motivation in embarking on this course is that we believe it to present the most promising long-term context in which the existing business can grow, and that for Croydon, as well as other companies who are similarly placed, internal development of each unit on its own cannot keep pace with, and stay invulnerable to, the competition of large integrated companies.

(iii) A fundamental feature of this group is that its size must be limited to ensure genuine operating and 'way-of-life' advantages over the giants. The group must be versatile enough to obtain long-term independence in an industry in which either quite small national companies, or international corporations that are strong in relation to their fields of work, will tend to flourish. Limited size implies a maximum overall sales volume determined by the number and size of companies that the board can control.

(iv) Some loss of independence is inevitably involved for every unit that becomes part of the group. However, we would hope to minimise this loss of independence for the type of company we have in mind, so that they, their customers and their suppliers may continue to benefit from each others' experience within their field.

(v) In terms of management structure, this implies that member companies should not become divisions, should retain their own boards, and that their management should not be weakened by syphoning off the best talent into a heavy central corporate structure. Notwithstanding this principle, the concept relies on securing the involvement of member companies in the affairs of the group as a whole. This must be achieved by creating a balanced holdings board, by providing important group services, and by involving senior managers of member companies in the preparation of proposals for the strategy of the group as a whole.

Specific criteria for acquisition candidates were formulated. Mr Hartley explained the thinking behind these criteria

> The starting point of our analysis was our interpretation of what the market (our actual and potential stockholders) expected of us. We concluded that a 15 per cent per annum compound growth in earnings per share was an appropriate target. Examination of our profits forecast (Exhibit 6) revealed that the years up to 1971 had a very flat gradient of profit increase, while the year 1972 onwards showed a profit increase in line with the 15 per cent growth target. There was a profit gap for the next two years, and in view of the close range of this gap, acquisition appeared to be the most effective means of filling it.
>
> Although we believed that in the long run a viable chemical company would have to be international, we had not yet developed the overall strength to embark on major foreign operations. We decided that our top priority for the next two years should be to generate added strength by giving concentrated attention to internal product development and to complete one or more UK acquisitions. Such acquisitions should be initially smaller than Croydon, preferably in the private sector because such companies would be cheaper and there would be less chance

of a rival bidder. We decided to confine ourselves to those chemical manufacturing companies which would give Croydon either new products or new technical skills, or established positions in new markets. With this in mind we drew up a list of concerns which could be suitable for acquisitions.

During the first half of 1969 we approached several companies which were at the top of the short list, but nothing positive emerged. We decided that we would not attempt any acquisition without securing the approval of the board of directors of the company concerned. This prevented us from going any further in two cases. For various reasons, we concluded that the other companies were not really suitable partners. In one case we could not get information, in another the shareholders of Croydon would have been in the minority in a shared company. One company had a major interest in inorganic chemicals, involving possible conflict with other Croydon customers. In two other companies we judged the management insufficiently competent, and the final company we approached did not have the space to expand its site.

In July 1969 the six members of the corporate development committee reviewed their objectives and the criteria for selecting acquisition candidates. Other than increased earnings, the main objective was to achieve market diversification and new technology to give more scope for management, new management strength and greater ability to attract new funds, while retaining management control. The committee decided that, rather than looking at companies, they would first of all attempt to define more specifically attractive areas of market and technology diversification. This would allow a sharper focus on a small number of companies. It was decided that Mr Swift and Mr Ashton should independently hold meetings of their functional groups to select three areas of diversification on the above lines.

The commercial group listed four possibilities for further consideration: chemical merchanting, adhesives, printing inks, and broadening Croydon's base as a supplier to the plastics industry. The technical group came up with six areas for the acquisition of companies and three areas for the acquisition of know-how. In the former category, in order of preference, they listed: (1) chemicals for sterilising, disinfecting, and industrial cleaning, (2) synthetic lubricants and oil additives, (3) formulation of agrochemicals, (4) adhesives, (5) surface coatings, and (6) water treatment chemicals. In the latter category, they listed (1) flame retardants, (2) paper chemicals, and (3) long-chain amines.

The subsequent meeting of the corporate development committee put the two proposals together and developed a common order of preference. Two categories of priority—areas for company acquisition and areas for seeking know-how—were used. The final lists in descending order of priority, were

(1) Areas for company acquisition
  (a) Adhesives
  (b) Printing inks
  (c) Water sewerage, slime and mineral treatment chemicals
(2) Areas for seeking know-how
  (a) Flame retardants
  (b) Specialised chemicals for processing and treatment of disposable paper articles
  (c) Long-chain amines
  (d) Plastics additives

Each of these areas was characterised by its relatively high rate of growth and the opportunity it represented for Croydon to build on its technical strength—particularly its process technology. The research and development group, which had developed Croydon's basic products, had not been able to make further major product breakthroughs as the technology matured. Mr Hartley commented.

The hardest thing for a company like Croydon to do is to enter new product/market areas by internal development. We have successfully done so three times in the past, but it is getting more difficult to do it again and again. We have grown to a size where to be significant to us a new development must itself be large. We are now sufficiently large for other companies to take notice and probably retaliate if we were to enter a field that they regarded as their preserve. These facts strengthen the arguments for buying an existing company in a new market area for Croydon, but one which nevertheless will use our skills in chemical engineering and chemical sales. We are really looking for product/market inputs from an acquired company similar to those we looked for in potential buyers of Croydon in 1967. We ourselves can now provide financial and management strength to such a company if we bought it.

The areas listed by the corporate development committee are the most promising, but the type of company we purchase may well be determined by availability as much as anything else.

EXHIBIT 1 Croydon's products and markets

Product line	Major raw material suppliers	Major competitors	Major customers	Croydon's estimate of % UK market share 1963	Croydon's estimate of % UK market share 1967	Approximate % of total sales revenue 1963	Approximate % of total sales revenue 1967	Estimated rate of market growth (% per year) 1968–71	Approximate added value (% of sales)
Plasticisers and stabilisers	ACE, Drake, Morley	UK Chemicals, Priestley & Sons, Todd	ACE, Todd	27	29	55	53	10	23
Polyurethanes	Drake, ACE	Urey, Drake, ACE, Bunsen	Didcot Rubber (Several others)	60	40	21	16	12	29
Surfactants	Drake, ACE, Jonothon Brothers	Drake, Priestley & Sons (several others)	Specialist detergent manufacturers (many others)	Not meaningful	Not meaningful	15	27	5	34
Herbicides	UK Chemicals	Various	Many	Very small	Very small	5	3	15	60
Leather chemicals	Various	Various	Many Leather finishers	7	5	4	2	3	48

Source: Company files and casewriter's notes

EXHIBIT 2 Croydon Chemical Company
Sales and profits

Year	Sales (£'000)	Pretax profits (£'000)	Pretax profits (as % of sales)	After-tax return on equity (%)
1952 (a)	711	9	1.3	NA
1960 (a)	5,592	232	4.2	NA
1961 (a)	6,314	374	5.9	26.2
1962 (a)	6,489	404	6.2	18.3
1964 (b)*	8,689	584	6.7	23.2
1965 (b)	8,127	288	3.7	17.2
1966 (b)	8,525	361	4.2	9.6
1967 (b)	9,640	403	4.2	8.7
1968 (b)	10,840	496	4.7	9.7
1969 (b)	12,937	717	5.5	11.3

*Accounting year end changed to end of February; therefore 1963 to February 1964 = 14-month year.

(a) Year ends 31 December
(b) Year ends 28/29 February

Source: Company records

EXHIBIT 3   Croydon Chemical Company

Selected balance sheets   (£'000's)

	Fiscal years to end of February					
	1964	1965	1966	1967	1968	1969
Current assets						
Cash	21	1	3	3	1	2
Accounts receivable	1,424	1,601	1,851	2,102	2,465	2,825
Inventory	875	1,124	1,088	1,366	1,322	1,541
Total current assets	2,320	2,726	2,941	3,471	3,788	4,368
Net fixed assets	1,561	2,084	2,153	2,246	2,242	2,248
Other assets	43	56	58	80	85	66
Total assets	3,924	4,866	5,152	5,797	6,115	6,682
Current liabilities						
Overdraft	253	879	874	1,020	933	253
Accounts payable	1,709	2,016	1,368	1,577	1,725	2,119
Other	230	155	238	376	459	602
Total current liabilities	2,192	3,050	2,480	2,973	3,117	2,974
Long term liabilities	—	—	22	22	22	267
Capital and reserves	1,732	1,816	2,650	2,802	2,976	3,441
Total liabilities, capital and reserves	3,924	4,866	5,152	5,797	6,115	6,682
RATIOS						
Accounts receivable turnover	6.1	5.1	4.6	4.6	4.3	4.6
Sales/inventory ratio	9.9	7.2	7.8	7.1	8.2	8.4
Sales/fixed asset ratio	5.6	3.9	4.0	4.3	4.8	5.7
Sales/total asset ratio	2.21	1.67	1.65	1.66	1.78	1.94
Current ratio	1.06	0.89	1.19	1.17	1.22	1.47

Source: Company records

EXHIBIT 4   **Extracts from Mr Hartley's Report**

FUNDAMENTAL ASPECTS OF FUTURE POLICY FOR CROYDON

Table of Contents
1. Summary
   (a) Background and introduction
   (b) Conclusions
   (c) Recommendations
2. Appraisal of Croydon's needs
3. Review of acquisition possiblities
4. The independent role
5. Financial comparison of alternatives for shareholders

Exhibit 1   New 6-year forecast for existing product lines with varying assumptions on profitability and calculations reflecting the impact of a selected group of specific development projects. (Note: the 'most likely' forecast is shown as Exhibit 6 in the case.)

Exhibit 2   Commercial outline of selected development projects with accompanying manuals on initial design and cost implications covering these projects.

Exhibit 3   Criteria developed by X (the consultants) for identifying suitable acquiring companies.
(Note: shown as Exhibit 5 in the case.)

Exhibit 4   'The consultants' selection of candidate companies in accordance with criteria developed in Exhibit 3.

Exhibit 5   Report on discussion with Y (a potential buyer).

Exhibit 6   Public issue share value projections,

Graph 1   Six-year net profit before tax projections on varying assumptions.

Graph 2   Six-year return of shareholders' funds projections on varying assumptions.

Graph 3   Various six-year tonnage forecasts.

Graph 4   Comparison of alternative financial gains for shareholders.

1. SUMMARY

(a) Background and introduction

1. This report was commissioned by the Board and Shareholders in June 1966, in order to decide

   'on means by which the Company may be strengthened and may gain in potential to an extent greater than can be brought about by internally generated development and funds, and which are likely to lead to changes in equity holdings.'

   An integral part of the brief was to determine a firm direction for resolving the problems of ownership by the Waldner family.

2. Two major alternatives were to be examined

   (a) Acquisition of Croydon by a larger industrial company

   (b) The growth of Croydon in an independent role

3. In approaching the task, X (management consultants) were brought in to provide an outside view of Croydon's strengths and weaknesses, and to develop therefrom criteria for identifying suitable acquiring companies.

4. At the same time management provided means of assessing future profitability as an independent company by extending to 1974 comprehensive financial forecasts in relation to existing business, and by establishing an initial group of possible new development projects with provisional estimates as to their cost and earnings potential.

(b) **Conclusions**

The analysis contained in sections 2, 3, 4 and 5 of this report have led me to the following conclusions

1. Croydon's present business position and capabilities form a basis on which a growing company in the field of chemical intermediates and specialities can be developed and can achieve increasing profit stability.

2. If profits are to remain satisfactory and be improved upon, changes in Croydon's present operations are necessary. Profit contributions from new products are definitely required to offset the effect of likely market erosion in present products, even where sales of these continue to rise in keeping with forecasts. I regard a 12 per cent return on shareholders' funds after tax as a sound and attainable objective.

3. The addition of new products generating sales of approximately £1m per annum within a five-year period is a target which can be achieved by the marketing and technical resources which are at our disposal and which can, where appropriate, be expanded.

4. In order to embark on this programme, there is an immediate requirement for new loan finance of at least £500,000 in addition to the funds now available.

5. The pursuit of an independent role expresses the desire of management and shareholders alike to perpetuate the identity of the company, and would now require the creation of a public company with all possible assurance of genuine long-term independence.

6. The (consultants') study of acquisition possibilities indicates that a number of potentially attractive acquiring companies can meet many of Croydon's needs and offer considerable advantages towards growth. Potential acquirers do not, however, show any interest in any situation involving less than total ownership of Croydon's equity.

7. Acquisition of Croydon's equity by a suitable company will for at least five years yield to shareholders considerably greater monetary rewards than the pursuit of an independent role. Even in the longer period discriminating reinvestment of funds obtained from the sale of Croydon's equity will in all probability outstrip the value of publicly held Croydon stocks backed by satisfactory earnings.

8. Drake's present equity holding in Croydon does not impair Croydon's independence. It adds stature to Croydon, and there are indications that the overt restrictions of the Drake/Croydon relationship to far-reaching arm's-length transactions, has enhanced the image of both companies.

9. If Croydon is to use effectively the strengths which it possesses to pursue a long-term independent role, management and shareholders would have to agree and act upon certain preconditions, the most important of which are

    (a) The agreement between the Vendors and Drake is in its present form incompatible with the concept of Croydon as an independent company and, therefore, must be set aside or fundamentally renegotiated. The clarification of shareholder relationships brought about by these means can lead to an extension of mutually profitable business in the area of raw materials and other spheres where conditions for meaningful arm's-length cooperation exists.

    (b) Long-term independence requires a commitment of management to change; the focal point of this change must be to participate as a team in the definition, agreement, and execution of specific objectives for expansion. Such expansion includes internal product development and an opportunistic approach to the use of outside know-how and to acquisition of other companies by Croydon. The greatest management strength we are able to deploy must be concentrated in this sphere and organisational changes which can promote new product expansion must be resolutely implemented.

    (c) The present structure of Croydon's board membership and titles must be reviewed and adjusted in order to reflect the needs of an independent public company, and the responsibilities which are carried by individuals.

(d) The stability of shareholders' relationships must be safeguarded after the completion of any initial sale of Croydon shares to the public by undertakings from the Waldner family and Drake to the effect that they will not dispose of their holdings without prior consultation of the Croydon Board, nor seek to increase their holdings without the consent of the Croydon Board.

10. In our present business position, the time is favourable to pursue either of the two alternative courses. If the independent role is selected, implementation is particularly urgent.

(c) **Recommendations**

I recommend that Croydon remain an independent company. This recommendation is based on my belief that the combination of a potential for satisfactory returns and the preservation of the company's identity outweigh for both shareholders and management the larger financial gain and diminution of risk arising from the sale of Croydon to another company.

I recommend that Croydon shares be sold to the public in such a fashion that no single shareholder is able to exercise absolute control and in quantities sufficient to obtain a quotation according to the rules of the London Stock Exchange. At the same time arrangements for an appropriate long-term loan should be made.

I am assuming that to grasp the opportunity which is presented major shareholders and directors are willing to forgo some capital appreciation over a period of years and that consultations which should now take place among shareholders and management will lead to effective agreement on the preconditions set forth in the conclusions.

EXHIBIT 5   Criteria for selecting companies for Croydon

No. of points available per criterion

A. *Criteria based on fit with Croydon's strengths*

   1. *Sales-service aspects* (Strong reputation, including good product, strong technical service, mainly in UK)   4
  - PVC processors (film, sheet and coated fabrics, flooring, wire coating)
  - Producers of flexible urethane foam (mainly for use in auto and furniture)
  - Surfactant formulators (liquid detergents, textile auxiliaries, agricultural chemicals)
  - Tanneries (e.g. for shoes)

   2. *Chemical engineering, process design and manufacturing*   3
  - Medium scale (500 to 20,000 tons) organic processes
  - Quality control
  - Process scale-up from research
  - Personnel base for expansion (in UK & elsewhere)

   3. *Management*   2
  - International orientation (including language capability)
  - Capacity for managing expanded business (in UK & elsewhere)

   4. *Good relations with ACE and Drake*   1

B. *Criteria based on filling Croydon's needs*

   1. *New Products*   5
  - Make use of Croydon's strengths (e.g. existing markets, related markets, forward integration, engineering and manufacturing)
  - Large outlets (relatively few customers)
  - UK market potential attractive
  - Possible exclusivity (based on proprietary position in patents, know-how, mineral rights, etc.)

   2. *Research capability* (continuing)   2
  - strong application research

   3. *Marketing capability*   2
  - Strong commercial development

   4. Sophisticated planning   1

C. *Criteria based on compatability with Croydon*   3
   1. Business philosphy (attitudes)
   2. Reputation
   3. Retention of Croydon's autonomy
   4. Risk-taking factors
   5. Interest in European expansion (UK and/or EEC) and elsewhere (e.g. Australia)
   6. Relations with ACE and Drake

D. *Criteria based on financial factors*   2
   1. Growth and profit potential
   2. Desire to go public
   3. Resources for expansion

                                                  Total points available   25

EXHIBIT 6   **Mr Hartley's 1967 forecast of Croydon results 1969-74**

Fiscal years to end of February

	1969	1970	1971	1972	1973	1974
Sales (£'000)	10,700	11,950	13,400	15,050	17,000	18,900
Stockholder equity at beginning of period (£'000)	2,955	3,105	3,295	3,482	3,641	3,900
Profit pretax (£'000)	489	512	550	648	853	1,058
Profit after tax (£'000)	279	294	300	371	442	579
Proposed dividends (£'000)	202	202	202	243	243	334
Rate of dividend %	20	20	20	24	24	33
After tax return on equity	9.4	9.4	9.1	10.6	12.1	14.8
Pretax profit as a % of sales	4.5	4.3	4.1	4.3	5.0	5.6

All figures are expressed in 1967 pounds

Assumptions for forecasts:
1. Corporation tax at $42\frac{1}{2}$%
2. Wage and salary costs increase at 5% p.a.
3. £3 per ton decline in value added from 1968-9 on
4. No change in equity base
5. Research expenditure to double between 1967 and 1972
6. Exports (as a % of total sales) decline from 24% in 1969 to 21% in 1974.
7. Year ends 28 February

Source: Company records

EXHIBIT 7   Directors in 1968

Name	Age (1968)	Qualifications	Pre-reorganisation title (1967)	Post-reorganisation title (1968)
Dr Waldner	65	Dr Phil, FRIC	Chairman	Chairman*
G. Hartley	44	MBA	Deputy Chairman and Joint Managing Director	Executive Chairman*
J. W. Swift	46	BSc (Tech) MI ChemE	Joint Managing Director	Technical Managing Director*
R. P. Ashton	46	AMCT	Commercial Director	Commercial Managing Director*
R. N. Reddington	48	BSc	Development Director	Development Director*
G. A. Bowman	50	BSc, ARIC	Research Director	Research Director*
Dr. E. J. Lang (Due to retire from employment in 1969)	64	Dr Phil PRIC	Personnel Director	Personnel Director
F. Jones	63	ACIS, FACCA	Non-Executive	Non-Executive

*Members of the newly formed corporate development committee

Source: Casewriter's notes

9 Big Buy Supermarkets (A)*

Big Buy Supermarkets[1] was one of the early pioneers of the supermarket revolution in food retailing in the United Kingdom. Originally founded in the early 1950s by Mr Phillip Green, the company initially consisted of 6 small food stores based in East London. Mr Green, however, had noted the trend toward self-service retailing and supermarkets emerging in the United States and proceeded to experiment with the concept for his own small operation. Mr Green had a simple formula for retailing success. His policy was to offer good quality merchandise at the lowest possible prices and to supply all the housewife's basic grocery needs. The business flourished and by 1959 Mr Green had to open a small warehouse in Deptford to service a growing number of retail stores which were all converted to self-service outlets and, as new stores became larger, to supermarkets. The East London warehouse soon proved inadequate to service the additional stores and in 1963 Mr Green moved the company's head office and central warehouse to Sevenoaks in Kent. Big Buy expanded rapidly during the early 1960s as a supermarket food retailing company and in 1964 made a public share issue of part of the company's equity capital which was oversubscribed a staggering 112 times. After the public flotation new store openings proceeded even faster and by 1966 Big Buy was operating over 40 supermarkets and superettes, while pre-tax profits had reached £0.7 million on sales of £16.9 million.

Then in 1966 Mr Phillip Green died suddenly and he was succeeded as Chairman by his son who has been involved with the company since his father had founded it in 1953. Despite going public in 1964 the Green family was still left with a majority of the ordinary capital and following his father's death Mr David Green had effective control of some 54 per cent of the stock including his own holdings of some 30 per cent, and those of his mother and various family trusts holding an additional 24 per cent. This case describes the subsequent strategy of the company under Mr David Green against the background of trends in the industry up to the middle of 1972.

THE FOOD RETAILING INDUSTRY

Although food sales in Great Britain were the largest single shopping item representing a market of some £7,000 million per annum or 20 per cent of total consumer expenditure this share was steadily declining. It had dropped from 22.3 per cent in 1966 to 20.7 per cent in 1971 while forecasts by the National Economic Development office suggested a continuing decline to 1980.

The number of grocery stores was also declining, from some 261,000 stores in 1961 to 202,000 by 1971. This decline was largely attributable to the rapid growth of self-service and supermarket stores and was more marked among grocers than specialist food retailers. At the same time, self-service and supermarket outlets had grown substantially in number from 7,100 in 1960 to almost 30,000 by 1971. The development of supermarkets, with at least 2,000 sq.ft of selling space, accelerated in the mid 1960s, reaching an estimated 4,800 stores by 1971. At this point the opening of new stores was being increasingly offset by the closure of smaller units. An estimate of outlets by size for 1971 indicated that 78 per cent of self-service stores were under 2,000 sq.ft in size and a further 13 per cent were between 2,000 and 4,000 sq.ft. Only 0.4 per cent were over 10,000 sq.ft, but since 1969 the trend to larger store sizes had increased markedly with the advent of superstores and hypermarkets, and in 1971 27 per cent of new supermarkets were over 10,000 sq.ft.

Food retailing was also beset by relatively low price mark-ups in comparison to other goods. Packaged groceries, for example, typically offered a gross margin of less than 10 per cent to traders, against a 25 per cent mark up on household textiles or 30 per cent on domestic utensils. Competition was intense and margins on many basic goods were often reduced to break-even point.

Food retailers had two advantages however. First, the overall market was the largest single retail area in the United Kingdom. Secondly, food retailers dealt in

---

[1] This case was made possible by the cooperation of a company that wishes to remain anonymous. All names, places and operating results have therefore been changed.

* Copyright © Manchester Business School 1973

necessities. Thus stock turns were high and shopping patterns meant that housewives visited grocery stores between 2 and 4 times per week, although only one of these trips resulted in major purchases. The large multiple supermarket groups were attempting to capitalise on these advantages.

In 1972 the retail industry was going through a period of dramatic change and renewal. It was estimated that 25 per cent of stores standing in 1975 would not have been in existence at the start of 1969. These major changes were occurring where new towns were being built, where existing towns and suburbs were being extended and where deteriorating older areas of towns were being renewed. New developments were therefore of three main types. First, there was the development of neighbourhood precincts replacing small rows of shops or providing new centres for suburban neighbourhoods. Second, new town centres or suburban precincts were being developed frequently as extensions of existing store groupings. Finally there were major new 'greenfield' developments in new towns or on the edges of suburbia. Such developments included 'out-of-town' hypermarkets and superstores, although reluctance to grant planning permission was slowing the growth of these large stores.

During the 1960s there had been a significant gain in the share of the food market held by the leading multiple retailers. These groups had exhibited rapid growth, increasing their share of trade from 25.3 per cent in 1961 to nearly 40 per cent in 1972. This growth had been given a special impetus by the abolition of retail price maintenance in 1964 and the introduction of selective employment tax in 1965 which had allowed the multiples to emphasise a price differential over traditional retailers. The multiples were also able to demand improved discounts from suppliers over small independent stores, could build their own private label sales, and engaged in considerable promotion principally by the use of local press advertising.

The major multiples were all attempting to develop large store sites which would enable them to broaden the range of goods offered and better cater for car-borne shoppers. As a result competition for good sites was intense and the largest groups with the best financial resources tended to be offered the best opportunities. Shoppers were, however, fickle and store loyalty was low for most of the food retailing groups.

In 1972 five major groups dominated the grocery trade: Tesco, Fine Fare, Allied Suppliers, J. Sainsbury and International Stores. In addition Marks & Spencer had developed its food activities to such an extent that it was a leading competitor. These six groups accounted for approximately 30 per cent of grocery expenditure nationally but their relative shares differed considerably from region to region. Sainsbury was the market leader in the South East but held a minor share of other southern regions, was growing rapidly in the Midlands, but was unrepresented in the north. Tesco was very strong throughout the South Midlands and North West. Fine Fare had a good base in Scotland and was important in the North and East Midlands. Allied Suppliers operated nationally but traded under a variety of names. The group was the major multiple in Scotland and was important in the North, East Anglia and the South West. International was represented in most areas under various names but was strongest in East Anglia and the South West. Marks & Spencer held a small but significant share in all areas. The five main grocery multiple groups had a turnover of some £1,216 million from over 4,600 stores of which some 50 per cent were supermarkets.

Tesco (turnover £395 million from 679 stores of which 421 were supermarkets) pioneered self-service stores in the 1950s. The company grew rapidly in the 1960s assisted by the introduction of stamp trading and low prices. The company had also moved away from traditional grocery lines by introducing household goods and clothing which by 1972 were stocked by 75 per cent of stores in addition to 60 exclusive Home 'n' Wear outlets. This product range was still being extended to furniture, footwear and consumer durables and it was estimated that non-foods made up some 40 per cent of turnover. Small stores were also being converted to Fresh Food units, off licences were included in all new stores and own label wines were sold. The company had developed over 500 private label lines. By 1972 Tesco had adopted a policy of only developing superstore sites with more than 20,000 sq.ft of selling space. Some 250,000 sq.ft of new selling area was being introduced in 1972, 600,000 was planned for 1973 and over 1 million more was in the pipeline. Many of the new developments were to be stores of over 50,000 sq.ft located at the edge of towns.

J. Sainsbury was a family firm, expanding rapidly, based on a reputation for high quality fresh perishable foods which had been successfully transferred to a wide range of own label dry goods and a growing non-food range. By 1972 the company had some 196 stores, 138 of which were supermarkets, and turnover had reached nearly £300 million.

Allied Suppliers with a turnover of some £330 million formed part of the Cavenham

Foods retail division which also included the Wrights/Moores chain. Most of the 2,650 stores operated by the group were small grocery outlets trading under a variety of names. The group was being rapidly rationalised to strip away unproductive property assets and it was intended to concentrate developments on supermarkets in the future.

Fine Fare, with a turnover of £205 million from 1,000 stores, was a subsidiary of Associated British Foods. 471 of the groups stores were supermarkets. Increasing emphasis was being placed on the development of large stores and increasing non-food sales which by 1972 were approaching 10 per cent turnover.

International Stores operated some 930 stores mainly of small size. It was acquired in 1972 by British American Tobacco, the world's largest tobacco company, as part of a major diversification programme. Only some 50 of International's stores were over 4,000 sq.ft and it was considered that substantial investment would be needed to make the group into a leading competitor.

In addition to the leading multiple groups there were a number of smaller chains operating, which were composed essentially of two types—subsidiaries of major companies or independent groups strong in a limited geographic area. MacFisheries (owned by Unilever) and Keymarkets (a subsidiary of Fitch Lovell) each operated some 200-400 stores emphasising fresh food. Safeway Stores, a subsidiary of a major US chain, operated some 50 supermarkets using American merchandising methods. The regional, groups included Big Buy, F.J. Wallis, and Pricerite in the South East, Lennons in the North and the Wrensons, David Greig and Redmans in the Midlands and North West.

A recent development in food retailing had been the rapid growth of discount stores whose positioning was based on the establishment of low prices mainly on national brands. These stores varied in size and the number of lines offered: at one extreme Kwik Save Stores carried only some 700 lines compared with some 4,000 in the average supermarket; at the other was Carrefour a hypermarket operator selling a complete range of goods in one location. By 1972 discount operators accounted for some 5 per cent of total grocery turnover although their importance in dry goods was greater. Discounters such as Kwik Save and Asda had established the highest recent growth of retail food operators, and due to better availability of sites this form of trading had developed most rapidly in the Midlands and North.

The largest retail organisation in the UK were the cooperatives, with 15,000 shops owned or controlled by retail Cooperative Societies responsible to their own membership. The Coops had been losing ground despite efforts started in 1968 to create a national identity and a drive for greater marketing coordination.

To combat the competitive thrust of the multiples two developments had occurred to assist the independent retailers. First, many small retailers had joined voluntary groups, the most successful of which were linked to one or more wholesalers with

EXHIBIT 1 Big Buy Supermarkets—profit and loss statements 1966-71
(Year ended 25 December £000)

	1966	1967	1968	1969	1970	1971
Sales	16,905.1	23,019.4	29,039.9	32,119.3	33,368.2	38,072.9
Profits before tax	699.7	906.6	1,014.8	1,077.8	772.4	579.9
Taxation	293.4	384.3	464.9	505.5	328.9	261.8
Profits after tax	406.3	522.3	549.9	572.3	443.5	318.1
Dividends						
Declared (net after tax)	96.9	100.3	103.4	129.3	131.7	134.8
Less waived	55.8	55.1	41.4	57.3	60.0	67.4
	41.1	45.2	62.0	72.0	71.7	67.4
Retained earnings	336.3	445.3	444.3	450.0	323.9	208.1
Depreciation	136.5	195.6	357.2	323.5	378.1	404.5
Directors' emoluments	22.9	21.5	40.8	46.5	43.9	69.3

Source: Company records

EXHIBIT 2 Big Buy Supermarkets Ltd
Balance Sheet as at 25 December 1966-71 (£000)

	1966	1967	1968	1969	1970	1971
Current assets						
Stocks at lower of cost or market	1192.4	1348.6	2587.8	2409.6	2665.0	3275.4
Debtors and prepayments	174.9	258.5	278.0	439.1	354.5	375.2
Cash at bank	71.5	29.7	81.0	140.0	4.1	0.0
	1438.8	1636.8	2946.8	2988.7	3023.6	3650.6
Fixed assets						
Freehold properties	677.6	1252.9	1133.8	1238.4	1535.3	1731.5
Leasehold properties	—	—	570.8	738.1	850.8	866.6
Fixtures, fittings and motors	790.9	1082.3	1521.8	1733.3	1908.1	2029.6
	1478.5	2335.2	3226.4	3709.8	4294.2	4627.7
TOTAL ASSETS	2917.3	3972.0	6173.2	6698.5	7317.8	8278.3
Current liabilities						
Creditors	1202.3	1622.5	2722.3	3041.2	3202.5	4068.6
Bank overdraft (secured)	—	—	436.6	—	193.7	231.2
Current tax	98.0	132.6	330.0	404.5	459.1	345.3
Proposed dividend	18.6	24.3	31.4	48.2	57.8	68.8
Tax payable 1 January	94.7	124.6	388.9	470.3	310.2	198.0
	1413.6	1904.0	3909.2	3964.2	4223.3	4911.9
Share capital in 25p shares	275.0	1100.0	1100.0	1100.0	1100.0	1100.0
Reserves	1228.7	968.0	964.2	1395.6	1737.1	1945.2
Future tax	—	—	199.8	238.7	257.4	321.2
	1503.7	2068.0	2264.0	2734.3	3094.5	3366.4
TOTAL LIABILITIES	2917.3	3972.0	6173.2	6698.5	7317.8	8278.3

Source: Company records

centralised buying control. The largest ten of these groups had approximately 25,000 members and in all some 33 per cent of independent grocers were participants in voluntary groups. The top four Mace, Spar, Vivo and VG had a combined turnover of over £400 million, provided merchandising know-how, private label products, promotion and advertising, and assisted with finance for conversion and modernisation. Second, cash and carry wholesaling had developed rapidly to provide lower prices for independent grocers.

BIG BUY IN 1966

When Mr Phillip Green died in 1966, Big Buy operated some 40 stores principally in London and the home counties. During the early 1960s the number and size of stores had expanded resulting in a rapid growth of sales and profits. Details of recent financial performance are shown in Exhibits 1 and 2.

Mr Green had operated the business in a highly personalised style. He personally had taken all the major decisions and had not been over-concerned with sophisticated accounting and control systems. In 1963, in response to the growing number of branches, a computer system had been introduced under Mr Simon Henderson to help control purchasing, stock levels and goods movements between the central warehouse and the stores. Wage payments were later also dealt with on the computer. Nevertheless, little information was available to guide top management decision making. No budgetary systems were in force and the only full-scale corporate accounting undertaken was the result of annual visits from the company's auditors, Peter J. Cobb and Company, a small accounting firm who also acted as personal accountants for the Green family. Mr Green, however, was able to maintain adequate control by knowledge of store sales, goods bought in and estimates of gross margins. This was supplemented by frequent visits to the branches by Mr Green from his office at the company's headquarters and central warehouse at Sevenoaks. As a result, profits had grown by over 500 per cent between 1960 and 1966 and Big Buy's performance was considered to be amongst the best of retail food companies.

The company organisation was also kept along simple functional lines. Apart from Mr Green, the Big Buy Board consisted of his wife, Mrs Sara Green, his son David and the family solicitor and friend, Mr Abraham Goldstein. Mr Green called board meetings at irregular intervals, with the meetings being used to approve formally the annual results or to sanction specific decisions Mr Green wished to undertake. Apart from Mr David Green, the remaining board members were not involved in Big Buy's operations.

A small number of senior executives reported to Mr Green (see Exhibit 3). Apart from Mr Henderson who had joined the company when the computer system was introduced, these executives had joined Phillip Green shortly after he had entered the food retailing business and their responsibilities had grown with the expansion of the company. Mr David Green, who started in the company first as a store manager, then as a supervisor and store controller, was responsible for sites and property developments, but also maintained a strong interest in retail operations.

EXHIBIT 3   **Big Buy Supermarkets Ltd—Organisation structure 1966**

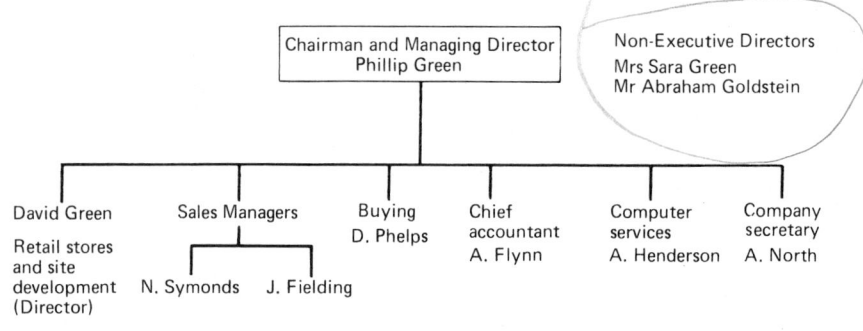

```
                    Chairman and Managing Director          Non-Executive Directors
                            Phillip Green                   Mrs Sara Green
                                                            Mr Abraham Goldstein
        ┌───────────────┬───────────────┬───────────┬───────────────┬───────────────┐
    David Green      Sales Managers   Buying      Chief          Computer        Company
                                      D. Phelps   accountant     services        secretary
    Retail stores                                 A. Flynn       A. Henderson    A. North
    and site         ┌─────────┬─────────┐
    development    N. Symonds  J. Fielding
    (Director)
```

Source: Company records

DEVELOPMENTS TO 1970

Following the death of his father, Mr David Green assumed the chairmanship of Big Buy late in 1966. He decided that the policy of rapid expansion should continue at all speed mainly by means of a substantial new store opening programme and within the next four years the number of Big Buy stores more than doubled to over 100. In addition, Big Buy extended a number of its existing stores wherever this was possible. As a result of new openings, Big Buy began to expand its geographic coverage with new stores being opened in South Wales and the West Country. The company also moved northwards and into the eastern counties from its base in the south of England. To help service the new stores two new warehouse operations were opened, a major depot in Bristol to service South Wales, the West and the Midlands and at Micheldever in Hampshire to service the western home counties.

The company also began to expand its range of private label merchandise wherever possible and made a number of applications for off-licences for its stores to enable it to include wines and spirits in the product range. Big Buy began to develop non-food sales in its larger outlets as well as improving its range of fresh foods and meats for which specialist packaging operations were set up at the Bristol and Sevenoaks warehouse. In addition, the company extended its stamp trading operations offering alternatively Green Shield or Sperry and Hutchison pink stamps in its stores.

EXHIBIT 4   Big Buy Supermarkets Ltd—store size and location 1972

Location	less than 2000	2-4000	4-8000	8-25,000	over 25,000	Total
Area 1						
London	3	8	6	1	—	18
Kent	3	6	5	2	—	16
Sussex	2	5	5	1	1	14
Surrey	—	3	4	—	—	7
Essex	—	1	2	1	—	4
Area 2						
Hampshire	2	4	3	1	—	10
Berkshire	1	3	1	—	—	5
Wiltshire	1	2	2	—	—	5
Dorset	2	2	3	1	—	8
Somerset	—	3	2	—	—	5
Devon	—	2	—	—	1	3
Cornwall	—	2	1	—	—	3
Area 3						
South Wales	2	2	2	—	—	6
Gloucestershire	1	2	1	1	—	5
Oxfordshire	—	1	1	—	—	2
Buckinghamshire	1	2	1	—	—	4
Northamptonshire	—	1	2	1	—	4
Cambridgeshire	—	1	1	—	—	2
Norfolk	—	1	2	—	—	3
Suffolk	—	1	1	—	—	4
Leicestershire	—	1	3	—	—	4
Lincolnshire	—	3	1	—	—	4
Nottinghamshire	1	2	2	1	—	6
Derbyshire	—	1	2	—	—	3
TOTAL	19	59	53	10	2	143

Sales area in sq. ft

Source: Company records

The new stores opened by Big Buy tended to be of increasing size in line with a national trend toward larger food stores. However, being one of the smaller supermarket chains, Big Buy tended not to be offered the prime sites in new shopping developments and in consequence many of the new stores were located either in smaller towns, and outside city centre or other major shopping centres. It was also Mr Green's conscious policy to seek outlets in locations where there would be no direct competition with the largest supermarket operators especially Tesco and to a lesser extent Sainsbury's who Mr Green considered were the most aggressive competitors Big Buy faced. In addition, relatively few stores had their own parking facilities. The location and size breakdown of the principal Big Buy stores in 1972 is shown in Exhibit 4.

At the same time, Big Buy was faced with increased pressure on trading margins caused by increased operating costs including higher bills for wages, higher rents and rates and the introduction of selective employment tax. More important, the company was faced with greatly increased competition from other supermarket operations, which were also expanding rapidly. Some were substantially larger than Big Buy and thus able to obtain better supply terms or improved promotional deals, which provided increased margins that could be passed on to their customers in lower prices. Moreover, despite Big Buy's store location policy, the increased geographic coverage by other supermarket operators meant that Big Buy began to face new competition in many areas where its early stores had been established. The major groups in expanding into these areas with new stores, which were generally larger than the earlier Big Buy stores, represented a considerable threat and led to significant pressure on Big Buy's trade margins in an attempt to maintain the turnover of its smaller outlets. Commenting on the increased competition, Mr Green stated 'At a time when we had to absorb sharply increased operating costs we were also faced with intensive competition in many areas in areas in which we operated, mainly from new supermarkets with a far greater sales area than our own. Aggressive competition, is of course a fact of life for us, but in 1970 for example we were particularly hard hit by the opening by major competitors of new stores in no less than 30 areas in which we operate, nearly one in every three of our stores was faced with competition from new and larger stores.'

The result of this increased competition was some reduction in sales turnover per square foot in 1970 although overall turnover continued to advance as a result of new store openings. More important, trade margins declined markedly and profits reached a peak of £1.1 million in 1969 before falling back to £0.77 million in 1970.

Big Buy's managers were poorly placed to make a careful response to the pressure on margins largely due to continued deficiencies in the company's control system which had little changed since the death of Mr Green's father. The personalised system developed by Phillip Green became increasingly inadequate, however, as the number of stores increased and strong localised competition emerged at branch level. Mr David Green recognised many of the inadequacies in organisation and control left by his father and took a number of steps to correct these. First, shortly after his father's death, which in turn had made Mrs Sara Green seriously ill, Mr Green invited his uncle, Mr Michael Jacobsen, who had been a close friend and confidant of his father, to join Big Buy as managing director. Next, early in 1968, he took steps to strengthen the main board by appointing Mr Phelps, Mr Symonds, Mr North and Mr Fielding as directors. Then, early in 1969 he took advantage of an offer from one of Big Buy's main suppliers and called in Mr Gerald Battersby the managing director of the British subsidiary of international consultants, Muller Day Associates Inc., to undertake a brief examination of the company's organisation and control systems.

THE MULLER DAY REPORT

Mr Battersby, who had previously held a senior executive position with a leading food retailer before turning to consultancy, had also acquired a reputation as a successful company doctor reviving the flagging fortunes of several companies in various industries.

In February 1969 Mr Battersby, after a brief examination of Big Buy, reported to Mr Jacobsen and made recommendations for organisational and control system changes.

He considered that changes in the administrative systems were required as a matter of urgency in view of the prospective growth in shops and turnover. A proper budgetary system was also required as soon as possible including capital expenditure and cash flow, purchases and sales, stocks, expenditure, profit and loss account and balance sheet.

Mr Battersby considered that the company's computer system was adequately staffed and Mr Henderson appeared confident that the systems he had designed were adequate. Nevertheless, he felt that independent advice upon computer performance might be useful and if the company's auditors were not up to this task Muller Day would be a suitable alternative. Mr Battersby also believed that, despite Mr Henderson's reluctance, some new systems should be contemplated, namely four-weekly profit and loss accounts for each shop, the bought ledgers and purchase invoices, the issue of cheques, statistics to buying and selling departments, and expense accounts.

Big Buy's accountancy systems were considered to be under pressure largely due to physical space restrictions. Mr Flynn was considered competent but again Mr Battersby thought that independent advice might be useful on the efficiency of the accountacy department and its paperwork systems and, failing the use of the auditors, Muller Day were recommended as suitable. Mr Battersby also believed that the production of monthly or four-weekly profit and loss accounts within two weeks of the end of a period for the company and for individual departments and shops was an urgent necessity, if senior management was to maintain their existing sensitive control over operations.

Mr Phelps was seen as a competent buyer, who had poor support from his team. Further, the buying department was thought to have too little knowledge of the detailed pattern or real profitability of purchases of 'directs'. Comparisons of 'direct' suppliers' invoiced prices, with buying department's negotiated prices, and with consequent adjustments of selling prices, was by test sample only. As a result, until goods inward or delivery notes could be endorsed with the buying department's cost and selling prices, profit and loss accounts for the shops, individual departments and the company itself could not be produced.

Mr Battersby reported that at present the computer gave a detailed analysis of warehouse stocks and of their movement, from which the 'average number of weeks' stock holding could be seen. Stocks requiring reorder were starred. On the other hand he felt less attention seemed to be given to overordered, slow-moving or 'special' stocks and of the consequent finance locked up in these stocks. The stock position had been excellent, but in view of the present cash position and of high interest rates, the size of the stock holdings was of increasing importance.

It was not clear to Mr Battersby exactly how the buying department worked out their gross margin policy on individual commodities so as to reach a desired overall gross margin for individual shops or indeed for the company as a whole.

Mr Battersby visited a number of Big Buy stores and was impressed with the quality of their personnel, the good control of staff costs, low wastage figures and small stockholdings. He considered lines of communication and management structure to be well planned and well under Mr Fielding's control. Mr Battersby also received the impression, however, that profit and loss information and budgetary controls were not deemed to have a high priority.

He discovered that most managers were not given information on gross margins as a matter of policy, and their results and rewards were judged solely on total sales. He believed that although this observation had little present importance it could be a weakness as the company grew to be a major national group.

The warehouse operation seemed extremely well managed and efficient compared with other supermarket groups. Space occupancy at Sevenoaks was 95 per cent and 75 per cent at Bristol. Mr Battersby was somewhat concerned however about large stocks of 'special' purchases which could be in the warehouse for several months, so tying up capital, despite the fact that they represented additional discounts from manufacturers when purchased. In addition, large consignments of 'own label' products were also taken from manufacturers.

Mr Battersby personally believed in education for top management and recommended that both top and middle managers should spend on average between seven and ten days per annum attending conferences, lectures, seminars, exhibitions and the like to keep themselves abreast of affairs.

Finally, Mr Battersby considered the size of Big Buy and its plans for expansion meant that the managing director would find it necessary increasingly to divorce himself from detailed operations. He therefore recommended the appointment of a new director of administration to coordinate and control all the administrative systems throughout the company. This individual should be about forty with a professional qualification and a successful background as a financial controller. Mr Battersby believed that this appointment should be made with urgency before the present strains on the administrative system led to a breakdown in financial controls.

MANAGEMENT RESPONSE

Although Mr Battersby's report made a number of recommendations these were not all acted upon immediately since Big Buy were in the process of moving to a new administrative building being completed at Sevenoaks. During 1969 a number of new computer systems were introduced but little progress was made on the introduction of new accountancy procedures, budgetary controls or long-term plans. In April 1970, following further discussions with Mr Battersby, it was decided that a director of administration should be appointed and subsequently Big Buy's auditors, Peter J. Cobb, who had merged with the large city accountants, Fitch, Henry, Sullivan and Company, were requested to undertake a comprehensive review of the company's basic systems and control procedures relevant to the accounting function.

Muller Day Associates, for a fee of 20 per cent of initial remuneration, were requested to draw up a specification for the new board post and to submit a short-list of suitable candidates. This was done and a specification submitted in May 1970 and, as the consultants did not recommend advertising the position, an initial candidate was put forward. This individual eventually proved unavailable and Muller Day suggested a second candidate, Mr Cyril Mellor, for consideration. Mr Mellor had had two years' experience in computer systems with the same major food retailer that Mr Battersby had worked for, but had left following a disagreement with a member of the main board to join a major electrical products manufacturer.

Mr Mellor was accepted by Mr Green and Mr Jacobsen and joined the company in October 1970. As administration director Mr Mellor was initially responsible for the introduction and maintenance of accounts and statistics, for the introduction, operation and control of budgets, and for finance and financial policy as laid down by the chairman and managing director. He was also to assist in the formulation of short- and long-term policy planning and was responsible for all accountancy, computer and administrative personnel, including Mr North, Mr Flynn and Mr Henderson.

Following his appointment Mr Mellor moved swiftly to fulfill his new function. He initiated a review of the company's computer-based systems by International Computers, introduced a new system of warehouse stock control, requested Muller Day to help recruit additional accountancy help, and in December, before the report on control procedures by Fitch, Henry, Sullivan, commissioned Muller Day to provide consultancy services to produce an expense control system capable of later computerisation. This contract, worth £2,500 plus expenses, was later increased to £4,500 as the Muller Day assignment was widened to include help in the preparation of a budget for 1971.

Following the completion of this project, Muller Day reported to Mr Green that in the course of its investigation a number of other defects had emerged which they wished to bring to his attention. Muller Day considered first that there was no agreed organisation structure or reporting structure in Big Buy and they had therefore defined the responsibilities of each manger within the existing day-to-day working arrangements. It was still felt that a detailed organisation structure should be spelt out; that the relationships between buying and marketing should be clearly established; that buying and selling operations for meat and fresh produce under the nominal control of the sales director was too flexible; and that the sales operation was weak, with some question as to the existing personnel being sufficiently forward-looking to manage a modern budgetary system. Second, it was considered intolerable that the company only knew its gross profit once a year as the existing accounting system could only give an indication of trends in gross profits. Third, their investigation of sales per square foot on the most recent sales figures revealed that the least successful stores were those opened in most recent years and it was recommended that formalised systems of site appraisal be introduced.

Then, early in 1971, following a series of disagreements between Mr Green and his uncle, Mr Jacobsen left the company. Mr Green turned to Mr Mellor as his new deputy, appointing him in effect the company's chief executive. This position was confirmed by the board in August 1971 on the appointment to the board of Mr Stephen Cleary. He had been recruited by Muller Day from Mr Mellor's former company to fill the slot left vacant by Mr Mellor's promotion.

CHANGES IN STRATEGY AND STRUCTURE

With the approval of Mr Green, Mr Mellor moved quickly: first, to place the existing business on a new footing by improving Big Buy's eroding competitive position; and second, to prepare the company for a new leap forward so as to become one of the major food retailers by 1980. Mr Mellor proceeded to accomplish the first of these objectives by reorganising the company and introducing new professional management; introducing new control procedures; broadening the company's retailing formula and expanding non-food sales in particular. To implement the second, in 1972 he brought in consultants to assist in the development of a corporate long-term plan which would provide the blueprint for Big Buy's proposed expansion.

The 1971 Reorganisation

Following the comments from Muller Day, Mr Mellor wrote to all branch managers outlining a revised structure for Big Buy with the objectives of creating lines of communication where these did not exist, giving each manager the authority that went with

EXHIBIT 5   Big Buy Supermarkets Ltd—Organisation, October 1971

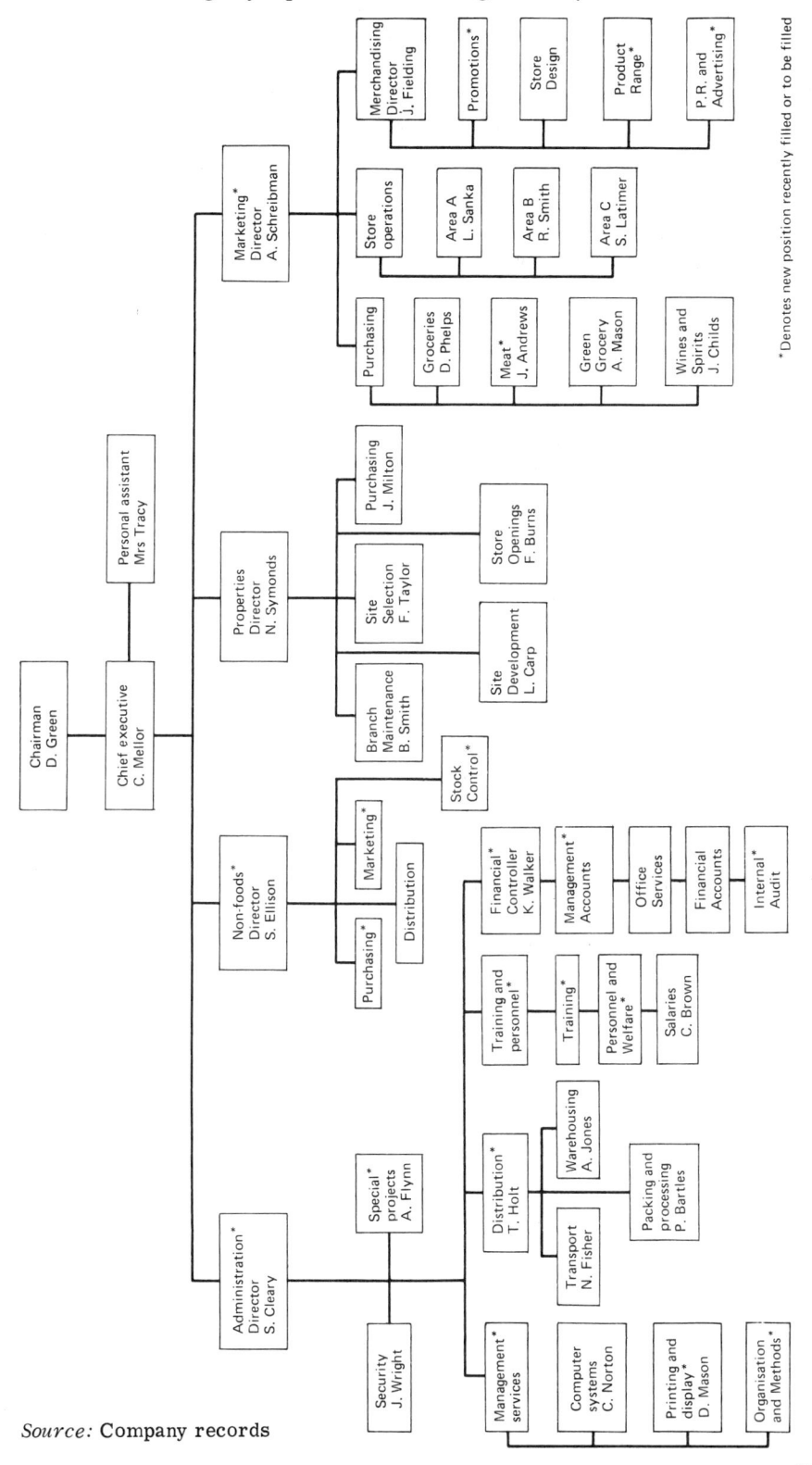

Organisation chart:

- **Chairman**: D. Green
- **Chief executive**: C. Mellor
  - Personal assistant: Mrs Tracy
  - **Marketing* Director**: A. Schreibman
    - Merchandising Director: J. Fielding
      - Promotions*
      - Store Design
      - Product Range*
      - P.R. and Advertising*
    - Store operations
      - Area A: L. Sanka
      - Area B: R. Smith
      - Area C: S. Latimer
    - Purchasing
      - Groceries: D. Phelps
      - Meat*: J. Andrews
      - Green Grocery: A. Mason
      - Wines and Spirits: J. Childs
  - **Properties Director**: N. Symonds
    - Branch Maintenance: B. Smith
    - Site Selection: F. Taylor
      - Site Development: L. Carp
      - Store Openings: F. Burns
    - Purchasing: J. Milton
  - Stock Control*
  - **Non-foods* Director**: S. Ellison
    - Purchasing*
    - Marketing*
    - Distribution
  - **Administration* Director**: S. Cleary
    - Special projects*: A. Flynn
    - Financial Controller*: K. Walker
      - Management Accounts*
      - Office Services
      - Financial Accounts
      - Internal Audit*
    - Training and personnel*
      - Training*
      - Personnel and Welfare*
      - Salaries: C. Brown
    - Distribution*: T. Holt
      - Warehousing: A. Jones
      - Transport: N. Fisher
      - Packing and processing: P. Bartles
    - Security: J. Wright
    - Management* services
      - Computer systems: C. Norton
      - Printing and display*: D. Mason
      - Organisation and Methods*

*Denotes new position recently filled or to be filled

Source: Company records

113

responsibility, which was to be carefully determined jointly between the individual and top management and, having established agreed performance targets, adequately rewarding managers who met their targets. In this way, Mr Mellor intended forging a closely knit organisation which would act as a team with the common aim of improving the profitability of the company.

The Big Buy organisation was subdivided into a series of major functions as shown in Exhibit 5. The first of these functions covered finance and administration and was headed by the newly appointed Mr Stephen Cleary. Reporting to Mr Cleary were a series of departments covering management services headed by Mr Jack Strong, responsible for computer operations, organisation and methods and printing and display; financial control headed by a financial controller Mr Ken Walker, a new cost accountant from manufacturing industry recruited by Muller Day; training and personnel for which no overall manager was initially appointed; and distribution, responsible for warehousing and transportation. No head of distribution was appointed initially pending a comprehensive review of all distribution systems and procedures by International Management Consultants Ltd. Subsequently, distribution was hived off as a separate function under Mr Tony Holt, a new appointment and former distribution manager with another leading food retailer. Mr Henderson, formerly responsible for computer systems, resigned shortly before the reorganisation and Mr Flynn was appointed to a new post responsible for development projects. Mr Mellor considered that in this position Mr Flynn's long experience in Big Buy could be utilised on financial aspects of new ventures and later on corporate planning, when an executive had been appointed to take charge of this activity.

All aspects of purchasing and retail operations were centralised under a new marketing department led by Mr Al Schreibman, a newly appointed marketing director. Mr Schreibman was a Canadian recruited from the British subsidiary of a North American food retailing company. Reporting to Mr Schreibman were purchasing, which was in turn subdivided into grocery purchasing, headed by Mr Phelps, a main board director, and separate buying functions responsible for meat, fresh produce and beverages; merchandising, headed by Mr Fielding who was responsible for advertising and promotion, store design, and product range; and retail stores, which were divided into three geographic areas, each the responsibility of an area manager.

The third major area was the property development function headed by Mr Symonds whose department was responsible for site selection, store development and equipment, new openings and store maintenance.

The final area was non-foods which was expanded in responsibility since Mr Green and Mr Mellor intended to develop this area substantially as part of Big Buy's plan for future expansion. Mr Stan Ellison was recruited to head non-foods from his position as sales director of a leading non-food variety retailer and appointed to the board of Big Buy. Mr Ellison then built up a team to incorporate buying, marketing, distribution and stock control staff, in line with the planned expansion of the non-food operations.

With the final appointment of Mr Mellor as chief executive and the introduction of a number of new professional managers to lead the functional areas, Mr Green's position as chairman meant that he needed to spend less time on Big Buy's day-to-day operations. As a result, it was agreed that he would in future concentrate his efforts on the all-important search for new store sites which would be vitally needed if Big Buy were successfully to accomplish its ambitious expansion objectives.

New Control Procedures

During the remainder of 1971 and the first half of 1972, new controls and systems were gradually introduced by members of the new management team aided by the supplementary assistance provided as a result of previous or new consultancy contracts. In particular, new computer systems were introduced to replace those developed originally by Mr Henderson, new accounting controls were developed by Mr Walker, a system of management by objectives was introduced, a new incentive plan for store managers was adopted, annual budgeting became fully established, and in May 1972 the company began to draw up its first long-term strategic plan.

Nevertheless, in 1971 although turnover continued to grow to £38 million, pressure on margins caused profits to fall yet again to £580,000, and Mr Green and the executors of his father's estate waived their entitlement to dividends on 5 million of their shares. Big Buy were therefore continuously searching for new ways of reducing costs and improving efficiency, and in April 1972 Mr Mellor and Mr Cleary reported to the board on an encounter they had had at a seminar on 'Store Profitability'. There they had met an executive of Starshine Inc., an American retail food company. Mr Mellor and Mr

Cleary had been extremely impressed with the results claimed for the Starshine control system that they had visited Starshine in the United States to see the system in use. As a result the board agreed that Starshine executives should come to the UK to install their methods experimentally in two Big Buy stores at a cost of $15,000 on condition that they achieved their specified targets. If the system was as successful as it was claimed, resulting in substantial improvements in efficiency, reduced labour requirements and more rapid stock turnover, consideration was then to be given to converting all Big Buy stores.

Changes in Retail Policy

In an effort to halt declining profit margins in the retail branches Big Buy introduced a number of policy changes in its trading formula. In August 1971 Big Buy operated 111 stores with a total sales area of 480,000 square feet, 107 of which offered trading stamps and of these 61 gave Green Shield with the rest offering S and H pink stamps. Although the average size of the stores was around 4,500 square feet, 10 were over 7,500 square feet and 53 were considered to be supermarkets. The remainder were self-service superettes, 19 of which had a sales area of less than 2,000 square feet. By mid-1972 the number of stores had grown to 143 and the company's total sales area to 620,000 square feet. These stores were serviced either from the company's three warehouses or direct from Big Buy's suppliers. Approximately half of deliveries were made through the company's own warehouses.

In its average supermarket Big Buy reckoned to have a product range of some 4,000 drygoods grocery lines which made up some 80 per cent of group turnover. Private label merchandise sold under the Big Buy brand name represented some 15 per cent of turnover and covered a product range, including beverages, biscuits, bakery products, canned fruit and vegetables, soups, cereals, confectionery, desserts, fats, frozen foods, jams and preserves, dairy products, pet foods, prepared meats, cooking aids, household and paper products, and soaps and toiletries. In all, some 350 items in various pack sizes. Meat, fresh provisions and greengrocery represented a further 14 per cent of total turnover with the larger supermarkets offering a wider range of merchandise. In addition, the larger stores provided a choice between prepacked or counter-assisted service in meat and counter-assisted service in greengrocery.

Non-foods represented only 5 per cent of total turnover and because of the limited availability of selling space in the majority of stores the product range offered was usually limited to household products, such as kitchen accessories. Larger stores where more space was available for home and wear products carried an extended range of household goods and cheap men's, women's and children's clothing and footwear.

In order to improve Big Buy's competitive appeal and to reduce the rate of obsolescence of its small first generation superettes, a number of changes were made to this pattern.

Conversion to discount operations

In September 1970 Mr Green introduced discount trading in one store as an experiment aimed at combating intense local competition. A small superette store in Wandsworth was converted from normal trading stamp operations to discounting. Under this method of trading the number of lines sold was substantially reduced from around 3,000 in the average superette to about 1,000, the merchandising displays were largely converted from the traditional supermarket gondolas to more emphasis on cheap, cut-case display, trading stamps were terminated and gross margins were reduced from the average of between 19 per cent and 20 per cent obtained in normal trading stamp supermarkets to an average of between $12\frac{1}{2}$-14 per cent. Furthermore, prices were cut across all lines of merchandise to at least some extent whereas in conventional supermarkets only certain lines were reduced, and although some lines were treated as loss leaders or special offers, most were sold at recommended prices or even in some cases 'bunced' to above recommended price. For discounting to be successful a turnover increase of between 30-40 per cent was necessary to break even in comparison with conventional operations.

The Wandsworth experiment proved highly successful and during 1971 and the first half of 1972 a further 26 of Big Buy's stores were converted from superette operation to discounting and 7 new discount stores were opened all operating on a 'baby shark' limited product range. Not all of these new stores were equally successful, however, and although Mr Green and Mr Mellor anticipated further increases in the number of discount stores a number of outlets were still considered to be too small to remain viable.

Changes were also made in the stores which remained unconverted. The budget for advertising and promotion was stepped up to over £80,000 in 1972. This was primarily spent on special promotions and local newspaper advertising. Increased attention was paid to store layout, changes were made to the product range offered placing increased emphasis on sales of fresh food, garden produce and meat, and in some stores changes were made in trading stamp policy, switching from pink stamps to green wherever this was found to be possible under contracts and franchise arrangements with the trading stamp suppliers.

The Opening of Superstores

Most important, however, was the opening during 1972 of Big Buy's first two out-of-town stores at Eastbourne in Sussex, and Plymouth in Devon. These new stores had a sales area of at least 25,000 square feet, together with ample parking places for between 150 and 250 cars. The Eastbourne store was typical of the new superstores. It formed the major part of a new shopping centre established some 3 miles from the town centre as part of a large new housing development on reclaimed shingle beach, and first became available as a site early in 1970. Big Buy submitted plans to the local council which gave planning approval in October 1970. Construction began immediately and was completed on schedule in March 1972, when shop-fitting began, leading to the new store opening in May. Details of the store are shown in Exhibit 6.

These new stores were expected to provide Big Buy with valuable experience in the management of large, out-of-town centres which Mr Mellor believed would provide a major source of the company's future growth. In particular, these stores provided the opportunity for a substantial increase in the sales area available for non-foods which were the largest single department in the new superstores with nearly 50 per cent of

EXHIBIT 6   Eastbourne Superstore details

Gross area	36,480 sq. ft	Departments:	
Sales area	27,640 sq. ft	Bacon	— open service
Warehouse area	4,170 sq. ft	Provisions	— "
Preparation area	1,930 sq. ft	Delicatessen	— "
Car parking	176 places	Fruit & vegetables	— pre-packed
Check-outs	15	Meat	— open/pre-packed
		Fish	— open service
		Frozen food	
		Bakery	— open service
		Cigarettes & tobacco	— "
		Wines & spirits	— "
		Home and wear	
		Car accessories & tyre services	— (Associated Tyre Services)

Size of departments: %

1. Refrigerated   23
   - Cooked meat (incl. Deli & Bacon)   8 m single side
   - Provisions (incl. Dairy)   14 m island
   - Produce   5 m 2 deck
   - Meat (fresh)   8 m single side
   - Meat (frozen incl. Home Freezer Pack)   16 m
   - Poultry   8 m
   - Ice cream   2 × 6' × 3'6"
   - Patisserie   1 × 14 m island; 1 × 9 m s/s
   - Frozen food   9 m single side

2. Produce   36' gondola   12' wall fitting   4

3. Home & wear   508' "   198' "   48

4. Grocery   340' "   36' pallet   25

Source: Company records

the available selling space. As a result, the range of non-food goods was broadened to include a wide range of soft goods, clothing and footwear. Many of these goods represented new additions to the non-foods catalogue and to cope with this increase in activity, Mr Ellison rapidly built up a team of 30 non-food staff responsible for buying, marketing and merchandising, promotion and display, and stock control. As many of the new lines were imported and made for Big Buy under contract, the buying function tended to differ somewhat to grocery buying, requiring a number of visits to suppliers, frequently including trips overseas to Western Europe, Hong Kong and the Far East in order to secure the best deals.

THE FOODFAIR ACQUISITION

Mr Ellison considered that non-food retailing was sufficiently different in that not only did it require a specialist staff but it would also be best if it were able to undertake its own warehousing and distribution function. This problem was solved in January 1972, when Big Buy acquired Foodfair Ltd, a company formed by Mr Michael Levene and operating a chain of 23 supermarkets and superettes mainly in South and West London, Surrey and Middlesex. These stores were serviced from a small 25,000 square foot warehouse with office accommodation in Putney near the South Circular road which was made available to Mr Ellison as a headquarters and storage area for the non-food operation.

Foodfair, with an annual turnover of some £5.5 million, had moved into a loss position during 1971 and in the half year to December 1971 losses had increased to nearly £80,000. At this point, Mr Green had approached Mr Levene who was a personal friend and suggested that Big Buy purchase his company. This was agreed and terms of £300,000 cash were offered and accepted, Mr Levene joining Big Buy to help Mr Green in the search for new store sites.

Big Buy moved quickly to rationalise the new acquisition in an endeavour to turn Foodfair around as well as utilising the additional purchasing power the increased turnover provided. Within 6 months, 5 of Foodfair's stores had been shut down realising nearly £45,000 and the remaining operations restored to profitability. In addition, Foodfair's purchasing, administration and distribution functions had been integrated into Big Buy resulting in the saving of over 50 staff. It was estimated that Foodfair's remaining stores had a profit potential of over £100,000 p.a. pretax which Big Buy hoped to achieve by 1974, and these earnings would be protected by the accumulated tax losses of some £300,000 incurred earlier by Foodfair.

HYPERMARKET DEVELOPMENTS

Mr Mellor believed that for the future large out-of-town stores with a minimum sales area of 40,000 square feet and ample parking facilities would become an increasingly important aspect of Big Buy's retail strategy. Mr Green and Mr Mellor had therefore undertaken a special study of hypermarket developments in France, where this type of store had shown spectacular growth in the late 1960s and early 1970s, and stores of up to 250,000 square feet had been developed.

Mr Mellor reported to the board in November 1971 that despite this spectacular growth there had, however, been 30 hypermarket failures in France. He therefore considered that despite the opening of Big Buy's own superstores which were in effect small hypermarkets, Big Buy had neither the personnel nor the expertise to risk the development of hypermarkets on its own. Mr Mellor was in favour of being able to call on the expertise of successful French hypermarket operators for at least the company's first hypermarket. Although some members of the board disputed the necessity to obtain this help, it was eventually agreed that Mr Mellor should explore the possibilities of working with a successful French operator.

As a result of further investigations, Mr Mellor was able to present to the board in April 1972 a draft agreement for consideration between Société Générale des Grands Magasins Provinciales S.A. (SGGMP) and Big Buy. SGGMP was a company registered in France formed by a group of French retail operators for the purpose of developing hypermarkets in the southern and central part of France and especially around such cities as Lyons, Toulouse and Marseilles. The company operated a total of seven hypermarkets with net selling areas ranging between 44,000 and 110,000 square feet under the trade name Hypermarché de Lyons.

Under the suggested agreement with SGGMP it was proposed that a new company would be created, 51 per cent owned by Big Buy, 49 per cent by SGGMP, which would own and operate hypermarkets in the United Kingdom. SGGMP were to provide the initial expertise for the new company in exchange for 33 per cent of the shares in the new company worth £75,000 which would be paid for by Big Buy. Apart from this, however, all further capital in the new company would be provided jointly in proportion to their shareholdings. SGGMP were also to train Big Buy's own personnel in France in hypermarket operations. Although Big Buy had no specific sites available for hypermarket operations, it was hoped that an initial site would be found to permit opening of the joint venture's first store by the end of 1973 or early in 1974.

PLANS FOR THE FUTURE

Mr Mellor believed that Big Buy should become one of Britain's leading retailers by 1980. He hoped that by 1976 the number of Big Buy stores would be reduced from 143 to about 110 but that the average store size would be increased from around 4,500 square feet to nearer 17,550 square feet of selling space due to a strategy of concentrating on new superstores while phasing out superettes.

Having introduced a budgetary system in 1971, Mr Mellor moved on in 1972 to the preparation of Big Buy's first 5-year plan which would serve as the basis for identifying what needed to be done to fulfil the company's objectives for 1976. To help in the preparation of the company's plan, Mr Mellor turned to Total Strategic Systems Inc., an American consultancy company whose president, Mr Harvey Wainwright, had developed a unique system of strategic planning. This system included both top down and bottom up features in order to ensure the active participation in the planning process of all the company's senior and middle management.

As a result of the planning exercise, Mr Mellor predicted that Big Buy would reach sales of £180 million in 1976 or, allowing for an annual rate of inflation of 7 per cent, £236 million. Retail store selling space was expected to expand to nearly 2 million square feet with a major expansion coming in non-foods which were expected to account for 880,000 square feet in 1976 as compared with only 80,000 in 1972 and as a result non-food sales were expected to reach £41 million by 1976 (in constant £). Although pressure on trade margins was recognised and margins were expected to continue to decline, Mr Mellor nevertheless predicted pretax profits would expand to £5 million by 1976. Mr Mellor, commenting on Big Buy's expansion plans, added

> Food and non-food retailing to the mass consumer market is steadily growing and providing an increasing market for those companies interested in retailing. This pattern of expansion has been demonstrated in America and hypermarkets have opened on the Continent. British consumers are as price conscious as consumers elsewhere, and this presents a massive opportunity to service their requirements for both foods and non-foods.
>
> Tesco, for example, during 1971 and up to February this year, expanded their retail space by 500,000 square feet. Their business increased by about 16 per cent to almost £300 million. Forty new stores were opened in 1971 alone with an average floor space of about 12,000 square feet or more and they are planning 5 to 10 years ahead.
>
> Sainsbury too pushed up their sales in 1971 by 18 per cent. During the past 3 years they opened 26 stores with a total of 353,000 square feet and in the next 3 years they plan to open 50 new stores adding a total of 800,000 square feet more than they are managing now.
>
> Our strategy, therefore, can be seen in these terms. First, administratively we must get the company into a streamlined, efficient and well-run operation. Second, we have to design and maintain an organisation and a management style which will maximise individual participation, provide good communications, gain above average motivation and keep our employee skills high. Third, we have to improve our corporate marketing image so that our sales per square foot go up to £2 per week on foods. Fourth, we want to establish distribution as a viable business so that we can distribute ourselves up to 96 per cent of the products sold through our retail space both internally and by joint ventures and acquisitions so that by 1976 we are operating over 1.5 million square feet of retail space.
>
> This is an ambitious plan but with the new management team we have built I am confident it can be readily achieved.

Critical to the success of Mr Mellor's plan was the search for new large store sites. Mr Green, who was especially involved in this activity, sounded a note of caution

EXHIBIT 7   Big Buy Supermarkets Ltd
Trading and profit and loss account to 13 May 1972
(£000)

	Actual	%	Actual	%	Budget	%	Variance	%
Sales			15805.6	100	15498.3	100	(392.7)	
Cost of sales			12360.0		12668.7		308.7	
BRANCH GROSS PROFIT			2845.6	18.7	2829.6	18.2	16.0	0.5
Add depot operating margins								
Meat			66.0					
Greengrocery			44.4	0.7	—		110.4	
GROSS MARGIN			2956.0	19.4	2829.6	18.2	126.4	1.2
Add Promotion allowance			68.7					
Cash discount			81.5	1.0	—		150.2	1.0
Less Stock losses			(27.2)	0.2	(61.9)	0.4	34.7	0.2
Cost of trading stamps			380.8	2.5	310.0	2.0	(70.8)	0.5
Stamps issued	405.2							
Deduct allowance and discount	24.4							
NET MARGIN			2698.2	17.7	2457.7	15.8	240.5	1.9
Deduct Branch expenses			1697.5	11.2	1648.4	10.6	(49.1)	0.6
Net rents	270.8	1.8						
Rates	101.4	0.7						
Light and heating	140.0	0.9						
Insurance	25.2	0.1						
Wages and salaries	933.0	6.1						
Cleaning	40.8	0.3						
Repairs and maintenance	49.7	0.3						
Depreciation	117.3	0.8						
Other	17.9	0.1						
BRANCH NET PROFIT			1001.7	6.5	809.3	5.2	191.4	1.3
Deduct Distribution expenses	200.6							
Retailing expenses	174.7							
Administration expenses	374.1		749.4	4.9	597.7	3.8	(151.7)	1.1
COMPANY NET PROFIT			252.3	1.6	211.6	1.4	40.7	0.2

* Excluding Foodfair Ltd, which showed a net profit of £11,000 over the period
Source: Company records

on this. 'Our main problem, as I have often told the board, is that we never get the "first bite of the cherry" as far as property is concerned and we only get offered the "leftovers" from the larger supermarket operators.' The South of England was proving extremely difficult for good sites especially for superstores of hypermarkets and as a result he and the property development department had begun investigating sites in the North of England. Indeed, in view of the company's proposed expansion the property development department's brief had been broadened to allow them to consider sites anywhere in the British Isles although 'adequate consideration of every circumstance was to be given to all aspects in each new instance'.

Nevertheless, Mr Mellor was confident, that, despite Mr Green's claim that Big Buy got last bite of the cherry on new sites, good sites would become available. 'Furthermore,' he added, 'the company has now embarked on an ambitious expansion programme, and if we cannot find enough space in the South, it is therefore inevitable that we move North.'

BOARD CHANGE

In March 1972 Mr Abraham Goldstein died, and in April Mr Green and Mr Mellor recommended to the board that this loss meant Big Buy urgently needed someone with financial and management expertise to assist the company. It was therefore agreed that Mr Gerald Battersby of Muller Day be invited to replace Mr Goldstein. Mr Battersby therefore joined the Big Buy board in May 1972.

THE SITUATION IN MID-1972

Following 1970's profit decline the first half of 1971 saw a further sharp fall in pretax profits to only £163,000 on sales of £18 million. But in the second half of the year the first benefits started to show through from the various changes made, and profits began to recover. Although traditionally the second half of the year was better than the first half, sales expanded to £20 million and profits to £416,000.

The early results for 1972 now available monthly to management showed a continuation of the improved trend. By June the latest available figures for Big Buy's fourth 4-week period (see Exhibit 7) revealed sales and profits running ahead of budget. It appeared that for the year overall pre-tax profits would comfortably exceed the £825,000 budgeted as a result of the opening of the company's new superstores and further developments of new discount operations.

10 Big Buy Supermarkets (C)*

In May 1972 Mr Cyril Mellor, chief executive of Big Buy Supermarkets,[1] considered that it was an opportune time for the company to undertake the development of its first five-year strategic plan to enable the company to reach its primary objective of becoming a major force in food retailing in Britain by 1980. In view of the lack of planning system expertise amongst Big Buy's management, Mr Mellor decided it would be most appropriate for Big Buy to engage specialist planning consultants to aid in the preparation of the first plan. Further, to ensure continuity of planning for the future, Mr Mellor's personal assistant, Mrs Tracy Blair, an attractive thirty three year old divorcee, was appointed as head of corporate planning activities.

Mrs Blair, commenting on the Big Buy approach to planning, said, 'There are several different planning procedures; you have probably heard of Management by Objectives (MBO), as sponsored by Urwick and Orr, and the American consultancy company of McKinsey's approach—namely, Corporate Strategy. We have reviewed both techniques, and have elected to adopt a planning procedure which permits the employees to participate in developing the future hopes and aspirations of the company.'

The planning method adopted by Mr Mellor was that developed by Mr Harvey Wainwright, who was president of his own consultancy company Total Strategic Systems Inc., (TSS). The unique characteristic of the TSS approach was its involvement of all sections of line management in the planning process. Rather than merely planning from the top down by the main board or a specialist planning department, the TSS system was participative, and the company's strategic plan was largely created from the bottom up. By introducing participative management into the planning process, Mr Wainwright considered plans developed could take advantage of the employees' own ideas, skills and knowledge, stop internal politics, ease a company facility for change, make top management listen to lower levels of management and ensure commitment to the ultimate plan throughout the organisation.

THE TSS PLANNING SYSTEM

Mr Wainwright described the TSS system as follows:

> Participative planning as TSS have developed it is a complete system. It is used where companies are interested in achieving a consistent increase in earnings per share. To achieve a consistent and constant growth pattern, it is critical that
>
> 1 All the voices of employees are heard
> 2 All middle and senior management see their personal impact on year-end profit
> 3 Top management sees and is constantly reminded of their role in the direction and growth of the company

Under Mr Wainwright's planning method, a general plan for the organisation as a whole was first developed with the chief executive; this laid down in detail the corporation's objectives and a detailed financial strategy for the company's planning period. Within this framework each subunit of the corporation then prepared its own strategic plan with all the senior and middle management of each unit participating in the planning process. Subunit plans were then collated with all functional overlaps being discussed and agreed between relevant management groups. The collated plan, which incorporated a series of action programmes, was compared with the original corporate master plan, which was modified in the light of the subunit plans to produce a fully-fledged corporate plan, to which all levels of management were committed.

The TSS system of planning could be readily divided into three distinct phases.

1. Preplanning procedures
2. The planning process
3. Post planning review and recycle

---

[1] This case was made possible by the cooperation of a company that wishes to remain anonymous. All names, places and operating results have therefore been changed.

* Copyright © Manchester Business School 1973

Preplanning Procedures

Prior to the construction of a new plan or the recycling of an existing one, a number of detailed procedures were undertaken to ensure that all participants in the planning process were fully briefed. In the case of new plans, close attention was paid to informing participants as to the mechanics of the system, what was expected of them, why they did it and how the plan was assembled and implemented. In the case of a recycle, the emphasis was on progressing the state of the planning art and in obtaining constant improvements in the operations and development of the unit being planned and managed.

A critical step at the preplanning stage was the appointment of a planning secretary for each unit to be planned. This person, apart from preparing for the planning session and maintaining the plan once formulated, worked closely with the TSS outside consultant in managing the planning process. The planning secretary was responsible for collecting together the preplanning data which, apart from the financial, budgetary and operational information available to the management of the unit to be planned, consisted of a series of Preliminary Points for Action (PPA).

The PPAs were strengths, weaknesses, threats and opportunities, identified by each and every member of management team engaged in formulating the plan. All such points for action were recorded on form TSS 1 (Exhibit 1) and it was the planning secretary's task to ensure that the PPAs put forward covered all areas of the unit's operations.

EXHIBIT 1   Form TSS 1

PRELIMINARY POINT FOR ACTION

TITLE

- NATURE OF ACTION POINT

  Please tick as appropriate

  STRENGTH

  WEAKNESS

  RISK

  OPPORTUNITY

- DESCRIPTION OF THE ACTION POINT
- POSSIBLE ACTION RECOMMENDED

PPAs were prepared throughout the year when the TSS system had been fully introduced, but in the case of a start-up situation, individuals were requested to write PPAs prior to the first planning session. The PPAs were anonymous to ensure that every individual could bring forward issues considered important, without fear of reprisals by senior management. As a result, a substantial proportion of PPAs dealt with faults or threats to present operations, although a number of opportunities were also generated. The planning secretary and the head of the functional area then appointed the planning team consisting of the six or eight senior executives within the area to be planned. Having completed the preplanning procedures and collected PPAs, the actual planning process took place over a period of five days, when the planning team were totally cut off from their normal operational duties.

The Planning Process

The planning process, after an initial introduction, began with sorting the PPAs into six categories according to product, process, market, distribution resources and administration, or suitable analogies for these areas depending on the specific nature of the unit to be planned. Thus the session chairman was encouraged to see his unit as a small business, cut off temporarily from the parent company.

The PPAs in each category were then allocated to a two-man team, considered to be least expert in the subject area assigned. Each team was then expected to integrate all the PPAs in each pile into a series of initial action proposals (IAPs), which were recorded on TSS Form 2 (Exhibit 2).

As many as twenty PPAs could be integrated into a single IAP, which might be

EXHIBIT 2   Form TSS 2

INITIAL ACTION PROPOSAL
PLAN TITLE
Definition of problem:
Evaluation of resources needed:
Functional involvement:
Description of proposed action:
Accountability:
Priority:

significantly broader in scope than any of the individual PPAs. Under no circumstances could PPAs be destroyed if they did not fit easily into any of the IAPs. Such PPAs could form the basis of a separate IPA, be buried in an overall 'dustbin programme' or if they related to another department's area of responsibility, passed on to the unit concerned.

As each two-man team completed the process of deriving IAPs from the PPAs, the titles of these proposals were recorded on a blackboard. When all teams had finished the analysis of the PPAs assigned to them, the full planning group assembled around the blackboard and the IAPs were reviewed with the team responsible outlining their views, plan by plan, to the others. As this process evolved with frequent reference to the PPAs, all other IAP titles were screened for duplication and for those so close as to justify integrating them with the proposal under review. The Form 2s of the IAPs which passed through this screening process were modified accordingly, and set aside for further detailed consideration at a subsequent stage.

After all the IAPs had been reviewed, the head of the unit being planned stated his desire to see the proposals converted in executive action programmes (EAPs). Each IAP was assigned to a two-man team, chosen to produce the best combination of talent to deal with the specific area of the IAP. A detailed programme of action to implement the agreed IAP was then drawn up by an individual member of the two-man team and recorded on TSS Form 3 (Exhibit 3). This EAP then became the responsibility of the individual who drew it up. All the EAPs were then reviewed phase by phase and section by section by the group as a whole. The rest of the planning team questioned whatever seemed doubtful to them and noted the effect of the EAP on their own work. Modifications were made by general agreement and, after the EAP had been essentially approved, a crude financial budget and bar chart timetable were made up and responsibility for implementation assigned to a specific individual. In addition, the key assumptions on which the EAP was based were recorded and the budgets summarised by a financial executive. The EAPs were then reviewed again in the form of negotiation between the individual planner responsible for each EAP and the chief executive. At this review the individual who had drawn up the EAP was seated next to the chief executive in the 'hotseat'. Other functional executives were assigned to summarise the sales planned, the key financial assumptions being made and the expense and capital budget required. The chief executive then carefully read the EAP work statements, timing, budget and expected results and control systems to be used. Negotiation then followed, during which the individual committed himself to budgets and targets based on the recorded assumptions. Even at this stage, it was common to find that differences of opinion existed within the planning group and where these differences were severe, discussion continued in an effort to reach a broad consensus of opinion.

After this process, when the EAPs had been generally agreed with the chief executive, the planning team made its first attempt to set priorities. This was done using a Delphi technique, whereby each member of the team ranked all the EAPs in his considered order of their priority. The individual priorities assigned to each EAP were then summed and the entire programme was then assembled in overall rank order of priority. At this point a check was made to ensure that the priorities decided were compatible with the time horizon of interdependent EAPs, the workloads of the individuals concerned or, where other departments were involved, with their priorities.

The group then prepared a basic statement of objectives and strategy, outlining the overriding reasons for the EAPs in the plan; listed the key assumptions on which the EAPs were based; and developed the detailed profit and loss expense statements,

EXHIBIT 3   TSS Form 3

EXECUTIVE ACTION PROGRAMME   Action Programme No. _____

PHASE 1 — PROBLEM DEFINITION

_____   Title _____

_____

_____   Executive

_____   Responsibility

                                         Control: _____

PHASE 2 — RECOMMENDED ACTION

_____

_____   Action: _____

_____

PHASE 3 — EXECUTION AND CONTROL

_____

_____

EXECUTIVE ACTION PROGRAMME (Timing & costs)

          19___   19___   19___   19___

	JF MA MJ JyA SO ND	JF MA MJ JyA SO ND	JF MA MJ JyA SO ND	JF MA MJ JyA SO ND
PHASE 1				
PHASE 2				
PHASE 3				
BUDGET £	BUDGET ACTUAL	BUDGET ACTUAL	BUDGET ACTUAL	BUDGET ACTUAL
RESULTS £ ADDITIONAL PROFIT COST SAVINGS				

Control Systems: _____   Assumption: _____

balance sheets and financial assumptions for the following five years, which were expected to result from the planning exercise. The entire package of plans was then collated and distributed to each member of the group and other relevant parties. The planning secretary and the department head were then held responsible for the monitoring of progress against each individual EAP.

Post Planning Review and Recycle

Following the preparation of the initial plan, a six-stage review procedure came into effect. This consisted of a close audit and quality control of the plan, presentation to the next level of authority in the organisation for approval and authorisation to proceed, monitoring of progress, constant update of the plan documents, a regular series of review sessions and a full recycle on a twice-yearly basis.

Following the planning session the rough draft plan was checked for accuracy and summary forms typed for presentation and distribution. The cleaned-up plan was then presented to the next highest level of authority, in the case of Big Buy to the chief executive. At this presentation the plan was put into context by the department head preparing a special statement, which described the current market situation with respect to the size, number and names of key competitors, including their particular activities or characteristics likely to affect operations; size and trends in the market, including the company's market share; price range in which it operated, and the effect of changes expected on sales and margins.

Following authorisation to proceed with the plan, a detailed time-table of the plan's EAP schedule was drawn up to keep a close check on programme completions. If major developments occurred which affected the plan an interim group conference was called to recycle the plan. It was considered that profit and loss and balance sheet statements could be calculated in about an hour and a revised set of financial targets could be readily produced. In addition, plan documents were kept regularly updated.

To improve control, the first year of the plan was broken down by month. Progress on EAPs could then be monitored by the chief executive or director concerned, either directly with the individual responsible or by means of a planning group conference. The frequency of such review meetings varied according to the rate of change being imposed on the organisation by the plan. In Big Buy regular recycling, apart from less formal individual or group review sessions, took place at six-monthly intervals. While one of these two annual occasions consisted of the full five-day plan recycle session, calling for the generation of new PPAs and a total system review, the second lasted for only two days and consisted of an in-depth review of progress achieved on each EAP, the basic premises of the plan and the generation of updated financial proformas.

THE BIG BUY STRATEGIC PLAN

Planning in Big Buy commenced in May 1972, with a planning meeting between Mr Mellor and Mr Wainwright. This session, lasting for one day, established Mr Mellor's overall master plan for Big Buy, which would act as a guideline and framework for the subsequent detailed planning sessions conducted in each of Big Buy's functional departments.

Following the development of Mr Mellor's plan, which detailed his ideas on Big Buy's future growth to 1976, the distribution division led by Mr Tony Holt met to produce its own plan at the end of May. Throughout the summer and autumn of 1972, each of the other Big Buy functional divisions met to produce their own plans and by the end of October a strategic plan had been produced for distribution, marketing, store operations, administration, properties, finance and control and non-foods. These departmental plans were then consolidated by Mrs Blair prior to the preparation by Mr Mellor and Mr Wainwright of the revised Big Buy master strategic plan on 20 November 1972. The key elements of the master plan are reproduced as Appendix 1.

The master plan, which Mr Mellor considered to be Big Buy's blueprint for expansion, was made up of a near-term strategy of some forty executive action programmes, covering all aspects of the company's operations, and established a clear set of corporate goals and objectives against which progress could be measured. Commenting on Big Buy's planning approach, Mr Mellor added, 'There are three basic principles behind the TSS method. First, it is participative; all the key executives take part in the process, and this obtains both their contribution and their commitment. Second, it is quantitative; the policies and plans that emerge from it are built into a five-year projection of the Budget and this projection is backed up with supporting evidence, with all the assumptions being clearly identified. Finally, it sets out the time scale for completion of each stage of the plans and projects that are evolved, and provides a monitoring system to keep a close check on progress. I am sure that by using this procedure in a disciplined manner, Big Buy will become an extremely successful company; this success will be reflected in increased earnings per share and hence a significant increase in Big Buy's share price.'

Despite Mr Mellor's optimism, not all the other executives were equally favourable to the system. This was especially true to of a number of the longer-term employees, one of whom commented, 'Some of us are calling the plan Mellor's Madness. We've been to the planning sessions because we were ordered to go, but we don't all believe that pie in the sky stuff. As far as I am concerned, I think Cyril Mellor was conned by that smooth-talking American. Those four-day sessions cost £2,000 a shot, and that's for every department in the company don't forget, not to mention the six-monthly review and the annual plan recycle. As far as I'm concerned personally it's a waste of time and I don't believe we'll ever make the targets Mellor's set for us.'

Commenting on this type of reaction, Mr Mellor said, 'You must remember that when I came to Big Buy it had been run by Mr Green's father in a very personalised way and had grown up from what was really a small shop grocery business. As a result, some of the older staff were not accustomed to the methods of modern management. Since becoming chief executive I have been building a top management team of good professional managers, accustomed to planning, budgetary procedures and the like, which will be necessary to ensure Big Buy accomplishes its objectives and is capable of managing a major food retailing company.'

Appendix

BIG BUY SUPERMARKETS LTD – STRATEGIC PLAN

Management Style

Big Buy Supermarkets Ltd management style calls for an above average expectation of performance from the company's professional associates and a high regard for creative business adventures within a relatively conservative financial posture.

Our style calls for an extreme concern for retail development and management.

STATEMENT OF CORPORATE OBJECTIVES

The basic purpose and objectives of Big Buy are to be a major factor in the food and non-food retailing industry, specialising in multiple shop management, supermarket and hypermarket retailing forms.

OUR PURPOSE is to be an important business in the field of distribution and transport, property development and management and knowledgeable of consumer requirements for new and improved products.

WE BELIEVE we should be experts in the field of product merchandising, store layout and product presentation, with especial skills in logistics and control.

WE BELIEVE that the interests of our employees, customers, suppliers, our respective communities, as well as stockholders and those who provide our financial resources are being served through this group's rapid growth in earnings as measured by our contribution to increased earnings per share.

WE BELIEVE that the fundamental purpose of our corporation is to contribute to the creation of wealth for each of our stakeholder groups.

Regarding our customers

WE BELIEVE our customer is served through our technical capability to supply need for quality, technical assistance, products/systems. We believe that our growth in profits permits our maintaining this customer support.

Regarding our Employees

WE BELIEVE that our employees' interests are served by creating an environment which permits maximum individual professional growth and economic participation in the work of the group as well as to enhance creativity and job enlargement. We recognise that all employees are not perfect and hence see the need for a willingness to work together as well as permitting candour in our interpersonal relationships.

Regarding our Shareholders

Regarding our shareholders' interest is served through our maximum use of corporate debt resources in the investments which generate high return on investments and hence to maximise long-term capital gain as opposed to near-term income.

Regarding our Financial Institutions

WE BELIEVE that our maximum use of debt/leverage with no near-term dividend payments enhances our earnings per share growth and hence is in the interests of both our stockholders and peripheral lending agencies.

Regarding our Community Interests

WE BELIEVE that our communities' interests are served through our profitable growth and so far as we provide an ever-expanding economic contribution to each community in which we operate as well as a social stability which accrues from growth and prosperity.

Regarding our Suppliers

WE BELIEVE that our suppliers are served not only through our own growth in terms of physical volume, but in our providing data on which our suppliers can plan their own business prosperity.

STATEMENT OF STRATEGY

United Kingdom Retail Market

Food and non-food retailing to the mass consumer market is steadily growing and providing an increasing market for those companies interested in retailing. This pattern of expansion has been exhibited in America and hypermarkets have opened on the Continent. British consumers will be as price conscious as consumers elsewhere, giving rise to a massive opportunity to service this consumer requirement for foods and non-foods.

Competitive Position

Tesco, during 1971 (ending in February of this year) expanded their retail space by 500,000 sq.ft. They increased their business by about 16 per cent to sales of almost 300 million. During 1971 forty stores were opened with an average floor space of about 12,000 sq.ft.

Tesco is negotiating for about 15 hypermarkets of 50,000 sq.ft or a total area of 750,000 additional sq.ft. Tesco is now planning 5 to 10 years ahead.

Sainsbury pushed their business in 1971 (ending in March of this year) up by 18 per cent. During the past three years they opened 26 stores with a total of 353,000 sq.ft. During the next three years Sainsbury plan to open 50 new stores, adding a total of 800,000 sq.ft. more than they are now managing.

Rationale

Because there is a growth 'retail market' in the United Kingdom, as well as in the Common Market and because we have an established retailing business here in the United Kingdom.

IT IS OUR STRATEGY in the near term

(1) Administratively, to get the company into a streamlined, efficient and well-run operation:

Finance	1	Accelerate and simplify budgetary control system
	2	Simplify and speed-up accounting system
	3	Generate sense of financial responsibility
	4	Evaluate economics of distributing similar and slow-moving products
	5	Improve financial evaluation of possible acquisitions
	6	Improve cut-off arrangements for branch and warehouse stocktakes
	7	Determine current rates of gross profits for each branch departmentally
Administration	3	Improve audio/physical communications systems
	15	Create consumable stores
	16	Improve on telephonist scheme already commenced
	18	Monitor MDS system to ensure catalogues up-to-date
Purchasing	1	Improve purchasing practices
Store operations	1	Improve retail control organisation
	4	Improve standards of handling goods in branches
	5	Establish retail manning standards

(2) To design and maintain an organisation and a management style which will maximise individual participation, effect good communications, gain an above-average motivation and keep our employee skills high.

    Administration   1   Introduce management incentive share programme

                              4   Improve information and decision links between all levels of management

                              5   Create corporate planning programme

                              6   Develop definite company career programme

                              7   Reorganise corporate structure

                              8   Create salary structure for company management

                              9   Establish company performance appraisal system

                             10   Improve company terms and conditions of employment

                             11   Improve recruitment programme

                             12   Improve welfare facilities programme

                             13   Improve employee and staff training programme

                             17   Improve catering arrangements at depots

(3) Marketing: To improve our corporate image so that our sales per sq.ft goes up to £2.00/wk on foods.

    Promotional   1   Improve advertising and promotion activity

                              2   Improve package design to present better company image

    Store operations   2   Accelerate shop refitting programme

    Merchandising   1   Improve vehicle livery to fresh food image

                              2   Create merchandising technique development programme

                              3   Establish viable policy for similar and slow-moving products

                              5   Create a sales promotion procedure and programme

Sales per sq. ft/week

	1972	1973	1974	1975	1976
£					
Food/soft	1.60	1.80	2.00	2.20	2.40
Non-food	0.75	0.80	0.90	1.00	1.00

(4) To become an efficient distributor of merchandise and to process up to 96 per cent of the products sold throughout retail Branches.

    Distribution   1   Establish distribution as a viable business

IT IS OUR STRATEGY in the longer term—

(1) To expand our retail space both internally and through joint ventures and acquisitions.

    Divers-1   Improve joint venture activity

    Divers-2   Improve acquisition programme
                    Improve new shop expansion programme

(2) To exploit benefits to be derived from 'own label' business.

    Purchasing   2   Improve and expand own label programme

RETAIL SALES PLAN

	1972	*1973*	*1974*	*1975*	*1976*
STAMP STORES					
Number	107	98	88	78	68
Sq.ft food	373	350	325	280	230
Sq.ft non-food	35	32	32	35	30
DISCOUNT STORES					
Up to 25,000 sq.ft					
Number	34	36	46	58	69
Sq.ft food	139	160	240	356	442
Sq.ft non-food	20	33	87	187	273
SUPERSTORES					
Over 25,000 sq.ft					
Number	2	3	15	26	32
Sq.ft food	25	50	190	340	415
Sq.ft non-food	25	40	270	480	570
TOTAL STORES	143	137	149	162	169
Sq.ft food	537	560	755	976	1,087
Sq.ft non-food	80	105	389	702	873
Total sq.ft	617	665	1,144	1,678	1,960

Assumptions: (1) That stamp trading be phased out over a period.
(2) That stores between 12,000 and 25,000 sq.ft will have roughly 50 per cent food and 50 per cent non-food.
(3) That stores over 25,000 sq.ft will have a higher non-food content.

PRO-FORMA BALANCE SHEET SUMMARY

(£ millions)

	1972	*1973*	*1974*	*1975*	*1976*
Capital Employed					
EQUITY in 25p ord. shares	1.1	1.1	1.1	1.1	1.1
Retained earnings	2.2	2.8	3.8	5.4	8.0
Debt	0	0	1.9	0	0
TOTAL CAPITAL EMPLOYED	3.3	3.9	6.8	6.5	9.1
Fixed Assets					
Land, bldg, plant and equipment	6.7	9.2	18.4	22.5	30.7
Less reserve for depreciation	2.2	2.8	3.9	5.7	8.1
NET FIXED ASSETS	4.5	6.4	14.5	16.8	22.6
Current Assets					
Cash	1.6	2.8	0	3.0	5.8
Debtors	0.4	0.7	1.0	1.5	2.2
Stocks	2.2	2.2	3.2	3.7	5.5
Current Liabilities					
Creditors	5.4	8.2	11.9	18.5	27.0
TOTAL CAPITAL EMPLOYED	3.3	3.9	6.8	6.5	9.1

PRO-FORMA PROFIT AND LOSS SUMMARY

(£ millions)

	1972	1973	1974	1975	1976
GROSS SALES	45.8	69.4	101.2	156.5	229.4
Less cost of goods sold	38.3	58.1	84.9	131.8	94.6
Gross margin on sales	7.5	11.3	16.3	24.7	34.8
Add gross profit from distribution*	0.2	0.7	1.1	1.7	2.4
TOTAL TRADING PROFIT	7.7	12.0	17.4	26.4	37.2
Less distribution expenses	1.4	1.8	1.9	2.6	3.3
Less retail/buying expenses	5.2	8.4	12.4	18.7	26.5
Depreciation	0.4	0.6	1.1	1.8	2.4
Interest	—	—	—	—	—
GROSS PROFIT BEFORE TAX	0.7	1.2	2.0	3.3	5.0
Tax at 45%	0.3	0.5	0.9	1.5	2.3
NET PROFIT	0.4	0.7	1.1	1.8	2.7
Dividends at 20% share capital	0.2	0.2	0.2	0.2	0.2
Less dividends waived	0.1	0.1	0.1	0.1	0.1
RETAINED PROFIT	0.3	0.6	1.0	1.7	2.6

* Distribution profits to be achieved by cost savings generated by increasing the level of distribution through the company's own warehouse operations from 43% to 96%. This to be achieved by the building of a major new warehouse complex at a cost of £12 million and located at Dunstable close to the M1 Motorway.

BASIC ASSUMPTIONS

1. Sales Growth

	1972	1973	1974	1975	1976
Actual gross sales—£million	45.8	69.4	102.2	156.5	229.4
Inflation factor	1.00	1.07	1.14	1.22	1.31
Gross sales (constant 1972 £ in millions)	45.8	64.9	89.6	128.3	175.1
Sales food—£million	43.0	59.8	74.5	101.1	135.2
Sales non-food—£million	2.8	5.1	15.1	27.2	39.9

2. Distribution of Food Sales (%)

% of Gross food sales	1972	1973	1974	1975	1976
Groceries	81.7	79.8	77.9	76.0	74.0
Produce[1]	5.4	6.8[3]	8.2	9.6	11.0
Meat[2]	8.9	9.4	9.9	10.4	11.0
Tobacco	1.9	1.9	1.9	1.9	1.9
Wines and spirits	2.1	2.1	2.1	2.1	2.1
	100.0	100.0	100.0	100.0	100.0
Food as % of gross sales	94.15	92.65	83.35	78.90	77.60

Notes
1. Produce to increase 19% over next 5 years due to EEC
2. Determination of meat percentage increase due to EEC not possible until import levies defined, but expected to be in the region of 10-11%.
3. Produce controller says 6% in 1973, but trading pressures due to EEC and lower prices will force a higher percentage up to 6.8%.

3. Pro Forma Margin Estimates

	1972	1973	1974	1975	1976
	%	%	%	%	%
Food margin	15.00	14.00	14.00	13.50	13.00
Non-food margin	30.00	29.00	27.00	26.00	25.00
Average gross profit or margin	16.35	16.32	16.11	15.74	15.14
Distribution (96%) and margin improvement	0.53	1.06	1.06	1.06	1.06
Trading profit	1.70	2.20	2.50	2.80	3.20

4. Share Price Estimates

	1972	1973	1974	1975	1976
EPS (£)	0.007	0.016	0.024	0.040	0.062
% change	—	131	54	66	53
PE ratio	25	35	40	50	60
5/- ord. share price (£)	0.17	0.55	0.97	2.42	3.70

11 Makepiece Company*

Two months ago at an operating committee meeting, the managing director of the Makepiece Company[1] asked Richard Peet, the general sales manager, and Paul Robb, manager of the organisation planning and procedures department, to get together and determine if better forecasts of sales and of inventory requirements could be made available in order to improve factory schedules, financial planning, and so on. David Kent and Charles Stevens, both of whom worked for Robb, and Robert Henry, Edwin Merrill, and David Entwhistle of the sales department were assigned by Robb and Peet, respectively to work on the problem. Stevens and Henry, being older and more experienced and being regarded as rather senior men, immediately became the informal leaders of the work group. The five men worked out the technical problems to the satisfaction of both Stevens and Henry. The group attempted to consult with their immediate superiors as the work progressed. After the study had been under way for some time, Robert Henry told Stevens that he, Merrill and Entwhistle seemed to be blocked by the opposition of the product division managers. Henry also told Stevens that he felt he 'could not go over the division managers' heads' to Mr Peet, the general sales manager, and he asked Stevens to have his boss, Mr Robb, ask the sales manager whether a conference might not be held to appraise the progress of the work. Stevens told Mr Robb of Henry's request and the reason for it. Accordingly, Robb talked over the matter with Peet, who acquiesced, as he believed the problem ought to be solved as rapidly as possible. Peet invited the four product division managers, Paul Robb, and the five-man working group to the conference and set the time for it. Peet told Henry to go ahead with Stevens and set up the presentation to be made at the conference.

As Henry and Stevens planned the conference, they decided that the group from the sales department—Henry, Merrill, and Entwhistle—were really on the spot. Henry, Merrill and Entwhistle all agreed that in order not to embarrass them or their bosses, the presentation of the joint conclusions of the working group ought to be made by Stevens.

At the meeting Richard Peet, the four product division managers, and the three men from sales who worked on the study were present, as were Paul Robb of the organisation planning and procedures department, and his two assistants, Stevens and Kent. When Peet asked who was going to report progress, Henry suggested that Stevens was the best man to present their findings. Peet asked Robb if that was all right. When the latter agreed, Stevens used half an hour to outline the concept of their work. He stated that both groups had agreed upon details, believed their recommendations would work, and were prepared to take personal responsibility for them. Both Merrill and Entwhistle asked Henry to amplify certain points during the presentation. It seemed to Robb that they had in mind clarifying matters for their own bosses who might be opposed or might not understand.

Following Stevens's statement, the sales manager asked his product division managers to give their reactions to the proposals. One of them gave the plan lukewarm support; the three others said it could not be accomplished. There was much discussion among the three who were opposed. Occasionally, Henry, Merrill and Entwhistle tried to get a word in edgewise without much success. Once, when David Kent asked Division B manager a question, the effect seemed to be mild anger at being interrupted.

Paul Robb watched the whole proceedings with interest. He recalled that it had seemed to him that for the past two years this same group of four product managers had opposed every step involving changes in methods or procedures. In his opinion, 'their delaying tactics' had been costly to the company. Robb knew that the managing director expected him to break some of these bottlenecks. Robb was only a staff advisor but he knew he had the ear of the managing director whenever he needed it. He considered the sales manager to be progressive and thought Peet could not tolerate these conditions much longer. It seemed to Robb that Peet had line responsibility to get something done in this area. Robb liked these 'old line' product managers, and did not want to hurt them if he could avoid it.

---

[1] All names have been disguised. A partial organisation chart of the company is attached as Exhibit 1.

* Copyright © London Business School

While Robb was in the midst of these musings and after two hours of apparently fruitless discussion, Richard Peet turned to him and said: 'Robb, you have heard this whole discussion, what do you think we ought to do next?'

EXHIBIT 1   **Makepiece Company—Partial Organisation Chart**

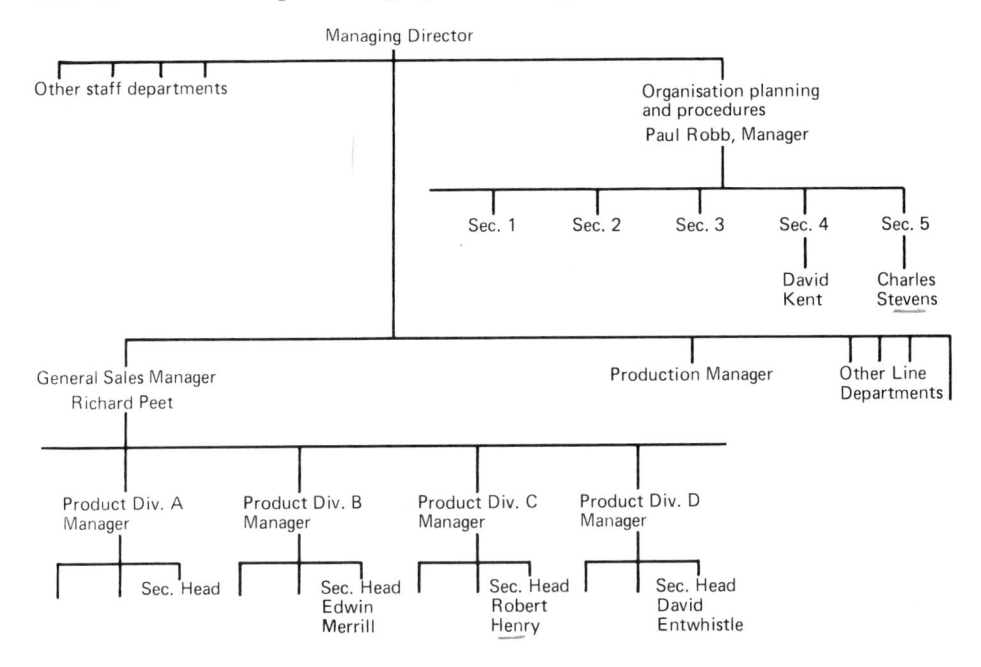

```
                              Managing Director
  ┌──────┬──────┬──────────────────┼──────────────────────────────┐
Other staff departments                              Organisation planning
                                                     and procedures
                                                     Paul Robb, Manager
                                          ┌──────┬──────┬──────┬──────┐
                                        Sec. 1 Sec. 2 Sec. 3 Sec. 4 Sec. 5
                                                               │      │
                                                             David  Charles
                                                             Kent   Stevens

  ┌────────────────────────────────────────┬──────────────────┬───┬───┐
General Sales Manager              Production Manager       Other Line
Richard Peet                                                Departments
  ┌────────┬────────┬────────┬────────┐
Product Div. A  Product Div. B  Product Div. C  Product Div. D
Manager         Manager         Manager         Manager
  │             │               │               │
Sec. Head      Sec. Head       Sec. Head       Sec. Head
               Edwin           Robert          David
               Merrill         Henry           Entwhistle
```

12 Barry McKenzie*

Barry McKenzie graduated in 1970 with a MSc degree in Business Studies. The following is his record of his approach to job selection in early 1970 and his impressions of working for an entrepreneurial electronics company—Hyper Dynamics Limited. (Exhibits 1, 2, and 3 indicate the scale of operations of Hyper Dynamics. This detailed information was not available to Barry McKenzie before he joined the firm.)

BACKGROUND

Barry McKenzie was born in Australia in 1943 and was brought up and educated there. Although not attending university in Australia, he became professionally qualified as an accountant and also took a postgraduate qualification in management accounting. He was employed by an international firm of chartered accountants and in 1966 was transferred to their London offices in order to gain 'overseas accounting and commercial expertise' and to 'see the world'.

In 1968 he applied and was accepted by a leading British business school to study for an M.Sc. in Business Studies. The motivations for this move were:

1. To achieve a greater understanding of the techniques of business administration.
2. Not having been to university, to undergo a university experience for its own sake.
3. To acquire a degree as an aid in subsequent career development.

McKenzie did exceedingly well on his master's degree course.

CHOOSING THE JOB

I found determining job objectives a bit difficult in that like most students, I didn't have a single-minded idea of what was the right thing for me to do. I started off pretty early in the year trying to evaluate what my average inclination was. I drew a chart above my desk which was what I called 'Mood Analysis', and under comments I listed the sort of thing I might like doing, i.e. company size, function, level, geographic preference. I also included what my overt capabilities were, which of course included finance. Probably a couple of times a day while working at home I would stop and think about a job and try to include it in the categories. However, in the end I don't think this helped much, apart from identifying for me some things that were more important than others.

I suppose I was looking for something that was interesting, challenging, exciting, which met a minimum salary criterion, and was also at a high organisational level. My reason for wanting a job at a high organisational level was that I left my previous company at a fairly high level and I didn't want to feel that I was slipping back. There was also the fact that I am not a particularly competent quantitative man, although I can appreciate what the quantitative man is doing. However, I cannot process figures as fast as a really competent quantitative man, and therefore I wanted to be in a position whereby if there was a lot of quantitative work involved, I could delegate this work and protect my own particular weakness.

My experience as an auditor had led me to believe that the level of brainpower used in determining a company's strategy was only one-tenth to one-twentieth of that used in implementing, and to me this was the wrong way round. If you weren't in the right business area, it wouldn't matter how well you were implementing your operational techniques, you would be wasting your time. This had resulted in my directing my studies at the business school to courses in business strategy. I didn't want to be pushed into a functional implementation position; I wanted a job at a high level where I would be determining the strategy, and hence I rejected any job requiring only technique and implementation skills. Fundamentally, I wanted a job where it would be quite

---

* Copyright © London Business School 1971

clear to anyone looking at my record that I had done a job that was really significant and perhaps a little unusual for someone of my age.

My interviewing schedule was based on companies coming to the school and on advertisements in newspapers. I felt that if I didn't find the job I wanted this way then I could commit further time and effort to job hunting after I had completed my studies. I didn't feel any urgency about the need to have a job before leaving the business school.

Hyper Dynamics did not arrive at the business school until late in the interviewing season. The company was an electronics company started by four senior design engineers who had been pushed out of their previous company after a fairly fundamental row. They had started their own company, Hyper Dynamics, and were confident that they were capable of developing some of their technical ideas into good commercial products, to their own financial advantage. They had a lot of technical expertise in the digital electronics area and were manufacturing automatic digital integrated circuit testers.

My first meeting was with the managing and sales directors who had asked specifically to see me, as they were looking for an accountant. I was pleased to see them as they sounded like interesting guys who had been doing some really interesting things. They showed me their product guides, explained what products they manufactured, what sort of money they were making and what their expectations were. I am impressed by people that do things, and they seemed to have done something. They talked very coherently and convincingly about what they were doing and where they were going, and on paper they seemed to be doing pretty well. I was also influenced by the fact that they had the backing of a very reputable merchant bank. At the first interview they defined the job rather loosely by saying that they wanted someone who could sort out their accounts and put in an information system. They also wanted someone with financial expertise to help them raise the money they were going to need in the future from city financial sources. I like the idea of entrepreneurial business and decided it would be worth following up.

So I went down for the second interview to the company's offices. We first discussed job responsibility and seniority at some length, as I wasn't prepared to join a small outfit unless I had an equal say in what was going on. This culminated in their offering me a job that put me immediately on the board as company secretary, and provided that things went well, in something like a year's time I would be offered the same equity share as the others, plus a directorship. This appeared to be a good offer if the company were successful, as there would be more than just a job involved: there would also be a fair bit of money. I would handle their finances and look after the development of an international organisation which would result from the export of their products. They thought it would take three or four years to get properly established overseas.

There were some other points at the meeting which made me begin to have second thoughts. They seemed to be taking on far too much, in that not only were they doing a lot of consultancy work in rather disparate technical areas, but they were also trying to build a computer. At this stage, they were fairly flush with money and were even thinking of investing in the local housing market—yet another dispersion of effort. Although disturbed, this raised another motivation to join them: that of helping them to sort out just what they should do, and of using my personal ability to set them off on a straight track with a clear corporate objective. In addition, some of the engineering staff, although very clever, appeared to be highly temperamental. I saw one senior employee in a responsible position, running around in circles not knowing what he was doing, because he was trying to handle too much. This sight disturbed me, but I thought I could be a big change agent and do a lot to help by lifting the weight off their shoulders.

It was such a different sort of company. It met my criteria of position and salary; it appeared interesting and exciting with potential for international growth. Other advantages which I saw were that I would be

1. Directly involved in the running of the company
2. In close contact with people who influence the destinies of firms
3. Able to see how a group of men tried to build a company
4. Able to learn something of the methods of operation of merchant banks in the city.

I wanted a job where I could make a very real contribution to a company.

What they had told me seemed credible, although I did not take the time to do my own research to substantiate their assertions. I reasoned that their backgrounds indicated that they should know what they were doing with their products in the market, and that the merchant bank would have verified this capability. My one major doubt was that they were trying to do too much in too many different markets. Even so, I thought that as they stood they had an even chance of being successful, and that my presence might make the odds more favourable. I decided then that joining them would be worth the risk.

EVENTS AT HYPER DYNAMICS

When I actually joined the company I was left very much to my own devices. I started prowling through their accounts and order books in an attempt to establish some financial picture of the actual situation. On a current basis their financial situation was really poor, but because they had a bank overdraft facility available to them, the overall situation was not too bad. I put some numbers to a set of sales forecasts and these suggested that things were going to be all right. It was only when I realised that none of these sales predictions had even remotely been achieved in the past that I started worrying. My fears increased as I saw them failing to meet their current sales forecasts. Their previous talk about an order book had been their expectations rather than real orders.

After three weeks, I realised I was on to a bad wicket. They hadn't been doing very well at all. I asked myself the question, 'Can I expect any better from an organisation at this stage of its life?', and concluded that maybe I shouldn't expect any better. I made a decision then that although things were bad I would stay on for one year, as I was too curious to leave. The risk of the company folding didn't influence me at the time, as being single, I didn't have to worry about financial risk. I thought that if it did fold it would take less than one year and I could set out again.

At this time one of the original four decided to leave. He was a very competent and likable young man who wanted to do well in business and had made a useful contribution to Hyper Dynamics. His philosophies in life were similar to those of the managing director. Unfortunately, their ways of achieving certain goals were different, and this resulted in his leaving. I was very disturbed about the effect his departure would have on the company's external financial resources at a time when the company needed external financing. In such a risky venture I thought it important that management should be seen to be united. I tried to persuade him to stay but my efforts were to no avail. His departure bruised my concept that Hyper Dynamics might prove that a group of highly technically competent people could work together.

I now began to appreciate some of the internal managerial conflicts. The other two directors were rather strange people. The production manager was phenomenally intelligent in analysis, very articulate and had an endearing personality, but somehow lacked some of the common commercial virtues: for instance, he would change specifications from one machine to the next irrespective of product bulletin specifications. The other director also had a fantastic analytical ability, but was simply not an administrator, and he thought he was superfluous to the organisation.

The managing director directed the whole show. He tried to give lip service to group management, but this didn't work, because if he didn't get his own way he would argue until he won. They had an abysmal 'formal' set-up, in that there was never a meeting of all the directors. The managing director would gather information by having people in one at a time to talk to him, thereby gathering information from all over the organisation. He would then correlate the information, and make some prescription for behaviour for the forthcoming period. The men obviously thought that they were being traded off. He was crazy to put himself in such an autocratic position as the only information coordinator.

At the time I joined Hyper Dynamics, my judgement was that anyone who starts off in business on his own is a pretty tough cooky. The insistence of the managing director on refusing to delegate control confirmed this judgement, and I reasoned that he wouldn't delegate much control to someone who was new to the organisation. This turned out to be true in that initially I was only a sounding board for the managing director's ideas. I took my role as a noisy influence, and also as someone who was trying to do something for the company. Realising the risks involved by the company taking on too much, I tried to influence the strategy of the company and became involved in some petty financial rows with the managing director. This did not affect our overall working relationship, however.

My increased involvement and responsibility in the company came in a sense by default. As the sales projections were not being met, cash became tighter and tighter and it became necessary for us to seek further financing. A two-page prospectus was put out, which was very rough. The figures didn't have much substance at all because they had pushed them about to make them look like the figures people would like to see. The prospectus attracted a lot of interest, but of course when prospective financiers began asking more detailed questions about the prospectus figures we couldn't answer them because the figures didn't really resemble our current performance. Fortunately, one financier became interested and suggested 'we formalise a little', which gave us a much needed breathing space. This is where the crunch came, as at this stage no one in the company had a clear idea of where we wanted to go or what we wanted to do. It seemed that many of the electronic design engineers wanted the financing so they could live a bit longer and punch out a few more designs.

I took this opportunity to force out a strategy for them which was what I thought they and the firm would commit themselves to. The firm was distinctive because of the excellence of its electronic engineering staff. I thought it was important that any strategy made full use of this strength. However, the engineers couldn't do anything which involved a lot of routine and had a need to be creative. On talking to the engineers I found that what interested them and what they wanted was continued effort to be made at developing the computer. The computer being developed was a process control hybrid computer. This type of computing is relatively small scale and Hyper Dynamics should have been able to compete successfully by tailoring the computer to a specific process installation. It was also my belief that we would only be able to raise additional financing by demonstrating future product potential and the development of a new computer fitted this strategy. Thus my strategy was that the emphasis of the company's efforts should be directed towards developing the computer and its future market potential should be the basis of our prospectus for seeking additional financing. This led to some very fundamental conflicts with the managing director. He realised he had to put down something concrete in his proposal, and it had to be something he wanted to do. However he was trying all the time to make past results look good, in order to justify the initial money raised two years before, and by using these results to develop future forecasts to raise the additional financing. Unfortunately the company had not achieved past potential, and as one of the things financial analysts do when you are raising money is to wait three months to see if forecasts are being met, to my mind there wasn't any hope of raising money by rationalising past failures. I felt we must focus on something potentially good, and hope they would back potential for a second time. The conflict came to a head at a board meeting when we argued through until 4.00 am in the morning before I was able to persuade the other directors that the future of the company and its financing must be based on the potential of the computer. The managing director was still worried about the computer being used as a basis for seeking future financing because it wasn't his idea. Strangely though, this conflict did not affect our relationship; once the argument was finished, we didn't show any resentment to each other.

My role in the company by this time had changed considerably. I was the only person in the company capable of drawing up the financial details for the prospectus and they needed the financial expertise. I became front man for the company in negotiating the external financing. However, because of this, I couldn't really consider leaving. I was unhappy at this stage because I felt that I was being a bit irresponsible in making financial forecasts which I didn't personally believe in. I felt pretty convinced the computer project couldn't succeed, not particularly from a market point of view, but more from a belief that the men themselves were not the sort that could build up a big company.

I was working phenomenal hours and physically I was taking a beating. This was another big decision period, and eventually I decided to stay. I realised that, if I pulled out, potential financial backers would immediately ask why, with the presumable answer that he knows what's going on, he's a money man, and he doesn't think the proposition is a runner.

The decision to stay was also in many ways a cultural one—I don't like resignation as a way of behaviour when you cannot get your own way. I knew what was in front of me when I joined the company, and that it might not be successful. However, I didn't realise how disappointed and frustrated I would be when I found I was being involved in something unsuccessful. I would have been irresponsible to myself to go and it would have been a dishonest thing to do. I went in with my eyes open and had balance in my mind to the extent that if things went badly I would just have to stick it out. That's a funny attitude but it's just the way I was brought up—I had told them I would stay for one year, so stay I would. I think therefore there were three reasons for my staying

139

1. Responsibility as the only financial man to the other people
2. A certain curiosity still to see how the company went and how the banks worked
3. A perhaps misguided sense of fair play

We got partial financial backing for the development of the computer but the overall financial position of the company grew steadily worse. The company wouldn't change its objectives and so the only alternative was to cut costs through the labour force. Eventually resources dwindled to the stage where the company couldn't afford me, and I left; at which time there was only the managing director left of the original four.

POSTCRIPT

I feel I have learnt a number of things from this experience.

To enter the electronics industry, if you have a good idea, does not require a lot of commercial sense of investment, but if you are to stay in the industry with its rapid changes, you require large development expenses. Even though a government agency was financing most of the development costs on the computer, we still couldn't generate sufficient funds to keep the company going.

We spent a lot of time just trying to establish credibility, justifying ourselves to people we needed. We didn't have those things called contacts. People in the technological world thought our engineers were extremely good, but that is essentially only a subset of the commercial world. You have to be known as the best in your business first, able managers second, and overriding that, you must be known as men of integrity who can be relied upon. When people are putting money into a company, they have to feel confident that you will go out and do what you said you would.

I now appreciate how difficult it is to start off and build up a company in terms of sheer human effort. I used to work some phenomenal hours and found it extremely painful, as my health suffered and I like to keep myself in good shape.

On a more personal note, I won't expect as much of myself as a change agent in future, neither will I let a situation influence my judgement about leaving. If I saw that things were going badly in a future situation, I would forget about the other people and get out—the reason being that when the crunch came at Hyper Dynamics, those guys moved out so fast it was untrue.

I would not work in an organisation where I saw a man as self-confident and bloody-minded as the managing director was; I just couldn't tolerate that; I'm a bit bloody-minded myself. A man who does get something going even on a small basis really does put a lot of effort into it, and if he is successful, I think he is likely to feel very confident in his own thinking. I think that is the sort of person you are likely to find at the helm of any small 'first generation' organisation, so maybe what I am saying is that I would never work with another 'first generation' organisation. What I would do is work with a 'second generation' company, with people I can get on with or learn from, so that I can establish a personal credibility. I think it's very important to work with people who can work towards a common goal, even if they think differently about how to reach it, provided of course that they discuss it. You get a much better decision in the end, because it is considered from all angles.

My next job I would expect to fit into an overall style of living. What I ask myself is not how important is a business career or business work now, but how will it fit into my ultimate objectives? I also ask myself what would be the stages of reaching this ultimate, and I think I found out for myself that I would be happier if I took it a bit more slowly for a while. The carrot with Hyper Dynamics was to be sitting on the top of an organisation with a fair bit of money at an early age. At the moment, I want a bit more security, although ultimately I will take the same risk again. I am also trying to get myself a lot of contacts to help in finding a job because I feel that if a contact does refer you to someone else, you don't have to talk yourself into a position to prove that you are worth being considered.

EXHIBIT 1   Hyperdynamics Electronics Limited—Sales (£)

Year and Month		Total	Products	Consultancy	Imports
1968	September	—	—	—	
	October	150	—	150	
	November	920	870	50	—
	December	—	—	—	—
1969	January	—	—	—	—
	February	215	215	—	—
	March	4,867	3,813	1,054	—
	April	5,555	1,543	4,012	—
	May	4,019	2,202	1,817	—
	June	1,777	177	1,600	—
	July	3,663	2,063	1,600	—
	August	2,130	530	1,600	—
	September	7,790	2,590	5,200	—
	October	5,395	4,395	1,000	—
	November	4,244	2,720	1,524	—
	December	4,290	3,266	1,024	—
1970	January	8,994	6,491	1,510	993
	February	10,650	10,250	400	—
	March	2,698	1,540	—	1,158
	April	1,551	1,551	—	—
	May	1,751	1,056	280	415
	June	4,702	4,517	—	185

EXHIBIT 2 Hyper Dynamics Electronics Ltd.
Unaudited Profit and Loss Account
9.9.68 to 28.2.70

	£	£	£
SALES			
Products	38,835		
less discounts and bad debt allowance	(3,093)	35,742	
Hire of Hyper Dynamics products		937	
Consultancy fees		22,042	
NET SALES			58,721
DIRECT COSTS			
Products			
Purchase at cost	29,920		
Labour (directors & staff)	10,267		
Depreciation of plant	162	(37,349)	
Consultancy			
Purchase at cost	2,102		
Labour (directors & staff)	8,122	(10,224)	(47,573)
GROSS PROFIT			11,148
INDIRECT COSTS			
Selling and Administration			
Wages, salaries, training and welfare	21,666		
Telephone, postage, printing and stationery	7,258		
Lease of equipment	2,065		
Travelling and motor expenses	4,132		
Advertising and exhibitions	2,729		
Others	4,938	(42,788)	
RESEARCH AND DEVELOPMENT			
R & D expense written off	25,294		
less administration cost charged to R & D account	12,050	(13,874)	
Legal, financial and professional charges		(5,637)	(62,299)
NET LOSS			(51,151)

EXHIBIT 3 Hyper Dynamics Electronics Ltd.
Unaudited Accounts

Date	31.3.69	30.9.69	28.2.70	31.6.70*
	£	£	£	£
LIABILITIES				
Long term				
Share capital				
Issued and paid up	4,820	10,000	10,000	13,120
Long term loans unsecured	9,000	30,000	38,000	95,800
	13,820	40,000	48,000	108,920
Current				
Directors' current accounts	4,103	4,331	1,943	—
Trade creditors	3,821	5,281	8,638	32,581†
Expense creditors	992	1,734	9,365	—
Outstanding hire purchase liability	2,278	4,033	4,101	3,996
Bank overdraft	—	—	5,682	14,013
Directors' PAYE reserve	816	1,277	1,757	—
	12,010	16,657	31,486	50,590
TOTAL LIABILITIES	25,830	56,657	79,486	159,510
ASSETS				
Fixed				
Motor vehicles	2,864	7,116	8,781	11,349
Plant and machinery	964	1,292	2,280	3,090
Lease of office	550	550	550	1,652
Furniture and fittings	258	340	600	1,007
less: accrued depreciation.	130	890	1,692	2,910
	4,507	8,409	10,518	14,188
Current				
Loans, short term	435	—	—	—
Stock and work in progress	3,082	13,296	12,681	33,517
Debtors	6,699	14,281	17,801 ⎱	22,956
Prepayments and reserves	342	1,591	3,745 ⎰	
Cash in hand	1,890	2,971	—	265
	12,467	32,138	34,227	56,683

Deferred expense

Start-up costs	323	323	323	427
R & D not written-off and other costs capitalised	1,500	5,094	12,222	482
	1,823	5,417	12,545	909
Profit and loss account adverse balance	7,032	10,692	22,194	88,157
TOTAL ASSETS	25,830	56,657	79,486	159,510

* The 31.6.70 accounts do not appear to have been prepared on the same basis as the earlier accounts.

† This figure covers all current liabilities other than those detailed.

13 Michael Parsons*

'Soda or water?' asked Michael Parsons. 'You know, Don, it's incredible, almost frightening when you are closing in on forty, how the future can change almost completely in a little more than a year. And it certainly feels strange to be thinking seriously about leaving the company after fifteen years.'

Donald Anderson accepted his drink, nodded his thanks and frowned. Having just returned to England on leave after nearly three years abroad, he had been looking forward to hearing his friend's news; neither man enjoyed writing letters. Now, he was not so sure, since it was obvious from Parsons's statement and expression that something was disturbing him greatly.

The two men had first met nearly twenty years earlier, at university. Although their subsequent careers had led in very different directions they remained good friends. Parsons had proved to be a very good salesman and an even better sales manager. Anderson had been pleased, but not surprised, to hear of the other's initial promotion to a general management position in 1965. After a year as assistant general manager in one of his company's larger plants, Parsons was selected to attend a three-month business school executive development programme, sponsored by his company.

Anderson left the country in March 1967 before the programme had ended: they met for a farewell dinner and Parsons had insisted upon buying champagne, because he had just heard that he was to become a plant manager on his return. 'A really great opportunity,' he told Anderson, 'it's been a loser for years. I can't wait to get my hands on it—and to see if some of the ideas I've picked up on this course make sense in the real world! Bill Martin, the division manager, is well known for leaving his plant managers pretty well alone to get on with their jobs, so long as they produce, which is fine by me. As regards my plant, I've heard that he has more or less given up hope that it will ever climb out of the red.'

Remembering Parsons's enthusiastic reaction to the news of that promotion, Anderson settled back in his chair and suggested that the other bring him up to date with his activities. 'As I recall,' he said, 'in 1967 Janet wrote on your Christmas card that she seldom saw you but that you appeared to be enjoying yourself. A year later she said that you'd had a promotion and that now she saw more of you, which sounded good to me.'

Parsons

It was, Don, but it might have been ever better. In fact, if things had turned out as I had been quietly praying they would, I might even have broken down and written that second card myself! But that's getting ahead of the story.

When I got back from the course, it took me nearly four months to fully understand and analyse the whole operation at my plant. There were no glaring weaknesses. If there had been I am sure they would have been spotted and put right, long before I got there. Rather, the complete system was a tangled patchwork of conflicting policies and uncoordinated procedures. Perhaps most important of all, there was a general atmosphere of 'what's the use?' I think the people had almost come to believe that, no matter what they did as individuals, the plant overall would continue to be unprofitable.

With a morale problem of that sort I'm sure it is a help to be a new face at the top. Anyway, I was pleased with the wholehearted acceptance of my ideas for change, throughout the plant, and by the way everyone set out to make them work. It took us another six months, but we made it; after February 1968 we were in the black to stay.

Anderson (smiling)

And you were pleased to find that you still had a wife and family.

Parsons

You're dead right! Curiously, I had to chase some chaps a little harder than before—I think they had lost a bit of perspective in the struggle to beat the breakeven bogey,

---

* Copyright © London Business School 1970

145

which for them had become an end in itself—but at least I would now get home most evenings before the children were in bed.

Also, we could do some entertaining and get to know people in the neighbourhood. As you know, we moved here when I became an assistant plant manager but, with getting on top of that whole new job, being away on that three-month programme and then licking my own plant into shape, there wasn't much time to play bridge or give elegant little dinner parties. Janet had met one or two people of course, but we had done very little together for two years or more. She knew it was an important period for me and never really complained but I knew she was beginning to wonder whether being a plant manager was forever synonymous with an eighty-hour week.

Consequently, I didn't say anything to her a few months later, after Bill had told me in confidence that there was a vacancy coming up at division management level and he had put me up for it. I really wanted that job, Don. It would be tough, but I believed I could do it and, in time, do it well. Not only that, I don't mind admitting I would have got a hell of a kick out of being made division manager at the age of thirty-eight—the average age of that group being forty-nine.

Well, I didn't get it. I knew the fellow they appointed, Frank Cartwright, quite well; he's a good man and it's clear already that he will be a very capable division manager. He is forty-six, by the way.

Anderson
Were you surprised by not getting the job?

Parsons
I can't honestly say that I was. I don't know whether or not Frank and I were the only two candidates, although Bill did give me that impression in our discussion, after he had told me that I was being promoted 'although not to the position that we might have liked to see you in'—he really can be a little pompous at times! Frank has been with the company ten years longer than I have and had managed two of the plants in that division, whereas I had no experience there, although I'm not convinced that would have been a major drawback.

But that is not really the point: what matters most is that now, unless anything quite unforeseen happens, I don't think there will be another such opportunity for seven or eight years. And I know I can't stand Draper for that long.

Anderson
Who is Draper and why has he got you so worked up?

Parsons
He's my boss and appears to be determined to prevent me from doing my job, as I think it should be done.

As I said earlier, when Bill Martin had to tell me I had not got the division opening he still had a promotion, maybe a consolation prize, for me. On 1 September 1968 I was to become plant manager at Amberton. It took me a little while to get over being disappointed but when I had, I realised that I had the top position at plant level. One of the older plants, Amberton, was due for complete overhaul and significant expansion over a six-year period, after which time it would be the largest, most modern and best equipped plant in the company.

Anderson
An important and interesting job, it seems to me.

Parsons
Yes, but unfortunately the decisions are not all mine: the classic situation of responsibility without corresponding authority. For instance, it is up to me to coordinate and analyse forecasts of market demand and translate these into capacity and capital equipment requirements. Then the major items have to be discussed with, and approved by, the division manager.

Very early in the game, I discovered that any attempt at 'discussion' was disastrous. 'I don't want to hear what your problems are,' he would say, 'I want to hear what you are going to do about them.' So I gradually stopped raising any questions and seeking his opinion, instead I would check all my assumptions and calculations at least twice, then go in with my conclusions and recommendations and fight for them. For a while there was very little fighting involved, but then, more and more, he started to ask how I could be sure of my predictions and estimates of future sales and industry trends. 'You marketing types are all the same' was an opening phrase I grew to detest! It invariably preceded a judgmental pronouncement that 'based on my experience, I think we should be a little less optimistic'. He was production manager at the Amberton plant something like twenty years ago, and sometimes I swear he sees the world still as he did then.

His latest gambit is to postpone decisions which I have to put up to him and which require prompt action. There are no obvious reasons for these delays and no explanations offered. The really infuriating thing is that he is not upsetting the head office timetable for the whole project. They see the construction, alterations and equipment installation taking five more years to complete, with a further three years being required to get everything running smoothly. In eight years time he will be up to retirement age: I'm convinced he sees this as a fitting capstone to his long and honourable service under the company colours.

Anderson
And do I sense that you think the project could be completed earlier, upsetting Draper's grand finale?

Parsons
Right, Don, damn right it could: probably in five years, certainly in six.

Anderson
Have you tried to convince Draper of this?

Parsons
Not just Draper—although as you might guess, he could not, or would not, accept my reasoning—I've been to the top. The whole Amberton project is really the managing director's brainchild, and the old man comes down once every three or four months to see for himself how things are going. I thought about it for a long time and eventually I decided I owed it to him to speak my mind. I told him what I thought, deliberately playing down the difficulties with Draper, although when he asked me whether or not we had discussed a possible telescoping of the timetable I had to say we had, and had disagreed.

The old man listened very carefully, asked some sharp questions which showed he recognised the critical issues, and said he would 'give careful consideration to my views'. I thought I might have convinced him, but when he next came around he merely said that he was pleased with progress to date and satisfied with the existing timetable. Not only that, he told me that Draper had told him that I was doing a good job and that he enjoyed working with me!

So there I was, stuck. I respected their differing points of view, but was becoming increasingly convinced that they were wrong. It seemed that head office was happy and convinced all was well, while I was becoming increasingly frustrated, and my job was becoming increasingly difficult. All of which seemed unlikely to change, except for the worse, for perhaps eight years, by which time I would be forty-seven.

Anderson
Yes, I can see that the prospect isn't as satisfying as it might be. But if you stick it out until then and continue to do a good job, in line with their expectations, I should think you would have an inside track on a division management position. You can spend more time with your family because you're under less pressure at the office than you would put upon yourself, if it was up to you to call all the shots, and more time doing things and developing friendships in the local community. You've always said the company pays pretty well. Could you do as well, or better, anywhere else?

Parsons
That's the very question which I asked myself a few weeks ago, after my last meeting with the m.d. And I realised that I had to try and find the answer pretty quickly. In a year's time maybe, or less, in many ways it might well be too late to ask it.

For one thing there's the children's schooling. You know the problems we've always had with Katharine. Well, she started at the High School this term and just loves it. Naturally we are both very relieved, especially Janet, who has had to cope with all the tears and tantrums and wails of 'But I can't go today, Mummy, I really do feel sick'. If she has settled down at last, would a move unsettle her all over again? I just don't know. Then there's Roy, who continues to frustrate his teachers, and his parents, by relying upon his innate ability, making just enough effort to get by. I've tried to talk to him but failed completely to convince him that he should set his own standards, and do his best at all times, even when the competition isn't there to stretch him. Here there is no eleven-plus and we are lucky in so far as there is a good eleven-to-eighteen comprehensive; although things might get sticky in a hurry if Roy's placement, following a move, depended entirely upon his headmaster's report.

Then there is the question of my pension. The company operates a non-transferable scheme and many firms are understandably reluctant to accommodate men who are, say, over forty when they join; while it wouldn't be worth my while to get in much less than twenty years with the scheme that will ultimately provide the company contribution.

Concerning my actual job at the present time, if I am going to leave it would certainly be fairer to the company—and to by successor—to do so sooner, rather than when the project is nearer completion.

Similarly, as time goes by we would get much more heavily involved with the community, while at present we are still almost newcomers and relative outsiders. So all in all, it seems to me that 'If it were done when 'tis done...'

Anderson
Yes, I see what you mean, although I'm not sure that the case for a move is yet proven. Do you have any specific openings to consider.

Parsons
Two opportunities have opened up recently, and one reason why I am bending your ear so much this evening is that I have to straighten out my own thinking sufficiently to make a sound, albeit a difficult decision within the next week or so.

The first came via an executive head-hunting organisation from such an unexpected source that it was a while before I could consider it seriously: it's a division manager's job with Hancock and Williams, our major competitors! Specifically, it is the division that competes with Bill Martin's, so as you might expect, when I was working for him I analysed that outfit quite thoroughly. In my judgement, they are coasting on their reputation and it is only because they grabbed such a commanding lead in market share over the rest of us, back in the late forties and early fifties, that they are still number one. As it is, we've climbed to within a few percentage points of them, which should never have happened. I certainly wouldn't have let things slide like that if I'd been in charge. The potential is still there and I think I could sort things out, so that it was realised. It wouldn't be easy—Bill's no pushover and he's got the bit between his teeth now—but it is the sort of challenge I would love to take up.

But therein lies the problem. Not only would I be going over to the chief opposition that I have been battling against, as a company man, for the whole fifteen years of my career, but I would be going head to head against a man I've worked for, whom I like and respect, who helped me become a good plant manager and showed me, by example, how I might become a good division manager. Much of the success I might have would be due to him, yet that same success would be to his cost.

Financially, the offer is extremely attractive, no matter how you look at it, and all round prospects are certainly as good as where I am, plus the fact that I would be (starting) at one, critical, level higher in the organisation hierarchy. Also, we would not have to move.

Anderson
I can see what you mean by a tough decision! Does the other choice seem any easier to resolve?

Parsons
In some ways, yes, but overall I think it is more complex, because of the greater number of uncertainties involved.

Many years ago, Marfax Engineering used to be one of my largest accounts. I was always struck by the attractiveness of its location, in a small country town, and by the pleasantness of its people; maybe it's a trite phrase, but it was a real pleasure to do business with them. I got to know Arthur Hammond, the managing director and chairman, quite well; he appeared to like me from the time we first met and we have kept in touch over the years. He founded the company just after the war and has run it almost single-handed. There are a couple of capable ex-engineers in management positions and a good accountant, but only recently, as the company has grown, has the need become apparent for more professional management, if you will.

Well, Arthur has decided to give up running the company full time and has asked me to come in as managing director; he will continue as chairman. He told me, and I believe him, that none of his present management group wants the job, although they would be happy to continue under whoever he likes to bring in—which tells you something of how his people think about him.

It is still a small company, with a current turnover less than a fifth of that of the Amberton plant. The growth potential is good, however, and I think I would have a pretty free hand to do what I want, and of course, at its present size it wouldn't take one long to get to know the whole company, it business and its people inside out.

Immediately, it would mean a cut in salary, not enough to really affect our standard of living, I don't think, but a cut nonetheless with respect to my present job; compared with Hancock and Williams of course, the difference would be quite substantial. And there is no pension fund. On the other hand, there are profit sharing and option schemes which, given the growth potential I mentioned, and if I am any good as a managing director, should enable me to come out later on considerably better off than I could by staying put or going with Hancock and Williams. It would also mean moving to the country, which would be fine as far as I'm concerned but Janet has always preferred city life. We would be very close to my family, which again I would like and my parents would love to see more of their grandchildren. But as you know, Janet has never really got along with my mother. My commuting would be cut from an hour and a half at the mercy of public transport to a ten-minute drive.

Schools? No problem for Katharine, assuming she has not become over-emotionally attached to the High School, and Roy could probably be squeezed into the local prep., although with his record as a 'scraper' it is by no means a certainty. From what little I know of it though, I am not impressed with the only independent school nearby—and the state schools are a write-off—so we could well have to think of a boarding school, weekly or otherwise. I acknowledge my middle-class prejudices against boarding schools but, seriously, I'm not sure at all that it would be the best type of schooling for that boy.

I suppose everyone thinks that he wants to run his own small company, at some stage in his life, and maybe that sort of grass is always greener. But perhaps it is also easier to slip up and fall flat on your face, and harder to pick up the pieces, particularly as one gets older.

So there you have it, and right now I'm damned if I know what to think!

Anderson
I'm sure I wouldn't either. Have you talked it over with Janet yet?

Parsons
No, to be frank I was waiting to run through it all with you, to help me sort it out in my own mind before getting her involved. Because I want to be able to lay it out for her as clearly, completely and objectively as I can. This will probably be the most important business decision of my career. This time I don't just want her to express an opinion, I want her to think it out and tell me what sort of life she wants to live, and to share, for the next twenty years, in all probability.

Thanks Don, you've been a grand listener. And give me that glass—if anyone ever earned another drink it was you tonight!

14 Crown Company*

Mr Edward Woodstock had recently received word of his appointment as general manager of plant X, one of the older established units of the Crown Company. As such, Mr Woodstock was to be responsible for the management and administration at plant X of all functions and personnel except sales.

The Crown Company conducted marketing activities throughout the United Kingdom and in certain foreign countries. These activities were directed from the head office by a director in charge of sales.

Manufacturing operations and certain other departments were under the supervision and control of a deputy managing director. These are shown in Exhibit 1. For many years the company had operated a highly centralised-functional type of manufacturing organisation. There was no general manager at any plant; each of the departments in a plant reported on a line basis to its functional counterpart at the head office. For instance, the personnel manager of a particular plant reported to the director in charge of personnel at the head office, and the plant accountant to the financial controller, and so on.

Mr Woodstock stated that in the opinion of the top management, in particular the managing director, deputy managing director and the sales director, the record of plant X had not been satisfactory for several years. The board had recently approved the erection of a new plant in a different part of the city and the use of new methods of production. It was anticipated that the relocation of plant X would take place quite shortly after Mr Woodstock's appointment as general manager. Lower costs of processing and a reduced manpower requirement at the new plant were expected. Reduction of costs and improved quality of products were needed to maintain competitive leadership and gain some slight product advantage. The proposed combination of methods of manufacturing and mixing materials had not been tried elsewhere in the company. Some features would be entirely new to employees.

According to Mr Woodstock the top managment of the Crown Company was beginning to question the advisability of the central control of manufacturing operations. The board had consequently decided to test the value of a decentralised operation in connection with plant X. They apparently believed that a general management representative in plant X was needed if the new experiment in manufacturing methods and the required rebuilding of the organisation were to succeed.

Prior to the new assignment Mr Woodstock had been an accounting executive in the financial controller's department of the company. From independent sources the case writer learned that Mr Woodstock had demonstrated analytical ability and general administrative capacity. He was generally liked by people; however, although he was personally acquainted with the head office executives, Mr Woodstock had met few plant personnel. From top management's point of view he had an essential toughness described as an ability to see anything important through. By some at the head office he was regarded as the company's efficiency expert. Others thought he was a perfectionist and aggressive in reaching the goals that had been set. Mr Woodstock was aware of these opinions about his personal behaviour.

Mr Woodstock summarised his problem in part as follows: 'I am going into a situation involving a large number of changes. I will have a new plant; new methods and processes but most of all I will be dealing with a set of changed relationships. Heretofore all the heads of departments in the plant reported to their functional counterparts in the head office. Now they will report to me. I am a complete stranger and in addition this is my first assignment in a major "line" job. The men will know this.'

'When I was called into the deputy managing director's office to be informed of my new assignment he asked me to talk with each of the functional members of his staff. The directors in charge of production, traffic and personnel said they were going to issue all headquarters instructions to me as plant general manager and they were going to cut off their connections with their counterparts in my plant. The other head office executives admitted their functional counterparts would report to me in line capacity. They should obey my orders and I would be responsible for their pay and promotion. But these executives proposed to follow the common practice of many com-

---

* Copyright © London Business School 1970.

panies of maintaining a dotted line or advisory relationship with these men. I realise that these two different patterns of head office plant relationships will create real administrative problems for me.'

Exhibit 2 shows the organisation relationships defined in these conferences.

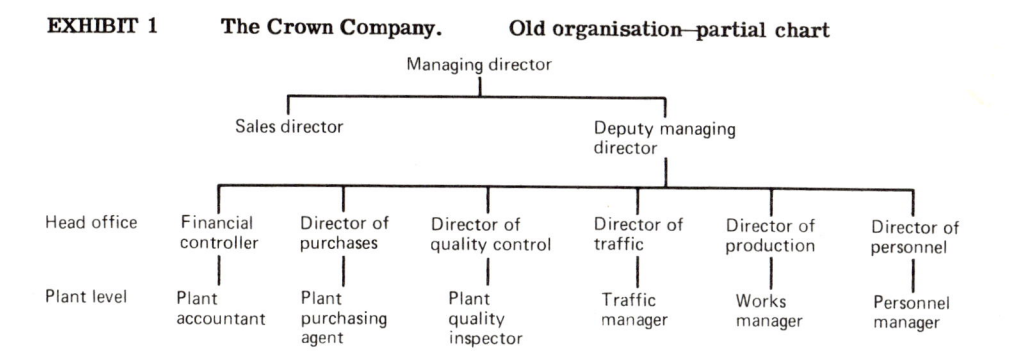

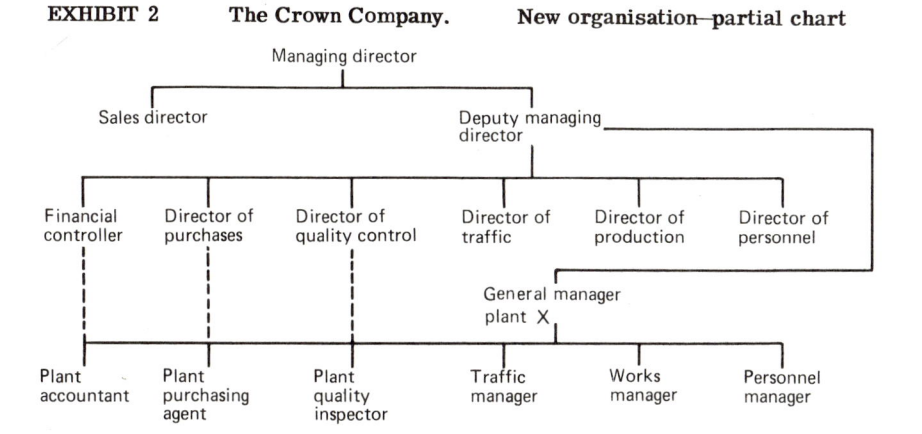

EXHIBIT 1   **The Crown Company.**   **Old organisation—partial chart**

```
                        Managing director
                               |
              ┌────────────────┴────────────────┐
         Sales director                  Deputy managing
                                             director
                                               |
        ┌──────────┬──────────┬──────────┬──────────┬──────────┐
Head    Financial  Director   Director   Director   Director   Director
office  controller of         of quality of         of         of
                   purchases  control    traffic    production personnel
           |          |          |          |          |          |
Plant    Plant      Plant      Plant      Traffic    Works      Personnel
level    accountant purchasing quality    manager    manager    manager
                    agent      inspector
```

EXHIBIT 2   **The Crown Company.**   **New organisation—partial chart**

```
                        Managing director
                               |
              ┌────────────────┴────────────────┐
         Sales director                  Deputy managing
                                             director
                                               |
        ┌──────────┬──────────┬──────────┬──────────┬──────────┐
  Financial  Director   Director   Director   Director   Director
  controller of         of quality of         of         of
             purchases  control    traffic    production personnel
      :         :          :          |          |          |
      :         :          :       General manager
      :         :          :        plant X
      :         :          :          |
  ┌───┴─────┬───┴──────┬───┴──────┬───┴──────┬──────────┬──────────┐
  Plant     Plant      Plant      Traffic    Works      Personnel
  accountant purchasing quality   manager    manager    manager
            agent       inspector
```

151

15 Burton Group Limited*

The Burton Group, first incorporated in 1929, was the largest retailer and manufacturer of men's outerwear in Great Britain in 1972. In addition the company was engaged in a variety of other retailing interests. Sales in 1971 exceeded £80 million, yielding record pre-tax profits of £7.43 million (for recent financial performance see Exhibits 1 and 2). The company owned or leased over 1,000 properties in the UK and in France, including some 600 retail stores and fifteen factories, engaged in the sale and manufacture of men's outerwear, over 100 women's fashion stores, and four manufacturing units and some seventy-five retail outlets for office equipment. In all the Group employed 27,000 people in the United Kingdom.

After successfully building the group over half a century, the death in 1952 of Sir Montague Burton had left the company with a dearth of management at all levels. To meet the situation, the board decided to acquire another multiple tailor, Jackson the Tailor. This group, smaller but similar in origins and philosophy, was controlled by the Jacobson family who took over the management of Burton for the next sixteen years.

In 1967, however, the board was again looking for new managers. Following government prevention of a merger with another multiple tailor, the board spent the next two years searching for an entirely new management team. In June 1969 they announced the appointment as chief executive of Ladislas Rice, a former Harvard MBA and management consultant, who had been chief executive of the Minerals Separation Company. Mr Rice, who subsequently became joint chairman of the Group with Mr Raymond Burton (the son of the founder and holder of the majority of the voting stock), was responsible for launching the group on a new strategy of becoming a group of specialist retail chains, each with a clearly defined market and distinctive face to the public.

The case describes the formulation and implementation of this strategy, discussing in turn the history of the organisation, the changes introduced since 1969, the outlook for the future and the situation as of January 1972.

COMPANY HISTORY

Montague (later Sir Montague) Burton opened his first shop in Chesterfield in 1901, with £100 borrowed from a relative. Initially, he sold a full range of men's and boy's clothing. The young outfitter then embarked on a radical new policy. In the early years of this century the men's suit market was sharply divided: ready-to-wear in a very limited range for the working men; and made-to-measure for the more affluent. Burton's crucial decision was to supply made-to-measure suits at the low price end of the market.

To carry out this new policy Burton contracted at first with a small Leeds clothing manufacturer to cut, sew and make-up the suits his customers began to order. By 1910 this supplier could no longer cope with the demand, so Burton opened his own workshops. He operated on the principle of maximising turnover on a modest profit margin.

From early on Montague Burton prided himself on paying good wages and providing good working conditions. He also attempted to build up a reputation for quality, so that satisfied customers would return. By the outbreak of the First World War he had laid the foundations of a multiple tailoring business.

Montague Burton grew fast during the war, winning large contracts for providing military uniforms. After the war it was decided to consolidate the company's manufacturing interests, and a large site was acquired in the outskirts of Leeds. The group's principal factory was still situated there.

In February 1929 the company went public. It was capitalised at £4 million. Two million 7 per cent preference shares at £1 each were put on offer; the 4 million 10s. Ordinary shares were taken up by Montague Burton himself. The company then had 300

---

* Copyright © Manchester Business School 1972

EXHIBIT 1 The Burton Group. Ten-year operating summary (£ thousands)

	1962	1963	1964	1965	1966	1967	1968	1969	1970	1971
Sales	44,300	45,880	48,591	52,422	57,273	60,973	65,605	68,309	70,264	80,049
Depreciation	736	854	899	993	1,128	1,232	1,341	1,303	1,405	1,583
Debenture and loan interest	160	477	536	528	512	488	474	458	685	1,227
Bank interest, etc.	274	109	80	189	334	503	311	254	494	681
Net profit before tax	3,255	3,160	3,627	4,227	4,413	4,952	6,543	7,188	6,280	7,426
Tax	1,722	1,655	2,063	1,645	1,711	2,020	2,847	3,386	2,824	2,886
Profit attributed to parent company	1,527	1,500	1,562	2,581	2,701	2,930	3,687	3,795	3,449	4,531
Retained profits	641	611	563	771	892	941	1,639	1,672	1,481	2,344

Source: Annual Reports

EXHIBIT 2

The Burton Group—Balance sheets for fiscal years 1962-71 consolidated (£ thousands)

	1962	1963	1964	1965	1966	1967	1968	1969	1970	1971
CURRENT ASSETS										
Stocks	10,271	9,835	10,864	11,418	13,273	12,975	12,298	14,545	16,241	21,155
Debtors and Prepayments	4,392	5,111	5,563	6,532	8,238	9,731	9,584	11,121	12,507	15,724
Investments	123	123	150	150	120	100	—	—	—	—
Cash	371	895	347	413	474	538	570	539	518	573
Total current assets	15,157	15,964	16,924	18,513	22,105	23,344	22,452	26,205	29,266	37,452
CURRENT LIABILITIES										
Creditors and accruals	4,826	4,657	4,865	5,485	6,883	5,822	7,039	6,544	7,015	10,159
Bank overdraft	2,593	1,241	1,654	2,880	5,963	7,534	2,424	3,981	7,430	8,082
Taxation	2,738	2,290	2,132	2,067	1,952	1,854	2,135	2,939	3,511	3,077
Dividends	597	599	709	785	1,337	1,516	1,575	1,650	1,594	1,823
Total current liabilities	10,756	8,787	9,360	11,217	16,134	16,716	13,173	15,114	19,550	23,141
Net current assets	4,402	7,177	7,564	7,296	5,971	6,628	9,279	11,091	9,716	14,311
FIXED ASSETS										
Freehold and leasehold properties	48,941	49,122	49,551	51,141	52,195	52,117	52,153	52,593	52,809	53,138
Branch fixtures and fittings and shop fronts	3,032	3,170	3,237	3,648	4,208	4,414	4,160	4,014	4,480	5,451
Factory plant, equipment and motors	1,691	2,110	2,315	2,691	3,273	3,844	3,803	3,710	3,845	4,648
Investments	238	292	319	207	128	119	149	146	138	127
Total fixed assets	53,902	54,698	55,759	57,696	59,805	60,493	60,265	60,453	61,372	63,364
Ordinary shares (50p)	2,229	2,229	2,229	2,229	2,229	2,229	2,229	2,229	2,229	2,229
'A' Ordinary shares (50p)	15,604	15,604	15,677	15,677	15,677	15,677	15,677	15,677	15,688	16,005*
Preference shares	2,970	2,970	2,970	2,970	2,970	2,970	2,970	2,970	—	—
Reserves	29,551	29,726	31,375	33,128	34,290	35,286	36,569	38,273	39,196	31,335
Future tax	1,244	1,773	1,750	1,820	1,781	2,020	3,386	4,056	2,843	3,206
Minority interests	173	166	187	171	158	178	182	151	126	196
Investment grants	—	—	—	—	—	248	263	286	331	303
Loan capital	6,531	9,406	9,133	8,996	8,670	8,513	8,267	7,911	10,575	23,974
Total capital employed	58,304	61,875	63,322	64,992	65,775	67,122	69,544	71,554	70,988	77,675

Source: Annual Reports

* includes 545,000 'A' shares issued of which 515,000 part paid balance due in 6 years as part of executive share incentive scheme

shops in Great Britain and Ireland, with nearly 200 of its sites owned freehold, while the factory employed 6,000 people.

The group continued to expand throughout the depression. It took advantage of depressed property values to acquire High Street sites at bargain prices. During this period the group went into the manufacture of cloth for its own use and cloth production became a major operation.

The Second World War again provided the group with opportunities for expansion in manufacturing. The group supplied one-quarter of all the uniforms required by the British armed forces; it then switched its vast productive capacity to the manufacture of civilian suits for the returning troops.

After the Second World War, Burton made the first move towards diversifying its retail activities. In 1948, Burton acquired Peter Robinson Limited, a department store group specialising in ladies' fashions and founded in 1833. When Sir Montague Burton, as he had then become, died in 1952, the company was the largest multiple tailor in the world, with 616 retail branches, and a workforce of 10,000. Sir Montague had won an international reputation both for the introduction of modern methods into the clothing industry, and for his conduct of labour relations. But he had failed to provide for the management necessary to take the group forward in the increasingly competitive environment of the post-war period.

In order to introduce new management in the highest echelons of the company, Burton acquired Jackson the Tailor Limited. Jackson was a smaller multiple tailor (with about fifty shops) concentrated in the north. It, too, was a family firm dating from the beginning of the century. The Jackson founder, Moses Jacobson, had (like Montague Burton) launched his business on a £100 loan; now his sons, Lionel and Sydney, joined the Burton board. Lionel was eventually to become chairman, and Sydney joint managing director.

The acquisition of Jackson and the Jackson management, however, was only the preliminary to solving Burton's most pressing problems, and then devising a long-term strategy. Burton had suffered a set-back in 1952/3 due to a fall in the price of wool. The new management team decided to get out of cloth manufacture. This immediately removed the group from further exposure to the cyclical swings of the wool trade. It also showed an appreciation of the future course of textile development. For, with the disappearance of post-war austerity, men's clothing was slowly beginning to break out of its characteristic drab uniformity. Burton's customers were not yet fasion-conscious, but at least they were coming to demand a more adventurous range of cloth than that mass-produced in the group's weaving mills.

The other problem was the sheer size of the retail chain. When Sir Montague died, Burton had 616 retail branches, and Jackson brought in another fifty. A programme of rationalisation led to net closures of about 100 branches. Many of the retail outlets which were closed during the early 1950's were let out on 21-year leases which would revert in the early 1970's. Rationalisation of the retailing side of the group's activities, however, did not consist entirely of retrenchment. In 1961 the company acquired Browns of Chester, a well-established department store; and it also began to look at prospects in Europe. In 1963 a small menswear factory in France was acquired together with four shops.

Other moves included a mail order venture in 1964, and the following year the Peter Robinson interest was expanded by the acquisition of the Arthur Bennett chain of twenty-eight shops.

By 1966, Burton had become one of Britain's major retailing concerns with sales of £58 million. The Jackson management that had come in to fill the higher echelons itself now consisted largely of men nearing retirement. Once again the group had to look around for new blood: once again its recruitment and management training policies had proved inadequate. For so long as the garment producing industry was not geared to High Street trading, managers of the calibre necessary to run a vertically integrated enterprise of this size were not likely to be found in many retail chains.

Initially, the company attempted to solve the seccession problem by merger. Negotiations, which had first been considered in 1964, were restarted in 1966 with United Drapery Stores. This company was engaged in similar activities to Burtons and was of similar size. It was, however, more profitable and in addition had proven expertise in the management of women's fashion retailing and mail order. Burton was particularly weak in these areas, the Peter Robinson chain together with Brown's of Chester only making a 2.7 per cent return on capital while the Burton mail order operation was losing approximately £1 million per annum.

Both groups considered that substantial benefits could accrue from introducing UDS management expertise into Burton's activities, and terms for a merger were agreed subject to clearance by the Monopolies Commission in April 1967. In September 1967 the government, on the recommendation of the Monopolies Commission, turned down the merger. The majority of the Commission considered that the merger could create 'risk to public interest resulting from the reduction of competition in the retail selling of mens outerwear, especially of men's suits'. The group thus had to find its own solution.

After the breakdown of the proposed merger with UDS the Burton senior management had to devote a considerable amount of attention to maintaining morale within the group—and to presenting a bold face to the outside world. Promises of higher turnover and increased profits were made, and the share price did not decline significantly. These promises were amply fulfilled. The spring of 1968 saw increased consumer spending in anticipation of tough government measures in the wake of devaluation.

In addition, the group benefited from the removal of the long-standing obstructions outside the Oxford Street store of Peter Robinson. In France lower export prices resulting from UK devaluation enabled turnover to be boosted by 19 per cent, and the venture moved into profitability. Even the mail order venture seemed to be doing rather better and losses were cut to £500,000. Increased cash flow and tighter stock control allowed the board to reduce the company's overdraft by £5 million.

In 1968 the directors decided to revalue their property assets which had last been valued in 1961. These assets were revalued at £71 million although they remained in the books at £52 million after depreciation. Return on capital on the book valuation had risen in 1968 to 1.5 per cent, yet shareholders criticised the reduced return based on the revised asset values. Nevertheless the revaluation strengthened the group's hand for the future. Management recognised a more active approach could provide scope for increased debt for future investment. The value of the property assets alone was well in excess of the stock valuation.

The problem of management succession remained. Many of the board were nearing retirement age and with the UDS merger barred the company had to find a new senior management team, and in particular a new chief executive. This proved no easy task.

The 1968-9 trading year was not as successful as the preceding one. Although some improvement occurred in sales, profits and margins, the tailoring business was slack. However the search for a new chief executive ended in June 1969 when Mr Ladislas Rice, a forty-three year-old Czech-born management consultant, accepted an offer to join the group. Rice was from outside the industry, having previously been chief executive of Minerals Separation. A Harvard MBA, with fourteen years' experience as a management consultant, Mr Rice was just the type of modern manager the board had been seeking.

MANAGEMENT REORGANISATION

Mr Rice's first decision was to launch his own search for a small, high calibre, top management team. This was begun in the two months between accepting his appointment and arriving at Burton to take up his duties as chief executive. On arrival he set up a small group headquarters in London for himself and his new team. This was deliberately removed from Burton's historic base in Leeds. 'If I was going to live on top of the shop,' Mr Rice said, 'I would have to see the shop steward every morning.'

While the incumbent managing director Sidney Jacobson had devoted a considerable amount of his time to labour relations, Mr Rice did not intend this to be his main role as chief executive. Further, while Mr Sidney Jacobson had been responsible for all major decisions relating to production and Mr Lionel Jacobson had been responsible for retailing activities, Mr Rice decentralised much of the responsibility for day-to-day operations and profits.

On 3 November 1969 a new corporate entity, the Burton Group Limited, was registered as the new name of, and successor to, Montague Burton Limited, with responsibility for that company and its subsidiaries. The Burton Group became in practice a holding company and its subsidiaries were grouped into operating divisions. Each division was regarded as a profit centre with its own chief executive responsible for divisional performance. The new organisation as of 1972 is shown in Exhibit 3.

THE GROUP EXECUTIVE

The small top management group at the new London headquarters consisted of no more than a dozen people including clerical staff. According to Mr Rice, 'The team concen-

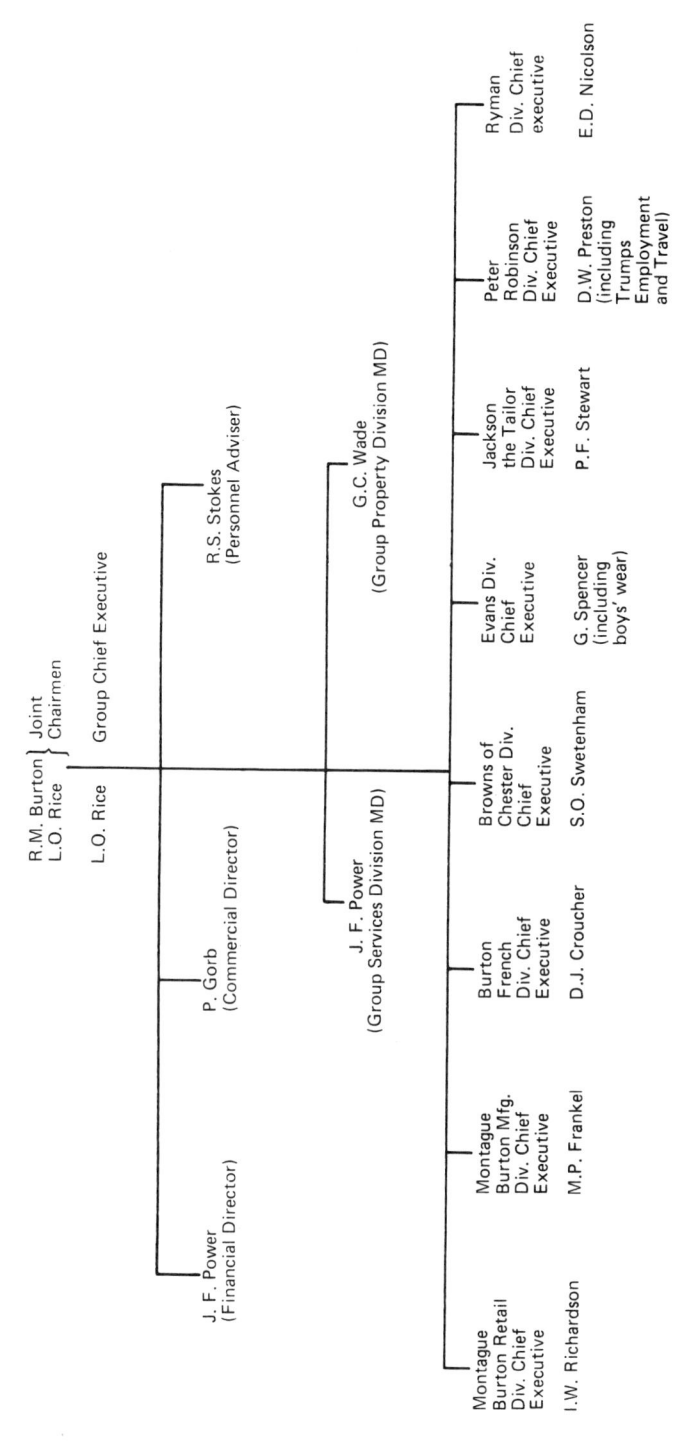

EXHIBIT 3 The Burton Group. Management structure

```
                                    R.M. Burton  ⎫ Joint
                                    L.O. Rice    ⎬ Chairmen
                                                 ⎭
                                    L.O. Rice
                                    Group Chief Executive
        ┌──────────────┬─────────────────┼─────────────────┬──────────────────┐
                                         │
   J.F. Power      P. Gorb          R.S. Stokes       J.F. Power         G.C. Wade
  (Financial      (Commercial      (Personnel       (Group Services    (Group Property
   Director)       Director)         Adviser)        Division MD)      Division MD)

┌──────────┬──────────┬──────────┬──────────┬──────────┬──────────┐
Montague   Montague   Burton     Browns of  Evans Div. Jackson    Peter        Ryman
Burton     Burton Mfg. French    Chester Div. Chief    the Tailor Robinson     Div. Chief
Retail     Div. Chief  Div. Chief Chief      Executive Div. Chief Div. Chief   executive
Div. Chief Executive   Executive  Executive            Executive  Executive

I.W.       M.P.        D.J.       S.O.        G. Spencer P.F.      D.W. Preston  E.D. Nicolson
Richardson Frankel     Croucher   Swetenham   (including Stewart   (including
                                              boys' wear)          Trumps
                                                                   Employment
                                                                   and Travel)
```

157

trated on matters of men and money; it was concerned with the groups overall strategy.' Conventional head office functions, including accounting, sales and marketing were still conducted from Leeds.

Mr Rice set up a small group executive committee consisting of himself and his three other key executives, Mr Peter Gorb, commercial director, Mr Jim Power, financial director and Mr Richard Stokes, personnel adviser. The groups chief communications officer, Mr Clifford Jupp, acted as secretary to the committee. With the exception of Mr Power these executives had all joined Burtons after Mr Rice's appointment. This committee planned and implemented the strategy of the Group. Mr Rice as chief executive was responsible for the group's performance to the board of directors, of which he was appointed joint chairman. Responsible to him were the chief executives of Burton's operating divisions.

The relationship among members of the committee was informal and Mr Rice deliberately shared his authority with his colleagues. 'We have a symbiotic relationship' was how one of them put it. 'We are the four faces of Rice.' Apart from the general informality of their working relationship, each member of the group executive had a broad area for which he was primarily responsible.

Mr Peter Gorb, former Harvard classmate of Mr Rice and the commercial director, had had long experience in the textile industry. He was Mr Rice's first appointment at Burton. He described his role as commercial director as a concern 'with our markets and our products.'

Specifically his task was to determine

what should be the distinctive faces of the Burton Group towards the public; and how the group should trade through its outlets;

the coordination of all meanswear retailing in the group, i.e. through the Burton, Jackson and French chains of shops; and in particular 'the balance of buying and selling relationship between manufacturing and retailing.'

the coordination of supplies: the Burton group had very large national and international purchasing resources—'this is when we make our gross profit. Product development was also highly significant.'

the shopping and consumer environment of the Group: 'What sort of places are Burton-owned shops to do business in? Are they in the right place?'

To carry out this fourfold task Mr Gorb could informally (through everyday liaison or formally (through his chairmanship of key committees) influence the commercial practice of the operating divisions, particularly the menswear divisions.

Mr Stokes was a member of the executive committee, because of Mr Rice's long-held conviction that the management of men was as important as the management of financial resources in running commercial enterprises. His brief was to ensure that never again would the Burton Group be in the position it was when it approached UDS. His immediate task was to recruit, from divisional managing director level downwards—with particular emphasis on the level immediately below managing director. Within a year fifty senior executives had been taken into the Group. Mr Stokes's second major task was to turn senior management into really professional management. This meant (ultimately) making sure that by the time an executive reached board level in one of the divisions he had served in two divisions and preferably in more than one functional capacity. This ideal, however, was still a long way from realisation.

This management development role required each operating division to have a strong personnel function. For example a special relationship existed between the personnel director and the divisional managing director (chief executive) of the Burton Tailoring division. The job specification for the post of personnel director in the division was to develop at board level the personnel function for 7,500 staff throughout the UK—covering every facet from labour relations to management development. The personnel director of an operational division was expected to aid divisional managing directors in a programme of individual performance improvement for senior staff. To further his policy Mr Stokes had set up a management centre for senior supervisor level and above, staffed by a director of studies and two tutors. This was not intended to be a permanent institution; its purpose was to instill certain precepts into a wide stratum of management within three years or so.

Mr Jim Power, financial director, was the only member of the group executive who was with Montague Burton before the arrival of Mr Rice. Formally he had five major responsibilities

> To determine the need for financial resources, develop techniques for their provision, and ensure for the Group the supply of adequate funds;
>
> To assist the Group chief executive in developing the planning activities of the Group, particularly in relation to long-range financial planning and to acquisition and merger studies;
>
> To report to the Group chief executive on the performance of the Group and divisions in the implementation of their agreed plans.
>
> To develop Group-wide policies and practices in respect of standard accounting and reporting procedures, coding, accounts classification, financial authority limits and financial control procedures.
>
> To provide to each of the divisions guidance and specialised services in planning, systems and procedures, data processing and distribution.

Describing the background to his task when he joined the newly-formed group executive, Mr Power said that the management information then available was rudimentary, slow and short on detail. Financial data, which might have to be used for control purposes was only available at top level. When Burtons had been a traditional made-to-measure business, the major decision affecting the group's results was cloth-buying at the beginning of the season—a matter of experience and judgement. Because only two or three people at the very top controlled ultimate profitability, this type of information was then probably sufficient.

But the market had changed very considerably in the previous decade: the proportion of made-to-measure to ready-to-wear business dropped from 80 per cent to 60 per cent. Success in the ready-to-wear business demanded considerable flexibility in the market place, high investment in stocks, and up-to-date data on prices and margins. In addition, the group was diversifying in other fields of retailing. All this, in turn, required sophisticated management information systems.

Thus, one of Mr Power's first tasks under the new regime was to create, as a separate profit/cost centre, a group services division, of which he became chief executive. Reporting to him were the company secretary, financial controller, treasurer, head of data processing and systems, head of long-range planning and the head of group warehousing and distribution. In some cases the functions were combined under one man.

Mr Power considered that treating each division as a 'business' in its own right could be taken too far. There was no overall group gain, for instance, in quoting rates for carrying Burton goods in Burton vehicles geared to showing a profit on transport, if the user division was thus forced to use a more competitive carrier outside the group. However, when a Burton vehicle had spare capacity, the transport section was encouraged to seek business from outside the group to fill it.

Mr Power did argue however that cash was a group resource. From this it followed that it should be managed on a group basis, optimising its use and cutting the cost of using it. Therefore the group services division managed the credit business of Burton's retailing division, with 500,000 accounts on a computer. For this service it made a charge to the retail division. Mr Power was also in the interim stages of moving from a divisional basis to a centralised basis for managing cash balances, since centrally-negotiated terms with a single clearing bank could bring large savings to the operating divisions. Again, it was intended that a service charge would be made to the divisions.

Apart from the executive committee, Mr Rice and his colleagues had a distrust of proliferating liaison committees; but there were some areas where a stream of decisions affecting different divisions were coordinated through committees, so that the Burton Group as a whole could reap the maximum benefit. An example of this was a committee to coordinate broad aspects of menswear retailing, with Mr Gorb as chairman, who frequently had to adjudicate between conflicting claims, 'taking a Group view'.

Much of the group executive's daily work was carried out on an informal basis: its members discussed issues with each other as and when they thought it appropriate and necessary. When the group executive committee did sit formally, each member was expected to, and did, have strong views on the various areas covered by his colleagues. 'It wouldn't work if we didn't get on,' members of the team admitted.

Suggestions that this 'structured informality' could confuse senior managers in the group's operating divisions were met by the claim that precedents had been quickly established. 'They generally know who to come to now,' it was said; 'and case history is being continually developed.' Mr Rice and his team believed that speed of response in running a complex group in a commercial environment outweighed more formal methods of communication and delegation.

THE OPERATING DIVISIONS

By 1972 the Burton Group had been divided into eight operating divisons, and two central divisions, each the responsibility of a chief executive accountable for profit performance. Four of these divisions were primarily concerned with the manufacture and retailing of men's outerwear in the United Kingdom and France, and this activity accounted for over 75 per cent of group sales and over 90 per cent of profits in 1971. Burton was the largest men's tailoring concern in Western Europe. Details of the group activities are shown in Exhibit 4.

In forming the divisions out of the cluster of companies which had made up the former Montague Burton interests, Mr Rice had taken a number of strategic decisions. First, he had split the Montague Burton retailing operation from the manufacturing interests. Historically the retail outlets had almost been regarded as order points for the integrated system of manufacturing plants. Second, an independent property division was created which was itself responsible for profit performance, thus early on confronting the retail divisions with demands for economic rentals. Third, the group services division was set up, responsible for distribution and warehousing amongst other things.

Mr Rice then concentrated on emphasising the role of retailing rather than manufacturing within the Group. 'The Burton Group,' he said,'is a group of specialist retail chains with supporting activities. Each retail chain has a clearly defined market and a distinctive face to the public. The Group has important property assets in the UK which it aims to use to optimum trading advantage through its retailing chains.'

Burton Retail

The largest interest of the Burton Group remained the men's outerwear market which the company serviced through its two main retail chains Burton Tailoring and Jackson the Tailor. The former of these two represented the retail function of what had formerly been the integrated Montague Burton retailing and manufacturing interest. The largest division in the Burton Group, Burton Tailoring, operated approximately 500 retail stores of various sizes in most major cities and towns, and overall the Group held about 25 per cent of the market for men's suits in the United Kingdom. The market for men's outerwear was undergoing substantial change in the late nineteen-sixties as the market moved away somewhat from made-to-measure clothing to ready-to-wear and consumers, especially the younger ones, demanded increasing emphasis on fashion.

When Mr Rice took up his position as chief executive, Mr Peter Gorb was immediately appointed managing director of the newly created retail tailoring division, a position he held until the end of August 1971. Mr Gorb saw his task as divisional managing director falling into three areas

> Building a team capable of buying and selling ready-made men's suits and outerwear, and in particular controlling the purchasing, sales and stocks of ready-to-wear garments.
>
> Establishing a distinctive 'face' to the consumer.
>
> Planning the staffing requirements of a widely dispersed retail team, to meet the changes brought on with a changing market and corporate strategy. He therefore decided to appoint three new assistant managing directors to manage the key areas of merchandising, sales promotion and stores operation, as shown in Exhibit 5.

The appointment of the assistant managing director merchandising was considered to be a key group appointment. Mr Ivan Richardson who was appointed came from Marks & Spencer and was responsible for the Burton Tailoring product line including

EXHIBIT 4 The Burton Group. Profit and sales breakdown (£000)

	Mens Tailoring UK		France and Belgium		Total		Other Fashion retailing		Mail order		Total	
	Sales	Profit	Sales	Profit	Sales	Profit	Sales	Profit	Sales	Profit	Sales	Profit
1968	NA	NA	NA	NA	56,373	7,487	6,452	311	2,780	(538)	65,605	7,260
1969	54,591	7,840	3,052	137	57,643	7,977	7,362	345	3,304	(428)	68,309	7,894
1970	55,859	7,583	2,675	73	58,534	7,656	7,882	189	3,848	(391)	70,264	7,454
1971*	NA	NA	NA	NA	63,356	5,633	16,497	587	—	—	80,049	6,106

* Excludes new ventures (sales £196,000, profits £114,000), and Property Division (income £2,949,000).

Source: Annual Reports

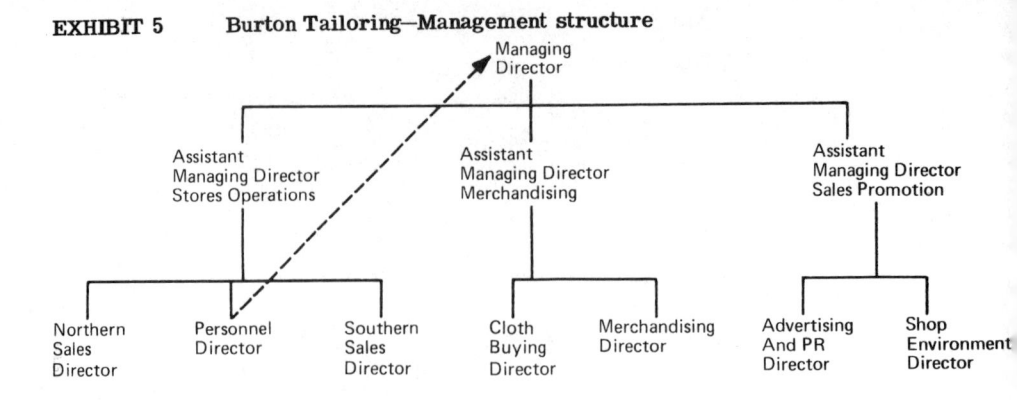

EXHIBIT 5 Burton Tailoring—Management structure

```
                              Managing
                              Director
                                 ↑
       ┌─────────────────────────┼─────────────────────────┐
   Assistant                  Assistant                 Assistant
   Managing Director          Managing Director         Managing Director
   Stores Operations          Merchandising             Sales Promotion
       │                          │                         │
   ┌───┼───┐                  ┌───┴───┐                 ┌───┴───┐
Northern Personnel Southern  Cloth    Merchandising   Advertising  Shop
Sales    Director  Sales     Buying   Director        And PR       Environment
Director           Director  Director                 Director     Director
```

purchase stock control, distribution, design and development. He succeeded Mr Gorb as divisional chief executive in 1971.

The assistant managing director dealing with sales promotion was responsible for advertising, window display, shop interiors and architecture and public relations. He had the key tasks of ensuring that Burtons was distinguishable from other tailors and seeing that such a distinctive image was consistent with the nineteen-seventies while not destroying entirely the image of Burton as a national institution.

The third assistant managing director appointed was in charge of stores operations. His immediate task was to ensure that a personnel function was established for the division with the direct object of recruiting and training amanagement. His longer-term and continuous responsibility however was to devise and institute new ways of selling merchandise and to run the shops.

Marketing Policy

Traditionally, the 500 or so Burton shops had been regarded as order points for the factories. Customers were shown a limited range of cloths and measured in the shops and their orders were then dispatched to the factory. Within three weeks or so the finished suit would arrive back at the shop. This meant that a few basic buying decisions by the factory management on cloth and colour—eighteen months ahead of the time at which a particular range of cloths was on offer to the customer—determined the stock of basic merchandise sold by Burton's retail outlets.

To introduce the flexibility necessary to sell successfully to customers who were both fashion-conscious and not prepared to wait three weeks for their merchandise, the first move was to establish the separation of the factory and the retail outlets, through the new divisional structure. 'The factories now produce what the shops say they can sell', was the new watchword.

The second move was to establish that cloth buying with all the concomitant ordering control over fibres, wool, synthetic or blends, over process, weaving or knitting, and over colour and design, was carried out by the retail division. Eventually it was hoped that, by close collaboration with the Yorkshire trade, the cycle from cloth buying to display in the stores and the intake of stock to the factory could be cut from eighteen to six months. As the division switched more of its business into the ready-to-wear suit market, this shorter cycle would become of increasing importance.

Third, the retail division was explicitly directed to optimise its return on capital. This meant that the shops, no longer order points for the factories, were to sell a wide range of men's clothing and accessories and to concentrate on overall profitability and not just high margins. Attention to traffic flow, display techniques, tactical pricing policies and the other tools of modern retail marketing were being employed.

The broad group philosophy of presenting through each division a distinct face to the public was particularly difficult to implement at Burton Tailoring. This was because very early on the new management found that the spread of its customers was considerably wider than had been traditionally believed. Research revealed that Burton Tailoring was selling more to AB consumers than had been expected. There were also regional differences in demand, which were particularly subtle in the made-to-measure business. There was also the difference in local reputation; in one town's High Street Burton might be considered very up-market; but have a rather different reputation a few miles away.

'There was a bit of Boots about us,' said Ivan Richardson, managing director of the division, 'a bit of Tesco and a bit of the specialised outfitter.' The problem, then, was to identify and create the right image for a wide number of differing people.

It was decided that the face which Burton Tailoring presented to the public need not be uniform. The basic criterion which had to be satisfied was a pre-determined rate of return on capital. To achieve this a number of experiments were made on a controlled basis. Several options were tried, including

Shops within shops

These could include special ready-to-wear units within traditional outlets, accessory 'boutiques', and so on.

One theme shops

These could be, for instance, ready-to-wear units only. They could compete with the Austin Reed type of store at one end of the market; or with the John Collier type at the other.

Mixed units

These could be on traditional lines, with more or less emphasis placed on ready-to-wear, made-to-measure and accessories.

Superstores

The group opened its first superstore in Leeds in February 1972. This embraced a number of the themes above and some others. It included a Top Shop, previously only in Peter Robinson Stores, for young women, a Mr Burt, offering a range of ready-to-wear menswear for the more fashion-conscious market, a traditional tailoring store, and a Director shop aimed at the higher price range of men's wear. In addition the store includes a section devoted to records, paperback books and cards.

The final pattern was still being worked out dependent on the results obtained from the experiments. It was possible that in future Burton Tailoring would replace its traditional nationwide, middle-of-the-road image not with any single uniform image, but with a variety of different styles, geared to different locations.

Just as the face to the public of Burton retailing division was the subject of considerable experiment, so too was the image of its merchandise. The current philosophy was to adopt a strategy of market segmentation. The division offered three ready-to-wear ranges—the New Director suit, the Town and Country suit and Mr Burt. The first two of these were aimed at the executive and higher price market. Mr Burt was in the words of Ivan Richardson, 'as many things as there are customers'. Launched in March 1971 in 120 branches, to the outside observer the Mr Burt suit presented a slightly 'trendy' appearance, youngish and 'with it'.

In addition the branches expanded the range of products they offered. Shirts, ties and knitwear were already sold in most branches, but the selection of other merchandise, and the establishment of house brands in other fields of men's clothing, was still the subject of review and experiment.

The division regarded its relationship with suppliers as an important part of the total marketing operation. Mr Ivan Richardson held the basic philosphy of close collaboration with suppliers by the retail division. As part of this philosophy the Burton group factories were treated as far as possible, without distorting the overall pattern of group operation, according to an arm's length relationship. The Burton manufacturing division was required to conform to standards set by the retailing division, just as any other supplier was required to do.

Burton Manufacturing

On 2 October 1969 Mr Martin Frankel, then production and personnel director of Daks Simpson,[1] was appointed managing director of Burton's newly formed manufacturing division. His initial responsibility was for eight factories (four in Yorkshire and four

---

* Daks Simpson is the clothing production subsidiary of S. Simpson Limited, the group owning the Piccadilly store.

in Lancashire), from which 10,000 employees turned out some two million suits a year.

The separation of Burton's manufacturing activity from the retail operations of the group was a key move in Mr Rice's initial strategy. The manufacturing division was to become a profit centre in its own right, with all that this implied in terms of planning, budgetary control and accountability.

In addition, Burton's factory management had to become market oriented. No longer were the group's 500 retail outlets to be order points for the factory: the retail division would become a customer in the market whose business might one day have to be won in more or less open competition. This move to an arm's length relationship would be intensified by the switch in the market from made-to-measure to ready-to-wear suits.

Translating this approach into practical terms, Mr Frankel said 'my job is to produce men's clothing, to quality standards and to the specifications required by my customers, largely the retail division, at the lowest cost and with the maximum efficiency'.

A number of formal objectives were laid down for Mr Frankel. These were

To ensure that manufacturing facilities reflected the changing requirements of customers.

To develop the basis upon which substantial increases in productivity could be achieved.

To reduce unit costs.

To improve quality, design and fit to required levels.

To achieve a delivery period of 3 weeks and to reduce overdue orders to an acceptable level.

To implement these objectives, Mr Frankel built up his management team. Three regional controllers reported to him in a line relationship and a number of staff functions were responsible to him including the technical director, the personnel and industrial relations director, the financial controller, the production control director, the contract departments manager, responsible for contract and uniform business, and the chief engineer.

Mr Frankel had three major areas where strategic decisions had to be implemented. These were specialisation and transfer pricing, labour, and garment technology.

Specialisation

The largest single factor in the men's suit market was the decline from 80 per cent to 60 per cent in the proportion of that business taken by made-to-measure garments. In order to maintain its 25 per cent share of total suit manufacture, Burton had to adapt its production facilities to reflect this switch in emphasis. Ready-to-wear suit manufacture does lend itself more to long runs, since the principal variants are of cloth, style and colour; whereas in made-to-measure production, individual fit is obviously a key factor. Mr Frankel, therefore, turned one factory at Doncaster into a specialist ready-to-wear plant.

One of the problems of suit manufacture was the seasonality of the made-to-measure business. Orders peaked in November (pre-Christmas) and in the period before Easter. Made-to-measure capacity had to be available to meet these peak demands. Before the war many clothing manufacturers would lay off labour in the periods between these peaks. Today such a policy was unacceptable. But, as Mr Frankel saw it, 'if the retail division requires the manufacturing division to supply made-to-measure suits to meet these peak periods of demand, then it must fill the troughs with ready-to-wear business.'

As part of his strategy of securing the optimum balance between made-to-measure and ready-to-wear, Mr Frankel changed the manufacturing division's pricing policy. Transfer prices between factory and shops had previously shown no distinction between made-to-measure and ready-to-wear suits.

Mr Frankel argued that since made-to-measure costs were higher, this ought to be reflected in the transfer price. He had, therefore, raised the transfer price of made-to-measure and lowered the price of ready-to-wear. This had two effects. First, budgetary control and costing could be carried out in a more realistic manner within the division. Second the retail division was now being charged less for ready-to-wear suits produced by the manufacturing division. This was an important factor in the retail division's buying calculations—since previously the retail division had argued that it could purchase ready-to-wear suits at lower prices outside the Burton Group.

Ready-to-wear suits produced within the group were now demonstrably competitive. This in turn could mean that the retail division would be more likely to place not only the orders necessary to fill the troughs between the seasonal peaks of the made-to-measure business, but also additional business.

Labour

Garment manufacture was a very labour-intensive industry. On an industry-wide basis there were serious labour turnover problems. Burton could claim a better long-term record than most companies in the industry. This was largely due to the enlightened welfare policies of Sir Montague Burton, and to the fact that at its Hudson Road factory, the largest clothing plant in the world, the company was one of Leeds's major employers.

One of Mr Frankel's first tasks within the division was to rationalise the wages structure. There was considerable labour unrest during his first six months, which brought certain anomalies to a head—in particular, the system whereby wage awards widened the differential between males, mostly employed in the cutting and pressing rooms, and females, the bulk of the labour force, employed in the machine rooms. After several major confrontations, a system of awards on an equal basis was introduced.

Garment technology

The increased emphasis on ready-to-wear production gave greater opportunities for design and production engineering. Manufacturing operations could be mechanised and this was expected to lead to better and tighter standards as well as a shorter training period which was important in an industry with a high labour turnover. 'We must make far better use of our labour than before,' said Mr Frankel, 'be more competitive with other industries in the skills we demand from our labour as well as in our payments.'

The technology of clothing manufacture had changed remarkably little over the last fifty years. The sewing-machine was still the principal item of factory equipment—and this was basically a hand tool. The other basic tools were band saws and steam presses.

Mr Frankel was pursing a policy of introducing greater mechanisation. Certain areas of machining such as pockets and buttonholes could be automated and machinery was being installed where possible.

The greatest potential savings in costs were expected to be in the cutting-room. Significant technical progress was expected in the industry from the development of new cutting methods and the use of computers to aid in controlling cutters instead of the traditional hand-chalked patterns.

Such systems, already well into the development stage in the United States, had important implications for Mr Frankel in his efforts to secure the right balance between made-to-measure and ready-to-wear. It had always been assumed that technological developments in the cutting-room would have their major impact on the ready-to-wear market through the obvious savings in cutting large piles of cloth into standard shapes. But if computer-controlled cutting became a reality, Burtons believed considerable savings could also be introduced in the made-to-measure business. Further, if made-to-measure cost—and the time lag between order and delivery—could be significantly reduced, this might, of course, reduce the progressive decline in the made-to-measure business.

Jacksons the Tailor Division

The second chain tailoring operation of the Burton Group, Jacksons the Tailor, operated some 150 stores and, like the Burton chain, had largely concentrated on made-to-measure suits. Jacksons were also experimenting with changes in retail design.

Like Burton Retailing there was an increased emphasis on fashion and ready-to-wear. The product line was being filled out to incorporate shirts, ties and accessories. In addition the division had announced plans for a chain of men's boutiques selling products made up by outside suppliers as well as made within the group. In February

1972 an experiment to sell Peter Robinson women's wear in a shop within a shop scheme was announced since it was considered that Jacksons clothing range was more complementary to Peter Robinson than that of Burtons.

Burton French Division

Burton was one of the few British store groups to have a stake in retailing overseas. The original entrée was made by the acquisition of the French Alba chain in 1964. By mid-1971 the group owned some thirteen 'Burton of London' outlets in France, six of them in the Paris region, with a turnover of £2.5-3 million a year. In August 1971 Mr Rice announced that the group was to pay nearly £1.7 million for an 85 per cent stake in the equity of the St Rémy group.

The St Rémy chain consisted of thirty-five stores. These were widely scattered throughout provincial France selling both meanswear and womenswear in the ready-to-wear market. At the time of the acquisition St Rémy's turnover was in the region of £4.4 million.

Burton's manufacturing interests in France at the time of the St Rémy acquisition consisted of the original Alba factory in Paris and a plant at Boulogne opened in 1969.

The principal reason for the decision to increase Burton's involvement in the French market was to provide additional outlets for Burton's Boulogne factory. This plant began production just one month after the French government cut back on consumer spending. With the Paris factory included, capacity in September 1969 was some 1,900 suits a week, while demand had fallen to 1,500. There was still plenty of spare capacity two years later. The up-to-date Boulogne plant, with its lower costs, could quite easily double its output. The addition of thirty-five St Rémy outlets, where made-to-measure suits could be introduced, provided an important captive market.

Further, the investment at Boulogne could not be liquidated for two reasons. First, Frenchmen required clothing made to French, not British, specifications with a distinctive French style, however 'English' the Frenchman buying Burton suits in France might consider the Burton style to be. It would therefore have been very difficult to make suits for the French Market on the same production lines as suits for the British market. Second, French customers demanded a seven day delivery for made-to-measure suits. This meant that a separate factory, geared to a short cycle, located in France was essential.

There were other reasons for the purchase. Men's retailing in France was entirely the reverse of the UK market. About 75 per cent of French men's outerwear sales were sold through small independent retailers. This allowed large groups to boost sales by acquisition—and hopefully, to reap the cost advantages of bulk purchasing.

In addition, France was the only country in continental Europe with a good market for made-to-measure clothes. If anything, Burton managers believed the made-to-measure market in France was gaining at the expense of ready-to-wear. British cloth had a particular cachet in France (which was exploited by the original 'Burton of London' stores). About 50 per cent of the suits Burton made in France used British cloth: they carried a Union Jack on the breast pocket label. All styling, however, was left in the hands of French designers.

Burton had an 85 per cent stake in St Rémy, and the original owners, the Bernheim family, held the remainder. Strategy and management decisions for all operations of what was now a single French division were the province of the Burton group. The menswear buying and sales organisation of 'Burton of London' and St Rémy had been merged; financial control of the two chains, which were being integrated, was now part of regular division-to-group head office reporting procedures. Store management, of course, was French, and executives controlling the division's operations from Paris, including two US-trained MBAs, were French speaking.

At the time of acquisition, St. Rémy was a chain selling menswear and womenswear, in the ready-to-wear business. Burton saw opportunities in France for introducing made-to-measure suits, and this required some restructuring of the retailing operation. As in the United Kingdom, the group was attempting to present a variety of faces to the public within the field of outerwear retailing. Some of the larger St Rémy shop premises were being split, so that a Burton store and a St Rémy one were adjacent to each other, to handle menswear and womenswear respectively. Other St Rémy shops were being converted fully to Burton menswear retail outlets. Smaller stores with the St Rémy fascia were continuing to trade under their original name, but might carry a Burton boutique as a shop within a shop. CDG Design Consultants, a Burton subsidiary, was working on the production of a new design theme for all the stores of Burton's French division.

Property Division

When Mr Rice was appointed as chief executive in 1969 the Burton group's financial structure was characterised by its great range of well-located properties and its low gearing. Mr Rice was concerned with unlocking the vast potential of Burton's property assets and a separate corporate property division was set up as a profit centre with control over all the group's property assets.

In 1969, Burton's properties had just been revalued at £71 million, an increase of £18 million over their book value. A subsequent revaluation was taking place in 1971-2. In all the group owned or leased over 1000 properties in the UK and France, a considerable number of which were sublet to others, and many of these were due to revert in the early nineteen-seventies. It was intended that many of these should then be used by the group for retailing activities in new fields.

To ensure that properties were put to their best use, the property division was charging a realistic market rent to the operating divisions. This provided a basis for a more flexible use of trading sites. A programme of new shop openings, extensions, modernisations and inter-divisional transfers was started in 1970/71. This programme was to be intensified in 1972 when 120 shops with more than 130,000 sq.ft of additional trading space would be involved.

Mr Rice was also prepared to sell properties not required for trading. In 1970/71 Burton disposed of twenty properties for £1.8 million and in September 1971 sold a prime site on the corner of Park Lane and Oxford Street for £2.4 million. The large Peter Robinson store in the Strand was sold for more than £500,000, and Peter Robinson's trading was now carried on in smaller premises next door.

The properties in many High Streets, acquired freehold by Sir Montague Burton between the wars, housed a wide variety of tenants. There had been, for example, many billiard saloons on the first floors, while the basements had rarely been used for anything beyond storage purposes. Mr Rice intended to unlock the retail potential of both upper storey and basement areas, either through running Burton activities in them, or by leasing them to tenants who would generate the revenue to provide Burton with more attractive rental income. Typically, an employment agency might be a suitable tenant for a first floor position or these areas could be used for the shops within shops concept.

Other Divisions

The company operated two concerns, Browns of Chester and Peter Robinson, engaged in department stores and women's fasions when Mr Rice was appointed as chief executive. These had been acquired in the post-war period as a conscious effort at diversification. These two concerns formed two of the operating divisions set up under the new divisional structure.

The larger of the two, Peter Robinson, was concerned with the retailing of ladies' fashion wear through a chain of some thirty stores the largest of which was in Oxford Street, London. The company was expanding the outlets for Peter Robinson's house name ready-to-wear clothes, Top Girl, by setting up shops within shops in a number of the menswear outlets.

Browns of Chester was a relatively small department store, localised to the North of England, retailing a general line of merchandise rather than clothing alone.

ACQUISITION AND DIVESTMENT POLICY

In addition to the divisions mentioned above which constituted Burton's interests before the appointment of Mr Rice a number of new divisions had been added in the past two years by acquisition. Mr Rice summarised his acquisition policy as 'to seek well-managed retail businesses, in any field, capable of expansion but needing, for real growth, the kind of property and financial strength which we can offer.'

However, before he could begin to implement this policy he took a decision which outside commentators felt to be long overdue. In July 1970 he sold off the unprofitable mail order business. Burton-by-Post began operations in 1965, dealing directly with the public and without the usual network of agents. Estimates put its cumulative losses at £3 million by 1970, when it was losing about £300,000 on a turnover of £4 million.

Mr Rice then launched five takeover bids in the autumn of 1970 and the spring of 1971—one of which was unsuccessful and one, the acquisition of St Rémy, that extended Burton's overseas operations.

The first of these was an acquisition conducted through the Peter Robinson division whereby Burtons acquired control of a small employment agency, Trumps, which joined the group in December 1970. Trumps traded—often in or next to Peter Robinson stores—in package holidays and office employment vacancies. In marketing terms, the ideal aim was to persuade the typical young, mobile Peter Robinson shopper to finance her holiday plans by taking well-paid temporary employment. Peter Robinson management already claimed remarkable increases in profit per square ft over what could be achieved through selling such traditional merchandise. At the time of acquisition Trumps had five outlets: by 31 August 1971 it had fifteen. In February 1972, however, it was decided that this investment would be better placed inside a larger employment agency concern. It was therefore decided to merge Trumps with the Alfred Marks Bureau in exchange for a small shareholding in Alfred Marks.

In November 1970 Rice bid nearly £4 million for Evans (Outsizes). This offer was successful and Burton acquired the whole of the issued Ordinary share capital, and 63 per cent of the preference shares. £3.4 million of this offer was in the form of $9\frac{1}{4}$ per cent unsecured loan stock 1998/2003.

Evans (Outsizes) was incorporated in 1936 and was principally a retailer of ladies fashions and underwear for the fuller figure. Through its seventy-six branches the company supplied ready-to-wear clothing in the medium price range, the vast majority of which was purchased from outside suppliers. The company did have some manufacturing facilities which supplied garments to the retail branches and other retailers. In addition, it operated a fast-growing mail order division and had recently acquired a double jersey weft knitting mill and a similar small retail chain, Outsize House Ltd, specialising in a similar market segment.

There were three principal reasons for the acquisition of Evans (Outsizes). First, the chain had a virtual monopoly in catering fashionably for women with fuller figures —and showed a very high return on capital. Second, Evans had a highly sophisticated, computerised, stock control system. For these two reasons Evans's existing operations were attractive to Burton. Third, if Evans was to establish itself nationwise, it needed the properties Burton could offer.

Since joining Burtons, Evans had provided the vehicle for another market segment experiment conducted by the Group. In August 1971 the first of a distinctive chain of specialist stores catering for five to fifteen-year-old boys was opened. Trading under the name Orange Hand, this chain of walk round stores offered a range of ready-to-wear fashionable leisurewear under Mr David Thomas, trained in retail management in the USA and recruited from Aquascutum.

Burton had for a number of years owned 36.2 per cent of the equity in Wallis, a chain of ladies' outfitters. In January 1971 Burton bid roughly £500,000 for the outstanding ordinary and preference shares, offering cash or loan stock. The offer was worth more than four times the last market deal in the ordinary shares (the previous October); but the Wallis directors and their associates, who held 52 per cent of the ordinary shares, were not enthusiastic.

Burton argued that it was not consistent with the group's policy to retain a minority investment of this nature and size. 'Particularly since the results of Wallis and hence the return on the investment, have been disappointing.' Mr Rice was confident that the return could be significantly improved if Wallis became a member of the Burton group.

However, the Wallis board remained adamant in their oposition. They argued that Burton's offer was based on an 'out-of-date and incomplete picture'; and they promised a big rise in profit. Holders of 72 per cent of the uncommitted ordinary shares had accepted the initial Burton offer by the beginning of April; and Burton indicated that it was prepared to increase its offer from 100p to 125p—on condition that the increased offer was recommended by the directors of Wallis. With their holding of 52 per cent, the Wallis board remained unmoved; and on 2 April the offers lapsed. Burton still retained its stake in Wallis; the value, however, and return on the original investment, had improved considerably.

Early in March 1971 Burton offered nearly £9 million for Ryman Conran, the office suppliers, made up of £6 million nominal of 7 per cent unsecured loan stock with warranty to subscribe to A shares between 1975 and 1985, together with £3.6 million nominal of $9\frac{1}{4}$ per cent in secured loan stock. The Ryman board agreed to accept the bid—as did Mr J.D. and Mr H.N. Ryman, who between them controlled 64 per cent of the votes.

Originally founded in 1893, Ryman had become the leading supplier in the UK of a complete range of office equipment comprising commercial stationery, office furniture and small business machines. It had seventy-five outlets including those of W. Straker Ltd, a similar concern acquired in mid-1970. To support the retail outlets Ryman had four manufacturing units, and other activities included a design group with one of the largest industrial design practices in Western Europe.

At the time of the bid Mr Rice gave the following reasons. 'First, we believe that the retailing of products for the office is an exciting growth industry and Ryman is the industry leader. Second, there are important areas of the country where Ryman is not represented and can benefit from our property spread. Third, Ryman needs funds, which our low gearing and high asset value enable us to provide'.

There were several subsidiary advantages. For example, Burton had a national distribution network which could be linked with that of Ryman. Ryman also controlled a leading design group which would bring the important benefit of independent creative thinking on shop design and environment.

The immediate results were disappointing. The postal strike in the spring of 1971, and the generally low level of business activity hit earnings in the first four months following Ryman's formal incorporation into the Burton group at the end of April. Reorganisation was being carried out and new products were being introduced. Additional branches were to be opened, to give Ryman national coverage and double its size over the next four years. The Conran side of Ryman Conran was 'hived off' within the group to become an integrated design service, specialising in corporate identity work including the Burton Group as a client.

PLANNING AND CONTROL PROCEDURES

New planning and control systems were being implemented for the first time within the Burton group, revolving round the creation of distinct profit centres. The operating divisions were obvious profit centres, but the dividing of the old Montague Burton tailoring concern into three divisions—manufacturing, retailing and property—each one a profit centre, had been perhaps the biggest single step in this exercise.

Planning within the Burton Group was carried out against the overall background of the group's capital structure, both current and as it should be in six years or so. The group's property, for instance, was valued in the books at £53 million, in 1969 it was assessed at £71 million, and a further revaluation was in hand.

The basic premise from which Mr Rice and Mr Power operated was that the group's assets were under-utilised in two ways: for financial purposes, and for the actual business of retailing. Once the new team took the basic decision that the group was to become a holding company for a cluster of retailing operations, then their strategy was based on these two premises. As a result of that it was decided that cash should be raised against these assets to finance the acquisition of more retailing businesses and existing retailing operations should be expanded into areas of greater profitability.

Mr Rice and Mr Power, however, emphasised that what they planned for the long-term must not jeopardise their profitability in the short term. They considered that 'what we do in the short term must justify a price/earnings ratio which allows us to pursue our long-term goals'.

A number of basic planning procedures had been established. There was a detailed annual divisional commitment to an operating and to a financial plan. This was subject to a six-monthly revision. Divisional chief executives sent in monthly reports on progress on both of these plans. The involvement of the group executive was in group planning, while the divisional chief executives were required to state their needs in terms of men and cash.

At the beginning of 1972, the group executive spelt out to the divisional chief executives the group objectives for 1972/3. 'We want your division to do this,' was the basic message, 'Please give us your initial reaction; and make your best estimate of what you can achieve.' Detailed planning below this level involved the coordination of objectives for middle management. These objectives were tailor-made to suit the responsibilities of particular managers within the broad objectives of their division.

The performance of the profit/cost centres was monitored using formalised computer procedures for pulling off key data. 'What matters in retailing,' said Mr Power, 'is data down to gross profit level. After that a large proportion consists of fixed costs —numbers of employees, numbers of establishments, and so on. But any variations at gross level come straight down to the bottom line.'

Mr Power picked a number of key variables to examine in the tailoring divisions;

for example, for the ready-to-wear business, he considered sales, gross margins, price reductions (at the time of reduction, not at the time of sale) and forward stock commitments. For the made-to-measure business, where a few basic, pre-season decisions were crucial, the key data involved more conventional factory costing information, and accurate cloth costing. Stock problems here were akin to those of any manufacturer. Burton aimed positively at optimising return on capital through achieving a balance between meeting demand swiftly and avoiding tying up capital in warehouse stock.

New procedures were also introduced to monitor distribution. 'This is an aspect,' said Mr Power, 'where control procedures have been totally neglected.' He had therefore begun an operation to classify ready-to-wear merchandise by location, value and style. And within the last category he had to consider whether to create further subcategories such as size, colour and cloth.

Yet another variable to be identified and monitored was the seasonality of suit buying. The demand for made-to-measure suits, for instance, peaks in November (before Christmas) and again before Easter. If the Leeds factory was to work at reasonable levels of capacity, ready-to-wear manufacturing had to be scheduled to fill the troughs.

Mr Power had established a regular flow of information from divisional chief executives to the group executive. Weekly returns of turnover were made by all divisions; and some provided in addition a statement of their trading margins. Monthly returns were in the form of a full divisional profit and loss account, with an additional analysis of stock-turn. A number of key ratios were considered. Mr Power regarded these key retailing ratios as those between stock-turn and sales, and between gross margins and sales. The stock-turn criteria, by which divisional performance was judged, were necessarily varied. For example, high fashion had to show a quicker stock-turn than furnishings.

To improve commitment a share incentive scheme was introduced towards the end of 1969 for senior executives. Under this scheme, non-voting 'A' shares were issued to senior executives under fifty on a part-paid basis. The remainder of the issue price was to be paid up at the participants request, over/after a number of years from the date of issue of each third of an executives allocation. This payment, however, could only be made if either pre-tax profits exceeded £7 milllion or the market value of the shares was at least 150 per cent of the market value at the date of issue.

FUTURE STRATEGY

Mr Rice summarised his future strategy as follows: 'We intend to become a group of specialist retail chains, each with a clearly defined market and a distinctive face to the public, selling through more than 850 shops. We intend to maintain and develop our dominant position in the menswear market. We shall, however, become less completely dependent on it as our newer retailing activities grow. In addition to retailing, the Group has, of course, other important activities. We are the largest men's outerwear manufacturer in Europe, a major office furniture manufacturer and we have a leading European industrial design practice. It is, however, the Group's property business which gives it a distinctive strength.'

One of Burton's most important objectives was to ensure that the properties were put to the best possible use. All UK properties were being transferred to the new subsidiary property company. An independent professional valuation was last undertaken in 1961 and an up-to-date valuation was being carried out.

The group services division was another important factor in Mr Rice's strategy. The main effort of this division was in the fields of financial control and planning, the development of group cash management and the use of data processing facilities. It had also been responsible for the integration of the physical distribution and warehousing facilities of the group.

Mr Rice was pursuing a policy of running Burton as a group composed of profit-centred divisions, whose chief executives were responsible to the group executive for meeting previously agreed targets. Mr Rice himself, as group chief executive, was responsible to the Burton board for the performance of the group as a whole. This meant considerable autonomy for the divisions, within a framework of operations devised and monitored by the group executive.

This framework emphasised improving the use of resources, especially people. Following a major programme of recruitment at top level, middle and junior management was being strengthened. Training and management development—including the establishment of an in-company management school at Leeds—was an important priority.

Further acquisitions were not ruled out: companies for which offers might be made would have considerable earnings potential, and be able to benefit from the injection of property assets and management skills which Burton could provide.

The largest of the divisions, Burton Tailoring, would continue to be the major contributor to group profits. Better merchandising and distribution, and the sale of a wider range of menswear—particularly ready-to-wear—would be the basis of these operations.

The profitability of the Montague Burton Manufacturing Division was low, and one of Mr Rice's important objectives was to improve this. Surplus production capacity and an imbalance of labour had been reduced by the closure of a number of manufacturing units and by a successful voluntary redundancy scheme at the Leeds factory. A specialisation programme designed to improve productivity and quality was now under way.

The French division was considered to be a bridgehead in continental Europe, and Burton had indeed opened two shops in Brussels. The present contribution to profits was a minor one, but the division already accounted for 10 per cent of turnover. Clearly it could be used as a base for major expansion, within the enlarged Community, which would allow easier access for British cloth. Mr Rice was well aware that even if his formula proved successful in France, this did not ensure similar success in Italy and Germany. 'We want first to be profitable and strong in French-speaking Europe,' he said. Mr Rice believed that the group should not be afraid to experiment with such ventures—and did not rule out further expansion. 'In retailing,' he said, 'you soon know if you are right or wrong.'

In women's fashion retailing, Peter Robinson had strengthened its central buying organisation and new shop projects provided an opportunity to improve profit per square foot in certain areas. In addition Evans Outsizes, with its clearly defined market and its highly developed merchandising skills, had ambitious growth plans.

At Ryman reorganisation was being carried out and new products were being introduced. Additional branches were to be opened to give Ryman national coverage and to double its size over the next few years.

16 Reed International Limited*

Reed International Limited[1] was an international organisation based in the United Kingdom holding world-wide interests and investments. The principal activities of its subsidiary companies were the manufacture of pulp, paper, stationery, paper and plastic packaging, chemicals, textiles, furnishing fabrics, wallcoverings, paint and building materials such as timber, plastic piping and rainwater systems, pitch fibre pipes, and 'do-it-yourself' products. With its acquisition in 1970 of the International Publishing Corporation, it also became a major producer in the business of publishing and printing newspapers, commercial and trade magazines, books and business periodicals, and general printing.

In 1970/71, Reed's sales exceeded £500 million yielding pre-tax profits of £19.8 million on total net assets of £423 million. Net profits attributable to ordinary shareholders were £11.1 million on ordinary shareholders' equity of £247.9 million. In March 1971 the company had approximately 84,000 employees and 103,800 shareholders.

Exhibits 1-7 provide details of Reed's financial results and operations.

HISTORY

In 1894 Albert Reed borrowed £10,000 from his employer Sir Thomas Owen and bought an old newsprint mill at Tovil, near Maidstone in Kent. This was the start of Albert E. Reed Ltd, the name the company was known by for nearly sixty years. The business expanded steadily but slowly, first by adding the manufacture of packaging papers, and then by going into packaging itself, producing such items as corrugated cases, cartons and tubes.

In 1920, following the death of Albert Reed, the company's shares were put on the market. Lord Rothermere, who controlled the *Daily Mirror* and *Sunday Pictorial* newspapers, had heard that Lord Kemsley wanted to buy a paper mill, so

> ...he bought two-thirds of the ordinary shares and then offered them to Kemsley. Unfortunately, he had not read the articles of association with enough care. The preference shares had votes; and Kemsley, discovering that Rothermere's holding did not represent a controlling interest, refused to buy it. Rothermere was therefore left with Reed's on his hands. The Mirror holdings ... amounted to about 30 per cent.[2]

The company continued to progress, and in 1937 made its first acquisition by buying a paper sack manufacturer which became Reed Medway Paper Sacks. By 1950 the business had grown to the point where Reed had total assets of £6 million and employed 5,000 people.

POST-WAR EXPANSION AND DIVERSIFICATION

In 1950 with the appointment of Mr Philip Walker as managing director, Reed entered upon its second major phase, which lasted until 1963. During this period the business

---

* Copyright © Manchester Business School and Dr Avraham Meshulach 1971.

[1] All the information in this case has been collected from publicly available sources. No data have been provided by any of the companies involved. The case is not intended comprehensively to portray the situations of the companies.

[2] C. H. King, 'Organisation and Management of the Daily Mirror Newspapers Limited', *Seminar on Problems in Industrial Administration,* The London School of Economics and Political Science, 29 November 1955.

developed as a group with some diversification both within the conversion industry and new fields such as building products; it also embarked on its first overseas operation. 1954 marked the beginning of Reed's diversification into products other than paper. It began production in an entirely new field, pitch fibre pipe for the building industry. This activity formed the start of the Building Products Division. A year later Reed commenced its first overseas activity. It participated in the building and managing of what became the Tasman Pulp and Paper Company in New Zealand. This was a quoted company with an equity market value in 1970 of nearly £50 million, of which Reed owned 19 per cent.

In the early 1950s, following a dispute with the then chairman, Sir Ralph Reed, the Daily Mirror Group increased its holdings in the company. In 1959 Reed contracted to manage Imperial Paper Mills Ltd which was owned by the Mirror Group. The Mirror Group also had extensive paper interests in Canada, through the Anglo-Canadian Pulp and Paper Mills, and in 1960 it rationalised all its paper holdings by selling both Imperial and Anglo-Canadian to Reed in exchange for shares. As a result, the Mirror Group's interest in Reed grew to almost 50 per cent.

In late 1960 Reed also entered the Common Market by signing an agreement with La Centrale Finanzaria Generale, SpA of Milan, for the formation of a holding company in Italy which would own subsidiaries engaged in paper and board products and conversion in that country. At that time Italy's paper consumption was well below the average for the other Common Market countries. This venture proved a failure, however, and in 1965 Reed succeeded, after some difficulty, in disengaging itself, but only at a cost of £3.24 million.

Also in 1960 Paper Products Pty Limited was acquired in Australia. It owned companies making corrugated and solid fibreboard containers, cartons, rigid boxes and paper bags. Reed laid great stress on cooperation with local companies and local investment interests in all its overseas projects. Thus all the Australian companies when purchased continued to function under Australian management using Australian materials.

In 1962, following the formation of the European Free Trade Association, Reed entered into partnership with Sande Trestipen A/S, one of the largest Norwegian producers and exporters of mechanical pulpwood, to construct a £2 million pulp and paper mill at Sande, on Oslo Fjord, Norway. This was aimed not only at assuring pulp supplies, but subsequently at providing a new source of paper for the group's packaging interests.

These foreign acquisitions formed the basis for Reed's overseas expansion in the 1960s. In 1960 the profit derived from overseas manufacture was negligible. By 1970 it accounted for nearly 30 per cent of the total.

At the same time, the company was rapidly increasing its paper interests in the UK. It acquired a large number of paper mills and packaging manufacturers in the second half of the 1950s, moving into more specialised areas such as laminated plastics. It also went into the consumer-oriented tissue field by entering in a joint venture with the American firms Kimberley Clark and International Cellulose Products, to produce tissue products under such brand names as Kleenex, Kotex and Delsey.

As a result of these developments, Reed's assets increased from £6 million in 1950 to £113 million in 1963 and pre-tax profits grew from £300,000 to £12.8 million. However, despite the post-Korean war boom conditions which prevailed in the paper industry from 1954 to 1958, the return on shareholders' equity declined steadily during this period; this averaged 44.8 per cent during the period 1950-54, 25.2 per cent in 1955-9, and 14.6 per cent in 1960-64.

MANAGEMENT CHANGES

Reed was now effectively controlled by the Daily Mirror Group and its associated company the Sunday Pictorial, which in 1963 became amalgamated into the International Publishing Corporation. Mr Cecil King had been chairman of both the Daily Mirror and Sunday Pictorial from 1951 to 1968. In June 1963 Mr King replaced Lord Cornwallis as chairman of Reed, and within nine months Mr S.T. Ryder became managing director instead of Mr Walker. These changes have been described as one of the quietest managerial takeovers in the history of British Industry, so much so that at the following annual meeting no questions were asked about the reasons for the changes. Some years later, Mr Ryder gave his version:

> [Mr King] was deeply concerned about the future of Reed and announced out of the blue at an informal meeting of both the Daily Mirror and Sunday Pictorial companies' directors that, in his opinion, Reed would be bankrupt by 1970. He further

urged that I should move to Reed forthwith, and in twenty-four hours I was installed there.[3]

Mr S.T. Ryder began his career in 1950 as a financial journalist, and then as editor, on the *Stock Exchange Gazette*. In 1960 he became joint managing director, and between 1961 and 1963 sole managing director of Kelly Iliffe Holdings and Associated Iliffe Press Ltd—a part of the Daily Mirror Group responsible for trade and technical journals. Within three years Mr Ryder doubled Kelly Iliffe's profits and established for himself a reputation for dynamic management and implementing changes quickly. In 1968, following the registration of Mr King, Mr Ryder became chairman of Reed as well as chief executive.

Immediately following his arrival at Reed, Mr Ryder formulated a seven-year plan to make the company viable. In 1960, when the Treaty of Stockholm established the European Free Trade Association, Reed was heavily dependent on mass-tonnage grades of paper. The imminence of free competition with the Nordic countries, with their abundant forests and strong pulp and paper industries, put Reed in a very vulnerable situation, since it was precisely in the mass-tonnage grades that this competition was likely to be fiercest. Several people besides Mr King had already become concerned and several moves were initiated to change the company's direction. At the time of Mr Ryder's arrival, however, little physical change had occurred, mainly because the capital-intensive nature of the industry imposed a long time-scale on new developments. Mr Ryder's plan, therefore, had three prongs

(i) To fortify Reed in the UK in order to withstand successfully the onslaught from Scandinavia.

(ii) To build up overseas interests rapidly, including the manufacture of certain mass-tonnage papers which were no longer profitable to produce in the UK.

(iii) To diversify.[4]

DEVELOPMENT OF UK PAPER ACTIVITIES 1963-71

In the November following Mr Ryder's arrival Reed acquired Spicers Ltd, by far the larger paper merchant in the UK. The two companies had worked together over the years and Spicers handled a lot of Reed's products. But the need for a strong merchanting and sales network which Reed lacked became more important as Reed turned its attention in the UK to increasing the manufacture of special papers. Spicers also had considerable overseas trading operations. Throughout the sixties Spicers maintained and increased its home sales, but competitive pressures on margins, together with high costs of moving some production units to new premises, reduced profits in the United Kingdom.

In 1965 Spicers acquired Trade Loose Leaf Company and its subsidiary, Merlin Visible Filing, with its major share of the UK market for loose leaf wallets, files and index cards. The same year marked the first major developments in a programme in which certain no-longer-viable grades of paper were relinquished or transferred abroad, and attention was focused on new or increased business in more attractive lines. Spicers introduced 'Interplus', described as a 'revolutionary comprehensive range of uncoated banks, bonds, printing and duplicating papers'. In the following year Reed introduced 'Plus Fabric', a non-coated writing series. 'Plus Fabric' and Interplus' were both marked by the Reed and Spicers sales and marketing organisations.

In late 1967 part of Spicers was integrated with Reed's Paper and Board Division. Prior to that, in 1965, Reed had acquired Alex Cowan & Sons Ltd, a long established Scottish papermaker. Its major activities, which included the manufacture of writing, printing and specialised papers, complemented Reed's UK and overseas operations. In 1967 the Cowan merchanting operations were merged with Spicers, in a new company, Spicer-Cowan Limited, in order to promote a more comprehensive distribution service to customers both geographically and in product range. It was this company which became integrated in the Paper and Board Division. A smaller unit, known as Spicers

---

[3] S.T. Ryder, 'Diversification, Decentralisation and Decision—the Management Philosophy of Reed International', *Joint Evening Seminar on Industrial Administration,* London School of Economics and Political Science and London Graduate School of Business Studies, 15 December 1970.

[4] Ryder, op. cit.

Limited, remained separate from Reed Paper and Board (UK) Ltd. This company concentrated on the conversion of paper to stationery and similar products. A consequence of the success of this converting company was the undertaking of two major projects in 1969 and 1970. One was an envelope and book making factory at Washington, Co. Durham, and the other a continuous stationery factory in Skelmersdale, Lancashire. Total capital expenditure on these two operations amounted to £1.5 million.

To counter competition from foreign importers Reed followed various courses, centring around increasing the production of fine papers and decreasing the production of newsprint. In 1965 Reed introduced new coated printing papers from their new trailing blade coating machine at Imperial Paper Mills. By 1967 the company was reporting that the paper had already secured a 'high regard from our customers'. In 1967 Reed successfully completed the modification of a machine to produce coated board at their mills at Colthrop. This further expanded their range of qualities available to customers.

At the beginning of 1969 Reed entered into a joint venture with Bowater Paper Corporation Ltd, under which each purchased a half interest in the Donside Paper Company, formerly part of the Inveresk Paper Company Ltd. This was mainly involved in coated paper production, and the two companies signed a joint marketing agreement for coated printing papers. Throughout 1969 and 1970 Reed attempted to build up the market and the production of the high quality blade coated paper for which Donside was equipped. The Donside Mill, prior to the takeover, had been operating at a considerable loss and in the 1969/70 period Reed had to bear a loss of £304,000. But following a major reorganisation and rationalisation programme the losses were diminishing in the later part of 1970; and the quality of the mill's products was much improved. The Reed chairman believed that 'there can be no doubt that in the long term participation by the group is well justified'.

The development of a new pulp and paper mill at Prince George, British Columbia, in the early sixties led to Reed's production of kraft papers being largely transferred from the UK to Canada. By the end of 1964 kraft papers accounted for 4.2 per cent of UK production (compared with a previous average rate of 14 per cent), and by the end of 1965 the figure was down to 1.4 per cent. Several plants were closed, while Aylesford Paper mill ceased to make bulk grades of sack kraft. Major changes to existing plant and installations to enable the Aylesford Mill to replace the transferred tonnage with other grades were mainly carried out in the second half of 1964 and the first half of 1965. Characteristically in the British paper industry, machines when modified were upgraded to make smaller runs of more expensive paper. Aylesford was no exception, producing, for example, coated printings and more specialised krafts.

The record sales and profits in 1965 were accounted for, not simply by acquisitions and changing technology, but also by increased capacity utilisation brought about by changes in the shift system. Traditionally, Reed mills had worked three shifts per day from Monday to Friday, at normal pay rates, and then usually through Saturday and often into Sunday on overtime. This meant that even with employees working a $6\frac{1}{2}$-day week, machines costing millions of pounds were idle for anything up to one day per week. Reed thus introduced a four shift system whereby the labour force was divided into four groups, one of which was always 'stood down' while the others kept production going non-stop by running consecutive eight-hour shifts. Mr Cecil King stated that output increased by 10 per cent or more through the continuous running of machines.

The firm followed two directions in its attempt to decrease its dependence on imported pulp. In 1965 Reed installed the first de-inking plant at the Imperial Paper Mills. Later the firm announced plans to extend their de-inking activities with two projects, at Imperial and Aylesford Paper mills. These were mainly financed by a loan of £1.5 million from the Industrial Reorganisation Corporation. In 1970 Mr Ryder announced that these plans were functioning well and profits were in line with their forecasts. During Mr Ryder's first few years as managing director, machines were converted to manufacture paper from secondary fibres or waste paper. The procurement of waste paper for Reed's growing needs was mainly carried out by an associated company, J. & J. Maybank Ltd, which in late 1968 opened a waste paper processing plant at Charlton, London. This plant was believed at the time to be the most advanced and largest of its type in the world.

In 1970 and 1971, owing to adverse economic conditions and the pressure of Scandinavian competition, the company closed down one of its Darwen mills and five out of the thirteen paper machines at the Aylesford Paper Mills. According to Mr Ryder

> These actions are reshaping, strengthening, but not indiscriminately reducing our important position in the British paper industry.... We are maintaining invest-

ment and growth in profitable areas, particularly in products based on fibre recovered from waste paper.[5]

UK PACKAGING DEVELOPMENT 1963-71

Packaging and converting operations were rapidly expanded in the sixties, especially during the first three years of Mr Ryder's direction. In 1964 Field Sons & Co. Ltd, of Bradford, a leading carton manufacturer, was acquired; and in the following year Mr King claimed this had proved an outstanding success. Mr Ryder explained the reason for the purchase as follows

> Reed's sizeable interest in the production of cartons had never really produced a satisfactory rate of return on the capital involved. Field's had a dramatic success and growth record and a management revered by both competitors and customers. It was logical, therefore, to bring in Field's not only to increase our share of the carton market but also to extend the benefit of their managerial expertise to our existing carton operations.[6]

In 1965 Reeds opened a new carton plant at Killingworth near Newcastle-upon-Tyne. This replaced activities of Field which had formerly been conducted at eight different locations, as well as permitting increased production capacity. Factories at Bradford Thatcham remained, and contributed to Field's increasing sales and profits throughout the second half of the 1960s. Field was integrated with Reed's paper and board division in 1966, allowing it to increase its efficiency in both production and graphic and constructional design. In 1970 a new factory was opened in Scotland, primarily to provide a more closely integrated service of cartons and cases for the whisky trade, especially its export business. Another new venture was the acquisition in the second half of 1969 of H. Tramer Ltd, an organisation which produced boxes and fabricated acetate containers in the North West, and whose products fitted well into the Field range. In 1971 Field extended considerably its activities in transparent plastic packs.

Reed Medway Sacks, a major producer in its field, increased its sales considerably throughout the sixties, but profits were at times affected by increases in costs and pressure on prices through excess capacity in the UK. The market became increasingly competitive as plastics were introduced into the UK. But Reed's sales were increased by the development of existing applications, and the pioneering of others. In both 1965 and 1968, the only two years that Reed Medway Sacks was able to increase its profits in the second half of the sixties, the chairman emphasised the continual search for new applications and increasing attention to customer service and manufacturing excellence. From 1967 onwards Reed Medway Sacks derived considerable benefits from the use of sack kraft from Prince George Pulp and Paper. In 1970 its factory at Larkfield in Kent remained the largest of its kind in Europe and produced several million paper sacks each week, not only for packaging, but also for waste disposal applications.

Through Reed Corrugated Cases Limited, Reed was the largest producer of corrugated fibreboard bases and tubes in the UK. Its eleven strategically located factories produced packaging products for a wide range of items and materials from foodstuffs to delicate electronic components. After Mr Ryder's arrival at Reed this subsidiary continuously increased its sales and profits. Capacity was increased to cope with increasing demand which Ryder attributed partly to a 'very keen sales force'. Every year between 1963 and 1968 Reed Corrugated Cases broke its sales and profit record levels. In 1969 and 1970 this record-breaking run was halted by increasing costs of raw materials and labour reducing profits. The increasing costs also resulted in price increases, but previous sales levels were maintained, primarily because of Reed's reputation for quality and service. The company also introduced new products, notably paper furniture which Mr Cecil King claimed was symbolic of the 'versatility of thought and enterprise in this vigorous company'.

Capacity for corrugated case production was increased in 1964 by a new West Hartlepool factory, extensions to Reed's Northern Ireland branch, and the acquisition of a 330,000 square feet factory in Gloucestershire. Three years later further extensions, costing over £1 million, were begun at the West Hartlepool factory. These were

---

[5] Annual Report, 1971.

[6] S. T. Ryder, 'How to make rationalisation work', *Achievement,* May 1966.

completed on time in 1969, but the factory suffered a serious fire just after opening. Mr Ryder commented that 'adversity merely served to demonstrate the resourcefulness of our branch personnel, so that the effect on our customers has been minimal'.

By 1970 plastic components were used successfully by all Reed's paper packaging companies. In 1962 Reed acquired Green Plastic Packaging, which made extruded plastic film and polythene bags and sacks. Its profits prior to being made part of Reed Polyfilms (in 1965) never regained the profit level it had enjoyed in 1962 at the time of its acquisition. Although Reed Polyfilms, the one operation entirely devoted to plastics packaging, continually produced on an increasing scale and increased its sales in the period 1965 to 1970, it made a net loss. In 1970 Mr Ryder said, 'A great deal of attention is being given to the solution of this problem, especially to reducing the average costs of production.'

NORTH AMERICAN DEVELOPMENTS 1963-71

The expansion of overseas activities begun in 1960 continued to gather momentum under Mr Ryder. In 1960 sales from overseas operations were nil; by 1965 they accounted for 24 per cent of Reed's turnover, and in 1970 (before the merger with IPC) they were 30 per cent of the total. This increase was largely due to acquisitions. In 1964 Reed acquired the Acme-Molson Group, which was involved in the manufacture and distribution of corrugated paper containers, pulp, polythene bags and a wide range of other converted products in Canada.

In 1963, before Mr Ryder's arrival, Reed had made an agreement with Canadian Forest Products Ltd to construct a major pulp and paper project in Western Canada, at Prince George, British Colombia. This joint venture, in which Reed had a 50 per cent stake, was called Prince George Pulp & Paper Mills Ltd. A mill near Prince George with an initial capacity of 600 tons per day of bleached and semi-bleached pulp was opened in 1965. Adequate pulpwood supplies were secured, and in the summer of 1966 the mill began production of paper. In the first years of operation, low pulp and paper prices led to losses being incurred, which were aggravated by technical difficulties arising primarily from winter severity and other local conditions.

Adjacent to the Prince George Mills, the companies involved in that venture set up the Intercontinental Pulp Mill. Production began in May 1968, two months ahead of the original schedule, and was immediately successful. However, the floating of the Canadian dollar and a two-month strike led to losses being recorded in 1970. It was only in 1971 that Mr Ryder was able to report that both mills were operating profitably and were proceeding 'with programmed developments in performance'.

The existence of controlled sources of the supply of lumber was noted by Mr Ryder to be of great importance. During the first four years of production the companies involved in the projects acquired several timber firms. Mr Ryder expected the main source of timber after 1970 to be Takla Forest Products, in which Reed had a $43\tfrac{3}{4}$ per cent interest. In 1969 the trading operation of this company was small; but in 1970 a new plant began production and other sawmilling complexes were planned. By 1970 Prince George had the pulpwood harvesting rights over 8 million acres—an area a quarter the size of England.

Throughout the period 1963 to 1970 other overseas activities were considerably expanded. The Anglo-Canadian Pulp and Paper Mills, which Reed had acquired in 1960 from the Daily Mirror Group, while improving its sales volume in the sixties, often suffered reductions in profits. Increasingly, costs of labour and pulpwood meant that profits fell below the previous year's level in 1965, 1966 (by some 12 per cent) and 1967 (by as much as 55 per cent). Profits in 1968 remained at roughly the 1967 figure. But profits began to increase as sales increased, and prices for newsprint, packaging and market pulp were raised. Unlike the situation facing British manufacturers in the years 1969 and 1970, the price increases in both paper and pulp manufacture were more than the wage increases, while paper prices rose faster than the combined increase in materials, wages and services.

OTHER OVERSEAS DEVELOPMENTS 1963-71

Reed had pulp and paper interests in both Norway and New Zealand. It had a 51 per cent shareholding in the Sande Paper Mill in Norway which began production in the mid-sixties. Despite rises in production and sales until 1969, no profit was forthcoming from this venture. Nevertheless, the price of corrugated medium (which had hitherto been depressed) increased, and in 1969/70 the company recorded what Mr Ryder described as 'a most satisfactory result'. Reed's trade investment in the Tasman Pulp and Paper Company Ltd in New Zealand continued throughout the late sixties to be highly profitable. In 1968, for example, its profit increased by 50 per cent over the previous year's figure. Reed had several other manufacturing plants throughout the world. For example, in 1967 Reed Medway Sacks opened a small factory for multi-wall paper sacks in Trinidad, and in 1968 Field commenced production of cartons in Jamaica.

By 1970 almost every part of the world was serviced by a vast paper and stationery distribution and merchanting complex, comprising branches and offices in strategic cities. In addition, the group developed overseas agencies for a wide range of products and equipment. In Australia, New Zealand, Canada, South Africa, Eire and Trinidad, stationery operations were developed.

Three other notable developments took place in 1970. First, Reed signed an agreement with Hoechst, the German chemical firm, to examine and research jointly the possibility of mutually profitable enterprises in a number of countries. This move was especially centred around the future of plastic paper. Second, a growth market in Australia for wine was identified, and Reed purchased a vineyard of considerable local renown. Third, Reed Overseas Corporation was involved not simply in manufacturing and distribution operations, but in selling 'know-how'. In 1970 it helped in the development of a £10 million paper mill in Iran. Reed was reluctant at first to go into the project, but once in it, seemed likely to gain £500,000 by the time the mill was in full production, without putting in any capital.

DIVERSIFICATION 1963-71

The main thrust of Reed's diversification away from paper came with the acquisition in 1965 of Wall Paper Manufacturers Ltd and the fast-growing market-oriented firm of Polycell Holdings Ltd. Despite counter-bids from Courtaulds, Reed's offer for WPM, amounting to some £65 million in shares and cash, was accepted in April 1965. At the time, this was the largest takeover in British history, and it increased the size of Reed by 40 per cent.

WPM had long been an important customer of Reed, who provided them with about 15 per cent of their paperbase requirements. The rest of the paperbase for the manufacture of wallpaper came from three of WPM's own mills. There was considerable disharmony within the management and directorate of WPM, and Mr Cecil King, then chairman of Reed, stated that he was 'moved by the chance of putting things right in one of Britain's biggest companies'. He further noted that 'with three mills in Lancashire producing printings and stationery grades as well as large quantities of wallpaper base, its papermaking operations are obviously close to those of our own Paper and Board Divisions. Even more attractive, however, is the scope which WPM's other activities offer for the application of our established policy of expansion and development as a vertically integrated business with appropriate diversification.'

One week before the closing date of Reed's bid for WPM, Mr Ryder announced that if Reed was successful it would make an offer to purchase all the capital of Polycell Holdings Ltd. This company marketed a range of 'do-it-yourself' building and decorating products, and had been remarkably successful, growing in ten years from nothing to an after-tax profit in 1964 of over £400,000. A month after the WPM acquisition, the takeover of Polycell was completed for a cash price of £12,175,000. In the Annual Report for 1965, Mr King stated that 'the acquisition of this outstandingly successful company will not only complement existing WPM operations, but will also provide added strengths to the management team, particularly in the field of marketing and retailing.'

At the time of the takeover WPM was the largest British company in the decorating business. It had long enjoyed an overwhelming share of the wallpaper market, and by pursuing a policy of acquiring its competitors managed to maintain this share at about 80 per cent. The company was also a leading producer in the paint market, but had slipped from a position of market leadership in the early 1950s to a position where its share of the market was only 10 per cent, far behind the 40 per cent held by ICI.

Apart from these major lines, WPM had an important stake in furnishing fabrics. In addition, it had other manufacturing units, whose products included paint brushes, ground mica and plastic moulding powders. These products and others were marketed through a network of retail shops (there were 750 at the time of the takeover), depots and branches. The company also had considerable overseas operations.

Immediately following the merger, the papermaking operations of WPM were put under Reed's home paper and board organisation. There also began a great deal of reorganisation and replanning of marketing and manufacturing operations. The most noticeable change was the introduction of the brand name 'Crown' in the paint market. By 1966 Reed reported that with a vigorous and consistent marketing effort Crown paint was becoming established as a well-known brand. Sales of Walpamur water paint, however, had been seriously affected by the introduction of new products, such as emulsion paints. During 1967 'Crown Plus Two', the first thixotropic polyurethane paint, was launched on the market. In 1968 Mr Ryder described it as 'an outstanding success' which had assisted in securing a wider distribution of Crown paints generally, and provided the spur for Reed in 1970 to add to this range a vinyl-gel emulsion. Crown Plus was an outstanding promotion; the brand's sales increased so rapidly that it had secured in 1970 12 per cent of the retail market and pushed Reed's total market share to 20 per cent. The promotion also pushed WPM into second place ahead of Berger, Jenson and Nicholson (owned by Hoechst), whose market share over the four years 1966 to 1970 was estimated to have slipped by over a third. It also helped—along with supermarket own-brand sales (especially Woolworths)—to reduce ICI's market share from 40 per cent in 1967 to 35 per cent in 1970.

Other products were launched following Reed's takeover of WPM. In 1967 Reed introduced a new easily strippable form of wallcovering under the name of 'Cleenstrip' which in 1969 was reported as 'making good headway as the first example of this increasingly important class of wallpaper'. A Crown vinyl wallpaper was also marketed. Polycell, which after its acquisition became a division of WPM, introduced a number of new products to the market, including ceramic tiles, boats and boat equipment, and paper-based toys.

Reed continued its diversification into the decorative products field by a number of smaller acquisitions. In 1967 for example, the Briton Brush Company Ltd, a manufacturer of brushes, was taken over, and in 1970 Reed acquired Bradfield Brett Holdings Ltd, a company which was engaged in the manufacture and process of textiles.

A second branch of diversification for Reed was in the field of building products. The company made its first move in this direction as early as 1955, when it acquired Key Engineering Ltd; this company produced fibre pipe, which was used for such things as drains. Throughout most of the sixties it manufactured almost half the UK output of this product. In 1964 Key increased its capacity to produce pipes by 50 per cent. This was aimed at maintaining Key's share of a rapidly growing market, despite increasing competition. Improved plant efficiencies and increased capacity utilisation in 1968 enabled Reed to reduce its prices and thus expand its demand even further.

Developments in the building sector of Reed were mainly through mergers and developments (originally by L. & P. Plastics) in plastics. In 1964 Reed acquired Burn Bros (London) Ltd, which had been on the distribution side of the building industry for over 100 years. This company had developed the Terrain range of rainwater, soil and waste PVC systems, the markets for which increased to such a degree in 1964 that production had to be transferred to much larger premises at Aylesford. In 1965, Key took over Pitch Fibre Pipes of West Hartlepool. The demand for such pipes was largely dependent on the number of new houses being constructed, and the substantial increase in Key's activities in the late sixties reflected in the rise in the production of new houses. But the lack of activity in the less developed North East meant that in 1968 the pipe factory at Hartlepool had to be closed. Key Terrain plastics drainage systems were introduced on a broad basis throughout the country, supported by a series of regional depots. Throughout 1968 and 1969 Mr Ryder noted 'rapidly growing sales indicated that those systems were obtaining recognition for their out-standing quality'. During 1970/71, despite the worst conditions the building industry had faced for some years, Reed Building Products improved its profits and gained an increased share of the market for Key Terrain pipes and fittings.

After the acquisition of WPM, the building products were reorganised as a division of that company. In 1966 the chairman reported that the results of the new Wallpaper, Paint and Building Products division were encouraging, and that the year's profits were the highest ever in the history of WPM. However, from 1967 to 1970 profits did not reach the 1966 level of £8.6 million. In fact, although sales increased after 1967, profits from UK operations in the decorative and building products area declined. Expansion of overseas activities, however, helped WPM maintain an increase in profits from their low level of £6 million in 1967.

A major problem facing the wallcovering trade, according to Reed, was that it was subject to a two-year cycle. This arose from the industry's practice of changing pattern books every other year. In 1966 Mr King claimed that Reed had taken steps which would 'almost completely remove the great difference between successive years'. However, as late as 1970, Mr Ryder was still making reference to the problem of the two-year cycle. Profits for the 'good' year of the cycle, 1967-8, were higher than those for 1969-70, which was also a 'good' year, despite the fact that sales had increased by some 15 per cent over the level of 1968-9.

THE REED-IPC MERGER

In January 1970 the Board of Reed and the International Publishing Corporation jointly announced that because of a long-standing association between the two companies substantial mutual benefit would result from a merger. Reed was a major supplier of newsprint and other printing papers and products to IPC, and by this merger the group became involved in the business of publishing and printing newspapers, consumer and business magazines, books and business directories, prints and general printing. IPC had extensive interests in all these areas, and was in fact the largest communications group, not only in the UK, but in the western world. Despite its name, however, it was largely tied to Britain.

In April 1970 the merger between IPC and Reed was completed. Whereas in 1963 the IPC constituent parts had been controlling shareholders of Reed, the rapid expansion of Reed had substantially diluted the position to the stage where the shareholding was down to 27 per cent. Mr Ryder explained Reed's decision to acquire IPC as follows

> ... We were at the crossroads. IPC could not exercise positive control over Reed, but, by Reed's Articles of Association, it needed a 75 per cent majority vote to increase its capital. This was a valuable negative control for IPC and one which it could not reasonably let go. Neither could it afford cashwise to take its share of Reed's expansion. Thus there was a danger that Reed's expansion would be halted.
>
> On the other hand, IPC itself was in great difficulties and the likelihood was that it would be the subject of a takeover bid, not as a going business but as a break-up situation to realise its very rich assets. In turn, this could possibly have involved pressure to sell off some of the most profitable parts of Reed and get us back to the mass-tonnage manufacture position we were in at the time of EFTA....
>
> Naturally, we would not have gone ahead, based solely on a defensive purchase, but only with the conviction that, although profitability of IPC had virtually disappeared and little could be expected in the first year of ownership after that, by the implementation of our management methods, one could restore it to a good level of profitability. [7]

The development of IPC into its form when Reed acquired it was mainly the product of two major acquisitions and one basic capital reorganisation, all of which took place between 1959 and 1969. The capital reorganisation involved both the Daily Mirror Newspapers and Sunday Pictorial Newspapers, which had strong boardroom links and cross shareholdings amounting to over 20 per cent in each case. Their main assets were the *Daily Mirror,* and *Sunday Pictorial, Reveille,* and trade investments, notably an important holding in Reed. In 1963 a scheme of arrangement was implemented under which the assets of the Daily Mirror and Sunday Pictorial Groups of companies were transferred to the International Publishing Corporation Limited, which was incorporated on 31 December 1962. In terms of the structure of the group, one of the more important changes was that this involved the elimination of the cross shareholdings.

In 1959 Daily Mirror Newspapers acquired Amalgamated Press Ltd, which at that time was one of the largest integrated magazine publishing/printing houses in the UK. Daily Mirror saw its role as that of applying the expertise it had acquired in mass circulation newspapers to mass circulation magazines. In addition, Daily Mirror was also obtaining an important interest in trade and technical journals, directories and annuals. In 1961 Daily Mirror acquired Odhams Press Ltd (after a battle with Lord Thomson), which had become a broadly diversified publishing company. It owned two national papers (the unprofitable *Daily Herald* and the profitable *Sunday People*), major magazine interests (including *Woman*), book publishing interests, and trade and technical publications. Mirror's stated aim in acquiring Odham's was to rationalise the magazine interests, but it also acquired, through the non-magazine interests, a number

---

[7] S. T. Ryder, *Seminar.*

of problem areas, notably the *Daily Herald*. In fact, the obstacles to integrating Odhams into the broader framework of IPC were to prove unexpectedly large. Many of IPC's much publicised managerial problems derived from this purchase.

When Mr Ryder wrote his statement to accompany the accounts of the Reed Group for the financial year ending 31 March 1970, he concluded with reference to IPC: 'There is much to be done in this great publishing house. I will not hide from you that there are areas of unacceptable losses, which must be remedied or removed.' In July 1970 he announced plans to deal with two such areas: the weekly colour magazine of the Daily Mirror, and IPC's printing businesses. Mr Ryder said that the magazine had been launched on the 'expectation that the growth in the advertising industry would continue and that in the first year it would attract £7 million in advertising revenue'. Advertising was running at £4.5 million a year, and 'bookings made for the autumn were down to a level that made it clear that there was no chance whatsoever of the magazine having a future'. In the year ended 28 February 1970 the magazine lost £1,945,000, and in 1970 it was estimated to lose some £3 million. During 1969-70 IPC's five London printing factories incurred a loss of £1.36 million. The major part of this came from Fleetway Sumner Street (£507,000) and Southwark Offset (£703,000). The losses of these two units for 1970 were estimated in July 1970 to be £1.75 million.

In the 1971 report, which was the first to reflect the combined results of the merged companies, Mr Ryder announced that the Sumner Street plant was closed, because 'no combination of actions, even given the unions' fullest cooperation, could have bridged this [£750,000] gap'. The Southwark plant, although making even greater losses, was given a reprieve 'in an attempt to find a viable basis for this important modern printery'.

A consequence of reorganisation following the merger was the realisation of several items of IPC's property portfolios. In November 1970, in one of the largest single office property deals ever, Reed sold two buildings in central London to Amalgamated Investment and Property for £6 million. IPC's 50 per cent holding in Music for Pleasure also was sold to the other partner, EMI, and some of the wholly-owned operating interests were considered for sale. Mr Ryder himself directed and supervised the first phase of the reorganisation of IPC. Phase two was to come under the command of Mr Alex Jarrett, who joined the group on 1 October 1970 from the Prices and Incomes Board. Mr Jarrett became chief executive in charge of the operations in 1971.

ORGANISATIONAL DEVELOPMENTS

In Australia, in 1967, a reorganisation of the corporate structure of the group took place so that most of the companies were integrated under the single ownership of Reed Consolidated Industries. The activities covered by this company at the time of its inception included packaging, paper merchanting, paper converting, wallpaper and fabrics. A similar organisation was established in South Africa during 1969. In Canada the establishment of the same type of corporate structure was planned, and a start was made in 1970 to establish the desired organisation. Mr Ryder stated that he regarded 'the best organisational model to be a separate strong corporation in the country concerned, with its own board of directors, its own corporate responsibilities and its own chief executive, and with local shareholding participation'. The board of directors, which would not totally comprise local men, would be ultimately responsible to the Reed Overseas Corporation, one of the four divisions which resulted from the reorganisation following the acquisition of the International Publishing Corporation.

In July 1969 Reed Paper Group changed its name to the Reed Group Limited. Commenting on this decision, the chairman stated that the company had a long record in the paper making industry, with which it had always been connected, and they were fully committed to developing their paper operations to increase still further their competitive strength. However, they were also growing stronger in the manufacture and sale of converted paper and other products—so much so that these now accounted for over 65 per cent of their sales, and the proportion was still rising. Therefore 'they considered that the name 'Reed Paper Group' gave an unduly restrictive view of their activities'.

Following the merger with IPC, the company again changed its name to Reed International Limited. The combined group had a turnover of over £500 million per year, and was among the leaders in each major market in which it was involved. Not only was it the largest communications group in the UK, but it was also the largest paper making company with an annual production of some 1 million tons per year. In

1969 Reed had 15 per cent of the total stationery market, 25 per cent of the corrugated fibreboard case market, 13 per cent of the carton market and 25 per cent of the multi-wall paper sack market. In many of these markets Reed was the market leader.

Wall Paper Manufacturers produced around 80 per cent of the total wallpaper manufactured in the UK, while with their Crown paints Reed accounted for about 18 per cent of the total paint market.

In consequence of the IPC merger, the company was reorganised into four major operating divisions, each of which had a full divisional structure beneath them. They were

1. The Reed Paper Group, concerned with the manufacture of paper and packaging.
2. The Wall Paper Manufacturers, concerned with the manufacture of wall coverings, paints, building products, tiles, and other related products.
3. The Reed Overseas Corporation, which comprised Reed's overseas activities.
4. The International Publishing Corporation, concerned with the publication of newspapers, magazines, business journals and books, printing companies, and large trade investments notably in television.

The organisation structure is shown in Exhibit 8.

Mr Ryder was a strong advocate of decentralised decision making, not merely at the divisional level, but as far down to the level of operating units as possible. Mr Ryder's own description of how Reed practised this doctrine was as follows

> With decentralisation must come accountability. In Reed this takes the form of the annual presentation of business plans by each division covering short- and long-term objectives, sales, profits, manpower, capital requirements, and every aspect of the business. The Reed International Operations Executive consisting of myself, my deputy chairman (finance) and my deputy chairman (technical) examines the divisional plans in great detail and particularly the way in which they will fit in with group plans. When they are adopted for the ensuing year, very often after modification, they become the standard against which performance is monitored and rated.
>
> Once the business plan is approved, we say in effect 'You have told us how you want to run your business next year, we have agreed all the objectives, targets and budgets, now go away and perform and only refer back if there are variances or major changes you wish to make.'
>
> I exercise control over the group with the assistance of a very lean corporate centre—about seven key executives. I have a horror of huge HQ staff of people with authority but without responsibility for actually making profits. The main centre functions include finance, technical control, corporate planning, and personnel and manpower developments.
>
> The other major body concerned with the control of the Group is the Operations Executive which ... comprises myself and the deputy chairman (finance) and the deputy chairman (technical). We have no immediate responsibilities and are therefore free from divisional commitment. The Operations Executive monitors performance against budget and considers short-term policy of not more than a year.
>
> Each of the main divisional boards has an Executive Committee, which I chair, which carries out much the same function as the Operations Executive but at a divisional level. The purpose of this is to ensure that *decisions* can be made speedily and only on rare occasions is it necessary for a matter to go up the pipeline to the top Reed International board. That board can then confine its activities, as it should, to longer-term thinking and policy making and not be cluttered up with day-to-day operational matters.[8]

The monitoring of performance was carried out basically in two ways. Monthly reports were sent to headquarters by all the operating subsidiaries, and in addition Mr Ryder made frequent visits all over the world to the Reed operations, travelling some quarter of a million miles per year.

---

[8] Ryder, *Seminar*.

Management Development Policies

Mr Ryder frequently stressed that the development of professional management was the task to which he devoted the largest part of his time and energy. In his own words, 'It is a basic truth that management must always be the limitation because everything within our control results from the action of management'.[9]

Mr Ryder had pronounced views on management development and education, and also on the quality of British management.

> Shortage of management talent is our national economic plight; we just cannot afford to waste potential which gives a man of thirty-five a job which, under the right environment and training, he could have coped with successfully at the age of thirty.... I am concerned with the gap between what is created at business schools—that is, a graduate with certain management theories and techniques—and what is wanted, that is, professional managers....
>
> My constant dealings with large American corporations have convinced me that, by and large, most of our present top managements of large UK companies are equal in calibre to their counterparts in the large corporations in the States.
>
> What worries me, however, is that the second line management at the elbow of the presidents and chairmen of the large US corporations, the men who will be in command in, say, five years' time, are truly professional. Their counterparts here, I am convinced, are of just as good calibre, but we as yet haven't given them the tools with which to cope with the new technologies and the revolution which will occur in management methods.[10]

Reed's management development programmes reflected these views, and contained elements of which Mr Ryder was particularly proud. The company had its own permanent management school, at which senior company executives and Board members spent part of their time as faculty members. Mr Ryder himself participated actively in these programmes.

Mr Ryder also pursued a policy of appointing personal assistants with a view to promoting them to key executive positions within the Reed Group. By 1971 seven of his personal assistants had become managing directors in their own right.

FUTURE DEVELOPMENTS

With the acquisition of IPC, Mr Ryder saw the activities of Reed as being centred on producing 'media for communication'. But looking ahead to areas of future growth, he singled out the leisure market as being the most promising.

> ... it is going to be the big growth market. Where will all these extra wages go otherwise?
>
> We can see all this happening in all sorts of ways. The way that Polycell boats have gone ... is fantastic. And we foresee a time when any petrol station of any size will sell our boats in all shapes and sizes.... Or look at Australia, where we have bought a vineyard: wine drinking is going up fast not only there but all over the world—by leaps and bounds.[11]

Mr Ryder himself was a man of legendary energy. He frequently worked an eighteen-hour day and himself freely admitted that he enjoyed his exacting routine. 'If I were a rich man, I'd pay to do the job I am now doing'.[12] He also made it plain that he enjoyed the intricacies of mergers. 'I love negotiations and takeovers. If I were not a company chief, I would be a merchant banker'.[13]

---

[9] ibid.
[10] ibid.
[11] Eric Foster and George Bull, 'What Makes Ryder Run', *The Director,* May 1970.
[12] Foster and Bull, op. cit.
[13] ibid.

EXHIBIT 1   Reed International Limited

(£ million)

Year ending 31/3	1964	1965	1966	1967	1968	1969	1970	1971
Sales excluding intercompany sales:								
UK companies	76.6	108.8	n.a.	168.9	172.4	187.4	211.3	376.7
Overseas companies	24.9	40.4	n.a.	71.5	77.1	94.9	103.1	125.6
	101.5	149.2	226.1	240.4	249.5	282.3	314.4	502.3
Profit before depreciation	15.7	20.5	30.6	27.9	28.9	31.8	36.6	45.6
Depreciation	4.6	5.5	7.7	8.4	8.9	9.0	9.4	13.5
Trading profit	11.1	15.0	22.9	19.5	20.0	22.8	27.2	32.1
Investment income	—	—	—	.8	.9	1.1	1.1	2.2
	11.1	15.0	22.9	20.3	20.9	23.9	28.3	34.3
Interest on loans	1.5	1.7	3.5	6.8	6.7	7.0	9.0	14.5
Profits before taxes	9.6	13.3	19.4	13.5	14.2	16.9	19.3	19.8
Taxes	4.7	6.0	7.2	6.0	6.6	7.6	8.2	7.5
Net profits after taxes	4.9	7.3	12.2	7.5	7.6	9.3	11.1	12.3
Minority interests	0.3	0.3	0.7	0.5	0.5	0.7	0.9	1.2
	4.6	7.0	11.5	7.0	7.1	8.6	10.2	11.1
Profits attributable to Reed shareholders:								
Preference dividends	0.1	0.1	0.1	0.2	0.2	0.2	0.2	0.2
Ordinary dividends	3.3	3.8	7.2	6.6	6.7	6.7	5.8	10.5
Carried to retained earnings	1.2	3.1	4.2	0.2	0.1	1.7	4.2	0.4

Source: Annual Reports

EXHIBIT 2 Reed International Limited
Consolidated balance sheets (£ million)

Year ending 31/3	1964	1965	1966	1967	1968	1969	1970	1971
CAPITAL EMPLOYED								
Preference capital	2.6	2.7	2.7	4.1	4.1	4.1	4.1	4.1
Ordinary capital	34.2	37.3	53.9	53.9	53.9	54.0	55.3	84.3
Share premium account	36.5	42.0	71.2	70.8	70.8	70.7	72.3	112.6
Retained profit and other resources	21.4	25.3	24.3	26.2	28.6	29.7	34.8	46.0
	94.7	107.3	152.1	155.0	157.4	158.5	166.5	247.0
Deferred taxation	—	—	5.0	5.6	7.0	7.3	7.9	8.1
Minority interests	4.1	7.2	13.7	8.1	9.2	9.7	10.6	16.5
Provision for pensions	—	—	—	—	—	—	—	9.1
Loan capital	30.9	34.2	65.7	81.5	84.5	94.2	95.5	142.5
	129.7	148.7	236.5	250.5	258.1	269.7	280.5	423.3
EMPLOYMENT OF CAPITAL								
Current assets	64.2	72.4	117.1	113.0	126.4	139.9	166.1	234.1
Current liabilities and provisions	27.1	38.7	79.1	64.7	74.0	76.2	99.7	145.6
	37.1	33.7	38.0	48.3	52.4	63.7	66.4	88.5
Net current assets								
Trade investments	4.7	10.3	7.7	10.2	12.7	14.1	15.6	34.5
Fixed assets	60.5	67.2	126.8	127.5	128.3	127.0	130.9	171.1
Goodwill	27.4	37.5	64.0	64.5	64.7	64.9	67.6	129.1
	129.7	148.7	236.5	250.5	258.1	269.7	280.5	423.2

Source: Annual Reports

EXHIBIT 3   Reed International Limited

Group sales percentages by products (excluding intercompany sales)

	1964/5	1965/6	1966/7	1967/8	1968/9	1969/70	1970/71
Packaging products	29	26	24	24	26	25	18
Newsprint	18	10	10	9	9	8	4
Printing papers and stationery	23	15	19	19	19	19	14
Wrapping papers	13	11	10	9	11	10	5
Pulp	4	3	3	2	2	3	2
Wallpapers	0	14	12	13	12	12	8
Paint and building products	0	12	14	15	15	13	10
Printing	0	0	0	0	0	0	32
Other items	13	9	8	9	8	10	7

Source: Annual Reports

EXHIBIT 4   Reed International Limited.

Employment statistics

	1964/5	1965/6	1966/7	1967/8	1968/9	1969/70	1970/71
Employees	27,700	55,100	54,000	53,300	53,500	55,600	84,000
UK employees	N.A.	N.A.	N.A.	43,000	44,000	43,000	72,000
UK remuneration (£000)	N.A.	N.A.	N.A.	£39,950	£43,900	£45,900	£102,600

Source: Annual Reports

EXHIBIT 5 **Reed International Limited.** UK markets and market shares of principal Reed products, 1969

Company	Products	Market share	Market position	Principal competitors
Reed Paper & Board (UK)	Paper and board	18% UK production 12% UK consumption	1st	Bowater, Wiggins Teape, Thames Board, Scandinavian, Canadian and US suppliers
Reed Corrugated Cases	Corrugated cases	25%	1st	Bowater, Hygrade, Alliance
Reed Medway Sacks	Paper sacks	25%	2nd	Bowater, Dickinson-Robinson
Fields	Cartons	14%	2nd	Metal Box, Mardons, Waddingtons, Dickinson-Robinson
Reed Polyfilms	Plastic packaging (film)	N.A.	N.A.	British Visqueen, British Cellophane, B.X., Metal Box
Spicers	Stationery	15%	2nd	Dickinson-Robinson, Wiggins Teape, Chapmans
Wall Paper Manufacturers (Crown and Sandersons)	Wall coverings	80%	1st	ICI, Melody, Leyland, Graham & Brown
Sandersons	Furnishing fabric	5%	1st	John Lewis, Wardles, Mark Nutter, Sekers, Fischbacher
Walpamur (Crown)	Paint (decorative)	18%	2nd	ICI, Berger Jensen Nicholson, Courtauld International
Polycell	'Polycell' products	N.A.	1st	ICI, Johnson Richards, Harris, Hamilton
Reed Building Products	Building products (plastic plumbing systems)	15%	3rd	Marley, Osma

N.A. = Not Available

Source: Speech by Sir Don Ryder, London Business School, 1970

EXHIBIT 6 REED INTERNATIONAL LIMITED
Reed Group Sales and Profits

Group Sales and Profit	Sales (£m)							Sales (% of total)							Profit (£m before taxation)							Profit (% of total)						
	1966	1967	1968	1969	1970	1971		1966	1967	1968	1969	1970	1971		1966	1967	1968	1969	1970	1971		1966	1967	1968	1969	1970	1971	
UNITED KINGDOM COMPANIES																												
Paper and Packaging	135.2	138.3	136.8	150.5	163.3	178.7		49	48	45	44	44	30		9.2	8.0	9.0	10.9	13.9	12.9		39	41	45	48	51	40	
Wallpaper, paint and building products	73.7	74.4	82.0	85.4	99.0	107.4		27	26	27	26	26	18		7.9	4.9	6.0	5.7	5.6	5.5		33	25	30	25	20	17	
Publishing and Printing	—	—	—	—	—	174.5		—	—	—	—	—	29		—	—	—	—	—	5.3		—	—	—	—	—	17	
	208.9	213.7	218.0	236.9	264.3	460.6		76	74	72	70	70	77		17.1	12.9	15.0	16.6	19.5	23.7		72	66	75	73	71	74	
OVERSEAS COMPANIES																												
Canada																												
Pulp, paper and packaging	32.9	34.2	32.2	42.0	46.8	51.5		12	12	11	12	12	9		4.9	4.3	2.7	2.6	3.3	2.9		21	22	13	12	12	9	
Wallpaper, paint and building products	5.4	7.2	8.8	11.0	13.4	12.7		2	2	3	3	4	2		0.5	0.5	0.7	1.0	1.4	1.4		2	3	3	4	5	4	
Other																												
Paper and Packaging	20.4	25.3	28.6	31.5	35.5	43.9		8	8	9	10	10	7		0.9	1.2	1.3	1.6	2.1	2.7		4	6	7	7	9	8	
Wallpaper, paint and building products	6.7	11.8	13.7	17.9	16.0	17.9		2	4	5	5	4	3		0.2	0.6	0.3	1.0	0.9	1.2		1	3	2	4	3	4	
Publishing and Printing	—	—	—	—	—	8.6		—	—	—	—	—	2		—	—	—	—	—	0.2		—	—	—	—	—	1	
	274.3	292.2	301.5	339.3	376.0	595.2		100	100	100	100	100	100		23.6	19.5	20.0	22.8	27.2	32.1		100	100	100	100	100	100	
Less:																												
Intercompany Sales	48.2	51.8	52.0	56.9	61.6	92.9									—	—	—	—	—	—								
Interest paid less investment income	—	—	—	—	—	—									4.2	5.9	5.8	5.9	7.9	12.2								
	226.1	240.5	249.5	282.4	314.4	502.3									19.4	13.6	14.2	16.9	19.3	19.9								

Source: Annual Reports

EXHIBIT 7   Reed International Limited
Principal subsidiary companies 31 March 1971

OVERSEAS

Reed Overseas Corporation Ltd*

Australia

Butterworth & Co. (Australia) Ltd
J.Y. Tulloch & Sons Pty Ltd. 73%
McLaren Vale Wine Estates Pty Ltd, 73%
Paper Associates Ltd. 73%
Paul Hamlyn Pty Ltd
Reed Consolidated Industries Ltd, 73%
Reed Group Holdings Pty Ltd
Reed Paper Products Ltd, 73%
Wilson Fabrics & Wallpapers Ltd, 73%

Belgium

Intek SA
NV Polyfilla Products

Canada

Acme Paper Products Co. Ltd, 90%
Anglo-Canadian Pulp and Paper Mills Ltd, 90%†
Anglo Paper Products Ltd, 90%
Arthur Sanderson & Sons (Canada) Ltd
Butterworth & Co. (Canada) Ltd
Canadian Wallpaper Manufacturers Ltd, 67%
Crown Diamond Paints Ltd, 67%
Dominion Colour Corporation Ltd, 67%
Dryden Chemicals Ltd, 90%
Dryden Paper Co. Ltd, 90%
Empire Wallpaper & Paint Ltd, 67%
General Paint Corporation of Canada Ltd, 67%
Hamlyn Publishing Group (Canada) Ltd, 67%
Reed Paper Group Canada Ltd

France

Intek SARL
Polyfilla SA

Germany

Molto GmbH, 50%

Holland

Alabastine Holland NV

Irish Republic

Irish Paper Sacks Ltd, 51%
Spicer-Cowan (Ireland) Ltd
Walpamur Co. (Ireland) Ltd

Kenya

Walpamur Co. (Kenya) Ltd

New Zealand

Alex. Cowan & Sons (NZ) Ltd, 73%
Ashley Wallpapers Ltd, 44%
Butterworth & Co. (New Zealand) Ltd
E.H. Lund & Co. Ltd, 52%
Polycell Decorating Products Ltd, 37%

Nigeria

Spicers (Nigeria) Ltd

Norway

Sande Paper Mill A/S, 51%

Rhodesia

Phoenix Brushware Co. (Private) Ltd, 55%
Spicers (CA) (Private) Ltd

South Africa

Butterworth & Co. (South Africa) Ltd
Crown Cebestos (Pty) Ltd, 70%
Keartlands S.A. (Pty) Ltd, 50%
Key Terrain (SA) (Pty) Ltd
Polycell Products (SA)(Pty) Ltd, 51%
Polyfoil Packaging Pty Ltd
Reed Corporation (Pty) Ltd
Spicers (South Africa Holdings) Pty Ltd

Trinidad

Reed Trinidad Ltd, 65%

Uganda

Walpamur Co. (Uganda) Ltd

United States of America

Birge Co. Inc, 67%
Butterworth (Publishers) Inc.
International Computaprint Corporation, 88%
Montmorency Paper Co. Inc, 90%
W.H.S. Lloyd Co. Inc.

UNITED KINGDOM

Reed Group Ltd*

Reed Paper & Board (UK) Ltd*
Spicer-Cowan Ltd

Packaging companies

Field, Sons & Co. Ltd*
Reed Corrugated Cases Ltd*
Reed Medway Sacks Ltd*

Spicers Ltd*

Spicers International Ltd
Stationery Division
Data Papers Division

Service company

Reed Transport Ltd

Wall Paper Manufacturers Ltd*

Wallcoverings Division
Sanderson Division
Paint Division
Merchant & Retail Division
Texales Division
Polycell Division
Building Products Division
Household Textiles Division

International Publishing Corporation Ltd*†

IPC Newspapers Ltd
Daily Mirror Newspapers Ltd
Odhams Newspapers Ltd
Overseas Newspapers Ltd
Reveille Newspapers Ltd
Scottish Daily Record & Sunday Mail Ltd

IPC Magazines Ltd

International Printers Ltd

Odhams (Watford) Ltd

IPC Business Press Ltd

Hamlyn Publishing Group Ltd

Butterworth & Co. (Publishers) Ltd

---

* Direct subsidiaries of parent
† Preference shares not held by the group
All the equity is held by the group unless otherwise stated

Source: 1970 Annual Report

EXHIBIT 8 Reed International Limited.
Organisation of Reed International for 1970

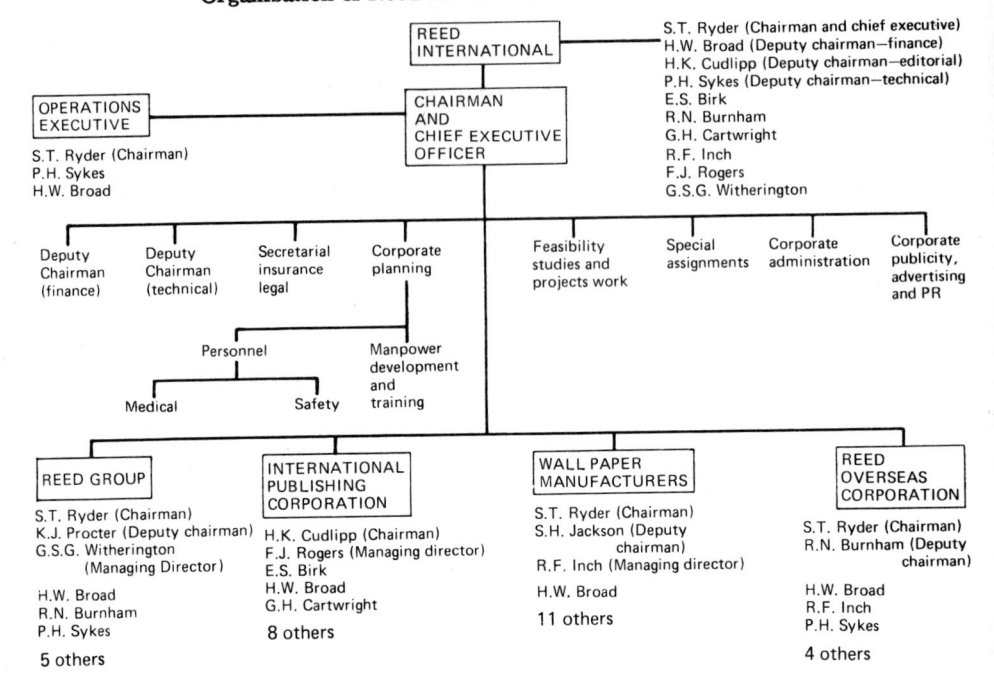

```
                                    ┌─────────────────┐   S.T. Ryder (Chairman and chief executive)
                                    │      REED       │   H.W. Broad (Deputy chairman—finance)
                                    │  INTERNATIONAL  │   H.K. Cudlipp (Deputy chairman—editorial)
                                    ├─────────────────┤   P.H. Sykes (Deputy chairman—technical)
  ┌──────────────┐                  │    CHAIRMAN     │   E.S. Birk
  │  OPERATIONS  │                  │      AND        │   R.N. Burnham
  │  EXECUTIVE   ├──────────────────┤ CHIEF EXECUTIVE │   G.H. Cartwright
  ├──────────────┤                  │     OFFICER     │   R.F. Inch
  │ S.T. Ryder (Chairman)           └─────────────────┘   F.J. Rogers
  │ P.H. Sykes                              │             G.S.G. Witherington
  │ H.W. Broad                              │
  └──────────────┘                          │
```

| Deputy Chairman (finance) | Deputy Chairman (technical) | Secretarial insurance legal | Corporate planning | Feasibility studies and projects work | Special assignments | Corporate administration | Corporate publicity, advertising and PR |

Personnel — Manpower development and training

Medical   Safety

REED GROUP	INTERNATIONAL PUBLISHING CORPORATION	WALL PAPER MANUFACTURERS	REED OVERSEAS CORPORATION
S.T. Ryder (Chairman)	H.K. Cudlipp (Chairman)	S.T. Ryder (Chairman)	S.T. Ryder (Chairman)
K.J. Procter (Deputy chairman)	F.J. Rogers (Managing director)	S.H. Jackson (Deputy chairman)	R.N. Burnham (Deputy chairman)
G.S.G. Witherington (Managing Director)	E.S. Birk	R.F. Inch (Managing director)	
H.W. Broad	H.W. Broad	H.W. Broad	H.W. Broad
R.N. Burnham	G.H. Cartwright		R.F. Inch
P.H. Sykes		11 others	P.H. Sykes
5 others	8 others		4 others

17 Norcros Limited*

In 1954 John V. Sheffield was concerned with preserving the assets of the Sheffield family from erosion by taxation. These assets, which had already been depleted by death duties following the death of Sir Berkeley Sheffield, mainly consisted of ironstone deposits near Normanby in Lincolnshire. The deposits were leased out for mining and were expected to be depleted by the mid-nineteen-seventies. Income from the mining operations was subject to surtax direction and hence by the time of depletion taxation would erode the majority of the asset value.

Mr Sheffield therefore decided to form a public holding company which would not be subject to surtax direction. Thus, in June 1956, 100,000 ordinary shares in a new company Norcros were offered to the public at a placing price of 5.25 shillings per share. In addition to preserving the asset position of his own family, Mr Sheffield considered, in launching Norcros, that it would meet similar needs of other successful family enterprises not large enough to be floated on their own yet not willing to risk a loss of identity by joining a large industrial group. At the same time an opportunity was offered to the investing public to participate in successful companies which would otherwise have remained private.

The initial assets of Norcros consisted of the Sheffield family ironstone deposits and a small label and specialist printing concern, Dapag (1943)—later renamed Tickopress—a company acquired by Mr Sheffield.

By 1971 the basic concept of Norcros had undergone significant change. The principal aim made in a statement to shareholders was 'to provide shareholders with the best possible capital and income return over the long term', which was to be achieved by a strategy 'of an industrially-based group which uses its resources efficiently to exploit its opportunities, in order to grow at a better than average rate as measured by its earnings per share'. In 1970 sales of the Norcros Group reached a record £33 million, producing pre-tax profits of over £3 million per annum on net assets of nearly £17 million. Recent financial statements are shown in Exhibit 1.

This case describes the evolution, strategy and stated policies of the Norcros Group from its inception in 1956 until 1971.

COMPANY HISTORY

The development of Norcros since inception in 1956 could be divided into three main phases. Between 1956 and 1961 the company expanded rapidly by a process of acquisition. From 1962 to 1966 problems created by the initial expansion became recognised and a gradual process of rationalisation took place. Following the rationalisation a new strategy and a new structure were forged to lead to the position found in 1971.

1956-61: The Acquisitive Growth Phase

Following the public placement of shares in 1956, Norcros expanded rapidly. The company became a kind of club, successfully attracting owner entrepreneurs concerned about reducing the threat of estate duty. The qualifications for membership of this club included a satisfactory past profit record and the availability of surplus cash. This cash was in effect used to finance the next purchase. This initial philosophy was clearly stated in a foreword to the early annual reports.

> Our subsidiary companies are wholly owned, and have been selected from a wide cross-section of British industry, and, prior to their incorporation within Norcros Ltd, they were controlled and managed by their founders or their families.
>
> Norcros enables the public to invest in some of the soundest and most progressive industrial companies of a limited size, which up to the present have been entirely in private hands.
>
> Norcros provides a means by which the private owners of these companies can avoid the destruction of their life's work by penal taxation and death duties, and yet retain an active interest by continuing to manage their companies, and by

---

* Copyright © Manchester Business School 1971

EXHIBIT 1 Norcros Group financial statements.

Year ended 30 November

(£000)	1960	1961	1962	1963	1964	1965	1966	1967	1968	1969	1970
Assets employed											
Stocks	1,821	2,939	2,931	3,165	3,367	3,658	4,411	4,379	4,210	3,873	4,468
Debtors	2,886	3,643	4,367	4,984	5,251	4,471	5,806	5,733	7,230	8,079	8,804
Liquid assets	503	10	19	27	168	1,757	132	124	318	1,480	807
Total current assets	5,210	6,592	7,317	8,176	8,786	9,886	10,349	10,236	11,758	13,432	14,080
Property, plant, equipment and motor vehicles	4,746	6,083	6,670	7,326	7,107	5,530	6,198	6,528	6,985	7,430	8,051
Goodwill	2,076	2,446	3,182	3,179	3,092	2,964	3,391	3,414	2,805	4,211	3,957
Investments	105	307	276	341	317	276	362	404	356	384	490
Total fixed assets	6,927	8,836	10,128	10,846	10,516	8,770	9,951	10,346	10,146	12,025	12,498
Total assets	12,137	15,428	17,445	19,022	19,302	18,656	20,300	20,582	21,904	25,457	26,578
Current liabilities	3,353	6,083	4,828	6,012	5,253	4,000	5,957	6,199	6,867	8,873	9,361
Net assets before longer-term liabilities	8,784	9,365	12,617	13,010	14,049	14,656	14,343	14,383	15,037	16,584	17,217
Loan capital	380	350	2,820	2,787	2,752	2,717	2,687	2,659	2,622	3,950	3,463
Other longer-term liabilities	1,239	1,129	1,162	1,202	1,338	1,077	1,080	1,080	1,316	1,554	1,532
Net group assets	7,165	7,886	8,635	9,021	9,959	10,862	10,576	10,644	11,099	11,080	11,882
Minority shareholders	62	211	182	205	239	510	232	238	244	109	195
Net assets of Norcros shareholders	7,103	7,675	8,453	8,816	9,720	10,352	10,344	10,406	10,855	10,971	11,687
of which: preference shareholders	1,943	2,038	2,198	2,198	2,198	2,198	2,198	2,198	2,198	2,198	2,198
ordinary shareholders	5,160	5,637	6,255	6,618	7,522	8,154	8,146	8,208	8,657	8,773	9,489
	7,103	7,675	8,453	8,816	9,720	10,352	10,344	10,406	10,855	10,971	11,687
Trading results											
Earnings per ordinary share	7½p	4½p	4½p	4½p	5p	6p	5½p	6p	8p	8½p	10½p
External group sales:											
UK	n/a	n/a	n/a	n/a	n/a	n/a	21,862	22,944	21,981	24,293	27,069
Exports from UK	n/a	n/a	n/a	n/a	n/a	n/a	2,706	2,648	3,196	2,085	2,717
Overseas	n/a	n/a	n/a	n/a	n/a	n/a	2,222	2,613	2,788	3,392	3,760
	16,670	19,750	24,340	25,860	23,000	22,301	26,790	28,205	27,965	29,770	33,547
Group trading profit	1,870	1,959	2,120	2,166	2,262	2,119	2,073	2,134	2,651	2,947	3,439
Profits available for appropriation	938	890	891	932	999	1,098	965	1,049	1,379	1,443	1,724
Preference dividend—gross	69	129	143	143	143	143	143	143	143	143	143
Earnings for ordinary shareholders	869	770	748	789	856	955	822	906	1,236	1,300	1,581
Ordinary dividend—gross	707	754	764	764	764	764	764	764	791	823	863
Tax retained from dividends	(301)	(342)	(352)	(352)	(362)	(372)	(38)	—	—	—	—
Retentions	463	358	336	377	454	563	96	142	445	477	718

Source: Annual Reports

investment in their parent company of which they become an active, participating member.

Care is taken when considering new acquisitions that management is progressive and assured for the future, that personalities and business outlooks are similar to existing members of the Group, and that relations with staff and work people have always been happy.

Lastly, great importance is attached to past profit achievements, encouraging growth possibilities and financial self-sufficiency.

Many family companies sought to join Norcros and some twenty-three acquisitions were made in the first five years, extending the interests of the group into a wide variety of product markets. Exhibit 2 contains a summary listing of the acquisition and divestments of the group and indicates the product markets in which the acquired companies were engaged. Profits expanded rapidly, increasing more than five fold in the three years up to financial year 1960 when profits reached £1.9 million before tax. This rapid growth was reflected in the share price which on an adjusted basis rose over seven times to 34 shillings in September, 1960 compared with the placing price of 5.25 shillings.

The typical formula adopted for acquisition was to offer one-third preference stock, one-third ordinary and one-third cash. The companies acquired continued to operate as autonomous units, with the original family managements being encouraged to retain all control over decision making. There was a minimum of central direction. Initially, central management was composed only of Mr Sheffield and a secretary. Rapid growth, however, led to an enlarged board, and in 1959 to the appointment of a managing director. This was the Honourable Geoffrey Cunliffe, former deputy chairman and managing director of British Aluminium who was chosen for his familiarity with financial management in a large enterprise. In 1960 an additional managing director, Mr John Boex, was appointed, a former colleague of Mr Cunliffe at British Aluminium. The function of Norcros central management was basically to provide finance and advice when and where called upon. Capital requests were never normally refused and the individual subsidiaries were free to spend and raise capital as they chose. Cooperation between subsidiaries, if it occurred at all, was accidental.

By the end of 1960 the financing of acquisitions and internal capital expenditure began to strain the available liquid resources. In 1961 it gradually became apparent that an overdraft position was developing but the lack of central financial data made precise estimating difficult. Although the rate of acquisition slowed, some new purchases were made. These were mainly for cash, thus further draining the short-term liquidity. For the first time profits failed to advance, causing a decline in stock price and increased the difficulties of continued acquisition.

1962-6: The Rationalisation Phase

The short-term liquidity problems of 1961 led to refinancing in early 1962. An issue of £2½ million 6¾% convertible loan stock was timed to coincide with the purchase of Dow-Mac Products Ltd. Profitability remained static throughout 1962 and acquisition was virtually halted. A chief accountant was appointed in an effort to improve financial controls, and late in 1962 a request for a short-term cash budget was sent out to the subsidiaries for the first time. Standardised accounting procedures were slowly introduced throughout the group but there were still no central controls on cash or capital expenditure.

In May 1963 Mr John Boex was appointed as sole managing director, on the resignation of Mr Cunliffe. Mr Boex began to rationalise the company in two main ways. First, a number of unprofitable subsidiaries were isolated and gradually disposed of or closed down to improve liquidity and financial stability. Between December 1963 and September 1965 five companies were disposed of and no new acquisitions were made until December 1965. Second, improved budgetary controls were gradually introduced by the central office over the activities of each subsidiary. This proved difficult at first and only slow progress was made. There was considerable resistance from the previously autonomous units to the concept of central controls. Further, central management was not available to attend in depth to the problems of the subsidiaries, and to develop the necessary information and control systems. Central management time was mostly taken up with day-to-day operations. However, in 1963 simple profit budgets were introduced, and the 1964 Annual Report noted a 'marked improvement in financial control and group management'.

In 1965 Mr Boex succeeded in reorganising the printing activities in the way he

EXHIBIT 2   Norcros Limited
History of principal acquisitions and disposals

Acquisition date	Name of company	Description of activities	Disposal date
1956 June	Norinco Ltd	Owners of land and properties in Normanby, Lincs, together with ironstone deposits therein	Dec 1969
1956 June	Tickopress Ltd	Specialist roll printers, etc.	
1956 Sep	Bramigk Ltd	Engineers and suppliers of machines to confectionery trade	Oct 1968
1956 Sep	Neil & Spencer Ltd	Manufacturers of dry-cleaning machines	Feb 1969
1957 Apr	CEC Ltd	Electrical engineers and contractors	Feb 1959
1957 Apr	Union Fibres Ltd	International merchants in textiles, etc.	Dec 1963
1957 May	John Tinsley Ltd	Designers and builders of haulage and winding machinery	Shut down
1957 May	Wescros Ltd	Iron, steel and metal merchants	
1957 Aug	Relay Vision Ltd	Rental, HP and sales of TV and radio sets	July 1964
1958 Mar	Autotype Co. Ltd	Manufacturers of photographic coated papers and films	
1959 Jan	Hygena Ltd	Manufacturers of timber and plywood kitchen units	
1959 Feb	Temperature Ltd	Manufacturers of air-conditioning equipment	
1959 Feb	Temperature (Vectis) Ltd (formerly Island Craft Ltd)	Manufacturers of air-conditioning equipment	
1959 June	Jensen Motors	Motor car manufacturers	July 1968
1959 Sep	S. Maw, Son and Sons (75 per cent interest)	Manufacturers of chemists sundries, etc.	
1960 Mar	Blythswood Ship-building Co. Ltd	Shipbuilders and heavy metal workers	Mar 1965
1960 June	Rotiss-O-Mat	Manufacturers of rotisserie equipment	Feb 1965
1960 July	Lantigen (England) Ltd	Manufacturers of oral vaccines	
1960 Oct	Fisher Clark & Co. Ltd	Tag and label manufacturers, printers	
1960 Nov	Harold Wood & Sons Ltd	Bulk liquid haulage contractors	Sep 1965
1961 Feb	Bulk Carriers Ltd	Bulk liquid haulage contractors	
1961 Nov	Aluminium Ingot Makers Ltd	Secondary metal refiners	
1961 Nov	Lowton Metals Ltd	Secondary metal merchants	
1962 Feb	Dow-Mac Concrete Ltd (formerly Dow-Mac Products Ltd)	Prestressed concrete manufacturers	
1965 Dec	Profile Publications (Publishers)	Publishers of profiles on aeroplanes, etc.	Dec 1968

1966 Mar	Ward Brooke & Co. Ltd	Plastics and instrument manufacturers, etc.		Mar 1969
1968 Dec	M. & S. Shifrin Ltd	Manufacturers of bedroom and dining-room furniture		
1969 May	Raymond Holdings Pty Ltd	Manufacturers of labels		
1969 Sep	P. P. Payne & Sons Ltd	Manufacturers of labels, ribbons and packaging materials		

Source: Annual Reports

wished later to apply to the group as a whole. Fourteen separate companies were welded together into a single company, Norprint, which integrated the activities of the individual concerns under a divisional executive group.

The reorganisation was carried out firmly yet considerately. Subsidiary directors were allowed to retain their directorship titles though their new functions were unquestionably those of managers. Minority interests were bought out and as a number of family managements retired initial annual savings of £75,000 were realised on executive salaries.

Nevertheless, profits still remained virtually static and the share price continued to decline as Norcros lost its growth image. By the end of 1965 it had become apparent that the rate of expansion which had characterised Norcros's early years could not be regained with the existing structure. It was therefore decided early in 1966 to conduct a study covering all aspects of the business. In June 1966 the group symbolised its desire for 'rationalisation and modernisation' by moving its head office from central London to a new centre at Reading some thirty miles from London.

1966-71: The New Strategy and New Structure

On the 7 July 1966 the following statement of corporate purpose was approved by the Norcros board:

> The policy of the Norcros group is to recognise its corporate and component structure by retaining in operation division form those companies which offer the highest potential in the fields of construction, consumer products, engineering and printing, and to achieve the specified rate of growth by concentrating all resources specifically to the expansion of those divisions, and to provide the necessary management to direct, coordinate and control the overall effort.

This statement marked the beginning of a new phase in Norcros's corporate life. Top management defined the task of the next five years as making the transition from a financially orientated holding company of widely diversified subsidiaries, each operating with a minimum of central direction, into an integrated group with a 'consistent purpose and common planned direction'. The group was to be made up of four operating divisions, namely printing, construction, consumer products and engineering, each having above-average growth potential, a coherent industrial structure and based on a solid industrial logic. Exhibit 3 shows the structure of the group in 1971, the divisions by then having been reduced to three.

In September 1966, with the board now behind him and the study complete, Mr Boex summoned the managing director of each subsidiary to a meeting at the Reading headquarters to advise them of the new strategy and structure.

Shareholders were notified of the change in a booklet circulated in March 1967 with the chairman's statement for the year. This included the following points:

> It was therefore decided we should aim to redefine Norcros Limited as an Industrial Group of Companies with the result that in future our energies should be concentrated on those of our businesses which have the strongest growth potential. Accordingly, the fourteen companies which best fit this requirement have been

EXHIBIT 3   Organisation of the Norcros Group

Board of Directors

Chairman
J. V. Sheffield

Executive
F.J. Briggs (Managing)
P.I. Marshall, FCA (Financial)
W.G.S. Tozer (Personnel and administration)

Non-Executive
D. Kirkness
A. Lyell
The Hon. P.M. Samuel, MC, TD
E.C.R. Sheffield

Norcros Limited
Managing Director
F.J. Briggs

Printing and Packaging Division

Chief Executive
D.M. Norman

Factories
7 in UK
Auckland, New Zealand
Bergen, Norway
Singapore
Sydney, Australia
Wellington, New Zealand

Products:
Photographic coated papers and films, paper labels, garment labels, tickets, tags, ribbons, overprinting machines and packaging materials.

Consumer Division

Chief Executive
D.H. Standen

Factories
5 in UK

Products:
Kitchen and bedroom storage units and dining room furniture; nursery goods and pharmaceutical products

Construction Engineering Division

Chief Executive
W.K. Roberts

Factories
7 in UK

Products:
Precast prestressed and reinforced concrete; air conditioning and refrigeration equipment fabrication and general engineers; metal merchants

reorganised into four main operating divisions each with a division chief executive who reports direct to top management. No further diversification will be made for the time being, allowing all resources of management, men and money to be concentrated on these four sectors.

The new divisions are construction, consumer products, engineering and printing. These are sectors which all have above-average potential for growth in a modern economy and at the same time are not industries in which massive investment in terms of research and development inhibit profitability.

Just as important is our intention to weld together these four divisions which will comprise Norcros Limited into a corporate body with a common identity having a common purpose and operating with a unified plan. It has always been our constant endeavour continually to improve the standard of management and financial control within the company. Management, although the least tangible, is the most important ingredient in any organisation, and a significant improvement in management standards and a much greater centralised control over all the operating divisions is a primary aim of the reorganisation.

Norcros has set itself high targets: a turnover of £50 million by the early 1970s and a coordinated plan designed to raise the rate of return on capital employed by over 18 per cent and before-tax profit margins by nearly 13 per cent. No operating part of the group, even those already bettering the target performance figures, is exempt from the obligation to aim for this standard of improvement. Again, a target attains nothing of itself. The means chosen to achieve the objective are critical and, in the case of Norcros, these means amount to an internal revolution.

Central financial control built on forward budgets imposes on every manager the necessity to think clearly about what he intends to do and how he expects to do it in the short, intermediate and long term, through his forward budget of profits and revenue: and how he plans to build the long-term growth of that part of Norcros under his control, through the capital budget. Capital spending, which means the allocation of the resources of the entire group, and thus the shaping of its future, is now rigidly controlled by top management.

These senior executives of Norcros, from the managing director downwards, now all have detailed 'position guides', or job descriptions, which lay down their precise roles in achieving the group's objectives. The managerial principle throughout is that unless a man knows what he is expected to achieve, and is forced to work out for himself how he will achieve it, the chances of success are seriously reduced, perhaps eliminated.

Managers will, however, receive greatly expanded central assistance in deciding on and arriving at their objectives. A new Management Services Division, providing consultant help in finance, industrial engineering, marketing and personnel, comes under a director of its own who also controls the financial system and who reports direct to the managing director. The separate marketing function of this division is unusual in a British company with only part of its interest in consumer products. The explanation is that Norcros is applying modern marketing techniques right across the group to ensure that the right products get to the right customers at the right price; and this will be a top management function in the subsidiaries.

Together with cost-cutting programmes, group-wide technical training, plant modernisation and other policies stemming directly from the board's July 1966 decision, these innovations will disturb many settled ways in the group. But growth is change; the alternative to dynamic expansion, which is stagnation, is in the long run far more unsettling for all those who belong to a commercial organisation.

Making its people realise that they do in fact belong to the group is one of the paramount objectives of Norcros and simultaneously one of the main methods by which it plans to achieve those aims. The intention is to build a group identity, to make out of a previously over-diversified holding company an operating unity with a clear and hard sense of purpose, whose members will identify themselves with the success and name of Norcros.

This statement of corporate purpose and organisation was backed up with a fifty-page formal statement of policies and procedures which was circulated to all managers throughout the group.

ACQUISITION AND DIVESTMENT POLICY

The new strategy anticipated that approximately two-thirds of the expected growth in turnover and profit before tax would come from external acquisition, with the remaining third being generated by internal growth. This ratio resulted from the identification of a so-called 'development gap'. The profit potential of the businesses Norcros wished to retain was identified and estimated to amount to approximately £3 million before tax by 1971. The difference between this sum and the 1971 profit objective of £4.5 million represented the gap to be satisfied by acquisition.

The financing of this programme was to be achieved partially by additional long-term borrowing but was expected to mainly come from divestments of interests which did not conform to the new strategy. In July 1968 Jensen Motors, a manufacturer of speciality cars, was sold for £60,000 after producing losses of £58,000 in 1967. This was followed by the sale of Bramigk Ltd, manufacturers of confectionery machinery. In February 1969 Neil and Spencer, manufacturers of dry cleaning machinery, was sold providing the main contribution in a total of £4.3 million raised by divestment. By the end of 1969 most of the former subsidiaries composing the engineering division of 1967 had been sold, and this division was combined with the construction division in 1968.

It was the strategy of the group to identify, in precise terms, appropriate growth sectors towards which the resources of the group could be directed and upon which they could be concentrated. Initially the areas chosen for concentration were to build up the consumer products division around the Hygena furniture interest and to expand the domestic and international interests of the printing division. Therefore, in December 1968 the group acquired M. & S. Shifrin, manufacturers of bedroom and dining-room furniture, followed in 1969 with the purchases of Raymond Holdings and P. P. Payne, manufacturers of specialist printings and labels. In May 1971 the overseas printing interests were further expanded by the purchase of a small specialist concern in South Africa.

PRODUCT MARKET STRATEGY

Each of the three main product divisions operated largely independently of the others. There was little or no interdivisional product flow and each division maintained its own contact with its respective markets. As a group Norcros did not engage in much basic long-range research. Concentration of research effort was made on product development and process improvement which was deliberately decentralised within the divisions. Extensive market research was conducted, however, aimed at establishing current and future consumer needs.

The largest product division, printing and packaging, accounted for 34 per cent of total sales in 1970 having grown steadily from 19 per cent in 1966. A breakdown of sales and profits by product group for the period 1966-70 is shown in Exhibit 4.

EXHIBIT 4 Sales and profitability by divisions 1966-70 (£000)

		1966	1967	1968	1969	1970
Construction and engineering	Sales	9,831	10,274	9,795	6,424	9,371
	% of total	37	36	35	22	28
	PBT	541	574	621	445	516
	% of total	28	31	26	17	17
Consumer products	Sales	5,403	6,099	7,372	8,702	10,148
	% of total	20	22	26	29	30
	PBT	296	401	466	431	508
	% of total	16	21	20	16	17
Printing and packaging	Sales	4,978	5,307	5,822	9,730	11,319
	% of total	19	19	21	33	34
	PBT	513	638	832	1,394	1,523
	% of total	27	34	35	53	50
Overseas and other interests	Sales	6,578	6,525	4,976	4,914	2,709
	% of total	24	23	18	17	8
	PBT	399	136	443	358	473
	% of total	21	7	19	14	16
TOTAL	Sales	26,790	28,205	27,965	29,770	33,547
	PBT	1,903	1,879	2,362	2,628	3,020

Source: Annual Reports

Printing and Packaging Division

In 1967 the printing and packaging interests of the group consisted of Norprint Ltd, the largest European specialist printer of tickets, tags and labels. Norprint produced over 14 million such labels per annum by all printing processes on almost every type of paper, board, film and foil. In addition, the company specialised in label systems and supplied a comprehensive range of machines, applicators and dispensers for printing and applying every type of label. These systems were sold for a variety of industrial purposes and were also widely used in supermarkets. Norprint was also an important producer of specialised coated papers and films for use in the production of photogravure cylinders and silk screens for the silk-screen printing industry.

Norprint extended the application of self-adhesive labels to the toy market in 1968 with the launching of its Simplay range of print-based charts and games for children. This consisted of a range of products such as Spotters Charts on such subjects as automobiles, wild flowers and Build-a-Map. Backed by advertising including spot TV and a specialist consumer products division, the operation achieved sales of over £100,000 in its first year of operation.

The addition of P. P. Payne in 1969 added further complementary strength to the printing division. This Nottingham-based firm was the UK market leader in printed fabric labels for garments and textiles. In addition Paynes produced decorative ribbons and had interests in packaging products especially heavy-duty industrial strapping and Rippatape, a built-in opening device for corrugated containers. Recent financial performance of the British subsidiaries of the Printing and Packaging Division are shown in Exhibit 5.

EXHIBIT 5   Printing and Packaging Division financial statements 1967-70

	Norprint 1967	1968	1969	1970	P.P. Payne 1968	1969	1970
	(£000)						
Sales							
Home	4,182	4,642	5,314	6,092	2,226	1,920	2,249
Export	770	895	1,051	1,312	441	418	499
Overseas	183	206	—	—	—	—	—
Total	5,136	5,556	6,365	7,404	2,667	2,338	2,747
Profit before tax	898	982	1,183	1,406	220	268	247
Profit after tax	523	607	752	1,066	133	149	169
Fixed assets	1,158	588	589	591	1,145	1,187	373
Goodwill, etc.	792	2,336	24	19	—	—	—
Unquoted investments	88	21	21	—	—	—	—
Current assets due from other subsidiaries	4	—	9	98	—	1	857
Stocks and WIP	825	777	938	1,119	402	348	353
Debtors and prepayments	1,122	1,448	1,886	2,294	429	661	720
Quoted investments	21	—	—	—	—	—	—
Cash	973	3	5	2	70	111	1
Total	2,945	2,228	2,838	3,513	921	1,121	1,931
Current liabilities							
Due to other subsidiaries	357	7	14	—	—	—	9
Creditors	488	657	960	1,114	349	295	252
Tax	653	808	871	399	11	90	126
Overdrafts	21	—	—	—	—	—	—
Dividends	506	522	732	1,078	45	50	157
Total	2,025	1,993	2,577	2,591	405	435	535
Net current assets	920	35	261	922	516	686	1,396

Source: Annual Returns

The acquisition of Raymond Holdings extended the divisions activities to Australia and New Zealand. Trading under the name of Label House Pty, Raymond had the major share of the Australian and New Zealand markets for labels, tickets and tags. Overseas interests were further extended in 1971 with the acquisition of a similar specialist printing concern in South Africa.

Construction Engineering Division

In 1967 this division was operating as two separate operations—a construction division consisting mainly of Dow-Mac Concrete, and an engineering division composed of a number of specialist engineering concerns. By 1968 these two divisions had been combined following the divestment of a number of the larger engineering interests, leaving two main subsidiaries Dow-Mac and Temperature Ltd, together with a number of small concerns engaged in secondary metal refining and trading. The remaining activities had been carefully chosen as growth areas where Norcros believed that success could be achieved through efficiency, service and technological innovation. The financial performance of the remaining subsidiaries is shown for recent years in Exhibit 6.

EXHIBIT 6   Construction Engineering Division financial statements, 1967-70

	Dow-Mac Concrete Ltd.				*Temperature Ltd.*			
	1967	*1968*	*1969*	*1970*	*1967*	*1968*	*1969*	*1970*
(£000)								
Sales								
Home	3,970	4,495	4,650	4,554	874	1,000	977	1,149
Export	—	—	11	38	365	634	328	602
Total	3,970	4,495	4,661	4,592	1,239	1,634	1,305	1,751
Profit before tax	356	339	370	426	44	125	129	101
Profit after tax	223	269	188	238	34	96	66	60
Net fixed assets	1,110	475	450	426	50	43	55	133
Current assets								
Stock and WIP	440	428	373	459	151	137	126	559
Debtors and prepayments	679	1,134	931	912	300	462	584	638
Cash	1	14	48	4	115	1	4	18
Due from other subsidiaries	—	5	24	17	3	116	—	—
Total	1,120	1,581	1,376	1,392	569	716	714	1,215
Current liabilities								
Due to other subsidiaries	—	—	—	—	20	—	29	—
Creditors	554	805	735	813	60	114	169	308
Tax	194	217	358	376	126	25	63	103
Dividends	433	161	349	239	65	124	80	63
Overdrafts	11	—	—	—	—	18	—	—
Total	1,192	1,183	1,442	1,428	271	281	341	474
Net current assets	(72)	398	(66)	(36)	298	437	373	741

Source: Annual Returns

Dow-Mac Concrete, the largest of the remaining subsidiaries, was the largest manufacturer of structural prestressed concrete units in the UK, and the world's largest producer of heavy structural units for motorway bridges and industrialised buildings. In addition, it had originated prestressed concrete sleepers for British Rail and currently supplied approximately half of the sleepers for an annual track-relaying requirement of 250 miles. Norcros estimated that in a notoriously unprofitable industry Dow-Mac's return on capital was the highest in its field.

The second main subsidiary, Temperature Ltd, was the largest British-owned air conditioning and environmental control manufacturing company. The British air conditioning market was expanding rapidly and was dominated by American concerns either producing locally or importing finished products. Norcros considered that some American equipment was not always wholly suitable for application in the UK and forecast an expanding future for Temperature Ltd. The company enjoyed a number of government contracts for air conditioning and environmental control in defence equipment. In 1969 the company moved to a new 78,000 sq. ft. plant on the Isle of Wight which had a further 15 acres available for future expansion.

Consumer Products Division

Norcros placed much effort into researching areas of consumer expenditure, attitudes and needs, and predicting future trends. As a result of this activity the efforts of the consumer products division had been concentrated in the fields of furniture, baby-care products and pharmaceuticals. Exhibit 7 provides financial details of these individual activities.

While the furniture industry was characterised by relatively slow growth, Norcros considered the industry was undergoing rapid change, with rationalisation into a smaller number of large efficient units. Two sectors of the industry had been identified as exhibiting above-average growth, namely kitchen and bedroom storage furniture. In 1967 the Norcros interest in this market was centred on Hygena Ltd, the largest manufacturer of kitchen storage furniture in the UK. Its main product line consisted of the System 70 range of kitchen units which sold towards the top end of the price range for kitchen furniture and was the brand leader in the UK. This was sold to both home owners and direct to developers, with each market representing about half of the £34 million industry sales reached in 1970/71. After investigating other sectors of the market Hygena launched its QA (Quick Assembly) range of units aimed at the do-it-yourself market in 1968. Backed by spot TV advertising this range had rapidly grown to be second only to System 70 in terms of the market share. In 1971 a further range, System 2000, was launched to appeal to the luxury market, incorporating a full range of built-in electrical appliances supplied by the German Bauknecht Company.

Norcros acquired M. & S. Shifrin at the end of 1968 in order to enter the market for bedroom storage furniture. Shifrin was primarily a low-price producer specialising increasingly in free-standing bedroom furniture. Wardrobes made up 50 per cent of sales with dressing tables and chests accounting for a further 30 per cent. The remaining 20 per cent of sales was split between dining-room sideboards, tables and chairs, wall units and room dividers.

The remaining subsidiary in the consumer products division, S. Maws Son & Sons was engaged in the manufacture, merchandising and sales of nursery and pharmaceutical products. Maws were brand leaders in teats and feeding bottles in the UK and also had substantial market shares in disposable nappies, baby pants and infant toiletries. A range of Junior Pharmaceuticals was sold through chemists including cough medicines, gripe mixture and teething balm. The company also produced a small range of proprietary and ethical pharmaceuticals including vaccines and eye care products. It was company policy to reduce Maws merchandising activities and increase the level of products manufactured within the group. At the same time substantial investment was being made in TV advertising and point of sale promotion to develop Maws's brand name in the baby products market.

Overseas and other interests

Apart from the overseas subsidiaries of the printing and packaging division, Norcros owned a subsidiary company in Canada. This company, Bulk Carriers Ltd, operated a fleet of about 200 'freight trains'—large bulk tractor-trailer tankers—carrying loads such as cement, fuel oils, chemicals and alcohol. This fleet operated mainly in Eastern Canada and the United States, from three bases in Toronto, Montreal and Windsor, Ontario. In 1970 Bulk Carriers made a profit of £91,000, a reduction of £59,000 on the 1969 results.

Other interests included a group property company which owned the freehold of the operating company buildings and a number of small investments.

THE ROLE OF THE CORPORATE HEADQUARTERS

The adoption of the new strategy and structure resulted in an increased role for the Norcros central office. In addition to Mr Boex and the company secretary, a finance director Peter Marshall was appointed from EMI in 1967. Mr Marshall was responsible for the introduction of improved financial procedures and played a major role in the acquisition and divestment programme. The staff of the finance director was

EXHIBIT 7 Consumer Products Division financial statements 1967-70

	Hygena Ltd			S. Maws Son & Sons Ltd				M. & S. Shifrin		
	1967	1968	1969	1970	1967	1968	1969	1970	1968	1969	1970
(£000)											
Sales											
Home	2,970	3,589	4,014	5,559	2,727	3,152	2,745	2,972	1,428	1,858	N/A
Export	34	36	48	76	90	97	164	171	—	—	N/A
Total	3,004	3,625	4,062	5,635	2,816	3,249	2,910	3,143	1,428	1,858	N/A
Profit before tax	244	338	286	684	147	187	57	(17)	274	185	N/A
Profit After Tax	222	335	212	399	85	106	33	(17)	156	113	N/A
Fixed assets	512	845	907	835	172	234	241	281	347	304	N/A
Current assets											
Stock and WIP	345	509	757	623	234	310	395	611	169	260	N/A
Due from other subsidiaries	—	—	—	1	152	—	—	—	—	—	N/A
Debtors and prepayments	734	1,158	1,473	1,758	682	896	713	865	210	218	N/A
Bank and cash	110	3	12	16	78	54	5	5	30	9	N/A
Total	1,189	1,670	2,242	2,398	1,146	1,260	1,113	1,481	409	487	N/A
Current liabilities											
Creditors	403	665	787	1,015	560	523	701	786	190	250	N/A
UK and overseas tax	92	20	13	117	97	143	109	30	64	166	N/A
Due to other subsidiaries	—	—	—	—	1	157	144	129	—	—	N/A
Dividends	410	334	283	399	85	99	22	14	—	50	N/A
Total	905	1,019	1,083	1,531	743	922	976	959	254	466	N/A
Net current assets	284	651	1,159	867	403	338	137	522	155	21	N/A

Source: Annual Returns

increased and a management services division was set up. Other appointments included an industrial engineer and a marketing adviser, together with a small staff for each. These appointments more than doubled the head office expenses from £147,000 in 1966 to over £320,000 in 1967.

In 1969 Gordon Tozer was appointed to the position of director of personnel and administration as the group came to recognise the need for developing managerial talent. In the same year John Briggs, formerly managing director of Norprint, was appointed director of operations.

The development of the central office led to the introduction of formalised procedures covering marketing, where annual marketing plans were prepared by the divisions; finance, incorporating both short- and long-term plans; and capital budgeting. Nevertheless the size of the central staff remained small and in 1971 totalled approximately thirty. The appointment of central office executives was restricted first to providing specialist advisory services such as taxation, pensions and legal functions, not normally available in the operating division, and second, for analysing incoming information from the divisions in order to control and monitor performance and allocate resources.

Financial Procedures

The new financial procedures developed to assist implementation of the new strategy were based on the concept of influencing future events through forecasting likely performance. The control exercised by head office centred mainly on two areas:

(a) a system of four-year plans and annual budgets

(b) central control of cash balances

A system of four-year, long-term plans was introduced for each division to be updated in May of each year, with the projections covering the full financial requirements for the growth of the business in terms of sales increase, capital requirements, cash flow and pre-tax profits over the following four years. These plans enabled Norcros to assess its future financial requirements in relation to its planned growth, and formed the basis for its policy on acquisitions and disposals.

Covering the short term a system of annual budgets was introduced. Each division agreed with Norcros (which was consulted throughout the planning stage) its annual budget in October each year for the following financial year (1 December-30 November). The annual plan was prepared initially at the level of the individual subsidiaries in consultation with the divisional chief executive. A plan for each division was then reviewed and renegotiated by the central office in the context of the group's target growth rates for each division. When finalised the plan became a divisional profit budget for the year and 'a solemn undertaking which local management was required to accept'.

Each division's performance was measured through its monthly management reports. These reports contained comparisons of actual achievement against budget and forecast performance. The monthly budget performance was phased at the time budgets were agreed. Forecast performance was revised monthly and indicated each month in advance how actual performance was likely to vary from budget.

Three days after the end of each month Norcros obtained a 'flash' report from each division containing estimated sales and pre-tax figures for that month. The period report containing actual figures was available to divisions and to Norcros fourteen days after the end of each month. The forms on which this information was supplied were specifically designed to provide data which divisional executives had to have for responsible, efficient management. The information required by head office was easily extracted for its control and accounting purposes.

Capital expenditure was approved 'in principle' at the time the budgets were approved. Each capital expenditure requirement had subsequently to be applied for with a full project justification. Once final approval was given, Norcros control then took the form of phasing the cash outflow.

Freehold properties of the subsidiaries were owned by a group property company and a fair market rental was charged to the occupier. The accounting result of the division was thus related solely to trading performance. For budget and management accounts purposes, a charge was also made by Norcros on each division in respect of interest on the assets managed. This was currently $6\frac{1}{4}$ per cent. The funds created by this charge were remitted to Norcros each month.

The major day-to-day control of the group by head office was through control of cash balances. No United Kingdom division was permitted a bank overdraft. Cash generated in a division's trade, less an agreed retention immediately required for its business, was transferred each month to Norcros Limited. Further cash required by divisions to finance trade expansion or the 'new' money required for capital assets was supplied by Norcros. All transfers were measured against the phased cash budgets and three-monthly rolling cash forecasts.

Recovery of Central Expenditure System

In November 1967, as mentioned above, the new finance director introduced a charge on capital employed by the subsidiaries. Throughout the group, operating companies bore a charge against their profits each month which was calculated at a standard rate on the opening balances of that month of fixed assets, stocks, debtors and creditors. These balance sheet categories were referred to as 'assets managed' and in the definition there was no deduction for depreciation, and all terms were valued at replacement cost so far as practicable.

The rate of interest charged on the 'assets managed' was determined centrally, designed for a longer term to avoid annual fluctuations and levied on all trading operations in an equitable manner.

The underlying principle of the system was to state the operating company profits at a level which was equal to the pre-tax equivalent of earnings for ordinary shareholders. The system yielded a number of advantages which included the following:

(a) Clarity of purpose—both operating and central managements were considering only one criterion of profitability—earning for ordinaries.

(b) Cost of time—interest charges were made on specific events, viz. the credit periods of debtors and creditors, the length of ownership of fixed assets, and the length of time goods remained in stock, or work-in-progress. The effect was valued and charged to the profit statement.

(c) Gross marginal costing was eliminated.

(d) Loss-making activities were identified in stark relief. Such activities usually contained excessive assets (under-utilised plant, slow-moving stocks, slow debtors, etc.) and these were fairly penalised by specific costs.

(e) Departmental profits were easy to measure. Since the interest was calculated on assets managed the charge to a given factory based on its fixed assets, work-in-progress, stocks, etc., could be further subdivided as required. In the marketing departments the interest charge on debtors could be divided readily between outlets of trade, individual customers, exports and so on, so that the particular manager involved could be aware of the situation.

(f) Overhead departments also bore interest charges so that the interest costs of their assets managed were specifically taken into account. This was particularly important in the case of works engineering departments, computer departments, etc.

(g) Piece parts passing from one department to another were priced including the interest content on the assets involved. Sub-assemblies passing between factories also contained the interest element attracted by the assets employed to that stage.

(h) Finished goods went into stock at standard prices which included the appropriate interest on the assets involved in their manufacture.

(i) Calculations for selling price guidance included interest according to the terms of trade. For example in the case of exports, interest would be provided on the length of time in finished goods stock, goods in transit, export debtors and cash in transit. This was frequently a surprising revelation to commercial managements.

(j) Plant and machinery attracted interest without a deduction for depreciation, so that factory managements were stimulated to dispose of under-utilised or inefficient items. This encouraged modern plants of optimum size.

(k) Profit-sharing schemes for management could be fairly devised, automatically containing the vital element—cost of time.

(l) The interest charge was dynamic, based on monthly opening balances. If stock went up in a month there was an immediate increase in the charge—if debtors went down in a month there was an immediate benefit in the profit statement.

Personnel Policy

The adoption of the new strategy led to substantial change in the top management of the subsidiaries. Many of the former family managements left the group in the first two years of the change in policy. Norcros recognised that to achieve better than average performance it needed skilled and highly motivated managers. Where possible it remained group policy to promote from within; however, to fill the vacancies created by the new strategy which could not be met from inside the organisation, Norcros began actively to recruit business graduates from leading British and American universities. In 1968, as a result of recruiting, one PhD in operations research from Lancaster, one DBA in business policy from Harvard and two MBAs joined the group. Exhibit 8 indicates the top management team at Norcros in April 1971.

EXHIBIT 8   Top Management Team

Chairman

John V. Sheffield. Chairman. Norcros Ltd. Age 57. Educated Eton, Magdalene College. Cambridge (MA). Chairman: Portals Holdings Ltd, Anderson Finch Villiers (Insurance) Ltd. Director: British Assets Trust Ltd, Second British Assets Trust Ltd, Atlantic Assets Trust Ltd, Clarke Chapman—John Thompson Ltd, Green's Economiser Group Ltd, Royal Exchange (City Branch), Normanby Estate Co. Ltd. Was High Sheriff of Lincolnshire 1944-5.

Executive Directors

F. John Briggs, Managing Director. Norcros Ltd. Age 47. Educated William Hulme Grammar School. Served in RAF from 1942 to 1946. Joined Tickopres Ltd, a founder company of Norcros in 1946. Was appointed Sales Director 1953. Became Assistant Managing Director in 1955, joint Managing Director in 1958, Managing Director in 1960. In 1962 became joint Managing Director Tickopres and Fisher Clark Limited. In 1965 was appointed Managing Director Norprint and Chairman of subsidiaries. In 1966 was appointed Director of Norcros and Chief Executive Printing Division. Appointed Director of Operations in 1969. Is now Chairman of ten Norcros companies. He is President of the World Packaging Organisation. Director of the European Packaging Federation (Past President), and Chairman of the Board, Institute of Packaging. He is also a Freeman of the Worshipful Company of Tylers and Bricklayers, a Fellow of the Institute of Directors, a Fellow of the Institute of Marketing and a member of the BIM.

Peter I. Marshall, Financial Director of Norcros since 1967. Age 44. Educated Buxton College, Derbyshire. Became Chartered Accountant in 1955. Financial Accountant for Mullard Ltd in 1956. Was Group Accountant of EMI Ltd, from 1960 to 1963 when he became Financial and Commercial Director of their Industrial Electronics Company to June 1967. Is a Fellow of the Institute of Chartered Accountants. Also a Licentiate of the Royal Academy of Music, conductor and pianist.

W. G. S. (Gordon) Tozer, Director of Personnel and Administration. Age 50. Educated at Harrow, Sandhurst and Joint Services Staff College. After serving in Grenadier Guards from 1940 to 1957, he became Sales Manager then Export Manager for Formica Ltd. In 1962 was appointed General Manager of Formica India Limited and in 1966 became involved with Overseas Development for Formica International Ltd. Joined Norcros in 1967 as Chief Executive, Consumer Products Division and the same year was appointed a Director. Present appointment made in 1969.

Secretary

Victor C. Yaldren, Secretary of Norcros since 1963. Age 51. After education at East Grinstead Grammar School, served in the Army from 1939 to 1946. Qualified as Chartered Accountant in 1948. Specialised in taxation and financial investigation. Worked on Norcros's financial affairs from 1956 while with Deloitte, Plender, Griffiths & Co., and joined Group in 1962. Is Fellow of the Institute of Chartered Accountants, Member of Society of Investment Analysts and Member of BIM.

Chief Executives

David M. Norman, Chief Executive, Printing and Packaging Division, and Managing Director of Norprint Limited. Age 30. After attending McGill University, Canada, where he obtained a BA Degree in Economics, he worked on the West Coast for the US Meat Packers, Armour & Company. Then worked for the Corporate Financial Department of Merrill Lynch on Wall Street. Returned to the UK and joined Dunlop's Central Marketing Department in 1964 and became Marketing Manager of Slazengers, UK. In 1965 he attended Harvard Business School, specialised in Marketing and Corporate Finance and received his Masters (MBA Degree) in 1967. Returned to the UK and joined Norcros Marketing Services. In September 1968 became Marketing Director of Norprint and one year later was appointed Managing Director.

W. K. (Ken) Roberts, Managing Director, Dow-Mac Concrete Ltd since 1954. Age 47. Educated: Dominican Friars School, Bangor, and Bath Technical College. Served in the Admiralty from 1942 to 1946. Joined Dow-Mac in 1946. Is a Justice of the Peace.

Donald H. Standen, Managing Director, Hygena Ltd since 1967. Age 46. Educated at Crofton School. Member of the Institute of Cost and Works Accountants and Chartered Institute of Secretaries. War service with Royal Air Force. Was Navigator, Bomber Command, Europe, Middle East, Far East. Industrial experience covers light engineering (general machine shop ferrous and non-ferrous foundries, hydraulics, metal sintering processing), instrumentation (including airborne navigation equipment), textiles (spinning, weaving, dyeing and making up), electrical engineering (including transformer manufacturing), pharmaceuticals (including toiletries), and confectionery. Previous board appointments: Sterling Industries Ltd in 1956, William R. Warner & Co. Ltd in 1961.

The company began a series of in-company group training courses in 1968 covering the functions of general management, accounting, marketing, production and purchasing. This was later expanded in order to facilitate the building of a strong team of executives in top, second and third line positions who could see a permanent career for themselves with Norcros.

A comprehensive and integrated programme was started to enable each individual to develop his career in the group. The career development programme was closely tied to the annual review of the four-year plans. From the plans information was extracted about future manpower, organisational requirements, succession and career development. These requirements were coordinated centrally in close consultation with the divisions and plans based on a minimum two-year training and development cycle. The training which each individual required in order to further his career with Norcros was planned with him and the recommendation detailed in the four-year plan.

In December 1970 Norcros introduced a special share-incentive scheme for executives making the greatest contribution to growth. These shares were only of value if specific targets were met over a period of time. The scheme was designed to increase profitability in terms of earnings per share and to attract and retain executives of the highest calibre.

In addition, an incentive bonus scheme was introduced for all executives who controlled profit centres. This was based on the achievement of an agreed annual pre-tax profit budget and there were substantial increments for results in excess of budget.

Change of Management

Mr John Boex resigned as managing director of Norcros on 20 March 1970 on the grounds of ill health. He was succeeded by John Briggs formerly managing director of Norprint from 1966 to 1969, when he became director of operations.

RECENT MARKET PERFORMANCE

The result of the new strategy and structure resulted in a rising market price for Norcros shares as shown in Exhibit 9. Nevertheless, market reaction did not result in much change in the company's price/earnings multiple.

Commenting on the 1970 results, the *Guardian* of 23 February 1971 stated:

> The fortunes of Norcros show how hard it is to convince investors that you are the exception that proves the rule. Norcros is a mixed holding company which is not a fashionable form of organisation. Its management is strong in young business

EXHIBIT 9   Monthly share prices (pence)

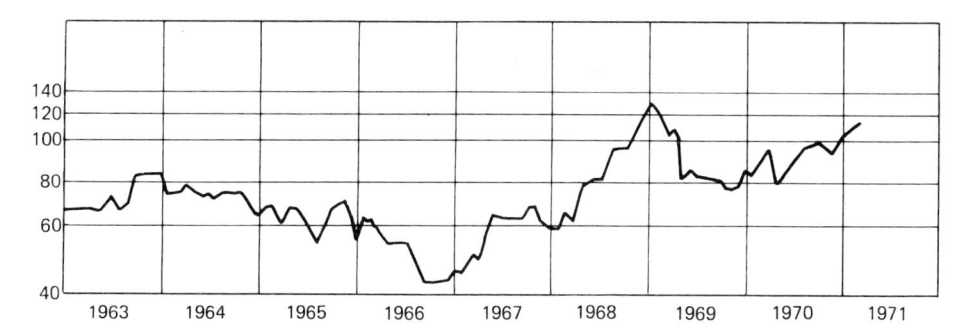

Source: Moodies Investment Handbook

graduates, who have yet to convince the stock market that the methods they learn work in real life.

Result: figures which are excellent by any test were greeted yesterday with little more than a shrug. Pre-tax profits are up 13.6 per cent, and the share price rose $2\frac{1}{2}$p—just over 2 per cent—to $118\frac{1}{2}$.

The profit is a record for the third year in succession, yet the p/e on the new earnings of 10.3p per share is only 11.2. Little recognition here for a consistent record, nor for the more remarkable fact that Norcros managed a shade of improvement in trading margins—from 9.9 to 10 per cent—in a year which has been disastrous for so many companies.

The profits picture is complicated by acquisitions and sales of subsidiaries, but apart from the recession in North America which made life difficult for the Canadian group, the preliminary statement gives the impression of an 'all-go' business.

In fact, all three of the operating divisions, construction engineering, 'consumer' (nursery supplies, pharmaceuticals and furniture) and printing and packaging made 'significant' contributions, to the peak earnings performance.

Given reasonable conditions, the improvement in profits could continue, for after the 12.5 per cent profits rise in the first half, growth accelerated to a 14.4 per cent increase in the second half. The synergy, fostered by the Payne and Raymond acquisitions was clearly a stimulus to the printing division.

Norcros now surely deserves a better rating. But it may be some time before investors can believe good news when they see it.

18 Lonrho*

The London and Rhodesian Mining Company (Lonrho)[1] was found in 1909 to acquire mining rights and shares in mining companies in Rhodesia. Over the next fifty years Lonrho developed these assets and also acquired interests in property, ranching and agriculture, which by 1961 were earning pre-tax profits of £158,000 on assets of £3.41 million.

A decade later, Lonrho had been transformed into a multinational conglomerate of some 400 companies, employing 100,000 people throughout fifteen countries in Africa and five in Europe. Interests ranged from automobile sales franchises and mining to electricity generation and ground nuts, giving an annual turnover of £216 million by 1972. A summary of Lonrho's principal activities is shown in Exhibit 1. Over this period pre-tax earnings had risen to £19.2 million on total assets of £231.6 million with an (unadjusted) earnings per share of 11.32p, and the share price increased by more than eight times. Recent financial performance is shown in Exhibits 2 and 3, while the history of the company's share price is given in Exhibit 4.

Lonrho owed much of its transformation to its managing director and chief executive, Mr Roland Rowland, who joined the board in 1961 at the request of Harley

EXHIBIT 1

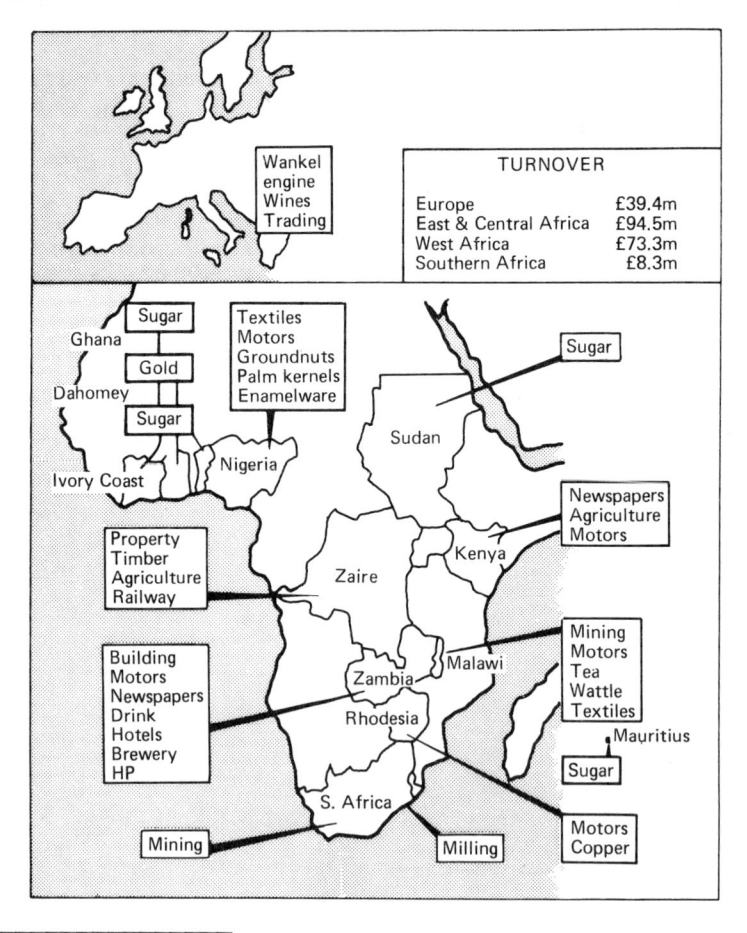

---

1. All the information in this case has been collected from publicly available sources.

*Copyright © Manchester Business School 1973

EXHIBIT 2 Lonrho Group Consolidated six-year operating summary
(£ millions)

	1967	1968	1969	1970	1971	1972
Turnover	N/A	101.0	154.00	184.00	191.88	215.90
Net profit before tax	3.60	6.83	13.75	14.23	15.06	18.28
after Depreciation	1.47	2.37	4.39	5.29	5.75	6.49
Long-term interest	0.08	0.20	1.16	1.23	1.45	1.38
Short-term interest	—	0.98	1.64	2.22	2.36	2.86
Tax	1.38	3.04	6.79	6.67	8.05	10.38
Minority interests	0.79	1.50	2.78	2.83	2.63	3.01
Profit attributed to parent Co.	1.42	2.04	3.19	4.73	4.19	4.89
Dividend	0.81	1.42	2.48	3.13	1.38	2.43
Retained profit	0.61	0.61	0.71	1.60	2.81	2.46
Earnings per share (adjusted) (pence)	5.60	5.60	6.75	9.00	7.95	7.85

Source: Extel Statistical Services Ltd

Drayton's 117 group, a major shareholder. After successfully building up Lonrho's operations in Rhodesia in the pre-UDI phase (Unilateral Declaration of Independence, Autumn 1965), Mr Rowland embarked on an ambitious acquisition programme, taking over well-established colonial companies which were sensitive to the new political climate of the emergent African states. Earnings before tax for 1969 were boosted to £12.5 million and the share price reached a peak of 316p in March of that year.

Then, a turn of fortune saw a number of promising mining ventures fall through when talks collapsed with the African governments concerned. Technical difficulties in the development of a major venture in South Africa, the Western Platinum Mines, caused a serious drain on capital and in September 1971, the acquisition of the Wankel Group, owners of patents of the revolutionary Wankel rotary engine forced a liquidity crisis over which two directors and Lonrho's financial advisers, S. G. Warburg, resigned. Simultaneously news arrived of the arrest of four directors in South Africa on fraud charges.

Peat, Marwick and Mitchell, the accountants, were called in to review the company's financial and managerial state of health. Their subsequent report, issued in March 1972, made certain recommendations which led to a strengthening of the board.

However, by March 1973 the board had split over a resolution to remove Mr Rowland from office, on the grounds that he was unsuitable to administer the diversified conglomerate Lonrho had become. Mr Rowland immediately sought a court injunction to prevent his dismissal. The issue was finally resolved at an Extraordinary General Meeting requisitioned by Mr Rowland in May 1973.

This case describes the development of Lonrho's strategy under Mr Rowland's leadership and its implementation, leading up to the liquidity crisis in 1971, the subsequent boardroom controversy, together with the reactions of governments and other interested groups in the 'Lonrho affair'.

MR ROLAND ROWLAND

Mr Rowland's invitation to join the board arose after the 117 Group, an investment group owned by Mr Harley Drayton, acquired an equity interest in Lonrho in 1960. The following year, Lonrho's profits fell sharply and the slump in share price prompted Mr Drayton to send Mr Angus Ogilvy, a junior member of the 117 Group and husband of Princess Alexandra, a member of the British Royal Family, to find someone capable of putting the company back on its feet. Mr Ogilvy's enquiries brought him into contact with Mr Rowland, 'Tiny' Rowland, a successful six-foot entrepreneur from Salisbury, who had built up a substantial fortune in Rhodesia.

EXHIBIT 3 Lonrho Consolidated Group Balance Sheets (£ 000)

(Year ended 30 Sept.)

	1967	1968	1969	1970	1971	1972
FIXED ASSETS						
Freehold and leasehold properties		36,780	45,053	48,128	51,980	52,680
Mining properties		4,807	23,662	26,904	33,400	33,230
Plant, equipment, vehicle, aircraft and others	N/A	13,376	48,940	54,398	62,200	66,240
Pipeline		3,590	3,590	3,590	3,590	3,590
Less Depreciation	8,244	14,574	33,964	35,973	45,160	45,920
	19,106	43,979	87,281	97,047	106,010	109,820
Nationalised assets suspense accounts	—	1,081	1,252	2,143	1,160	530
Investments	1,413	4,835	11,201	12,715	11,650	14,920
Wankel patents rights[1]	—	—	—	—	12,170	12,250
TOTAL FIXED ASSETS	20,519	50,793	99,734	111,905	130,990	137,520
CURRENT ASSETS						
Stock and W.I.P.	—	—	34,410	38,682	47,780	47,540
Project expenditure[2]	8,597	15,797	1,344	1,260	760	—
Debtors	8,213	14,514	27,447	37,743	36,300	34,060
Cash and deposits	1,631	2,774	8,899	8,191	7,120	12,440
TOTAL CURRENT ASSETS	18,441	33,086	72,100	85,876	91,960	94,040
CURRENT LIABILITIES						
Bank Overdraft						
Secured	}6,569	8,638	}19,551	6,260	6,830	6,020
Unsecured				15,840	17,160	11,790
Creditors and accruals	8,879	17,035	33,878	44,153	52,210	47,350
Taxation	3,045	5,850	10,714	10,621	13,670	13,410
Dividends	490	1,424	2,483	3,128	1,380	2,430
Others	46	61	—	—	—	—
TOTAL CURRENT LIABILITIES	19,029	33,008	66,626	80,000	91,250	81,000
Share capital	3,860	7,061	12,286	12,521	12,521	16,210
Surplus on consolidation of net assets	325	3,956	6,467	6,004	5,440	4,240
Capital reserves	313	7,332	33,532	35,132	30,020	40,720
Revenue reserves	1,989	2,376	3,429	7,482	9,810	14,480
Future tax	—	926	1,899	2,413	2,500	3,970
Minority interests	6,570	22,075	23,489	29,060	31,470	33,920
Convertible loan stock	1,916	546	12,400	11,810	12,980	12,520
Long-term loans	1,142	2,520	5,508	6,199	15,940	10,220
Short-term loans[3]	3,816	3,181	6,198	7,160	5,760	12,340
Deferred Purchase Consideration	—	—	—	—	3,260	1,940
TOTAL CAPITAL EMPLOYED	19,931	49,973	105,208	117,781	131,700	150,560

SOURCE: Annual Reports

Notes: 1 Increase in 1972 due to currency realignment.

  2 The amount represents expenditure on mining and other projects in course of investigation or development.

  3 Repayable in less than five years.

EXHIBIT 4 Lonrho Share Price Movements 1962-72

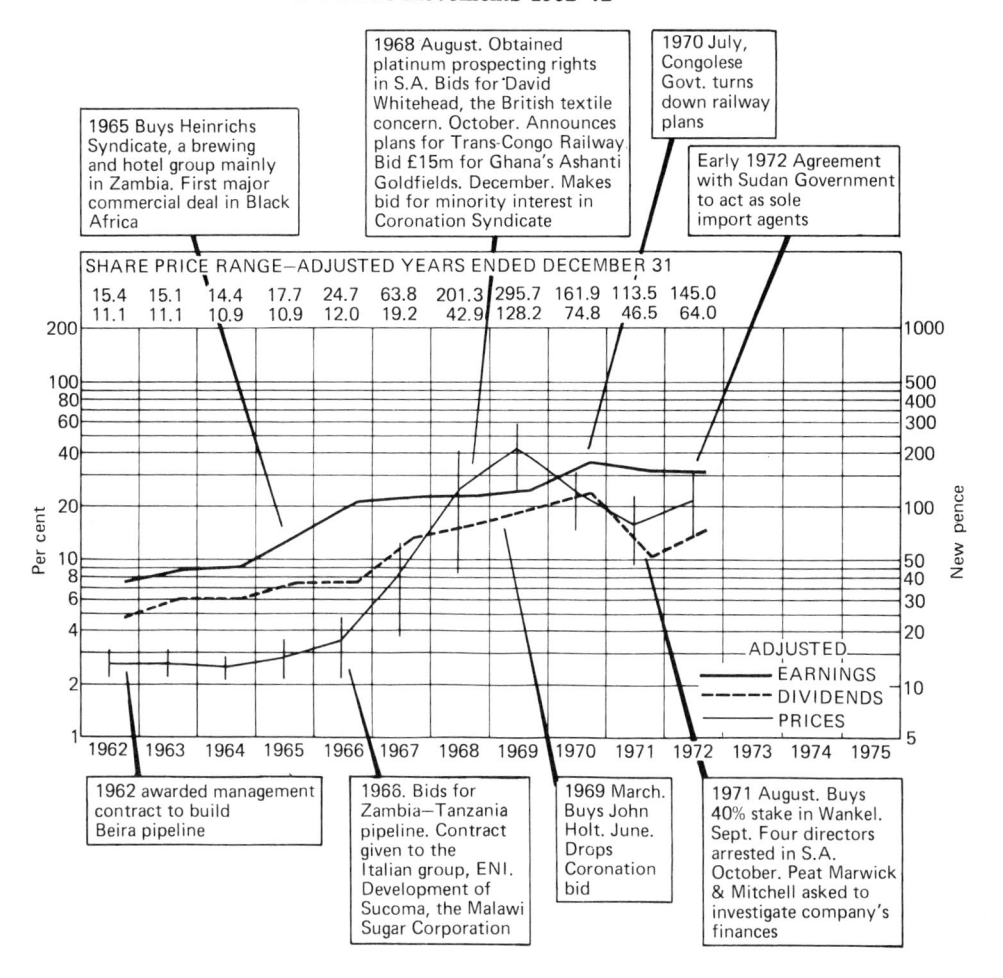

1965 Buys Heinrichs Syndicate, a brewing and hotel group mainly in Zambia. First major commercial deal in Black Africa	1968 August. Obtained platinum prospecting rights in S.A. Bids for 'David Whitehead, the British textile concern. October. Announces plans for Trans-Congo Railway. Bid £15m for Ghana's Ashanti Goldfields. December. Makes bid for minority interest in Coronation Syndicate	1970 July, Congolese Govt. turns down railway plans
		Early 1972 Agreement with Sudan Government to act as sole import agents

SHARE PRICE RANGE—ADJUSTED YEARS ENDED DECEMBER 31

| 15.4 | 15.1 | 14.4 | 17.7 | 24.7 | 63.8 | 201.3 | 295.7 | 161.9 | 113.5 | 145.0 |
| 11.1 | 11.1 | 10.9 | 10.9 | 12.0 | 19.2 | 42.9 | 128.2 | 74.8 | 46.5 | 64.0 |

ADJUSTED
——— EARNINGS
- - - - DIVIDENDS
——— PRICES

1962 1963 1964 1965 1966 1967 1968 1969 1970 1971 1972 1973 1974 1975

| 1962 awarded management contract to build Beira pipeline | 1966. Bids for Zambia–Tanzania pipeline. Contract given to the Italian group, ENI. Development of Sucoma, the Malawi Sugar Corporation | 1969 March. Buys John Holt. June. Drops Coronation bid | 1971 August. Buys 40% stake in Wankel. Sept. Four directors arrested in S.A. October. Peat Marwick & Mitchell asked to investigate company's finances |

Mr Rowland was born in Rawalpindi, West Pakistan, in 1917, son of a well-to-do German merchant who, he claimed, was financial adviser to the Dalai Lama. The family settled in England before the Second World War, and when war was declared Mr Rowland and his father were interned as a security precaution. He was released before the end of the war and started his entrepreneurial career.

When peace came he moved to Holland, where he used his salesman's skills to persuade a number of Dutch local authorities to allow him to act unofficially as their buying agent in England. Large purchases of goods were made at substantial discounts, on which Mr Rowland was able to make a handsome profit by way of commission. But then, after a spell as a director of a London-based refrigerator company, he moved to Rhodesia.

On his arrival in 1955, he set up as a farmer, growing maize at Gatooma, a small town some ninety miles from Salisbury. He quickly made a number of important Rhodesian friends, among them a government minister of foreign affairs. At the same time he expanded his interests, buying among other things the Mercedes motor dealerships in Salisbury and interests in two gold mines. Just as significant, he started to act as contact and go-between for a number of mining companies, the most prominent being Rio Tinto (Rhodesia), a subsidiary of the international Rio Tinto Mining Company of London. During the next seven years he brought Rio Tinto a number of important deals. One of the first was the Isandhlawana Emerald Mine, discovered by Mr Rowland on his own initiative, who then organised its sale to Rio Tinto in return for a substantial commission.

Mr Rowland's first encounter with Lonrho came in 1960, when he succeeded in persuading Lonrho to sell its most profitable asset, the Cam and Motor gold mine, to Rio Tinto. Mr Rowland arranged that three of Lonrho's directors, the late Sir Arthur Ball, his son Alan Ball and Brigadier Thorburn, representing the 117 Group, be paid 'compensation for loss of office' of £11,000 each.

It was this operation that convinced Angus Ogilvy, a year later, that Mr Rowland was the man for Lonrho. Mr Rowland joined the board on 29 August 1961. Mr Rowland's strategy for the transformation of the company from a somnolent ranching and mining company to a multinational conglomerate in the space of ten years can be conveniently divided into three main phases.

PHASE 1: DEVELOPMENT IN RHODESIA (1961-5)

The first phase of the strategy brought growth primarily in Lonrho's Rhodesian operations from the time of Mr Rowland's accession to the board until UDI was declared by Rhodesia in 1965. Upon joining the board Mr Rowland agreed to the transfer of assets held in his Rhodesian holding company, Shepton Estates, to Lonrho. These included two gold mines, the Mashaba and the Kanyemga; two companies dealing in cars, one of which dealt in spare parts, while the other, Morton Developments, owned a chain of distribution outlets and held the sole franchise in the Rhodesias for Mercedes Benz vehicles; and a company negotiating to build an oil pipeline from Beira in Portuguese Mozambique to Umtali, Rhodesia. In exchange he received the managing directorship of Lonrho, and together with the chairman, Mr Alan Ball and executive director, Mr Angus Ogilvy, these three formed the main executive body. In addition, Shepton Estates received 1.5 million Lonrho shares, which represented 19 per cent of Lonrho's equity, and an option to buy 2 million more at 35p in five years' time.

After the negotiations Mr Rowland also offered to Lonrho his interest in the Shamrock Copper Mine in Rhodesia, the sole assets of a Rhodesian company, Nyaschere Copper (PVT)Ltd. This interest comprised a 50 per cent holding in Nyaschere and the management rights. Lonrho made an engineering appraisal which showed development to be uneconomic and the offer was declined. Lonrho also immediately appraised the prospects of the Kanyemba gold mine. Although it was believed to have a commercial life of twenty years, the appraisal showed that the mine had commercial prospects for less than one year.

These were the only initial disappointments, for there remained Lonrho's acquired interest in building the Beira pipeline, one of Mr. Rowland's most profitable deals, and described by a colleague as 'his masterpiece'. Mr Rowland formed a company called Associated Overland Pipelines in which he had a 51 per cent interest after spotting the profit potential in supplying land-locked Rhodesia with oil, via pipeline, from the port of Beira. It was reputed that Mr Rowland made no less than sixty-five journeys to Lisbon in an attempt to gain Portuguese approval and he was finally awarded the management contract in 1962. Backed with South African money, the pipeline came into operation seven months before UDI was declared, showing a profit potential of £1 million annually before it was shut down.

In 1962/3 Mr Rowland also managed to extend Lonrho's interests to neighbouring Malawi, (formerly the British colony of Nyasaland) when he bought the management contract of the almost profitless Nyasaland Railways. After selling off the monopoly fuel rights to Total, Mr Rowland approached Mozambique with the offer to sell them the company's railway bridge over the Zambesi. Malawi was approaching independence, and this proposal was fiercely contested by her (British) civil servants. However, Mr Rowland succeeded in gaining the support of the President of Malawi, Dr Hastings Banda, in return for the promise of additional investment in the future. The cash raised from this deal then enabled Mr Rowland to undertake further expansion.

Lonrho expanded further into ranching with the acquisition of Willoughby's Consolidated and into more motor dealerships in both Rhodesia and Malawi. At the end of 1963 Lonrho strengthened its position in Malawi with the formation of Lonrho (Nyasaland) to administer Lonrho's estates and to conduct a feasibility study for a £4 million sugar scheme.

In South Africa Lonrho acquired a controlling interest in a gold mining company, Coronation Syndicate, which owned several mines in Rhodesia. The deal enabled Lonrho and Coronation to rationalise their holding into one Rhodesian subsidiary, Corsyn. This was followed by the acquisition of Klanderson's Transvaal Estates, owners of substantial coal assets in Rhodesia, via its subsidiaries, Tweefontein United Collieries and Witbank Consolidated.

At Lonrho's general meeting in March 1964, Mr Ball advised shareholders that he estimated 65 per cent of the group's investment was represented by mining, 4 per cent by railways, 11 per cent by tea and 20 per cent by commercial and industrial activities which were spread mainly in Central Southern Africa, but with a 16 per cent interest in the UK.

However, recognising the political uncertainties facing Rhodesia, Lonrho strengthened its ties with neighbouring African countries. By 1965 the company had made significant acquisitions in Zambia (formerly the British colony of Northern Rhodesia), including interests in brewing, hotels, a newspaper company and the formation of the Lonrho Construction Company to meet Zambia's growing economic needs.

PHASE 2: EXPANSION NORTH OF THE ZAMBESI (1965-9)

In the mid-1960s Africa was undergoing a dramatic change, emerging from the grasp of past empires into a collection of new and independent countries. Europeans, who had established businesses in the colonial days had become nervous about their future, fearing that hotheads in the new administration would push through threats to expropriate or nationalise foreign-owned assets. Mr Rowland sensed however, that the new Black African leaders wanted to reassure world opinion as to their stability and responsibility. He therefore embarked on an acquisition programme to purchase such assets with a singular display of initiative, drive and business acumen which earned him an image which the *Observer* described as belonging to 'a man of action who hops from country to country in his Mystère executive jet, clinching deals and building up goodwill, so that if there is business to be done, it will come Lonrho's way. He is not a man who works through committees and close consultation with colleagues.'

European businessmen were moving out of Africa as fast as they could sell. Mr Rowland offered them low cash multiples, and mopped up valuable earnings and debt-free assets at knock-down prices. Moreover the businesses acquired had a well-trained and sound local management so that Mr Rowland foresaw little need for reorganisation. He used Lonrho's new acquisitions to secure loans which were then ploughed back into the newly independent economies, and high returns on low outlays created impressive earnings and growth records. Mr Rowland gained the new leaders' favour, the new states prospered, and Lonrho boomed.

In the four years between 1963 and 1966 the group's equity base expanded by just five per cent from 15.7 million to 16.5 million shares. But earnings over the same period multiplied fivefold, from £0.22 million to £1.22 million, and earnings per share rose from 1.4p to 7.41p. Net assets per share doubled from 17p to 34p, against a fivefold expansion in capital employed from £3.21 million to £15.84 million. The group spread rapidly in Zambia, Zaïre (the former Belgian Congo), Uganda, Lesotho, Botswana, Swaziland, Kenya and Malawi, acquiring companies dealing in newspapers, cars, sugar, tea, ranching, bricks, electricity, textiles, beer and others.

Rhodesian operations were also built up with the acquisition of more mining interests in 1966. These included a 50 per cent holding in Nyaschere Copper, which formerly belonged to Mr Rowland's partner and acceptance of the mine's management duties together with the acquisition of the Luyati Copper Mine which lay just inside the Rhodesia/Mozambique border.

In 1967 and 1968 Lonrho's growth rate slowed a little. The group doubled its equity from 16.5 million to 33.9 million shares with a successful bid for Anglo-Ceylon and General Estates that took it into Sri Lanka (formerly Ceylon), a one-for-five scrip issue, and Mr Rowland's subscription for his option at 35p per share against a market price of 71p.

Nevertheless, just after the end of the group's financial year in October 1968, Mr Rowland pulled off his biggest coup with the acquisition of Ashanti Goldfields Corporation Ltd in Ghana. The Ashanti mine, reputed to be the richest in the world, was typical of Mr Rowland's style and was the culmination of this period of rapid expansion. First, Mr Rowland had made an important political contact in the inspector of mines for the Ghanaian government, which was threatening to revoke Ashanti's mining leases. Lonrho, with government backing, then made an offer of £15 million to the Ashanti board, which at that time included Mr Duncan Sandys, the former Commonwealth Secretary, and chairman Major-General Sir Edward Spears. This offer was accepted and Sir Edward Spears joined the Lonrho board as a director with a salary of £10,000 p.a., while Mr Duncan Sandys remained as a director of Ashanti, although he was subsequently engaged by Lonrho South Africa in the summer of 1971 as a consultant for £10,000 p.a. The acquisition was completed in December 1968 and the political difficulties facing Ashanti were solved by making the Ghanaian government a partner by giving it 20 per cent of the equity together with an option for a further 20 per cent.

Simultaneously news broke of a highly significant platinum discovery in South Africa. It was known as the Western Platinum Mine, and Mr Alan Ball, Lonrho's chairman, announced that it was destined to be 'one of the major producers of the world', and Lonrho reported its reserves were worth up to £600 million.

By the end of 1968 Lonrho had grown into a multinational conglomerate operating well over 300 companies involved in a variety of mining interests such as diamonds in Lesotho, rare earths in Malawi, copper in Rhodesia, asbestos in Swaziland and platinum in South Africa. Mining interests had become less important, however, being estimated to account for 40 per cent of profits; agricultural activities consisting of tea, sugar and cattle ranching were estimated to account for 10 per cent of profits. Industrial and commercial interests, such as motor trading throughout Africa, hotels in Zambia, building and construction in Zambia and Malawi, and printing and packaging in Kenya, Uganda and Tanzania, had expanded in importance at 45 per cent of profits; finally, finance and other activities, including building societies in Malawi, made up the remaining 5 per cent.

PHASE 3: CHANGES OF FORTUNE (1970-71)

The pace of acquisition continued. In February 1969 and in the aftermath of the Nigerian civil war, Lonrho launched an £8 million bid for the John Holt motor trading group in Africa and then followed up its West African success by buying Slater Walker's wattle and cattle ranching interests in Central and East Africa for £6 million. By March Lonrho's shares had reached a peak of 316p.

In September Lonrho made its first venture into shipping with the acquisition of The Watergate Steamship Company Ltd, which was expected to yield profits of £200,000 p.a. This was quickly followed by the acquisition of a 51 per cent interest in Rogers and Company Ltd, a merchant shipping company in Mauritius which also had extensive interests in aviation and tourism.

However, towards the end of 1969 the first problems of expansion by acquisition began to appear. With a head office staff of only eighty personnel and no formal corporate planning, rationalisation proved difficult to achieve and, as one director observed, 'Tiny' (Mr Rowland) is the only one who knows the whole picture'.

In some African countries various motor franchises were competing with each other, and in Zambia nationalisation of the commercial vehicle fleet operators, Smith and Youngson, had provided little compensation. The many makes, depreciation and spare parts difficulties made valuation difficult and finally Lonrho paid the Zambian government £210,000 to wipe out losses and provided a loan of £1.08 million for working capital, in return for a nominal amount which bought 100 percent of the equity.

Nevertheless, Lonrho's successful past growth was emphasised by Mr Rowland in his message to shareholders in the 1969 annual report: 'The pre-tax profits for last year were £14.4 million on a turnover of £154 million. This was a record. Assets have risen to £172 million and there are now nearly 100,000 employees in the group spread over 25 countries.'

But it was the group's mining ventures that were gaining the attention of management. At the AGM in July 1969, Lonrho's chairman, Mr Alan Ball, stated, 'I want to emphasise that we regard ourselves primarily as a mining finance house and there is certainly no intention of changing this policy .... we will look at mining propositions of all sorts anywhere in the world.'

In Ghana, Ashanti Goldfield's expansion continued at a cost of £1 million annually, and through its South African subsidiary, Coronation Syndicate, Lonrho was busily extending its Rhodesian copper interests. Coronation Syndicate, which held all Lonrho's Rhodesian mining interests, was itself fully engaged in developing the Inyati copper mine which lay close to the Mozambique border. In August 1969 Lonrho's 50 per cent holding in the Shamrock copper mine was transferred to a wholly-owned Rhodesian subsidiary, after which locally-raised development expenditure of £3.05 million was made. In Mozambique, Coronation Syndicate acquired an option on the Edmundian copper mine in September 1969, and then transferred the mine to a wholly-owned Lonrho subsidiary in early 1970 for development. The Western Platinum Mine in South Africa produced highly favourable drill test results and Lonrho stated, 'the first mine should start production early in 1971 and it is planned that the second mine should begin operations during 1973'. Development costs amounting to £26 million were estimated to be recoverable in three years, eventually yielding profits of £3.5 million per annum.

Other mining ventures, however, were not so successful. In mid-1969 Mr Rowland attempted to secure a marketing contract for Sierra Leone diamonds in a deal involving the Sierra Leone government. At the time, diamonds worth £11.5 million were being mined by Consolidation African Selection Trust (CAST) along with William Baird. It was reported that if Lonrho managed to secure the marketing contract, they planned further deals with Tanzania, Russia and Israel to establish a world-wide marketing organisation. A 'shell' company, Diminco, was formed in which Lonrho originally aimed for 51 per cent control, but as talks continued a new company, Cominco, was formed with the Sierra Leone government taking a 55 per cent stake. However, Mr Rowland was distrusted by Sierra Leone top civil servants and strongly opposed by De Beers, the diamond marketing concern responsible for over 80 per cent of world diamond sales. Unfortunately, Mr Rowland's main contact, the Governor-General, had no executive power and resigned at a critical time in the negotiations. Finally, a *coup d'etat* occurred during which the president was deposed and the mines nationalised, although the management contract was eventually awarded to CAST.

At the same time Lonrho sought to gain a major share in the management contract of the Congo's Copper Mines and untapped mineral wealth, which was held by the Belgian group, Union Minière. Mr Rowland's plan was to link the management contract with an offer to build a £300 million railway in Zaïre to be independent of the Benguela railway which ran through Portuguese West Africa, and managed by a major shareholder of Union Minière. Finance was to be arranged with the World Bank by the Zaïre government. Originally the deal appealed to the Zaïre government on the basis of a partnership with Lonrho and removal of Union Minière, who were perceived as supporters of the former colonial regime. However, in July 1970, the Zaïre government issued a statement accusing Lonrho of publicising as a certainty a deal yet to be concluded and refused to have any future dealings with them.

The collapse of a partnership with the Nigerian government to build and run an oil tanker fleet and a change of government in Ghana emphasised the political uncertainty of operating in Black Africa. In March 1971 Lonrho found Ashanti under the axe of annexation, with the Ghana government taking 55 per cent of the equity instead of the negotiated 40 per cent. Zambia too was posing problems for Lonrho's substantial motor vehicle distribution franchise. In an effort to reduce the balance of payments deficit in late 1971 Zambia restricted imports of all cars under 1200 cc, and imposed a double import tax on those of over 2000 cc to assist the penetration of locally produced Fiat cars. Tanzania too followed up its 1967 nationalisation of sisal estates with the purchase of Lonrho's two local newspapers.

PROBLEMS OF EXPANSION

The explosive growth of Lonrho into a multinational conglomerate had also brought special problems. After UDI all Rhodesian profits had been blocked, although Lonrho continued to foot the annual maintenance bill of £300,000 for the Beira pipeline. Capital expenditure had been mounting and the 1970 accounts showed commitments of £13.3 million of which three ships accounted for £11 million, Ashanti Goldfields for £1 million, without accounting for the Western Platinum Mine. Furthermore not all African countries allowed profits to be remitted to the UK. The 1972 accounts showed that £2.40 million of 1971 profits were remittable and £3.56 million remittable in 1972.

To improve the return of income earned abroad, Lonrho appointed Mr A.S. Sardanis in early 1971. Formerly a prominent secretary in the Zambian Ministry of State Participation and managing director of Zambian Industrial and Mining Companies Ltd, he had particular expertise in rationalising diversified organisations in Africa. Mr Sardanis was given the post of joint managing director (together with Mr Rowland) of a new subsidiary, African Industrial and Finance Corporation (AIFC), as well as a directorship of Dominco for the purposes of the Sierra Leone negotiations. AIFC held all the group's interests in Africa north of the Zambesi and these were to be regrouped and rationalised with a view to further expansion from a firmer base.

In May 1971, however, Mr Sardanis resigned, 'because I found myself in basic disagreement with Lonrho's objectives and its style of management.' He added that foreign investment must have capital to supply and earn its profits through efficient management, in order to be consistent with the interests of the developing countries.

He also found that Lonrho's policy was geared towards acquisition and in his view not enough attention was paid to long-term management. Meanwhile technical difficulties had arisen at Western Platinum and the downward spiralling commodities price caused doubts about the forecast profitability of the operation. Lonrho had entered into partnership with Falconbridge Nickel and Superior Oil in July 1970 to offset development costs. Falconbridge paid £2.9 million for a 49 per cent stake and a further £2.1 million for subscription rights and the intent to raise long-term capital for future development. Fifteen months later Mr Rowland estimated that Western Platinum had spent around £13.3 million in development and a further £8.3 million was planned to bring the first stage into production by the end of 1972. Full production was now postponed until 1975.

To finance their 51 per cent commitment, Lonrho applied to the First National City Bank to form a syndicate to raise a further $8 million, in addition to their original $8 million loan towards development of Western Platinum. This was rejected on the grounds that it was not advisable, although Lonrho's main bankers, The Standard Bank, agreed to increase its stakes to $20 million.

At the same time the company had made a commitment to purchase the Wankel rotary engine patents. These were held by Wankel GmbH and Rotary Engines GmbH (the Wankel Group), and in the summer of 1971 a partnership of Lonrho, Rio Tinto Zinc and British Leyland had made a bid when the opportunity had arisen. This bid was rejected, but Mr Rowland decided to bid again, this time alone, and successfully acquired the Wankel Group on 30 September. Lonrho claimed that the deal would eventually be self-financing in terms of income from subscription rights, and details in the press indicated the deal involved a sum of £10 million, of which some £6.8 million was required immediately as a down payment to give Lonrho a 40 per cent share in future licence income. Finance was arranged by a $7\frac{1}{2}$ per cent Swiss loan repayable over five years. As a result of this commitment, however, Lonrho's merchant bankers, Warburg's, and two of the group's main board directors, Andrew Caldecott, a director of Kleinwort Benson and Philip Hunter, former chairman of Cammell Laird, resigned. Further, rumours of a liquidity crisis spread in the press and the London Stock Exchange urged Lonrho to give more details to shareholders on the Wankel deal.

Then came the news that the South African government had issued warrants of arrest for four directors on fraud charges and that one director, Mr Fred Butcher, had been arrested on 25 September. In South Africa, the government made allegations that Lonrho had been engaged in intercompany dealings to the detriment of outside shareholders and charged four directors in all. Three of the directors charged were directors of local South African subsidiaries, Tweefontein and Corsyn, a Rhodesian subsidiary of Coronation and the financial director on the board of Lonrho's South African subsidiary. Mr Fred Butcher, the main board finance director, was charged on behalf of Lonrho.

According to the *Observer* the origin of the events precipitating the charges could be traced back to 1967. An 'administrative error' then occurred when the local Rhodesian subsidiary of Lonrho sold its 50 per cent share of Nyaschere to the Rhodesian subsidiary of Coronation Syndicate, Corsyn. In August 1969 this holding was retransferred by Fred Butcher to a wholly-owned Rhodesian subsidiary. Over time, a variety of mining claims were transferred out of Coronation in this manner including the Edmundian mine which lay near the Mozambique-Rhodesian border. Then, in January of 1969 Lonrho made a bid for the minority holdings of Coronation Syndicate and Tweefontein Collieries which controlled Coronation Syndicate via a 60 per cent holding. The bid fell through, but it gave rise to later allegations that the offer document did not disclose an important copper find in Rhodesia, thereby undervaluing shareholders claims. Although this referred to the Inyati mine, allegations were also made that Lonrho bought the Edmundian mine from Coronation at a bargain basement price. Eventually the charges were withdrawn in the Regional Court, Johannesburg on 12 January 1973, but the papers were passed to the South African attorney general for a final decision.

As a result of these events Lonrho's share price sank to 48p and shortly afterwards, in mid-October 1971, Mr Angus Ogilvy insisted on calling in Peat, Marwick and Mitchell, the accountants, with the mandate to conduct an independent audit of the group's affairs and a complete reappraisal of its management methods.

PEAT, MARWICK AND MITCHELL REPORT

At the beginning of March 1972, Peat, Marwick and Mitchell (PMM) submitted a report to shareholders, providing information on the group's operations and recommendations to the Lonrho management. The report included details of unaudited results for the year ended 30 September 1971 and a profit forecast for 1972. The report also provided information such as analysis of turnover which had not been available to shareholders before (see exhibit 5).

The main findings of the report were as follows:-

Accounting Procedure

When a subsidiary was acquired it was Lonrho's practice to include in their accounts that subsidiary's profits from its previous accounting date. It was recommended that only that part of the accounting year's profit from the date of acquisition should be included.

Expenditure incurred on projects under examination or in the negotiation stage was carried forward in stock and work in progress. This project expenditure was either capitalised or written off when it was known the project was to succeed or be abandoned. PMM recommended that such expenditure should be capitalised as an asset only when there were reasonable prospects of the development producing revenue in the near future.

It was also Lonrho's practice to include extraordinary items in the profit-and-loss account, for example, the £2.1 million subscription rights fee from Falconbridge. Since this was not recurrent income, PMM advised that such items should not figure in profit before tax but should be shown separately in the accounts.

Nationalised assets were kept on Lonrho's books at the old book value without provision for depreciation, the argument being that the company would be in a better position to negotiate greater compensation. It was recommended that a consistent depreciation policy on mining assets should be adopted throughout the group, which PMM showed would reduce profit before tax by £0.3 million and constitute an assets write-off of £5.3 million.

Capital Commitments

At 30 September 1971, capital commitments totalled £12.7 million of which £1.4 million was authorised but not contracted for.

Finance external to the group had been arranged for £6.3 million of this capital expenditure, and liabilities amounted to £3.8 million.

PMM noted that the Western Platinum Mine had demanded an increasing investment on the part of Lonrho. Although Falconbridge were responsible for 49 per cent of the capital development, they were unable to raise long-term finance! This had so far involved Lonrho in development costs amounting to £4.8 million which were in addition to its original investment of £3 million. Further costs of £2 million seemed likely before the first sales of platinum, which were scheduled to commence in late 1972. Lonrho had also agreed to build a precious metal refinery for £1 million near the mine, with finance arrangements under negotiation in South Africa.

In Peat, Marwick's view, Western Platinum was the major cause of Lonrho's liquidity problems. However, another project was also discussed which, together with Western Platinum, had involved Lonrho in a heavier cash commitment than any it had undertaken in the past—the Wankel deal of 30 September 1971.

It was revealed that Lonrho had paid £12.2 million for Wankel GmbH and Rotary Engines GmbH which had a 40 per cent interest in the exploitation of patents in Europe and Japan. Of the principal, £7.8 million was payable immediately on acquisition with annual instalments of £1.28 million for three years and the remainder in the fourth. This was financed by a Swiss loan of £7.9 million bearing $7\frac{1}{2}$ per cent interest, of which 8 per cent was repayable in December 1972, and the remainder in eight equal half-yearly instalments. Third party interests arose over the outstanding claim of another party to buy a 100 per cent interest in the Wankel companies. They agreed to accept a 20 per cent equity interest at no consideration although the management rights had yet to be settled.

PMM further noted that provided income was received in accordance with the terms of existing licences (although dependent on successful renegotiation with one important licence holder) and no dividends paid, the cash forecast of the Wankel group indicated that the total cost of this deal would be recovered by the end of 1976. Lonrho had agreed to issue a circular giving full details of the Wankel takeover.

Liquidity Crisis

Since late 1970 remittances had been inadequate to finance the group on projects such

EXHIBIT 5   Analyses of Turnover, Profit Before Tax and Net Assets (Year Ended 30 September 1971)

(£ millions)

	East and Central Africa	West Africa	Southern Africa	Europe and other	TOTAL
Turnover	104.0	57.0	7.0	24.0	192.0
Profit before tax					
Agriculture	1.2	—	0.9	0.6	2.7
Finance	0.1	0.4	(0.2)	(2.4)	(2.1)
General trading	2.5	1.2	—	0.5	4.2
Mining	0.3	2.8	0.2	—	3.3
Motor distribution	2.7	0.5	—	—	3.2
Printing and publishing	0.8	—	—	—	0.8
Shipping	—	—	—	0.1	0.1
Textiles	1.6	—	—	0.2	1.8
Wines, spirits and beers	0.8	(0.2)	—	0.4	1.0
TOTAL	10.0	4.7	0.9	(0.6)	15.0
NET ASSETS (before deducting minority interests)	37.9	28.2	26.1	(0.5)	91.7

Territories included are as follows

East and Central Africa: Kenya, Malawi, Rhodesia, Tanzania, Uganda, Zaire and Zambia
West Africa: Ghana, Ivory Coast and Nigeria
Southern Africa: Botswana, Lesotho, South Africa and Swaziland
Europe and other: Belgium, Ceylon, France, Mauritius and UK

PROFIT AND FUNDING RECORD (£ million)

Year ending 30 Sep	1962	1963	1964	1965	1966	1967	1968	1969	1970	1971
Profit before tax	0.4	0.5	1.0	1.8	3.0	3.4	6.1	12.5	15.0	15.0
Profit after tax	0.2	0.3	0.6	1.1	1.8	2.1	3.5	6.8	8.8	7.0
Profit attributable to Lonrho[1]	0.2	0.2	0.3	0.6	1.2	1.4	2.6	4.0	7.7	5.0
Shareholders' funds	2.6	3.0	3.7	4.8	5.7	6.5	21.6	55.7	61.1	60.22[2]
Bank overdrafts						6.6	8.6	19.6	22.1	24.8
Loan stocks						1.9	0.6	12.4	11.8	13.0
Debentures and other loans						5.0	5.6	11.7	13.4	21.7
Total borrowings						13.5	14.8	43.7	58.7	28.7

Source: Peat, Marwick & Mitchell Report (March 1972)

Notes: 1 Profit attributable is stated after crediting extraordinary income.

2 Decrease in shareholders' funds due to provision of £5.3 million for diminution in value of nationalised and mining assets and the write-off of £0.5 million project expenditure incurred in prior years.

as Western Platinum and Wankel, and pay dividends. In particular bank overdrafts had risen to £24 million and, due to the diverse nature of the group losses arising in a number of subsidiaries, these were not available to relieve profits earned elsewhere so that the company's tax rate had been high.

Cash flow projections indicated that Lonrho's overdraft with its main bankers, the Standard Bank, would increase from £6.1 million to £11 million by 30 September 1971. Standard Bank's expectations were that the overdraft should be reduced to £2 million by that date. PMM estimated that if this was to be met, funds of the order of £10 million were needed. Apart from not making the approaching dividend payment they therefore recommended that, if an actual loan was not forthcoming, the sale of a major asset should be considered.

Management

PMM observed: 'The group is currently managed in effectively the same manner as it was in the early 1960s. Due to the rapid expansion of the group in recent years, the existing management organisation is now unsuitable for administering the complex and diversified group that Lonrho has become.'

They further disclosed that the group's chairman since 1947, Alan Ball, had announced his intention to leave this post to become executive deputy chairman and Mr Rowland would become chief executive as well as managing director. Mr Fred Butcher, who had been with Lonrho since 1944, had also expressed a wish to resign his post as group finance director, as soon as a successor could be found. He would remain on the board as an executive director.

At the same time recommendations were made to appoint an independent chairman from outside the group, along with two independent non-executive directors, and to increase the number of permitted main board directors from twelve to twenty. Subsequently, three of Lonrho's senior executives, Mr T.R. Prentice, Mr W.H.M. Wilkinson and Mr R.F. Dunlop, were then invited to join the board.

The future

Peat, Marwick argued that ventures such as Western Platinum were entirely dependent on the vagaries of a currently depressed platinum price, although they saw a good potential in Wankel on the basis of licences already granted. For the immediate future, they saw current operations yielding profits for the year ended 30 September 1972 at least equal to those of 1971. This represented a return of 8 per cent on shareholders' funds, which they regarded as adequate.

However, they stressed that the liquidity problem should not be recurrent and made recommendations to maximise the remittance of funds to the UK, dispose of assets which showed an inadequate return on capital employed, and obtain finance for overseas developments and projects from sources outside the UK, in order to reverse the flow of funds from the UK. In conclusion, Peat, Marwick and Mitchell remarked of Lonrho that 'in common with other groups of this nature profits must be viewed in the light of the territories in which they arise and the ease with which profits and capital can be remitted to the UK'.

THE AFTERMATH OF THE REPORT

Following the report's recommendations, the group's management structure was strengthened by the appointment of Mr Roger Moss to the post of group chief accountant on 28 February 1972. Initially he found Lonrho to be a 'group rich in assets and people with demonstrable entrepreneurial genius which had not been subjected to central financial controls'. He added, 'The [group's] legal structure was like a cat's cradle ... the only management control information that was centrally available was the sum of 165 profit-and-loss accounts and balance sheets submitted each quarter and added up.'

Mr Moss immediately organised back-up teams in financial accounting, management accounting, development accounting and tax to strengthen the group accounting function; he also restructured group reporting. 'Basing the changes principally upon the former regional offices we now have seventeen standard regional operating statements coming into London monthly ... instead of the 260 standard quarterly submissions and the great variety of other forms...,' he reported.

In addition two non-executive directors, Sir Basil Smallpiece and Mr Edward Du Cann MP, and a new chairman, Mr Duncan Sandys MP, were appointed to the board in April 1972. Sir Basil Smallpiece, aged sixty-six and an experienced professional manager, was formerly managing director of BOAC and chairman of Cunard until 1971. He joined the board as non-executive deputy chairman after Lord O'Brien, Governor of the Bank of England, and Sir Ronald Leach, senior partner of Peat, Marwick and Mitchell had expressed the hope that he would be appointed. Mr Edward Du Cann was also chairman of Keyser Ullman, the merchant bank that had agreed to succeed S.G. Warburg as the group's financial advisers. Keyser had subscribed for 500,000 new shares involving an initial outlay of £350,000 with an option on another 500,000. The new chairman, Mr Sandys, had been associated with Lonrho for some time, and had extensive knowledge of those parts of Africa in which the group traded. Known as a strong personality and respected but not too well known in the City, he was appointed chairman of a board of sixteen directors at a salary of £40,000 p.a. Of the appointments and boardroom moves in general, Mr Ball commented that the board were 'unanimous that we have come up with the right sort of package for Lonrho'.

In line with the recommmendations to divest loss-making and incompatible activities, the annual report for 1971 gave details of five holdings sold in its 'rationalisation programme'. Among these the shipping and general services company, Rogers and Company, of Mauritius, was sold in October 1971, and a 50 per cent interest in Chibukeu Holdings, the group's only brewing interests south of the Zambesi was sold in December, both at a profit. Other interests sold in December included diamond mining in Lesotho and an insurance company in Mauritius, and by March 1972 a motor parts distributor, Consolidated Motors Ltd, and a road transport company, Freight Lines Ltd. Sales of these assets realised £2.5 million.

More cash was raised on 25 May 1972 by a rights issue of over 14 million ordinary shares of 25p nominal. These were readily subscribed for at 73p per share and raised approximately £10 million, thus reducing the group's short-term borrowings to £1.5 million. Mr Rowland took up his rights at a personal cost of £1.8 million, although this was partially offset by the repayment of a £1 million loan he had made to Lonrho during the previous year's liquidity crisis. As a result of the successful issue, the Standard Bank agreed to increase substantially its £2 million overdraft facility.

Shareholders were then provided with more information on the Wankel deal in a circular issued in March 1972. The circular gave details of complex arrangements between Wankel, Audi-NSU and Curtis Wright in the United States that reduced Lonrho's nominal 40 per cent share of royalties to 36 per cent of most non-American sales, 22 per cent of payments from General Motors, and 10 per cent of other American receipts. It also provided some guide to the overall value of Wankel royalties by pointing out that Audi-NSU had issued non-voting participatory warrants which shared in the royalties on a decreasing income basis, and that the market price of those warrants effectively capitalised the royalties as a whole at £61 million.

The group was also able to report the completion of the first stage of development of the Western Platinum Mine, and that shipment of milled ore to the refineries had begun. At the AGM in April, Mr Sandys informed shareholders that production had reached 60 per cent of the designed capacity and that capital expenditure was falling away, although he noted, 'the viability of such a venture depends very much on the price of platinum'. However, in July, Ford announced that it had agreed to buy 0.5 million ounces of platinum from Lonrho on a three-year contract, and commodity prices for platinum began to rise. This was followed by General Motors' announcement to begin commercial production of Wankel engines in 1975 and to install them in some of their Chevrolet models.

New ventures were in accord with the group's policy of taking initial steps 'toward an expansion of our activities into North Africa and the Middle East'. In particular Lonrho Exports, a wholly-owned subsidiary, signed an exclusive purchase agreement with the Sudanese government to act as their sole agents for imports. The deal, which involved no financial commitment on Lonrho's part, provided income in the form of a fixed percentage of the value of goods involved.

Lonrho then announced in October their intention to undertake a feasibility study for a £45 million sugar project in the Sudan, in which Lonrho would participate on a 49/51 per cent basis with the Sudanese government. At the same time an agreement was signed between Lonrho and the government of Dahomey to survey, finance and manage a £24 million sugar project—Dahomey's largest investment project since independence.

THE BOARDROOM DISPUTE

By April 1973, however, public speculation was rife over the delay in the publication of Lonrho's mid-March accounts. Although unanimously approved by the board, the group's auditors, Peat Marwick and Mitchell felt that publication without revealing a deep boardroom rift would be unfair to shareholders.

Following the recomposition of the board after the 1972 Peat Marwick Report there had been mounting boardroom fears over a new impending liquidity crisis as well as growing criticism of Mr Rowland's style of management. In order to avert a major rift within the board Mr Rowland, backed by Keyser Ullman, produced a plan to inject a further £8 million into the company. This involved Mr Rowland, highly placed Zambian interests, and Dr Khalil Osman, a Sudanese and managing director of the Gulf International Group of Kuwait, subscribing for new capital at 115p per share, a premium of 23p per share. It was hoped that this would boost confidence in Lonrho as well as strengthen its finances and bring Middle East oil and African interests together.

However, the plan was rejected, and on 18 April a resolution calling for the dismissal of Mr Rowland as chief executive and managing director in the interests of shareholders was signed by eight of the Lonrho board. Those involved were Sir Basil Smallpeice; Mr Gerald Percy, one-time protégé of Mr Rowland and his proposed replacement; Mr Wilkinson, an ex-merchant banker; Major Colin Mackenzie, a director since 1963 and ex-rancher; Mr Stanley Dalgleish, non-executive director since 1970 and second largest single shareholder with 763,721 shares, which were acquired when his family shipping business, Watergate, was taken over in 1969; and a Swiss who became joint managing director with Mr Rowland of Wankel GmbH and an executive board member in 1972.

In opposition to the resolution were seven directors: Mr Rowland; Mr Duncan Sandys; Mr Alan Ball; Mr Edward Du Cann; Mr Prentice; Mr Dunlop; and Mr Butcher. Mr Angus Ogilvy, who represented the Drayton Corporation which had recently halved its 10 per cent holding, did not vote and resigned the following day. Mr Sandys was holder of 267,072 shares, 200,000 of which had been bought from Keyser by means of a loan from them—Keyser's holding being thus reduced to 300,000 shares.

Mr Rowland, Lonrho's largest shareholder with a 20 per cent holding, acted immediately by applying for a temporary injunction to prevent the passing of such a resolution on the grounds that his dismissal would be disastrous for Lonrho's African interests. This was granted pending a full court hearing in May. Kleinwort Benson came to the support of the directors headed by Sir Basil Smallpeice, while Keyser Ullman resigned as Lonrho's merchant bankers but remained as advisers to Mr Rowland. An extraordinary general meeting to allow shareholders to settle the issue was also called for 31 May by Mr Rowland.

THE COURT HEARING (MAY 1973)

The court hearing called by Mr Rowland to prevent his dismissal before the general meeting commenced on 8 May. Mr Rowland had received many affidavits from chairmen of Lonrho's overseas companies which Alan Ball described as 'all supporting Mr Rowland to a man'. Notable among these were statements from the Zambian President, the son-in-law of President Kenyatta of Kenya, Udi Gecaga (managing director of Lonrho East Africa), Colonel Gil Olympio, son of the former president of Togo (in charge of development in Central, East, and West Africa), and the governments of Ghana and Zambia. Mr Rowland also had the support of Mr Chapman, Lonrho's most senior executive in French-speaking West Africa, and Mr Hossy, the Lonrho Group's consultant mining engineer.

The essence of Mr Rowland's case was that Lonrho had substantially benefited from his personal commitment. He stated, 'Accounts show that the net profits before taxation of the company have grown from £158,000 in 1961 to £19.3 million in 1972.... A large part of this expansion is, I believe, due to my knowledge and understanding of Africa which I have obtained from living there for over twenty five years.... I have helped to build turnover from about £800,000 to about £230 million in the current year. I do not believe that this could have been achieved in the aftermath of the British Empire in the areas concerned without close personal knowledge and understanding.... Since I joined the company I have been solely responsible, with one or two minor exceptions, for the negotiations which brought about 400 subsidiary companies into the Lonrho group. In the course of my negotiations I have met the principals concerned. Many of them have become my friends.... When I am in London because of my personal connections I spend my time by day, in the evening, and at weekends, as all who know me will confirm, to the total exclusion of all social life, on the company's affairs.'

In putting the defendant's view, Sir Basil Smallpeice rejected this argument. He stated, 'I came to the conclusion that Mr Rowland was unfit by reason of his temperament and lack of commercial probity to be chief executive of a public company.... None of the defendants denies the vigour, energy, and speculative ability of Mr Rowland .... In the considered opinion of the majority of the board the time has now arrived when the damage which has been done ... by the irresponsibility of Mr Rowland greatly outweights any benefit to be derived from his abilities and contacts .... In order to get his own way, he is prepared not only to override and disregard decisions of the board and to refuse to consult with the board but also ... actively to deceive and conceal from the board material information .... In specific circumstances Mr Rowland appears to have acted without any regard whatsoever to the true interests of the company or indeed, to what are in my view, elementary standards of propriety. The total UK bank overdrafts are now forecast to grow from £1½ million immediately after the rights issue to approximately £9 million by the end of 1973.'

Mr Rowland, however, thought that he and Sir Basil were in opposition because they held 'ideologies so opposed as to make a meeting of the minds impossible'. He added, 'In the thirteen months he [Sir Basil Smallpeice] has been director of Lonrho he has never visited any of the group's mining operations, nor, I understand, any of its activities outside head office.' Mr Rowland also admitted that apart from board meetings he had rarely if ever spoken to Sir Basil since the latter's appointment.

In Mr Hossy's opinion the strength of Mr Rowland's management lay in his encouraging senior executives to manage their particular responsibility areas as if they were running their own businesses. 'Lonrho's metaliferous mining division [had built up] from a production rate including associated companies of £1.25 million per annum eleven years ago to the current annual rate in excess of £35 million. Profits have risen more than proportionally. I state categorically that this could not have been achieved without Mr Rowland's far-sightedness, drive, negotiating ability, guidance, inspiring example and firm backing .... I believe that the group's strong position in several African countries stems from and is dependent on Mr Rowland's personal relationships, based on mutual trust with heads of state and other influential personalities in these countries.'

These views were strongly contested by Major-General Sir Edward Spears. With reference to Mr Rowland he stated, 'He appears to be wholly convinced that no one but he can be right, and he has regrettably thought fit to add deceit of his co-directors to arbitrary, and even abusive refusals to listen to their views or abide by their majority decisions.'

Referring to the possible effect of Mr Rowland's dismissal on African and Middle East connections, Sir Edward went on: 'African companies and governments ... ultimately have regard ... to the interests of their shareholders and to criticism .... If, as in this case, their arrangements with Lonrho are beneficial to them, they will not terminate them out of pique or for sentimental reasons merely because Mr Rowland has been displaced from office.'

However, affidavits from the governments of Zambia and Ghana both strongly supported Mr Rowland. Furthermore, Mr Chapman testified that a change in the company's direction might not be acceptable to the group's Ivorian associates.

Mr Hossy saw Mr Gerald Percy as the only one who had made significant contributions to Lonrho and whose knowledge of its operations qualified him to express a meaningful opinion.

Mr Percy, however, came out out strongly against Mr Rowland and was described as a 'dirty double-crossing rat' by Mr Rowland for his stand. An executive director since 1967, Mr Percy said he had been concerned by 'the general manner in which Lonrho was being controlled' since 1968. He thought that, 'although Mr Rowland had an undoubted flair for business which played a valuable role in the growth of Lonrho during the sixties, his preoccupation with the long-term future, and his highly egocentric approach to business and management problems, coupled with his lack of interest in day-to-day management brought about ... serious management difficulties and liquidity strain.'

Mr Percy went on: 'A major difference of opinion between myself and certain other executives in Lonrho on the one hand and Mr Rowland on the other occurred in 1969-70, pursuing proposals whereby a certain African government should nationalise the assets of two other British companies in the country concerned and then transfer them to a new corporation which would be jointly owned and/or manged by such a government and Lonrho .... Ultimately Mr Rowland was prevented from carrying the proposals into effect by circumstances outside Lonrho's control. [The country concerned was later understood to be Sierra Leone]. A further matter which has regrettably caused much controversy within the board concerns Nyaschere Copper (PVT) Ltd, which is an associate company of Lonrho. Lonrho owns 50 per cent of the share capital of HCC Investments (Pty) Ltd, of which Nyaschere is the wholly-owned subsidiary, and during the year ended 30 September 1972, the position was thought to be ... that Mr Rowland owned the other 50 per cent. The development of Nyaschere has been financed by the group, and as at 20 September 1972 the total indebtedness of Nyaschere to the group was in excess of £300,000, whereas the equity capital of the company is equivalent to approximately £5,000.'

Both Peat, Marwick, and Mitchell, and Keyser Ullman, had previously indicated that they considered Mr Rowland's indirect interest in a company to which the Lonrho group had advanced substantial loan funds rendered both Lonrho and Mr Rowland open to criticism. Mr Percy added that, as a result of this criticism, Mr Rowland had offered to sell his interest in HCC to Lonrho for £600,000 in September 1972, but subsequently withdrew that offer in October. When the auditors suggested that the issue should be covered in the 1972 directors' report, Mr Rowland reoffered his interest for £750,000. The board rejected this proposal, whereupon Mr Rowland said he had already sold it to his father-in-law for £700,000. 'I find Mr Rowland's behaviour in ... this matter inexplicable and extraordinary,' commented Mr Percy. Mr Rowland, however, denied making a large profit out of his interest in Nyaschere and stated that in 1965 he could have acquired the outstanding interest for a nominal sum of £20,000 and made a very large profit by selling the whole. 'However, being opposed to UDI in Rhodesia, I decided that I did not wish to increase my personal interests in Rhodesia. I therefore agreed to pass the outstanding interest, without profit to myself, to the local Lonrho subsidiary, on the specific condition that I would not have to put up the capital or be involved in the management of the mine.'

More information in the hearing referred to Peat, Marwick's later discovery that Mr Rowland's stake in Nyaschere was in fact shared with Mr Ball and Mr Ogilvy, who had 10 per cent and 5 per cent interests respectively.

A further issue that emerged at the hearing concerned the appointment of Mr Duncan Sandys as chairman and cancellation of his contract as a consultant. On 18 November 1971 Mr Sandys had been appointed consultant to the group at a salary of £50,000 per annum, effective from 1 September. Mr Fred Butcher wrote to Mr Sandys on 9 February 1972 extending his contract for six years, terminable at twelve months notice, with remuneration of £51,000 per annum for UK and overseas services. The overseas part of the fee, £49,000, was paid via the tax-free Cayman Islands. It was at the board meeting of 22 March 1972 that Mr Rowland told the board of the contract, a fortnight after they agreed to appoint Mr Sandys as chairman at £40,000 per annum, 55 per cent of which was to be paid via the Cayman Islands.

Mr Percy, drawing attention to the consultancy agreement with Mr Sandys, stated, 'An important instance of Mr Rowland's failure to disclose matters to the board is exemplified in the conduct of the consultancy arrangements with the chairman, the Right Honourable Duncan Sandys MP.' Mr Percy said he had been totally ignorant of any compensation arrangements for Mr Sandys on his appointment as Lonrho's chairman. 'I believed, as the result of what Mr Rowland said at the board meeting of 22 March 1972, that the consultancy agreement would fall away on Mr Sandys's appointment as chairman.'

According to Mr Percy there was no mention of a £130,000 payment to Mr Sandys for termination of his consultancy contract. This allowed the rights issue prospectus of 25 May following to omit this information to shareholders, which was not revealed until 14 February 1973, when Peat Marwick found that Mr Sandys had been paid £23,000 accrued fees and £44,000 compensation as a first instalment. On finding the remainder of the board had no knowledge Mr Sandys had immediately repaid the compensation.

Mr Rowland's own affidavit denied these charges and gave his version of the agreement with Mr Sandys. 'With regard to matters raised in connection with the consultancy agreement entered into with Mr Sandys before he joined the board, I considered that his personal status and intensive experience of international affairs, particularly in Africa, and his acquaintanceship with leading figures in many foreign countries would be of great benefit to the group and fully justified the proposed remuneration. This view was amply borne out by the valuable missions abroad which he undertook on our behalf .... I offered to pay him fair compensation for the termination of his consultancy contract, which, although it could be legally terminated earlier, had been entered into on the mutual understanding that, except in unforeseen circumstances, it would continue for six years. Mr Alan Ball, the chairman, Mr Angus Ogilvy and I considered carefully what should be the amount of compensation to be offered to Mr Sandys for the termination of his consultancy agreement. We decided that £130,000 would be fair and reasonable.' Mr Rowland added that the method used reaching this decision had been in accordance with the pattern of management followed since he, Mr Ball, and Mr Ogilvy, first came together in 1961.

Mr Percy also answered allegations from Mr Rowland and his supporters that he was 'an unfit person to deal on behalf of Lonrho in Africa.' He said, 'I have never had any reason to believe that I was not welcome in any African country in which Lonrho trades.' He added, 'In my opinion there is much merit in developing the existing partnerships with the governments and/or citizens in the countries in which it operates, but I consider that at the present time the most important requirements is for Lonrho to expand its United Kingdom earnings ....'

Mr Rowland denied as quite untrue that he had opposed acquisitions in the UK to avoid dilution of his shareholding, and cited as an example. 'In February 1971 the opportunity had arisen to open negotiations to acquire Rolls-Royce Motors from the Official Receiver, 70 per cent of the consideration for which would have been in Lonrho shares. The combination of Rolls-Royce and Wankel, and the use of the Rolls-Royce engines would have produced an immensely valuable asset. Only the present boardroom dispute made it impossible to pursue such an enormous project.'

Another defendant, Mr Wilkinson, gave evidence primarily on the Wankel deal. Mr Wilkinson said he became aware in September 1971 that Mr Rowland on his own account had entered into some form of 'secret supplementary arrangement' whereby the two Wankel companies should receive an extra 36 million Deutschmarks (£4.34 million). Mr Wilkinson alleged that Mr Rowland had also involved Lonrho in a commitment of £12.14 million for an 80 per cent interest in the Wankel companies, whereas the transaction had been portrayed as one costing £7.8 million for a 100 per cent holding. He went on: 'Finally and perhaps most serious of all, Mr Rowland misinformed or allowed the board to be misinformed, on no less than four separate occasions between 9 August and 20 October 1971 on the true cost and nature of the purchase.' When Mr Wilkinson raised the matter of the extra 36 million Deutschmarks, he alleged that Mr Rowland indicated the money would be provided by himself and 'that if he died, the liability would fall on his estate.'

Mr Dunlop's affidavit, on the other hand, supported Mr Rowland over the Wankel issue. He stated that it was always clear that Lonrho would acquire 80 per cent of the Wankel companies for £12.2 million. Mr Rowland added that 'there had been references to both £7.8 and £12.2 million. The extra amount arose over the transfer to Lonrho of General Motors' obligation to pay Wankel £4.4 million over four years which would eventually be a self-cancelling exercise when Lonrho was in receipt of that income from General Motors.' He stated further that the precise terms of the acquisition had been known to both Peat, Marwick and the Lonrho board, as well as circularised to shareholders.

In his summary, Mr Stammler, QC, for the defence, drew attention to a recommendation in the original Peat, Marwick report which had criticised the tenure by three directors, Mr Ball, Mr Percy, and Mr Rowland, of substantial properties rent free. The three directors had given undertakings to the board that they would repay company loans for their houses by 30 September 1972. Mr Gerald Percy had honoured his undertaking, but Mr Rowland, whose loan was £350,000, and Mr Ball had broken theirs.

In answer to this, Mr Rowland said, 'I had always maintained substantial credit balances with the company on which I was credited with interest in the normal course. Against this, my account has always been debited with interest on the capital cost to the company of the property.' Mr Rowland's income in this case was the dividend payment to Shepton Estates, which had accumulated in Lonrho and on which Lonrho paid a rate of interest. His account stood at over £300,000 in credit.

The judge, in his summing up, described the case as one that 'involves issues which transcend the legal problems involved', and ruled against Mr Rowland. However, an agreement was reached between the two parties which allowed him to keep his position until the EGM on 31 May. At a press conference following the hearing, Mr Rowland stated that he thought the boardroom dispute had arisen because of a 'complete clash of personalities between Sir Basil Smallpeice and myself.' Mr Rowland explained that his vision of Lonrho's future would be to combine 'the potential of independent Africa', the cash resources of Middle East Oil and Western technology in an 'unbeatable force.'

GOVERNMENT AND INSTITUTIONAL REACTIONS

The case itself provoked a number of reactions from African governments and their spokesmen, some in affidavit form, and from government bodies and institutions in the United Kingdom.

The Zambian government, commenting upon the possible dismissal of Mr Rowland stated in an affidavit:

> 'The Government was strongly of the view that in these circumstances it should take immediate control of the assets of Lonrho in Zambia .... It was only as a result of urgent representation from Mr Rowland that the Government of Zambia has refrained from taking such a step.'

The Ghanaian government voiced a similar opinion:

> 'The Government of Ghana supports the stand taken by our brother countries of Zambia, Kenya and the Sudan ... and warns that it will not be party to any decision taken unilaterally which may be detrimental to the smooth and efficient operation of Ashanti Goldfields ... of which Lonrho is a minority shareholder. The Government would like to warn all concerned that it will not hesitate to take measures to protect its interests in any appropraite circumstances.

Kenya and the Sudan also supported Mr Rowland.

Messrs Udi Gecaga, Gil Olympio and Tom McFine, on behalf of Lonrho's operations in Central, East and West Africa, and representing Lonrho's major political contacts there, also issued a joint statement declaring in their affidavit, 'We decided to join efforts with Mr R. W. Rowland to implement programmes in Europe and Africa, which should bring substantial benefit to the people of Africa .... We are extremely disturbed that some of Lonrho's directors, a few of whom ... have very scanty knowledge of the African continent, should take a decision that is bound to alter Lonrho's basic orientation and policies without any communication or consultation with us at all to ascertain the full repercussions of their action. We are also deeply disturbed that proposals to allow minority participation by African and Middle East interests in the share capital of Lonrho has been shrugged off by these same directors. We reaffirm our support of Mr Rowland, what he stands for, his policies, and his breadth of vision.'

Nevertheless British public opinion was shocked by the disclosures of the hearing and in an unusually strong statement in the House of Commons, the British Prime Minister, Mr Edward Heath, called the Lonrho affair 'the unpleasant and unacceptable face of capitalism', but added that one should not suggest that the whole of British industry consists of practices of this kind. He went on, 'As far as the boardroom procedures are concerned they can obviously be examined by the department concerned from the point of view of tax affairs or from the point of view of company law.'

Although the Confederation of British Industry declined to comment specifically on Lonrho, a statement stressed its deep concern at the 'personal conduct and integrity' of directors, and in its annual report on the responsibilities of the public company issued in May 1973 declared, 'companies must recognise that they have functions, duties and moral obligations that go beyond the immediate pursuit of profit and the requirements of the law.'

Mr Anthony Wedgewood Benn (former Labour Minister for Trade and Industry) gave one view from the major opposition party. In a speech he stated, 'The abuse of business and financial power is now a direct threat to our democratic institutions and must be checked .... That is one reason why the Labour Party must allow the public to control or own key industries or financial centres on a far greater scale than in the past.'

SUBSEQUENT EVENTS (MAY 1973)

A further statement explaining the Zambia government position was made on 17 May by Mr Annock Phiri, the Zambia High Commissioner. He declared, 'The attempt to remove Mr Rowland represents to us a probable drastic change in policy in Africa—such a far-reaching change that Lonrho would cease to be welcome in Zambia as an independent company....' Zambia, in which Lonrho had acquired forty companies since independence in 1964, accounted for approximately £2 million of pre-tax profits on assets of £8 million. However, Mr Phiri modified Zambia's position by adding that 'any action by the Zambia Government would depend on whether the policy of the company changes.'

The eight directors then produced a seven-point plan on which, in their view, Lonrho's future policy should be based. In summary, these were:

To save £1 million in supporting Mr Rowland's personal initiatives, including £300,000 operating expenses for the Mystére jet and expenditure on 'uncontrolled development schemes' undertaken by him.

To implement the Peat, Marwick report in full and recruit top managers.

Develop a long-term strategy of backing activities where Lonrho is strong and dispose of weaker ventures.

Put greater concentration on remittable profits and acquire immediately £2 million of annual profit generated in Britain in order to close the current balance of payments gap in the Lonrho group amounting to £2.5 million per year.

Develop local management in independent Africa and build on broadly-based local support.

Meanwhile, under a section of the British Companies Act which covers 'miscreance or other misconduct, or when members (shareholders) have not been given all the information they might reasonably expect', the Department of Trade and Industry on 15 May announced their intention to conduct a full-scale investigation into the affairs of Lonrho.

This was immediately followed by a statement from Mr Rowland, disclosing details of his shareholding arrangements with Mr Ogilvy and Mr Ball. Mr Rowland explained that in March 1967 Yeoman Investments, a Bahamas company, had been nominated by him to take up two million shares in Lonrho on option at a total cost of £725,000. Yeoman had been formed in order to circumvent the problem of blocked dividend accumulation in Shepton Estates, Mr Rowland's Rhodesian Company. At the same time he gave Mr Ball and Mr Ogilvy a 20 per cent and 10 per cent participation respectively in Yeoman, accredited to their family trusts, in order, as he said, for them to benefit from likely growth in Lonrho stock.

Their association with Nyaschere came with the formation of HCC (Pty) Ltd in South Africa, and Borma AG in Switzerland. HCC was formed in early 1970 to hold both Lonrho's and Mr Rowland's interests in Nyaschere. The shares of HCC were issued in July 1970 (just after the British General Election) with Lonrho acquiring 50 per cent and Borma, formed as a wholly-owned subsidiary of Yeoman in mid-1970, acquiring the remaining 50 per cent.

Through later Lonrho scrip and rights issues Shepton's shareholding grew to 5.3 million with 7.2 million in Yeoman. All assets in Yeoman had been shown against Mr Rowland's name in the accounts since the condition that Mr Ball and Mr Ogilvy reimburse Rowland for their options on two million shares had not been fulfilled.

The press however continued with allegations and disclosures. The *Sunday Times*, posing the question, 'Did Sandys get fraud charge stopped?', referred to a remark made by a Lonrho South African director, Sydney Newman, in an ITV off-camera discussion, that Gerald Percy knew perfectly well why Mr Sandys was paid £50,000 p.a., and referred to Mr Sandys's frequent meetings with the South African foreign minister and London ambassador.

The *Observer* was more specific and revealed that on the 13 August 1969 the British government had sent a note to the United Nations, concerning 'a possible evasion of sanctions in the export of Rhodesian Copper.' The note went on 'Some time in 1968 a Johannesburg company purchased the Edmundian Copper Mine in Mozambique. The Edmundian Mine had not been worked for six or seven years and an expert who inspected it last year pronounced it to be a completely uneconomic proposition. Nevertheless, work has begun to reopen the mine and production is due to start in early August 1969. The purpose of this activity is understood to provide a cover for Rhodesian copper exports ... production has not yet begun at the Edmundian Mine but a shipment of copper has already been falsely documented and described as originating from that mine.'

This was corroborated by disclosures from an ex-director of Edmundian and employee of Hochmetals, Johannesburg in 1969, relating to his company's involvement with Lonrho subsidiaries in Rhodesia and South Africa. It was alleged that sanctions had been easily broken before the summer of 1970 by informing the South African Chamber of Commerce that the source of copper shipments was South African. In response to the United Nations' requiring more positive proof of origin, Hochmetals acquired the Edmundian Mine to redocument Rhodesian shipments, although the mine itself remained unworked. Via Coronation Syndicate, Lonrho subsequently purchased the Edmundian Mine with Gerald Percy and other Lonrho executives replacing the old Edmundian Board in July 1970.

THE FINAL DECISION

Against this background the shareholders of Lonrho were scheduled to meet on 31 May 1973, for an extraordinary meeting, where they were to determine Mr Rowland's future role in Lonrho by vote on two resolutions:

(a) Whether to retain Mr Rowland as chief executive.

(b) Whether to remove the eight dissident directors from office.

19 Slater Walker Securities Limited (A)*

Early in 1969 the board of Slater Walker Securities met to review the company's future strategy and to consider making changes in emphasis in the basic pattern of future activities. In the years between 1964 and 1968 Slater Walker Securities, led by Mr James Slater, had experienced phenomenal growth in sales, earnings and assets (see Exhibits 1 and 2). Since Mr Slater had acquired the almost defunct H. Lotery and Company Ltd in mid-1964 and changed its name to Slater Walker and Company Ltd, net capital employed had increased from £2,293,000 to £72,091,000 and profits before tax had expanded from £136,939 to £4,868,213. Net earnings per share after tax had increased from 3/5d in 1964 to 22/4d in 1968 and management were able to forecast a further increase in the range 34/1d-38/2d for 1969, at the same time net equity assets per share had risen from 4/3d to 24/- over the same period. By early 1969, due to a rapid rise in the company's share price, Slater Walker Securities had grown from very modest beginnings to ranking as one of Britain's top fifty companies measured by market capitalisation (see Exhibit 3).

Much of Slater Walkers's growth had been accomplished by the acquisition and reorganisation of a wide variety of companies operating in different industries in both Great Britain and overseas. These acquisitions, although operating in apparently unrelated industries, had increasingly been made as a result of careful screening of potential opportunities in the search for 'assets' situations.

In the case the student is confronted with the situation as of early 1969. He is asked to analyse the company's progress between 1964 and 1969 and to formulate his own ideas for the future development of Slater Walker.

Next, in the (B) case, the student is asked to appraise management's change in strategy and to analyse the development of the company over the next four years to the spring of 1973.

HISTORY

Jim Slater left school at the age of sixteen and trained as an accountant, qualifying when he was twenty-four. He later became secretary of Park Royal Vehicles Ltd, a commercial vehicle manufacturers, and a subsidiary of the Associated Commercial Vehicles Group. He was promoted to become commercial director of ACV and, when ACV was acquired by Leyland Motors Ltd, he became commercial manager of the Leyland Group and ultimately deputy to Donald (later Lord) Stokes, the sales director of Leyland.

Apart from his successful industrial career, Mr Slater began to take a serious interest in the stock market, in the early 1960s. Within three years he had converted his modest savings of £2,000 into £50,000. He then left Leyland to form his own company, Dayside Finance Ltd (which subsequently changed its name to Investment Analysis Ltd and later to Slater Walker Investments Ltd), specialising in investment consultancy and handling portfolios for large private investors.

In 1963 Mr Slater met Mr Peter Walker, a member of parliament (later a senior government minister) and the chairman of Walker Moate and Company, insurance brokers. Mr Walker, of a similar age and background to Mr Slater, proved an ideal partner and helped to finance the first acquisition made by Mr Slater in 1964, which formed the basis for the development of Slater Walker Securities.

At a board meeting of H. Lotery & Co. Ltd, held on 24 July 1964, Mr J. D. Slater, Mr P. Walker and Mr K. Meyer were appointed additional directors of the company and the rest of the board tendered their resignation. On 27 July 1964, at the annual meeting of the company, Mr Slater announced that he and his associates had acquired 48 per cent of the ordinary share capital for a total consideration of £720,000 or 10/- per share. The cash required for this transaction represented a personal stake of £25,000 from Mr Slater, some £325,000 from bank borrowing and a further £350,000 from a syndicate of friends and associates.

H. Lotery had previously operated as a small clothing and textile company, but these textile interests had been sold, leaving the company largely as a shell owning

---

* Copyright © Manchester Business School 1972

some freehold and leasehold property valued in the latest balance sheet at 9/9d per ordinary share.

The new directors announced that they intended to develop and expand the business, and on 27 July the company also purchased Dayside Finance Ltd from Mr J.D. Slater for a nominal value of £100. Mr J.D. Slater and the board recognised at an early stage the benefit that both the company and employees obtained by the company granting share options as an incentive to capable employees. At a board meeting on 24 September 1964 this principle was approved and at the same meeting the company's name was changed to Slater Walker & Co. Ltd; this was subsequently changed on 25 November 1965 to Slater Walker Securities Ltd.

On 2 December 1964 Slater Walker Industrial Group (SWIG) increased its issued capital from £2 to £2,500,000 by the issue of 2,499,998 shares at £1 each. This resulted in Slater Walker & Co. owning 1,000,000 shares (40 per cent), and Great Portland Industrial & General Investments Ltd (a substantial shareholder in Slater Walker & Co.) owning 200,000 shares. The balance of shares were spread amongst institutions and large private clients.

On 5 February 1965 Beaufort House, the main leasehold property asset of H. Lotery, was sold for £1.85 million causing a decline in rental income for the year. Investment counselling services continued to expand, however, and profits therefore increased during 1965.

1966

In 1966 the growth rate of the company began to quicken. The financial service activities experienced an increased volume and several small acquisitions were undertaken. In January the company purchased 260,000 shares in SWIG from existing shareholders, making its holding 50.4 per cent and in October the company made an agreed purchase of the outstanding capital of that company for £1.3 million. The main assets of SWIG were strategic shareholdings in Productofoam Holdings, a holding company owning a number of small subsidiaries in plastics and rubber goods, and George Wilson Gas Meters, manufacturers of gas meters, industrial burners and catering equipment.

In August 1966 Slater Walker made its first major takeover bid for Thomas Brown & Sons Ltd, a UK company operating in Australia engaged in wholesaling, wines and spirits, grocery distribution and food products. (For a detailed list of acquisitions 1964-April 1969 see Exhibit 4.) Slater Walker began buying shares in the market and by August 1966 had accumulated some 30 per cent of the ordinary and 31 per cent of the preference stock. Bid terms were announced valuing Browns at $3 million (Australian) and were eventually raised to $3.39 million (£1.35 million) before receiving 100 per cent acceptance.

Following the acquisition, draft accounts were prepared and divisional and subsidiary figures were analysed in detail as below. It was concluded that it would be difficult and time consuming to revitalise Brown's wholesaling business and this was sold off to other merchants. Credit terms were given to those who needed them and premises of certain branches were rented out to those companies which could not buy the properties.

Analysis of Thomas Brown & Sons

		Group capital employed		*Net profit before tax and interest*
		(millions)		
Wholesaling activities		$6.9	1.7%	$119,697
Brisbane companies (Manahans, Holsums, Tunleys, Caledonian House and distillery)		$1.2	22%	$257,121
Gross		$8.1		$376,818
Less: Net overdraft	$600,000			
Unsecured loan stock	$940,000			*less* interest and tax
Short-term loans	$460,000	$2.0		$293,393
Net tangible assets		$6.1	Net profit	$83,425

Source: Jos. Sebag & Co.

Conservative calculations were then made of the probable losses and profits resulting from the disposal of the assets of these businesses, resulting in the liberation of $5 million cash. Brown's assets then consisted of $5 million cash and the following four companies:

Tunleys (60 per cent owned), who were manufacturers of hessian sacks. Management was considered good and the return on capital seemed high enough for the company to be left alone.

Beenleigh Rum Distillery, which was part of the wines and spirits division of Thomas Brown. The distilling company had been treated as a captive supply of rum and its prices to other merchants and breweries were higher than all other rum distillers in Australia. Further, no worthwhile marketing effort of promotional activity was carried out for the consumer market. As a consequence, Slater Walker decided to convert the distillery into a separate company which in turn acquired the assets from its former parent, Thomas Brown. The company's price list was revised in line with competitors and a marketing manager employed. New products, including a colourless Bacardi type rum, called Dryandra, were introduced and launched with a progressive marketing programme.

Holsum Products, which were manufacturers of essences for the food industry, with additional interests in ground and packaged pepper and spices, packed fruits, bottled vinegar and concentrates.

The capital employed was divided almost equally between facilities in Brisbane and Sydney. However, analysis revealed that the net return on capital in Sydney was only 4 per cent against 16 per cent in Brisbane. The Sydney plant was, therefore, closed and activity concentrated in Brisbane.

A product analysis revealed that some product lines were unprofitable while others had a high return. All lines with a gross margin below a specific level were eliminated, the old premises in Brisbane were sold and work was transferred to a more modern and suitable rented plant.

H. A. Manahan, which operated a chain of thirty-one self-service grocery stores. Twenty of these were in country districts while eleven were in the city of Brisbane. The country stores were found to be profitable; however, competition from large stores made the city outlets unprofitable. As a result the city stores were shut down and efforts concentrated on building up more effective coverage in the profitable country districts. In addition, a policy of standardisation was introduced for country stores on such items as marketing policy and store layout. Two of the original stores were closed and a further seven were opened with more planned.

Manahans also operated its own warehousing operations which were found to be unprofitable and, in addition, more time by management was being devoted to wholesaling than to retailing. The wholesaling operation was, therefore, closed down thus releasing a further $250,000 of capital employed.

As a result of these reorganisation measures and improved liquidity control, some £1.2 million cash net of debt repayment was released. The remaining subsidiaries, plus property interests valued at about £750,000, were producing some £105,000 pre-tax for the subsidiaries and about £100,000 for the properties, against a net outlay of some £45,000.

By the end of 1966 Thomas Brown held a considerable amount of liquid assets as a result of reorganisation and improved liquidity control. In December part of this cash balance was, therefore, used to purchase, at a price estimated at £150,000 a 44.6 per cent interest in Wancol Holdings Limited, a quoted Australian company owning a coal mine and cash resources of £300,000.

1967

During 1967 rationalisation of Thomas Brown's 45 per cent stake in Wancol took place. Wancol's existing stock quotation was used to issue shares to acquire a number of other interests including the 60 per cent interest in Tunleys from Thomas Brown and the 82 per cent stake of Greengate and Irwell Rubber Company in Bramac Ltd. In December 1967 Wancol changed its name to Slater Walker Securities (Australia) Limited.

In January 1967 Slater Walker launched its first major move in the United Kingdom. Having built up a 16.3 per cent stake, the company bid for the Greengate and Irwell Rubber Company and by March the acquisition was successfully completed for a price of approximately £3 million.

Greengate and Irwell was a long-established company specialising in rubberised fabrics and conveyor belting. After the Second World War, growing competition in the company's traditional belting market led to reduced earnings and diversification into other industrial rubber goods such as hosing, mouldings and ropes. Chronic overcapacity continued in conveyor belting leading to depressed prices. These problems were exacerbated by management problems associated with the rubberised fabric portion of the business. Reorganisation began in 1959 and by 1964 the group had developed into a well-diversified rubber goods manufacturing company. In 1966, however, further problems arose outside the company's control resulting in a labour shortage and reduced profits. Then, early in 1967, came the successful bid by Slater Walker.

At the time of the acquisition Greengate and Irwell shares were on a price earnings multiple of 19 compared with a forecast of 16.6 for the shares of Slater Walker. However, Greengate's market capitalisation represented only 73 per cent of net book value whereas Slater Walker was capitalised at 150 per cent of book value.

Following the acquisition, reorganisation began immediately. Bramac, Greengate's Australian subsidiary was sold to Slater Walker Securities (Australia); the elasticated thread division was hived off and integrated with the rubber gloves division of Productofoam, another associate of Slater Walker. The canvas and rubber footwear units were shut down and Telemac, a women's rainwear manufacturer, was sold.

Initially, Slater Walker decided to concentrate on improving profits on general rubber products. These were increased from £81,000 in 1966/7 to £270,000 in 1968. This was achieved by negotiating improved prices for raw materials by concentrating buying, rationalising and formulating the number of rubber compounds produced, increased selling prices, improved exports and reduced overheads. A productivity deal was introduced with consequent savings being equally shared between the workforce and the company, and by 1968 productivity had increased by 15 per cent. Profits from other activities also increased slightly from £239,000 to £263,000 with the result that by the end of the year profits overall were approximately £533,000 on a reduced investment. Further, over £1.75 million in assets had been withdrawn including more than £1 million additional cash, which had been released elsewhere in Slater Walker, by the introduction of debt capital at Greengate, and reductions in working capital.

In August 1967 Slater Walker acquired the balance of the shares in Productofoam Holdings and George Wilson Gas Meters. The outstanding 56 per cent of Productofoam was acquired for £900,000 in shares, and was then rapidly rationalised. The unprofitable laminating and plastics interests were sold, the latex surgical products subsidiary was merged with Greengate's elasticated thread operation to form United Latex, and only a 51 per cent interest in Salisbury Parry & Company, a small shopfitting firm, was retained. Despite these attempts at rationalisation, however, the Productofoam investment and subsequent acquisition did not contribute much improvement in the profitability of Slater Walker.

George Wilson, which also became a wholly-owned subsidiary in August, first entered into an association with Slater Walker in December 1964. Then the business had consisted of three plants in Coventry (making radiators, meters and components), Jarrow (making components) and London (a repair works). Profits totalling around £40,000 per annum were declining and output of gas meters was only about 600 per week while 20 per cent of all the meters produced were rejects.

The Slater Walker central management analysed the company and decided that its basic product was inadequate, the method of production uneconomic, and goodwill was rapidly declining with area Gas Boards. A programme of reorganisation was therefore commenced. Over £40,000 was spent on developing a new gas meter, the Jarrow plant was closed, the Coventry plant reorganised and the workforce retrained from a craft basis to an assembly line operation. This was assisted by the introduction of a productivity scheme resulting in a 12 per cent increase in output in return for an 18 per cent increase in earnings. Rejects were reduced from 20 per cent to 2 per cent while increased selling effort resulted in an increase in orders of 30 per cent. Output rose from 600 to 2,000 meters per week and profits increased to £68,000 per annum. Further finance was provided for expansion by sale and lease back of the factory, and by the end of 1968 production had reached 3,000 meters per week. Profits were running at about £100,000 per annum with further increases expected and market share had risen from 7 per cent to 20 per cent in three years.

In July 1968 George Wilson acquired Thomas Braddock, a subsidiary of Peglers, which manufactured gas meters in London. This company's production was transferred to Coventry thereby releasing the London plant for disposal.

Constructors Ltd

By August 1967 a strategic investment of 16 per cent had been acquired in Constructors

Ltd. This was followed by a bid for the whole capital in September, and in November 1967 Constructors became part of Slater Walker. The group consisted of Constructors itself (shelving, steel partitions, cycle stands, steel office furniture, lockers, filing systems and materials handling equipment); Poles (overhead electric poles, street lighting columns and sign posts); A. W. Chapman (adjustable seat mechanisms for motor vehicles); and Rock & Taylor (liquid sampling machines, weather recorders, and other electronic devices). Rock & Taylor and Poles were disposed of by SWS at the end of 1967, and Constructors's office equipment, office furniture and cycle stand activities were terminated.

The Slater Walker bid was well timed in that Constructors's profits had fallen from £111,766 (before tax) in 1962 to a loss before tax in 1966 of £64,043. This decrease was largely due to the growing losses made by Constructors's Scottish factory which was finally closed in 1967. The loss from this factory in 1966 was £62,466. According to the offer document made by Slater Walker Ltd on behalf of Slater Walker Securities Ltd, the net asset value per share of Constructors as at 31 December 1966 was approximately 16 shillings per share. This was calculated from shareholders funds of £804,000 which included valuing several properties on a going concern basis and nearly £1 million of debtors stocks and work in progress. In October 1967 the board forecast a small loss for the first half of the calendar year necessitating a further omission of any dividend, and at that time it was warned that recovery would be a long affair.

Constructors's problems were chronic, if not unfamiliar. Static sales, too many products causing high fixed costs and preventing tenable runs—and loss-making products dominating the profitable lines; within that range, the primacy of product quality rather than marketing and ever-rising overhead costs, were all features of the company. One serious headache was the spreading of Chapman's business between five factories in London.

After the acquisition Slater Walker closed four of the London factories and concentrated production in Birmingham where the factory was sold and leased back. Loss makers were then sold or liquidated and the company's structure was rationalised by combining all subsidiaries into one operating company under the name Chapman Constructors (Birmingham) Ltd, with two sales companies, A. W. Chapman and Constructors. A Slater Walker managing director was appointed with full executive responsibility for profits. By these moves three-quarters of the purchase price of £720,000 in shares and cash had been recovered in six months.

Constructors's prices were cut and orders which had been at a standstill began to recover. The company's sixteen salesmen who had received no pay increase for three years, were low in morale. Three were made redundant and the resultant savings went to provide an increase for the remaining thirteen. Sales targets were revised and an incentive scheme introduced. Overheads were cut and aggressive buying cut raw material costs. An order for seat slides worth £350,000 was obtained from Ford in Germany thus reducing dependence of the UK automotive market. A 65 per cent increase was also obtained in the sales shelving units. Within six months losses had been converted to profits, which were estimated at £50,000 for 1968.

A further flurry of small acquisitions rounded out 1967 for Slater Walker, including Newmans Holdings, a company involved in footwear manufacture with a strong asset backing but poor earnings performance, and Nathaniel Lloyd, a fine printing and packaging company acquired for some £600,000, which after disposal of surplus premises and sale of the loss-making printing operations, reduced the net cost of acquisition to £380,000 against estimated 1968 profits of £85,000.

Before 1967 Slater Walker had acquired two small builders' merchants, and towards the end of 1967 two further companies, Kirby Bros and Wiggins Sankey were acquired. All these acquisitions were linked into a single structure, Metropolitan Builders' Merchants, whose operations were concentrated in greater London. The identities of the constituent companies were retained and Slater Walker management was concentrated primarily on optimising working assets usage, stock turnover improvement, reducing the multiplicity of products carried and integrating various management operations.

Financial Services, although somewhat overshadowed by the growth of Slater Walker's industrial activities, continued to do well in 1967. Considerable growth occurred in the volume of funds controlled by Investment Analysis Ltd, and in June 1967 the Invan Unit Trust was formed to cater for clients with less than £50,000 to invest. Although initially restricted, Invan performed extremely well in its first year of operation and in March 1968 was offered to the general public with a minimum initial subscription of 300 units worth some £500. The offer attracted a record of £8.2

million in subscriptions, the largest amount ever received for an initial public offer by a UK unit trust.

1968

Further rapid development took place in 1968. In March Slater Walker acquired Keith Blackman, heating and ventilation engineers, at a cost of £4.33 million in loan stock and shares. It was found, however, that the time involved in turning Blackman around to a really profitable basis would be unacceptably long and, therefore, the company was sold a few months later to General Electric for £3.7 million cash.

In May 1968 Mr Slater launched his largest acquisition to date by bidding for Crittall Hope, a move that effectively more than doubled the size of Slater Walker in terms of net assets.

Crittall Hope was formed in 1965 as the result of a merger between two family firms engaged primarily in metal window frame manufacture but with ancillary interests in heating and ventilation equipment, agricultural products and architectural metalwork. Sales in 1967 were approximately £30 million, of which £26 million came from window frames. In addition the company held a number of investments in supplying companies and operated a number of overseas subsidiaries, including interests in South Africa, the United States, Canada, Australia, Malaysia and West Germany, which contributed 40 per cent of sales.

Having built up a substantial stake in Crittall, Slater Walker made its initial bid in April 1968. This first bid was rejected but an increased offer was eventually accepted, valuing Crittall Hope at just over £18 million.

Rationalisation began immediately. The West German subsidiary losing £300,000 was rapidly sold, as was the Canadian company, making losses of £60,000. Assets of the South African and Zambian plants were sold, although the shell of the former company was maintained since it was quoted on the Johannesburg stock market.

In the UK plans were ready by October 1968 to reorganise domestic production. Crittall's Smethwick factory working at 40 per cent of capacity was halved and some workers made redundant. The Crittall plant at Wednesbury was closed creating further redundancies, although production was expanded at Crittall's Braintree plant involving an additional 420 workers. Various other losing subsidiaries were liquidated and Crittall's remaining oil and gas burner activities were merged with George Wilson Gas Meters.

Following these rationalisation moves, a programme of new product development was initiated. Crittall entered the market for double glazed metal window frames and began to develop activities such as metal greenhouses, which offered higher growth potential in profitable market sectors.

Mr Slater was able to report to shareholders in 1969 that 'since taking control we have sold ten of Crittall Hope's overseas subsidiaries for cash or shares in other companies, some of which were subsequently sold.... In the UK we have liquidated or sold six of the subsidiaries and incurred substantial reorganisation expenses on rationalising production facilities. As a result the capital employed in manufacturing windows and allied products has been reduced from approximately £21 million to £11.5 million and over £6 million in cash has been redeployed within Slater Walker.' At the same time profits had been increased, from £700,000 per annum pre-acquisition, to £930,000.

A series of further acquisitions was made before the end of 1968, including TWW, an independent Welsh television contractor whose franchise was withdrawn in July 1968, leaving assets consisting of two firms of opticians with surplus cash of some £600,000; a 51 per cent holding in three theatrical production companies; a 58 per cent share in an outdoor advertising company and £2.55 million cash arising from the liquidation of TV interests. Further acquisitions of Harrisons and Augustine Investments strengthened the Slater Walker interests in optical retailing giving the company the largest chain of optical retailers in the UK with some 300 branches and about 8 per cent of the market.

The most important acquisition in 1968 was that of Drage's Ltd. In October Slater Walker purchased from the Wolfson Foundation and other shareholders a controlling interest in Drage's Ltd, and an offer was made for the rest of the issued capital of the company. This acquisition restored the balance between SWS industrial and financial activities.

Drage's, according to their balance sheet as at 31 December 1967 (adjusted for the sale of the subsidiary in January 1968), had net assets of £23.7 million or 23/9d per share. With its shares worth 76/3d, the market value of the Slater Walker paper bid was around 33/10d per share and a cash alternative of 30/- was provided by N. M. Rothchild & Sons. The SWS earnings per share after tax and minority interests for the year ended 31 December 1967 were 10/4d per share, and for the year ended 31 December 1968 the earnings were 22.4d per share. This means that effectively SWS issued shares on a PE ratio of 88.0 using 1967 earnings or a PE ratio of 40.8 using 1968 earnings. Slater Walker also issued to the Wolfson Foundation £7.6 million of 8½ unsecured loan stock to replace the existing Drage's debt capital.

Drage's largest subsidiary, General Guarantee Corporation, was engaged in finance and hire purchase and in addition had a portfolio of quoted investments and cash. One of the most attractive parts of Drage's empire was its 50 per cent holding in Ralli Brothers (Holdings) Ltd. This company had two main subsidiaries, Ralli Brothers (Bankers) Ltd, which was an Eighth Schedule Bank with all the necessary authorisations to carry on all forms of banking business, and Ralli Brothers Ltd, which was principally engaged in commodity trading. The Ralli group owned a 75 per cent interest in the equity of Phillips Brocklehurst, a company with interests in textiles in the UK and South Africa, who had net assets of around £7 million.

These assets other than Ralli Holdings were rapidly liquidated for £23 million in cash while in January 1969 a further 25 per cent of Ralli Holdings was acquired for £4.5 million with an option to acquire the remaining 25 per cent at the same price. In March 1969 Slater Walker bid for and acquired the outstanding preference share capital of Ralli Brothers Ltd.

Overseas activity began to expand in 1968. Shortly after the change of name Wancol to Slater Walker Securities (Australia) Ltd in December 1967, Thomas Brown reduced its holdings in SWSA to 30 per cent by placing its shares with institutional investors in Australia and the UK. In August 1968 a rights issue was made which increased the Australian companies' liquidity to over $12 million and equity capitalisation to $33 million. A programme of acquisition began shortly thereafter including Plastalon Holdings Ltd which carried on very similar business to Bramac Ltd. Both companies were reorganised and the Plastalon activities were merged into the Bramac factory at Footscray. This resulted in the Conveyor and V-Belt manufacturing activities being disposed of and the name being changed to Bramac Plastalon Ltd. The Sydney-based Halifax Group of Companies who were importers and distributors of plastic materials and speciality fabrics were also acquired in September 1968. In July Lithgow Valley Colliery Company Ltd was acquired. This company had a substantial share portfolio and operated a coal mine in the heart of Lithgow. Further programmes of mechanisation and development at this and the Wallerawang collieries took place during the year, and exports to Japan were increased; the company also announced that it had determined substantial deposits of coal at Mt Tomah which was approximately thirty miles north of the Wallerawang Collieries.

Other SWSA acquisitions during the year were H. A. Manahan & Sons Pty Ltd—twenty five stores, Beenleigh Rum Pty Ltd and Holsum Products (Brisbane) Pty Ltd from Thomas Brown. SWSA also acquired the outstanding 40 per cent interest in Tunleys Pty Ltd, which it did not own.

In August 1968 Slater Walker acquired a 75 per cent interest in a Bahamian bank, Carden Withers (which was subsequently renamed Slater Walker and Withers), for £1.5 million in shares. This move was also made as a part of Mr Slater's plan eventually to develop financial operations inthe United States. It was announced that Carden would continue its existing role of portfolio management and currency dealing but would probably be expanded on the same lines as Investment Analysis, now renamed Slater Walker Investments Ltd. In December Slater Walker Trust Management (Bahamas) was formed, and in March 1969 this was followed by the launch of a new unit trust, Slater Walker International Fund, an open-ended fund aimed at capital growth with an international investment policy. While this fund was similar to a UK unit trust, it differed in that it paid no taxes and was able to arrange dollar loans to enable it to purchase securities outside the sterling area, thereby minimising risks associated with investment premium dollars.

In South Africa the quoted local subsidiary of Critall Hope was changed in name to Slater Walker Securities (South Africa), while its actual business and assets were sold to a local company in exchange for cash and a 24.2 per cent shareholding in the acquiring company Wire Industries Steel Products and Engineering Company.

COMPANY PHILOSOPHY

Mr Slater believed that profits and only profits were what primarily counted in business.[1] 'The key word is earnings. In business, one's primary job, and one's primary responsibility is to shareholders; it is their money that one is playing with.'

In pursuit of this objective Mr Slater had clear ideas of the way in which a company should be managed, which he outlined as follows:

1. It is essential for there to be very strong central financial control. In this context, accurate monthly profit and loss figures are vital, together with budgets and a detailed analysis of all variances from those budgets. Similarly, there should be very close central control of group liquidity.

2. There should be a strong central team, free of day-to-day routine, who can deal as a task force with trouble spots as and when they arise.

3. Each new acquisition should fit reasonably well into an existing division of the company or be of sufficient size to be the nucleus of a new division.

4. After deciding that a proposed acquisition makes general commercial sense and provides scope for substantial organic growth, the approach to it should be financially orientated. In particular, the main criteria should be whether or not it will improve the assets and earnings per share of the main company. The other critical question is whether or not it will impair liquidity. Each acquisition should be looked at with these three criteria in mind—the effect on earnings, assets and liquidity.

5. It is essential to be stock market orientated. In this context the main aim should be to achieve a 'smoothed-out growth rate'. By this I do, of course, mean a smooth and regular growth in earnings per share. This is essential to maintain a reasonably good price—earnings ratio which is again essential to make acquisitions relatively less expensive. It may seem to be an extravagant claim that one can achieve a smoothed-out growth rate. Obviously, if earnings are not in fact increasing, it it not possible to smooth them out. Provided growth is there, it is, however, possible to smooth it by, for example, the timing of acquisitions. Obviously, if a large *tranche* of stock is issued at the end of a financial year, this will have the effect of damping down earnings growth for the year in question. If, therefore, earnings are exceptionally good during a given year, it may pay to make an acquisition at the end of it as opposed to the beginning of the next financial year.

6. Industrial companies should be managed in the same way as an investment portfolio, the key to this is to cut out or improve loss makers rapidly and back winners. Money and effort should be channelled where management is succeeding in good, long-term growth areas as opposed to where it is pushing uphill in the wrong field.

7. Acquisitions should in general have a good asset backing, which will provide an essential buffer and reserve for bad times. It is a very dangerous policy to be purely earnings-orientated and this, to my mind, is one of the main reasons for past failures.

8. Acquisitions should in general be substantial in size. This is one of the most vital points of all as otherwise management becomes an almost insuperable problem. Relatively large companies usually have management in depth and are not wholly dependent on one or two men. The other extremely important advantage of sizeable acquisitions is that it enables the maximum leverage and advantage to be obtained from the talents of the top team of central personnel. It is not worthwhile, for example, for the top team to spend their time in looking in detail into the buying techniques of a mass of diverse, private companies. It would, however, be very much worth their while to look into the buying techniques of a relatively large company with a multi-million buying bill. Similar arguments apply to every facet of the business.

9. In addition to the central management being free to tackle trouble spots, they should also be free to assist in selling off loss makers where the task of putting them right is not worth the effort involved in doing so. Without this firm policy of selling off real trouble spots, one can easily develop the habit of chasing good money after bad and spending a disproportionate amount of time on endeavouring to recoup losses as opposed to developing profits.

---

[1] E. Foster and G. Bull, 'Jim Slater's Six Fat Years,' *The Director*, August 1970.

I believe that the basic theme should be to build up earnings per share and then reverse into assets. From these assets cash should be generated by selling off loss makers and reinvesting the proceeds in further earnings. As further earnings are generated, the cycle is again repeated. By doing this, assets per share are kept moving up in line with earnings per share and it is these increasing assets which provide a firm base for future development.

Pre-acquisition procedure

Initially the acquisitions made by Slater Walker tended to be opportunistic. Mr Slater noted that there had been no carefully-planned rationale and that several errors had been made, as in the case of Productofoam and Newman Holdings. Gradually, however, as the company grew, a systematic approach to the screening of potential acquisitions evolved which entailed a more rigorous investigation. Mr Slater described this procedure as follows:[2]

> If (the company) is private, we would get first of all an independent accountant's report as opposed to the auditors of the firm in question, and that would be along specialised lines, with a set of detailed questions to be answered. In particular we would break down the capital employed over the different areas of the business and ascertain the earnings in relation to that capital employed. Also, we would get opinions from the trade, especially if we had any businesses in that type of operation or allied to it. (We have a widespread group so it is fairly easy.)
>
> If it is a public company, one of the first things, obviously, would be to get details of the balance sheets, Exchange Telegraph cards, and then go back to the more detailed underlying balance sheets. Then we would go to the Registrar of Companies to get the individual balance sheet of the underlying constituents of the group and, in effect, to put on a bigger scale the sort of exercise we asked the independent accountant to do with a private company.
>
> In other words, we would break down the capital employed in the different facets of the business and the earnings in relation to them. We would pay particular attention to properties because they are in principle a very readily realisable asset, and we would have them independently valued by our own people (from the outside looking in, with ordnance survey maps and so on). I think, again, we would get what I call trade opinions as far as we were able to. But usually, as we are a very highly financially-orientated company, we would be much more concerned with the financial criteria. For example, property is always a very important asset which we look at first and value ourselves. We have our own way of valuing plant and machinery and usually take it in at 25 per cent of original cost. The current assets we usually write down to 90 per cent of book value. The total of these assets less liabilities then gives us a rough idea of the net worth of the business.
>
> If, for example, you have a business with property worth £1 million that you have validated, plant and machinery of £250,000, net current assets of £750,000, making a total of £2 million, and if it was earning a lot more than £300,000, I would be worried about it. There would be goodwill in the price, almost certainly.
>
> So, having got this, I would then look at how the £300,000 was made up, and it might well be made up of £500,000 of the assets earning £200,000 and £1½ million earnings £100,000. And, therefore, part of the business is earning 40 per cent and part is earning about 7 per cent. It is this analysis that we are interested in. Because, oversimplifying it, you can move in and close down or literally move the loss-making part from that area, and you are left with the good one.

Prior to making an actual bid, Slater Walker would normally build up a significant equity stake in a potential asset situation which would serve to reduce the overall price of the final acquisition, deter other potential bidders, and even if the bid were a failure, allow Slater Walker a capital profit on its holding built up at pre-bid prices.

Post-acquisition reorganisation

As soon as a bid was actually completed, a detailed procedure was immediately set in motion (see Exhibit 5) with the responsibility for action being shared between Mr Slater,

---

[2] E. Foster and G. Bull, op. cit.

Mr Richard Tarling, the managing director of Slater Walker Industrial Group, and Mr Malcolm Horsman. First, the acquired company was usually visited by Mr Slater, Mr Tarling, and by a divisional director, appointed responsible to the main SWS board, for the running of the new subsidiary. The divisional director would immediately be appointed to the board of the acquired concern.

The constitution of the board, directors' remuneration and their pension arrangements were all ratified, accounts as at the date of acquisition drawn up, and arrangements promptly made for producing a budget covering both earnings and liquidity from the date of acquisition to the end of the SWS financial year. It was also decreed that weekly cash positions be reported to the central office. Audit and legal arrangements were examined and amended as necessary, banking facilities examined and precise details of expected cash movements of any significance over the following six months clearly determined. All cash surplus of day-to-day operating requirements were transferred to Slater Walker Industrial Group. A full examination and review of pensions and insurance cover, together with careful scrutiny of property assets was then conducted.

Procedures for future board meetings were introduced and specific reports for presentation at future meetings were requested covering sales, production, research and development and finance, together with a review of immediate problems, capital expenditure, any other important projects and, most important, a review of available management.

The second stage of post-acquisition appraisal comprised an exhaustive analysis of all the new company's activities, its earnings, capital employed, overheads, buying policies and the introduction of group buying procedures. This stage included the completion of an extremely detailed questionnaire by the incumbent management supplemented by SWS staff, which exposed and documented activities in the minutest detail, as indicated in Exhibit 6.

As soon as these reviews were completed, rapid action took place to terminate unprofitable activities, the development of profitable ones, the introduction of new products, the reduction of capital employed, management development and intergroup commercial and technical cooperation. The closure, liquidation or sale of loss-making activities was considered of prime importance for the liberation of resources for the expansion of profitable products, or for the Slater Walker Group as a whole. Once the elimination of losses was complete, reorganisation proceeded on a sound financial basis.

Describing the respective managerial roles in the procedures involved after an acquisition, Mr Slater added, 'Mr Horsman, Mr Tarling and I have a look at the financial statistics of the business and at the business itself, and decide upon a course of action. Mr Horsman helps me on the disposal side. The process might be compared with an operation on a patient—he gives me help with any surgery that is necessary. At a certain point when the operation nears completion, Mr Tarling comes into the picture to help resuscitate the patient and give post-operative treatment. At this stage it is a question of building up the organisation's strength again and developing industrially along positive lines.'

'To take Crittall Hope as an example, Malcolm Horsman helped me with the reorganisation in South Africa and the sales of Hope Windows in America. He also helped with the sale of Silver End Village and other similar matters. Dick Tarling was, however, responsible for running the company and still is today. To some extent, as the one gradually moved out, the latter gradually moved in. It was like handing over the baton in a relay race and there were of course times when they were operating together during the hand-over period.'

While the specific techniques employed by SWS were not unique, it was considered that the speed and comprehensiveness of the approach was a distinctive feature. When integration was complete, operational management was left decentralised, largely autonomous and responsible for profitability. The central office controls consisted primarily of detailed financial returns and sanction over policy.

The financial monitoring system was used to identify carefully any potential trouble spots which, when needed, brought swift correcting action from a small group of central office executives. These central executives were a small, carefully-chosen group trained to identify and correct problems, and they were often supplemented by the use of external consultants.

Mr Slater reviewing his approach remarked

> When we take over a company, I believe in being firm in decision and considerate in execution. By that I mean if you take a firm over and, for example, it has the

wrong sales director, it is absolute idiocy to keep him because you have some vague moral feeling that you have a responsibility more to him than to the shareholders. You make a positive assessment: is the man any good and can he do the job? If he can't, he either has to have another position or he must go.

I don't personally believe in what I would call demotion. It doesn't really work. If there is no lateral or upward transfer for him, it is a question of his going. This is where the consideration comes in, and here our terms of settling with people are second to none because we are exceptionally generous in *ex gratia* and other payments.

It should of course be realised that when we move into an organisation it provides a great opportunity for the more able executives, many of whom will have been blocked in the past. We do tend to back winners and cut losses, and we develop positively the better aspects of any business. Again, in the case of Crittall Hope, we have substantially developed its double glazing and greenhouse business. To coin a phrase, it is a question of 'eliminating the negative and accentuating the positive.

ORGANISATION

The rapid growth of Slater Walker necessitated the introduction of what Mr Slater called 'a proper organisation'. Mr Slater's approach was, therefore, 'to organise, delegate and supervise' and by early 1969 he had built a small central office team of nearly 200 people who were responsible for the main operational activities of the group. See Exhibit 7 for the SWS organisation in 1968.

Apart from Mr Slater, the remaining directors of the group were all in executive positions apart from Mr Peter Walker. Mr Simon Pendock, an accountant, aged thirty-six, was responsible for Slater Walker Investments Ltd, which managed the unit trust, institutional and private clients funds. Mr Pendock was also responsible for overseas investment banking in the Bahamas and Australia.

Mr Richard Tarling, another accountant, aged thirty-six and, like Mr Slater, formerly with AEC, managed the Slater Walker Industrial Group and supervised industrial investments in Australia. The third key task of the group was handled by Mr Malcolm Horsman, thirty-five, who was responsible for 'bids and deals'. Mr Horsman and his staff were responsible for the investigation of potential acquisitions, the arrangement of disposal for the entire organisation, and the initial post-acquisition appraisal and action before transferring new subsidiaries to Mr Tarling's industrial group.

In addition to these three, the other board members were Mr Anthony Buckley, company secretary, legal and administrative director, and Mr John Ford, finance director.

The board members met each Monday morning for a policy meeting which reviewed the policy and implementation of the entire company's activities. These meetings were extremely comprehensive, intense and fast moving, and opposite every item on the long agenda was an 'Action By' column, which clearly recorded who was to do what, and usually by when.

The board members in turn, with the exception of Mr Ford, were chairmen of their own respective divisions where similar board meetings took place at two-week intervals. The same procedures were adopted with the minutes providing a clear record of what was to be done by whom and by when, rather than a record of what was said. In the case of the Industrial Group, there were a further series of subdivisions for the optical companies, Crittall Hope and the like, each with their own board meetings.

In every case the principle applied was of one man at each level being responsible for reporting to the meeting at the next level. The sequence of meetings formed a chain of communication through which information flowed both up and down at great speed. The emphasis everywhere was on precise decisions, rapidly taken and clearly defined responsibility.

Mr Pendock's investment group was separated from the rest of the central office group, being located in the City, but a considerable two-way flow of information was maintained. Beneath Mr Pendock were the fund managers, including three for the Invan trust and one for every twenty to twenty-five private clients. Each fund manager was given maximum responsibility and discretion and, irrespective of the collective view, which was determined thrice weekly at breakfast meetings, it was his decision alone to buy or sell any particular stock. The fund managers were also to some extent in competition with one another and on the large funds they had special bonus incentive fees.

Mr Pendock, however, regularly scrutinised every portfolio and kept special watch on any performing below average.

Mr Horsman, in charge of bids and deals, had two executives engaged in the identification of potential acquisitions. Much of his work, however, was in property disposal and, where formerly there was an emphasis on sale and leaseback, by 1969 this type of arrangement was diminishing. Much of the property disposal was part of the reorganisation task in acquired companies before they were handed over to Mr Tarling's division, and Mr Horsman was responsible for this initial rationalisation. Early in 1969, for example, the industrial investments of Ralli, Drages and Forestal Land were still being handled by Mr Horsman.

The Slater Walker Industrial Group, headed by Mr Tarling, was composed of Crittall Hope, Greengate and Irwell, the optical retailers and engineering together with industrial investments in Australia. After Mr Horsman's group had undertaken the initial reorganisation of a newly acquired subsidiary, Mr Tarling undertook to draw up a sound long-term plan for the revised concern.

This consisted of a detailed analysis of the past and projections for the future. These internal estimates were then usually checked against the assessments of external consultants. The adopted plans were then implemented, usually after the departure of a number of the previous senior management and the promotion of middle managers to senior positions. Mr Tarling was assisted in his task by three assistants, plus five subdivision directors, who also each had three subordinates. In view of the small size of the central team, therefore, it was necessary to time acquisitions carefully in order to avoid overloading the limited central management resources. At least one of these central office executives was attached to each acquired company to supplement existing management. These executives were hand picked and had wide-ranging experience in such companies as McKinsey, Shell, Plessey and Mars; but in Slater Walker they assumed an overall strategic responsibility to the Slater Walker board for the running of the subsidiary in their charge.

Recruitment and Incentive Policies

Mr Slater regarded himself as the leader of a young and successful group of entrepreneurs and considered the success of the company as being essentially due to good teamwork. Commenting on his approach he added

> The people one employs in an executive capacity divide broadly into ideas men and functionaries. The idea men are the most difficult to motivate and retain. Usually they are very able and creative people, who basically want to 'do their own thing'. They are motivated in the first instance by being able to develop their talents within the organisation in a relatively free way. We always give them a lot more responsibility than they would find elsewhere. They are also motivated financially with share option schemes and, in certain instances, shares in specific projects in which they are involved. Certain people do, of course, develop an absolute compulsion to 'do their own thing' in their own way outside our organisation. I have found that the best way of dealing with this is always to have an open door, and be willing to back them in their new ventures as opposed to trying to stop them from branching out. As far as the functionaries are concerned, they are, of course, vitally important to the success of an organisation, but they are usually very much more easy to motivate and retain.

New executives normally came to the company mainly through recommendation from City contacts, or through a management consultant, or from one of the company executives. 'And that is the best recommendation you can have,' commented Mr Slater, 'because they know your standards and will not recommend someone lightly.'[3]

THE POSITION IN APRIL 1969

In April 1969 Mr Slater was able to report to shareholders at the annual general meeting that earnings per share in 1968 had increased by 115 per cent, and that of increased profits of £3.71 million, £1.94 million came from companies already part of Slater Walker in January 1968.

---

[3] Foster and Bull, op. cit.

He also reported the sale of Metropolitan Builders' Merchants to Mercian Builders' Merchants and the £10 million acquisition of Forestal Land completed in March 1969. With nine major acquisitions in 1968, the Slater Walker Group was engaged in a wide variety of product markets, including metal windows, rubber and plastics, engineering, opthalmics, commodities, textiles, together with a range of financial services, including investment banking and trust management in the UK. In addition the company had begun seriously to establish itself overseas, with subsidiary operations in Australia, South Africa and the Bahamas.

FUTURE PROSPECTS

Commenting on the future prospects of the group, Mr Slater told shareholders in April 1969[4]

> Our industrial interests are in effect a portfolio of industrial investments in various stages of development. When we consider that an industrial investment has realised its main potential under our management, we consider making further acquisitions in that field or selling our own interests to another industry. In this way significant benefits can be obtained by taking advantage of the further opportunities for rationalisation and reorganisation.
> The acquisition of control of Ralli Holdings is a major step in the development of your company... and we intend during 1969 to establish our headquarters in the City of London by moving to Ralli House. All our operations will then be in the City... and from these bases we intend to further the expansion of our investment banking activities... we are continuing to concentrate on expanding the international operations... and we believe that the unit trust movement will continue to grow rapidly... and now intend to participate to the full in this major growth area.
> For 1969 your board has already forecast low range profits before taxation and after gross minority interests of £7.9 million and high range profits of £8.9 million. We are looking forward to another excellent and record year and see considerable growth prospects for the future. Last year the group achieved very substantial organic and internal growth and we see no reason why this should not continue for many years to come.

---

[4] Annual Report, 1968.

EXHIBIT 1 Slater Walker Securities and Subsidiaries.

Consolidated profit and loss accounts 1964-8 (£)

	1964	1965	1966	1967	1968
Turnover	n. a.	n. a.	n. a.	16,755,174	38,101,518
Expenses:					
Depreciation	1,817	11,350	54,253	326,579	579,736
Loan stock interest	—	—	19,339	182,789	674,887
Short-term loan interest	12,995	12,653	—	201,297	764,869
Other interest	15,992	5,764	30,271	30,271	81,710
Directors emoluments	7,205	12,458	23,764	30,135	52,361
Dividends and interest rec'd	6,525	93,678	99,856	225,132	641,783
Net rents rec'd	119,843	23,432	—	—	—
Net profit before tax	136,939	190,919	370,221	1,158,848	4,868,213
Taxation:					
Income tax and profits tax	71,656	73,276	72,292	—	—
Corporation tax	—	23,800	110,523	316,904	1,398,862
Overseas tax	—	—	—	94,980	468,725
Double tax relief	—	—	—	—	(124,955)
Over provision	—	—	(7,337)	(311)	—
Net total tax	71,656	97,076	175,478	411,573	1,742,632
Minority interests	—	—	23,296	99,503	188,435
Net profit attributable to parent Co.	65,283	93,843	168,408	647,461	2,937,146
Preference dividend	8,422	8,078	13,750	20,823	69,898
Ordinary dividend	45,938	52,875	114,255	392,411	976,810
EPS (adjusted to 1972)	.81p	1.28p	1.61p	2.89p	7.98p
Net equity assets per share (adjusted to 1972)	11.87p	16.87p	18.43p	25.31p	67.50p

Source: Annual Reports

EXHIBIT 2   Slater Walker Securities and Subsidiaries.
Consolidated balance sheets 1964-8 (£)

	1964	1965	1966	1967	1968
Current assets					
Stocks and work in progress	—	—	605,858	3,660,150	9,082,926
Debtors, loans and advances	1,031,552	1,171,980	2,900,579	5,483,907	50,418,760
Investments (at lower of cost and market)	215,219	82,489	369,631	1,514,922	19,230,146
Bank balances and cash	3,094	188,576	1,542,856	1,605,847	3,999,056
	1,249,865	1,443,045	5,418,924	12,264,826	82,730,888
Current liabilities					
Creditors	295,033	632,888	3,625,687	5,602,818	34,692,075
Bank overdrafts	55,486	21,206	555,012	2,169,460	4,828,379
Current taxation	106,399	75,693	186,025	600,320	2,259,724
2nd interim dividend	25,266	30,844	40,687	244,857	691,602
	482,184	760,631	4,407,411	8,617,455	42,471,780
Net current assets	767,681	682,414	1,011,513	3,647,371	40,259,108
Fixed assets					
Freehold property	38,253	38,253	975,106	3,508,783	10,956,002
Leasehold property over 50 years	1,410,611	63,611	89,563	441,586	904,723
under 50 years	11,300	7,020	3,384	156,347	529,119
Plant and equipment	4,740	30,355	234,882	2,103,828	4,416,084
	1,464,904	139,239	1,302,935	6,210,544	16,805,928
Investments at cost					
Quoted in UK	—	—	1,486,510	746,851	536,573
Quoted in Australia	—	—	151,667	—	2,672,333
Loans to unquoted companies	—	—	104,000	122,685	—
Unquoted in UK	5,100	1,044,317	109,196	213,945	6,969,216
	5,100	1,044,317	1,851,373	1,083,481	10,178,122
Capital					
5¾ cum. pref £1	250,000	250,000	250,000	450,000	1,762,500
Ord. shares of 5/- each	750,000	750,000	1,538,997	2,720,638	7,684,462
Reserves	334,267	755,862	948,829	3,351,864	26,631,215
Undistributed profit	53,418	86,308	185,202	457,492	2,533,226
	1,387,685	1,842,170	2,923,028	6,979,994	38,611,403
Unsecured loan stock					
7% ULS 1973[1]	—	—	—	—	9,545,750
8½% ULS 1988/93[2]	—	—	940,245	2,240,280	2,240,280
8½% ULS 1991/96	—	—	—	—	12,848,455
			940,245	2,240,280	24,634,485
Other long-term debt	850,000	—	—	—	748,525
Minority interests	—	—	171,838	1,297,092	1,715,655
Corporation tax	—	23,800	130,710	424,030	1,533,090
	2,237,685	1,865,970	4,165,821	10,941,396	67,243,158

Notes: 1.   7% ULS 1973 carries subscription rights entitling holders to subscribe to 15 ordinary shares for every £100 nominal of stock exercisable on the 31 October 1970, 1971, 1972 and on the 31 May 1973 at a price of 52/6 per share.
       2.   8½% ULS 1988/93 carries subscription rights for 5⅓ ordinary shares each for every £5 nominal of stock at the price of 12/- per share, exercisable on June 30, 1968, 1969, 1970.

Source: Annual Reports

EXHIBIT 3 Slater Walker Securities. Share price movement 1963-9

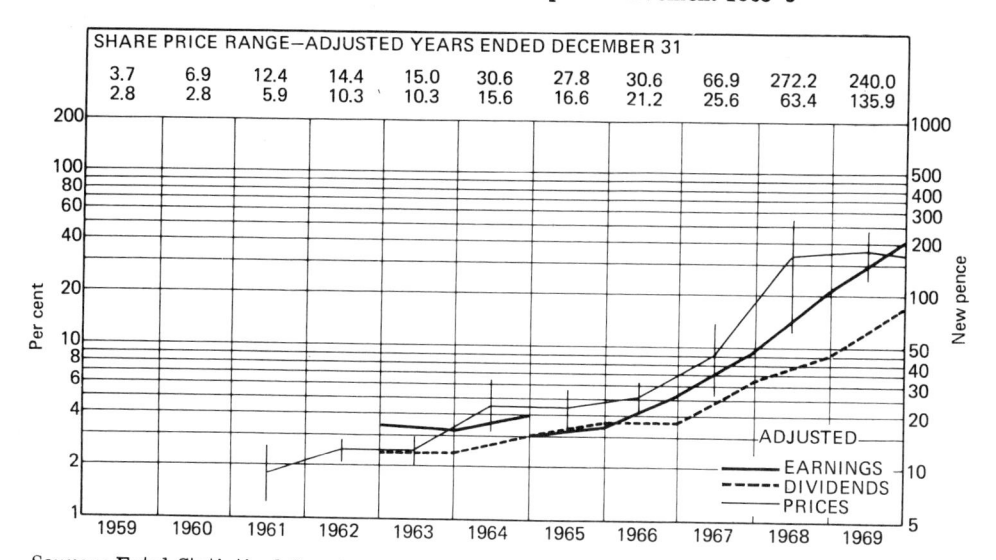

SHARE PRICE RANGE—ADJUSTED YEARS ENDED DECEMBER 31										
3.7	6.9	12.4	14.4	15.0	30.6	27.8	30.6	66.9	272.2	240.0
2.8	2.8	5.9	10.3	10.3	15.6	16.6	21.2	25.6	63.4	135.9

ADJUSTED
——— EARNINGS
----- DIVIDENDS
——— PRICES

Source: Extel Statistical Services Ltd

EXHIBIT 4   Slater Walker Securities Ltd.   Principal acquisitions 1964–April 1969

Date	Company	Main activity	% of equity held at time of bid	Bid value (millions)	Terms
1966					
September	Thomas Brown	Wholesaling, retailing food manufacturing and merchanting (Australia)	30	£1.35	915, 986 5/- ord. £335, 245 $8\frac{1}{4}$% unsec. loan stock, 1988/93
November	Slater Walker Industrial Group	Investment Holdings mainly in George Wilson Gasmeters and Productofoam	51	£1.3	1, 240, 000 5/- ord. £465, 000 $8\frac{1}{4}$% unsec. loan stock plus £217, 000 cash
December	Arthur Hill & Co. (London)	Builders' merchants	—	£0.13	£140, 000 $8\frac{1}{4}$% unsec. loan stock 1988/93 loan note of £50, 000 ($8\frac{1}{2}$%) + £35, 740 cash
1967					
March	Greengate & Irwell Rubber	Rubberised fabrics, conveyor belting, general rubber goods	16	£3.0	1, 858, 100 5/- ord. £1, 215, 507 $8\frac{1}{4}$% unsec. loan stock 1988/93
August	Productofoam Industries	Rubber and foam rubber products	44	£1.64	944, 785 5/- ord.
	George Wilson Industries	Gas meters	53	£0.45	224, 536 5/- ord. 50, 000 £1 $5\frac{3}{4}$% pref.
October	Constructors Ltd	Car seat slides, metal shelving	16	£0.72	417, 025 5/- ord. 150, 000 £1 $5\frac{3}{4}$ pref. £66, 029 cash
November	Newman Holdings	Footwear	29	£0.36	142, 120 5/- ord. £84, 528 $8\frac{1}{2}$% unsec. loan stock 1988/93
December	Nathaniel Lloyd	Fine printing and packaging	—	£0.76	444, 000 5/- ord.
	Kirby Bros	Builders' merchants	—	£1.2	696, 000 5/- ord.
1968					
April	Keith Blackman	Heating and ventilating engineers	2.5	£4.33	1, 638, 000 and £1, 160, 000 $8\frac{1}{2}$% unsec. loan stock 1991/96

June	British Building Supplies & Brooks Phillips	Builders' merchants	—	£0.47	203,815 5/- ord.
	Crittall Hope	Metal window frames	9	£18.32	2,386,438 5/- ord. 1,312,500 pref. £9,545,750 7% unsec. loan stock 1973 £525,000 8½% unsec. loan stock 1991/96
August	Carden Withers	Investment bankers	—	£1.5	411,950 5/- ord. issued for 74.9% stake
September	TWW	Opticians, investment interests, poster advertising	—	£7.07	1,859,399 5/- ord.
	Hanson Holdings	Small conglomerate	—	£4.76	1,186,652 5/- ord.
November	Drages	Investment banking, commodities trading, investment interests	36	£32.13	5,628,134 5/- ord. £7,600,000 8½% unsec. loan stock 1991/96 issued to acquire loan stock of Drages
December	Harrisons Opticians	Opticians	—	£3.45	1,008,000 5/- ord.
	Augustine Investments	Opticians	—	£5.31	762,923 5/- ord. and £2,746,520 8½% unsec. loan stock 1991/96
1969					
February	Forrestal Land, Timber & Railways	Tanning extracts, wattle, metal slating, paint driers, health foods	8.5	£12.00	1,221,856 5/- ord. £6.68 million cash
	Ralli Holdings Ltd	Bankers, commodity trading	50 (acqd. as part of Drages)	£4.5	£4,500,000 cash for 2 million ord. (25%)

Source: Extel/company records

245

EXHIBIT 5 Slater Walker Industrial Group.
Company acquisition procedures

Summary of points for investigation and action

Stage one
(a) Visit by group managing director
(b) Constitution of board, remuneration and pension arrangements and SWIG liaison
(c) Preparation of accounts as at date of acquisition
(d) Establishment of accounts and budgets for the future
(e) Audit and legal arrangements
(f) Banking arrangements and surplus cash
(g) Insurance arrangements
(h) Properties
(i) Meetings and reports, capital expenditure proposals
(j) Overheads
(k) Buying
(l) Vehicle fleet and purchasing arrangements
(m) Analysis of activities, earnings and capital employed

Stage two
(a) Termination of unprofitable activities
(b) Development of profitable activities
(c) New product development
(d) Reduction of capital employed
(e) Management reorganisation
(f) Intergroup commercial and technical cooperation

Source: Company records

EXHIBIT 6 Slater Walker Industrial Group.
Company acquisition procedures

Information required

1. Nature of business and brief history
2. Copies of profit and loss accounts and balance sheets, for the last financial year, and to date for current financial year
3. Detailed financial analysis covering:

Properties

(a) Freehold properties
   — book value
   — current value
(b) Leasehold properties
   — book value
   — current value
   — rental
   — subletting, change of use rights
   — term of lease
(c) Area of land
(d) Area of buildings, and allocation
   — offices
   — stores
   — works
(e) Utilisation
   — surplus land
   — surplus floor areas
   — shortage of space

Plant and machinery

(a) Book value, original cost and aggregate depreciation; tax written down values
(b) Average age and replacement policy
(c) Special/general purpose classification
(d) Plant register, and reconciliation with accounts
(e) Basis for valuing plant manufactured internally
(f) Surplus capacity
(g) Capacity required

Fixtures and fittings

(a) Book value, original cost, and aggregate depreciation
(b) Age and replacement policy
(c) Nature, i.e. associated with property, or plant and machinery

Patents, trade marks, research and development, goodwill, moulds and tooling

(a) Basis of valuation and extent to which justified
(b) Original cost, depreciation and current book value
(c) Tooling cost recovery arrangements

Stocks

(a) Basis of valuation
(b) Stock turnover ratios
(c) Obsolete redundant and damaged stocks

Cash

(a) Balance at bank
(b) Overdraft facilities and extent to which secured
(c) Bankers and charges
(d) Exceptional receipts/payments due
(e) Capital commitments

Investments

(a) Quoted investments — current value
(b) Trade investments — nature
 — basis of valuation

Creditors

(a) Cash discounts
(b) Normal supplier credit (aged credit schedule)
(c) Credit taken
(d) Disputes with suppliers
(e) Exceptional creditors
(f) Contingent liabilities

Debtors

(a) Cash discounts
(b) Normal customer credit
(c) Credit taken (aged debtor schedule)
(d) Disputes with customers
(e) Exceptional debts
(f) Contingent assets

Mortgages and loans

(a) Amount
(b) Interest rate
(c) Maturity date or redemption arrangements
(d) Security
(e) Restrictions applicable

Taxation

(a) Tax losses
(b) Investment grants
(c) Selective Employment Tax position
(d) Surtax clearances

Sales

(a) Analysis by product/service, with comparative figures for prior years
(b) Analysis of sales by area
   — home
   — export
(c) Sales organisation, methods, costs
(d) Selling price policy, basis and timing of reviews
(e) Trade and cash discounts

Materials

(a) Percentage to sales turnover by products
(b) Usage and prices
(c) Buying policy
(d) Alternative materials
(e) Alternative supplies
(f) Wastage

Labour

(a) Percentage of sales turnover
(b) Total labour force analysed
   — productive
   — non-productive
   — staff
   — management
(c) Rates of pay
(d) Union position
(e) Productivity agreements
(f) Restrictive practices
(g) Availability

Overheads

(a) Factory overheads
   — percentage of sales turnover
   — labour analysis
   — expense analysis
   — fixed/variable analysis
(b) General overhead (categories as above)
(c) Sales and distribution overheads (categories as above)
(d) Management overheads
   — percentage of sales turnover
   — labour analysis
   — expense analysis
(e) Miscellaneous overheads, i.e. charitable donations

General

(a) Patents and trademarks
(b) Products/services under development
(c) Competitors
   — prices
   — market share
   — product/service comparison
(d) Significant trends

Source: Company records

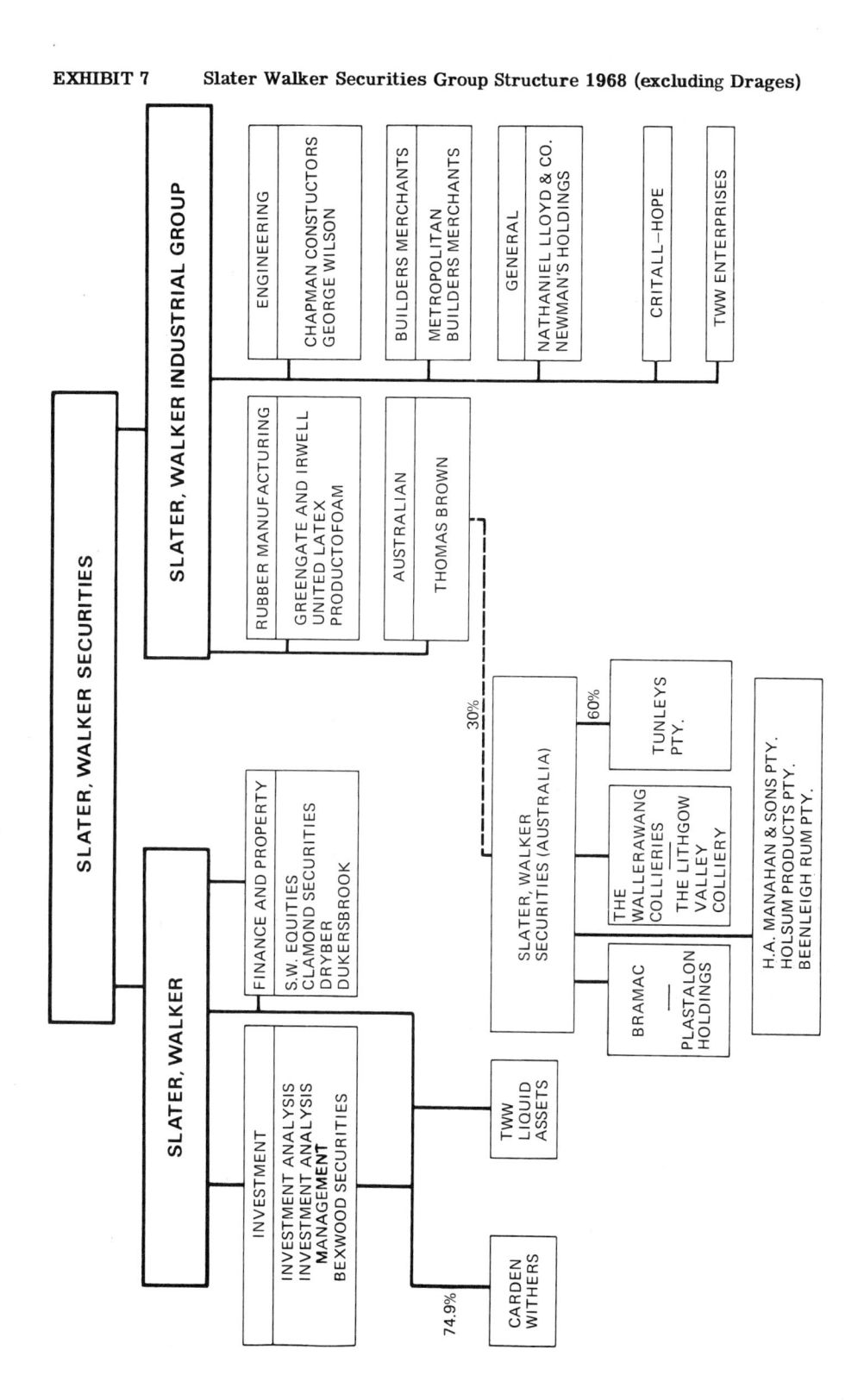

EXHIBIT 7 Slater Walker Securities Group Structure 1968 (excluding Drages)

20 Slater Walker Securities Limited (B)*

Early in 1973 Slater Walker Securities was moving rapidly towards the completion of its third major strategic transformation in nine years. During this period, under the leadership of Mr Jim Slater, the company had evolved first as an industrial conglomerate, then as a major British merchant banking and investment company. Latterly, the company had been extending its range of financial services to include commercial banking and insurance, was building substantial interests in property and extending its geographical coverage to include most of Western Europe, North America and Asia, together with interests formed earlier, in Australia and South Africa. In addition, the company had spun off or helped to initiate a large number of other similarly financially-oriented organisations, engaged in a wide variety of financial service and manufacturing industries. Despite the changes in Slater Walker's business interests, the company had maintained a consistently high growth rate, with earnings of 0.81p and net assets of 11.87p per share in 1964, rising to 17.10p and 160.36p per share respectively, by the end of 1972.[1] For details of recent financial performance, see Exhibits 1 and 2. By the beginning of 1973 Slater Walker was emerging as one of the world's leading multinational financial concerns; the company's shares were quoted in three major cities (London, Hong Kong and Toronto), with further quotations expected in the future as international coverage continued to expand.

This case deals with the evolution of Slater Walker Securities between 1969 and April 1973, during which time the company divested itself of many of its industrial holdings, accumulated over its first five years (see Slater Walker 'A' case, for details of this earlier period), and expanded its financial and geographical interests.

COMPANY HISTORY TO 1969

Slater Walker Securities owed much of its success to the strategies evolved by its chairman, Mr James (Jim) Slater. After a successful industrial career, Mr Slater formed his own investment consultant company, before joining with Mr Peter Walker in acquiring the almost defunct H. Lotery & Co., in 1964.

Having changed the name of the company to Slater Walker Securities (SWS) in 1965 and releasing the cash potential of the Lotery property assets, Mr Slater embarked on a series of industrial acquisitions between 1964 and 1968. These acquisitions were the result of an increasingly systematic search for 'asset situations', in which the market capitalisation of the acquired concerns tended to reflect relatively poor earnings performance and so neglect the strength of the underlying capital assets. As a result, having usually built up a significant strategic shareholding, Mr Slater was frequently able to purchase companies at a price near or below their asset value. Once acquired, these concerns were systematically evaluated; underutilised or unprofitable activities were terminated to release liquid resources; and the profitable activities were built up. This policy of careful divestment and exploitation of growth potential usually enabled the company to develop an improved stream of earnings from a significantly decreased capital base. Between 1964 and the beginning of 1969 SWS grew rapidly by the adoption of this policy, undertaking over twenty acquisitions. By the end of 1968 turnover had reached £38 million and SWS was engaged in a wide range of industries, including rubber and plastics products, retail and dispensing opticians, metal windows, textiles, engineering products, food and food distribution, coal mining and commodities trading in the United Kingdom, Australia and South Africa.

Apart from the expansion of industrial interests SWS had also begun to develop its financial service operations and to expand overseas. From Mr Slater's original investment consultancy interests, the company began to manage funds for the general public in 1967, when its Invan Trust was offered to other than private clients. A further offshore fund based in the Bahamas was started in 1968.

Then towards the end of 1968 SWS made what was later recognised as one of its most important moves, when it acquired a controlling interest in Drages from the Wolf-

---

[1] All EPS figures adjusted.

* Copyright © Manchester Business School 1974

son Foundation. In so doing, the company, after bidding for the remainder of Drages' capital, obtained a 50 per cent holding, later converted to 100 per cent, in Ralli Holdings Ltd, one of whose main subsidiaries was a full eighth schedule bank with the necessary authorisations to conduct all forms of banking business. Apart from Ralli, Drages also owned a number of other interests in textiles, engineering and commodity trading, as well as a considerable amount of cash and a portfolio of securities.

STRATEGIC DEVELOPMENTS 1969-72

Following the acquisition of Ralli between 1969 and 1972, a number of new policies were introduced, which were to change the basic character of SWS. These policies were:

1. Divestment of industrial interests in Britain
2. The creation of 'Associate' companies
3. The development of banking activities
4. Growth in investment management
5. Entry into insurance
6. Investment in property
7. Expansion overseas

As a result of these strategic developments SWS underwent a complete transformation in less than four years. Further, by the end of 1972 the company was already in the process of changing itself yet again into a broadly-based multinational financial services, property and banking corporation. One result of this change in strategy was an expansion of the company's central offices and the adoption of a new organisation structure, details of which are shown in Exhibit 3.

Industrial divestment in Britain

By the end of 1968 SWS had developed industrial sales of over £38 million, primarily as the result of acquisitions of British manufacturing companies in a wide variety of industries, including light engineering, metal window frames, textiles, rubber and plastic products, opticians and building supplies.

From the beginning of 1969 the number of industrial acquisitions in the UK began to decline, and gradually a reverse trend of divestments began to develop. The first of these occurred early in 1969 when Metropolitan Builders' Merchants was sold to Mercian Builders' Merchants, in return for cash and a shareholding in the combined concern.

Acquisitions did continue, however, and in February 1969 a bid was made for the Forestal Land, Timber and Railways Co. Ltd. Primarily engaged in the supply of tanning materials based on quebracho extract obtained from South America and wattle obtained from Eastern and Southern Africa, Forestal had built up extensive plantations, factories and land, principally in Argentina, Rhodesia, Central Africa and South Africa. However, after the Second World War the advent of synthetic leather had led to a decline in the demand for natural heavy leather and therefore for the tanning materials supplied by the company.

Despite attempts to diversify into new businesses, principally in the UK, the Forestal board considered that a takeover was inevitable. No approaches came however and consideration was given to liquidating the company. Then, late in 1968, SWS became interested in Forestal and by the end of January 1969 when a formal offer was made to shareholders a share stake of nearly ten per cent had been accumulated.

By the end of February the acquisition was completed at a cost of £12 million in cash and shares, against a balance sheet value of approximately £15 million and an estimated asset value of some £14 million.

SWS moved rapidly to rationalise its new subsidiary. The East and Central African wattle and tanning interests were sold to Lonrho for £2.5 million; the Argentinian land and properties were disposed of piecemeal to net £2.5 million, and the quebracho interests were combined with those of the French Rhone-Poulenc Company, to form Unitan, in which SWS initially held a 50 per cent interest valued at approximately £2.5 million. The British industrial interests in speciality chemicals, metal coatings and health foods were considered too small to keep and were sold to separate buyers for £3.4 million while Forestal's head office, properties and investments were sold for a further £1.2 million. The important South African-based Natal Tanning Company was sold to Slater Walker (South Africa), (SW(SA)), at terms agreed by independent advisers of 1.5 million shares in SW(SA), valued then at £7.13 million. In his 1969 report to shareholders, Mr Slater was thus able to announce 'we have disposed of many of [Forestal's] interests on very satisfactory terms'.

The other SWS industrial interests were not disposed of as rapidly. The acquisition of Ralli had provided SWS with a 75 per cent holding in Philips Brocklehurst, a company primarily engaged in textiles in the UK and in South Africa, via a subsidiary Berg River Textiles. With the intention of expanding these textile interests, SWS arranged for Philips Brocklehurst to acquire the Anglo-Portugese Telephone Company, a concern which had liquid resources of some £15 million. Suitable expansion opportunities were not forthcoming, however, and in October 1969 SWS itself offered to acquire the minority interest in Brocklehurst that it did not own in order to redeploy the liquid resources. The UK activities of Philips Brocklehurst were then rationalised. This released further resources of over £1 million, removed the loss-making section of the distribution and merchanting division and created some 600 redundancies. Three smaller subsidiaries were sold to G.R. Bodycote and the South African interests were sold to SW(SA) in each case in exchange for shares.

Other moves in 1969 included the acquisition of a rubber products company, P.B. Cow & Co. for £8.5 million. This company was integrated with SWS's existing rubber products subsidiary, Greengate & Irwell. Three optical subsidiaries acquired in 1968 were successfully integrated, their manufacturing operations centralised and a number of overseas interests disposed of. Further rationalisation occurred at Crittall Hope, manufacturers of metal window frames, resulting in the sale of a number of overseas subsidiaries and excess properties in the UK to release approximately £6 million. In May 1969 Slater Walker Ltd acquired from directors 43 per cent of the issued capital of Kent Castings (Gillingham) Ltd, manufacturers of patterns, mouldings and non-ferrous castings. The group holding was then reduced to 3 per cent and in August SWIG sold George Wilson Industries Ltd (its gas meter subsidiaries) to Kent Castings for the issue by it of approximately 2.3 million shares to SWIG, this resulted in the Slater Walker Securities Group owning approximately 64 per cent of the capital of Kent Castings. This shareholding was later increased to 77 per cent as the result of a further deal in which Kent acquired Picador Engineering Company Ltd, another subsidiary of Ralli. In December 1969 Chapman Constructors (Birmingham) Ltd, an SWS subsidiary engaged in automobile seat tracks and industrial shelving was sold. By the end of 1969 industrial activities in the United Kingdom had almost reached their peak, although the turnover from manufacturing interests continued to rise until 1971, as shown in Exhibit 4.

In 1970 SWS undertook the first of a series of steps, which in the space of two years effectively severed all direct links with British manufacturing industry. In July the small Frankenstein Group, manufacturers of survival equipment, was acquired. This company was integrated into SWS's other rubber and plastics interests as a prelude to a share floatation of the combined group under the name Allied Polymer in 1971.

In November 1970 the optical subsidiaries were sold to Gallahers for £10.2 million in cash, a premium of £6.4 million over the net asset value. At the year end, part of the textile interests, Horrocks019 Ltd & Dorcas Ltd, were sold to Spirella for £1.2 m.

During 1971 industrial disengagement contined. SWS sold most of its rubber and plastics interests when, in June, Allied Polymer was floated. All the engineering interests were combined via a complex series of moves, whereby Kent Castings, a quoted subsidiary, acquired Oxley Engineering in July 1970. Oxley in turn owned a subsidiary, Butterley Engineering and, following Kent's acquisition in July 1971 of Priam Investments, a holding company whose assets mainly comprised loans to other SWS Group companies, the combined engineering interests were renamed as Butterley Engineering. The final move came at the end of 1971 when Crittall-Hope was acquired by Butterley, which resulted in a further name change to Crittall-Hope Engineering, in which SWS initially held a 63 per cent holding. This was gradually reduced during 1972 and by April, Crittall-Hope Engineering, had been deconsolidated. The remaining textile interests of the Brocklehurst Group were treated similarly, being absorbed into Bodycote Holdings at the end of 1971. The reorganised grouping was requoted early in 1972, allowing SWS rapidly to reduce its holding. By mid-1972, in the short space of three years, Slater Walker Securities had deconsolidated all its British industrial assets.

Commenting on this change of policy, Mr Slater stated, 'It was a very positive decision to deindustrialise by selling a few companies. I think that very diverse conglomerates are fundamentally unsound. They are difficult to run, it is difficult to motivate all the people if they are not small enough units and it is difficult to keep a proper track of all the different businesses. You tend to get an equivocal high P/E ratio that tends to make you try and run instead of walk. Also there was the conglomerate scare coming from America that rather made them unpopular and with all these we decided to get out of the conglomerate business.'

The Creation of Associates

The policy of deindustrialisation led to the development of a number of 'associate' companies. Thus SWS retained a minority shareholding after redistributing the majority of the shares in Allied Polymer, Bodycote Holdings and Crittall-Hope Engineering. In addition, apart from the associates which developed as a result of deindustrialising, the company developed similar minority holdings in a wide range of other concerns. A list of the associates at the end of 1972 is shown in Exhibit 5.

The associates were usually led by financially-oriented executives, who had either been previously employed by SWS or who had demonstrated by their management experience a similar aggressive profit-seeking orientation. As a result the financial press had nicknamed the companies 'satellites' of SWS. The largest of the associates was Ralli International led by Mr Malcolm Horsman, a former director of SWS. This company was created as the result of a reverse takeover in 1969 by Oriental Carpet Manufacturers for Ralli Brothers (Trading), the commodity trading interests SWS acquired by its purchase of Drages. Following the merger with Oriental Carpets, 1.8 million shares in the renamed Ralli International were offered for sale at a price which allowed SWS to recover £1.4 million and still retain a controlling shareholding.

The new company under Mr Horsman began actively acquiring other commodity companies, commencing with Millars Timber & Trading Co. Ltd, whose main associates were in Australia, in which SWS had previously built up a 34 per cent interest. Rapid rationalisation of Millar then allowed Ralli to engage in further deals, often in conjunction with or assisted by SWS. As a result of share issues used to make further acquisitions, the SWS holding was gradually reduced to a minority investment.

Although not expanding as rapidly as Ralli International, the other associates also tended to develop in a similar manner, by acquisition followed by the rapid rationalisation and disposal of unprofitable or underutilised assets of the acquired companies.

Mr Slater considered that this development of associates represented possibly his biggest single contribution to the overall thinking of SWS and he actively encouraged the development of entrepreneurs. Further, instead of merely letting potential entrepreneurs leave SWS he believed in capitalising on them and was prepared to back them in their new concerns with a capital stake. 'As a result,' he added, 'any man that has left us—we've made a fortune out of him'.

THE DEVELOPMENT OF BANKING ACTIVITIES

In 1969 SWS completed the acquisition of Ralli Brothers (Bankers). Mr Slater then adopted the policy of developing SWS as a broadly-based financial service company. In line with the new emphasis Mr Slater moved the group head office to the former Ralli headquarters in St Paul's Churchyard in the City of London. The name of Ralli Brothers (Bankers) was changed to Slater Walker Ltd, and during the next few years this subsidiary was developed to cover a complete range of merchant and investment banking, and commercial banking services.

Merchant banking

The merchant banking activities of Slater Walker Ltd were the responsibility of Mr Ian Wasserman and Mr Michael Booth, who were appointed main board directors in July 1971 and February 1972 respectively. Mr Booth was responsible for running the bank in an administrative sense and for organising acquisitions, mergers and the like. Mr Wasserman was more responsible for development activities, especially with those companies who were emerging as either present or potential merchant banking clients. Apart from the two main board directors, the merchant banking team consisted of about fifteen other executives. Commenting on this, Mr Booth stressed, 'It is very necessary in merchant banking to maintain a very personal role for all clients, hence the tendency to remain relatively small and for each client to be carefully sponsored by an individual member of the banking team.'

The merchant banking team of Slater Walker Ltd was subdivided into three groups of four to five executives. Each of these groups was responsible for a number of specific banking clients and the company acted as merchant bankers for nearly sixty quoted companies, with a market capitalisation of almost £1,000 million at the end of 1972 in both the UK and overseas.

Slater Walker Ltd's clients tended to be smaller than the average industrial concern and to have an above-average growth rate, much of which was the result of acquisitions. Further, in nearly every case they were associate companies in which the Slater Walker Group had been involved at the formative stage of the business and/or held a significant share stake. Finally, the companies were usually financially oriented, above average in financial control and efficiency, and led by young ambitious entrepreneurs with a substantial share stake in their company. As a result the clients had an above-average requirement for merchant banking services, and Slater Walker Ltd was able to assist them in activating acquisitions and mergers through the Group's holdings in undervalued asset situations, which were often suitable merger candidates.

In addition, one executive was responsible for acting as a general advisor to the three groups of banking executives on acquisition schemes for client companies, schemes for blending together into viable units for floatation or merger concerns made up from private companies, or interests and subsidiaries acquired by SWS. Two further executives formed a situation search team looking for new potential situations either for purchase by client companies or for developing further into potentially viable floatation prospects. Such situations were primarily sought from amongst private companies to prevent undue overlap with the activities of Slater Walker Investments.

Mr Booth pointed out that SWS were very conscious of the potential conflict of interest and claims of insider trading between the group's banking and investment interests. He observed that strict security was maintained to ensure banking executives did not know the contents of the Group's investment portfolios, nor when the investment group was buying or selling specific securities. Nevertheless, the high percentage of merger business conducted, together with the bank's ability to initiate and implement such deals via the Group's strategic shareholdings, enabled the bank to charge above-average fees and reduced dependence on the normal, more passive, new issue role of merchant banking.

Mr Booth stated that Slater Walker Ltd was actually very selective in choosing private companies for injection into either existing corporations owned by the group or for direct floatation. 'We are not a venture capital company nor do we wish to be,' he added. 'We look very carefully for a successful, if short, track record on the part of the main participants in any such potential company.'

To keep abreast of events Mr Booth and Mr Wasserman met each morning with the three section leaders and the executive responsible for developing situations. Each Monday morning the group leaders in turn held a weekly processing meeting with their groups. All meetings used the action minute system, common throughout SWS. The merchant bank had proved the main area for developing new entrepreneurs for associates or new group activities, and this remained as a conscious policy.

Commenting on the company's approach to banking in late 1972, Mr Slater said

> I think 90 per cent of our clients are associates, which I regard as a good thing—it means they aren't going to run away. Some critics think the quality of earnings is not so good, saying it is captive business, but take for instance GEC, which is not captive business and has just moved from Hill Samuel to Lazards— now that's low quality in my view. I don't want clients that run away.
>
> We deal in equity like the Banques d'Affaires in Europe. We have a shareholding in most of our clients, who are associates. This isn't really enough to influence them and they are clients because the men are reared in the business and they know if they want to make money, there is no one better can make it for them. We have the network—we have got a stake in nearly every asset situation in Britain and if you were in that sort of business who would you want to be your banker? We have got the image, the money and we have got the shareholdings in the sort of companies they want. So if they go somewhere else how can they improve?

Commercial banking

Apart from merchant banking, SWS had increased its commercial banking interests, which included taking sterling and foreign currency deposits, issuing sterling certificates of deposit, dealing in foreign currencies, providing cash advances and acceptances and documentary credits for financing international and domestic trade and advising and arranging export finance.

The commercial banking activities formed part of the responsibilities of Mr Roland Rowe, the deputy managing director of Slater Walker Securities. Early in 1972 Mr Robert Valentine was appointed as joint managing director to the board of Slater Walker Ltd, with the specific responsibility for developing commercial banking, which was seen as an area capable of substantial expansion. In 1969 deposits received had been around £24 million, had reached £92 million by 1971, and by the end of 1972 were £187 million.

The rapid growth of deposits could be attributed in large part to the company's approach to commercial banking. While the method in which banking was practised was conventional, Slater Walker Ltd had adopted an aggressive approach in seeking out deposits. At first these had largely stemmed from the group's corporate, finance clients but the rapid growth in the 1970s came mainly from arms-length customers. These depositors had been carefully selected by research, such as the analysis of Extel cards and annual reports. Cash-rich companies so identified were then solicited either personally or by mail to see if they would care to place their excess cash on deposit with Slater Walker Ltd, where they could earn higher interest rates than those offered by the main clearing banks. Early in 1973 such commercial deposits represented som 60 per cent of Slater Walker Ltd's deposits, the remainder coming from the money market.

Deposits were normally loaned for short- and medium-term finance. However, although loans had expanded by over 50 per cent in 1972, they still fell short of deposits, reaching approximately £90 million at the end of 1972. Loan clients were also mainly arm's-length companies rather than the associates who had formed much of the bank's early accounts. Such arm's-length clients for loans were also identified largely by research and then specifically approached. Deposits not placed on loan were placed on the interbank market.

As a further means of expanding Slater Walker Ltd began to open regional commercial banking offices in 1972. The first of these, in Birmingham, was rapidly followed by others in Bristol, Glasgow and Manchester, while another in Southampton was to open in 1973. Mr Slater, commenting on the development, said 'We intend to extend the opportunities for generating new business and to offer, in each locality, corporate finance, instalment credit, insurance and investment management services. There will be strong local management for each activity housed at these offices, thereby enabling decisions to be taken speedily and on the spot. The response to the regional offices which have already opened has been encouraging and we anticipate they will provide a valuable source of future business.' By early in 1973 the branch offices had attracted an additional £10 million or so in deposits and were helping to spread the name of Slater Walker Ltd, resulting in new financing deals and clients for merchant banking.

The organisation of commercial banking was principally the responsibility of Mr Valentine, who was in charge of deposits and overseas banking relationships, Mr Paul Sanders, responsible for loans and advances together with the provincial offices and Mr George Le Friant who supervised activity on the interbank market. These three were all directors of Slater Walker Ltd. Control was maintained by means of regular meetings, the most important of which were weekly meetings to discuss new money propositions and a fortnightly management committee meeting.

Apart from the activities of Slater Walker Ltd, in 1971 Slater Walker Finance Corporation had been formed to offer instalment credit services. However, by early 1973 this subsidiary was also engaged in current and deposit accounts, as well as leasing, conditional sale, block discounting, personal loans and a complete mortgage service for private and industrial clients. The company was granted banking status in 1972. In its first full year of operation small profits were generated, although expenses were high as the company rapidly expanded its coverage of the market by the opening of local offices. Having started 1972 with only two branches, thirteen had been opened by early 1973 and it was intended that national coverage would be completed by the end of the year. Advances had risen rapidly to nearly £12 million by the end of 1972. Although related to banking, this financial service formed part of the responsibility of Mr John Ford, Slater Walker Securities' director of finance.

Growth in investment management

The portfolio and investment management business of the group was conducted by Slater Walker Investments Ltd (SWI). This subsidiary had expanded rapidly since 1971, and by the end of 1972 funds managed had risen from approximately £46 million to nearly £250 million. Under its chief executive, Mr Jim Nichols, SWI was deliberately located in a separate building, a short distance from the main SWS offices. This physical separation was necessary to minimise any possible allegation of insider trading or unfair usage of confidential information.

SWI was composed of a total of sixty-one people, including all administrative and accounting personnel. Under Mr Nichols were the investment director, Mr Brian Banks, with two investment assistants, a team of about a dozen investment analysts and a small marketing unit. Also reporting to Mr Nichols was a small dealing team led by another SWI director, Mr Eric Farrell.

Investment analysis performed by SWI was closely monitored as to the type of research conducted. At no time did the appraisal team analyse conventional blue chip stocks, but a great emphasis was placed on the identification of asset situations. Earnings were not given a very high rating. Having identified asset situations the investment group sought to build strategic stakes in them, with these holdings being divided up between the various funds managed. This was done in such a way that the size of the overall holdings was not readily identifiable.[2] Large holdings were normally purchased as blocks of shares, brought to SWS by banks, broking houses and the like, or were bought, in the market, usually through nominees. SWI adopted a policy of frequently changing its nominees to help preserve secrecy.

At the end of 1972 SWI was responsible for the management of some £30-35 million in private portfolios; some £70 million in nine separate unit trusts and, following entry into the area in 1970, some £100 million in five investment trusts. Details of the group's portfolio of unit and investment trusts are shown in Exhibits 6 and 7. SWI was also responsible for the investment of premium income received by Slater Walker Insurance, although this was mainly in non-equity securities.

The trusts managed by SWI tended to concentrate on two main types of situation. First, a number were devoted to investment in asset situation companies, and a second group invested in financially-oriented concerns, some of which were 'associates' of SWS. In addition, increased overseas activity had led to the development of two UK-based investment trusts, specialising in similar companies in the Far East and Australia. Overall, approximately one-third of funds invested were held in 'house stocks' or associates; some 50 per cent in strategic stakes and between 5 and 15 per cent in asset situations; and the balance in specialist stocks for particular funds. SWI adopted a policy of active dealing in the funds it managed, although the portfolios of investment trusts were subject to less change in order to protect their status.[3] In addition, the company dealt actively on its own account and in 1972 profits from investment dealing were £9.2 million before overhead deduction—some 45 per cent of profits from investment banking and other financial activities.

The largest investment trust managed by SWI was the split-level Dual Trust. The £15 million capital in 50p units of this trust was equally divided between income and capital shares and issued at 100p per share. All income generated from investment then went to income shareholders, while all capital appreciation went to the capital shareholders.

The launch of the Dual Trust in January 1972 provoked substantial press criticism,

---

[2] Under Section 33 of the Companies Act 1967 share stakes of more than 10 per cent of the equity in a quoted company had to be declared. Shares held by unit trust and private portfolios were not treated as part of the stake held directly by a company managing any such investments. In the case of shares held by investment trusts these were only treated as part of SWS's interest in that quoted company if SWS's holding in the investment trust exceeded 33 per cent. In 1973 Slater Walker Securities agreed to declare, in addition to its obligations under Section 33, the interest of its total funds under management in a quoted company if that interest was over 10 per cent of the issued capital of that company. This meant Slater Walker included in its wider interest the holdings by unit trusts and other fully discretionary investment clients.

[3] There were a number of significant differences between unit trusts and investment trusts, which affected investment policy. Unit trusts were open ended and were legally restricted from holding more than 10 per cent of total capital in any one company, with a further limit of no more than 5 per cent of the trust's funds in any one company. Investment trusts were closed ended and could employ up to 15 per cent of the fund in any one situation. Further, investment trusts could be geared. However, their portfolios could not be changed as frequently as unit trusts, otherwise they became reclassified and so lost their tax advantages, whereby they paid effectively $\frac{1}{2}$ the rate of capital gains tax.

because of its close linkage with SWS. The investments contained in the Dual Trust's portfolio were in the main shares, purchased from SWS, in the group's associates, and it was considered that any decline in investors' confidence in Mr Slater could seriously affect the value of the portfolio. Doubts were also raised as to the associates' ability to sustain growth under more adverse overall stockmarket conditions. Finally, there was criticism of the price paid by the trust to SWS for the shares, many of which were a narrow market. In launching the trust it was noted SWS had obtained a 2 per cent underwriting commission, an annual management fee, a profit of some £4.65 million on its holdings and increased liquidity. Mr Slater was very conscious of these criticisms and did not consider them well founded. Although the trust had not enjoyed an outstanding performance, results had been better than the average for investment trusts. Nevertheless, SWS had been forced to build up gradually its shareholding in the Dual Trust.[4]

The investment analysis undertaken by SWI was done by a team of ten to twelve analysts, divided in concentration by industry and geography. About half of the group examined investment opportunities in the United Kingdom, with the remainder concentrating on investments in Europe, South Africa, the Far East, Australasia and North America. Normally, investments were not made in any country until the group had formed a local subsidiary and the London-based analysts acted to supplement similar local efforts.

After using quick screen methods, such as a computer data bank to reject the majority of companies, a series of clearly-defined criteria were used in selecting the specific investments made. First, asset situations were identified, with large elements of cash and securities being preferred. Companies which were highly geared with little cash could still be acceptable with a high cash flow. The increased size of the group had reduced interest in small companies with less than £5 million market capitalisation and companies valued at less than £2 million were not considered. Particular attention was paid to identifying property assets, which might be undervalued. For this the investment team called on advice from Slater Walker Properties Ltd. Second, there was a requirement of accessability to the stock of the potential investment, and companies where the board had a large shareholding were generally not attractive. Third, serious consideration was given as to how quickly the potential in a situation could be achieved if an acquisition was made, and assessments were made in terms of the management/money, or both, required. Finally, clearly-defined ideas were established as to how any strategic stakes should be disposed of.

Four main methods of disposal were used. First, the group could bid themselves, although this was very unlikely in the United Kingdom, except for financial or property concerns. Second, an associate could be encouraged to make a bid, although as these companies had a free hand they might not bid as SWS hoped. Third, the stake could be sold to another bidder, as in the case of Cunard where SWS sold its stake to Trafalgar House Investments, and finally Slater Walker might hold the investment and wait. The second and third methods of disposal were most commonly used in the United Kingdom through the group's merchant banking interests, while overseas the first method was still common. Merely holding an investment was unusual and Mr Nichols commented, 'If we become involved with any company, we normally expect something to happen within two years.'

Apart from Mr Nichols, Mr Slater was kept closely informed of investment actions. He personally approved all major purchases of strategic holdings for Slater Walker Securities and its subsidiaries and handled all the disposals of these stakes, while Mr Nichols and Mr Banks made the decisions about non-group investment funds. Mr Slater received a daily report of all dealings and each week an updated listing of all investment holdings.

ENTRY INTO INSURANCE

In 1968 SWS entered the insurance market. The need originally arose to underwrite pensions for the companies within the group. Expansion and development was inevitable and the original insurance subsidiary became an autonomous insurance company within the Group soon afterwards. At this stage pension business was the primary

---

[4] In July 1973 SWS made a cash bid for the outstanding shares, offering 108½p for capital shares and 106½p for income. At the time of the bid, SWS held 23 per cent of the capital and 76.3 per cent of income shares.

function of the new company, until in late 1971 life business and general branch underwriting were added to the activities. The name of the company was then altered to Slater Walker Insurance Company Ltd (SWIC).

The three facets of the business activities were developed independently as the company continued to grow. The life department began to mature with the launching in April 1972 of the annuity income bond which, followed by two other similar bonds in late 1972 and early 1973, resulted in the considerable expansion of funds of the company from £8.5 million in December 1971 to £60 million in September 1973. SWIC also began to write conventional life business such as endowment and whole life assurances in early 1973.

Single premium contracts represented relatively low-risk business as the investment requirement could be matched by the choice of suitable investments. These investments were, therefore, principally in convertible loan stocks, which provided an interest requirement linked closely to the requirement under the policies and a maturity date equivalent to the maturity date of the liabilities under the contracts. The equity element in these convertible loan stocks provided the opportunity for profit to the company. Other favourable investments were short-term leaseholds.

The marketing of life business was conducted through established brokers and national press advertising in order to avoid the high cost of a direct-selling organization.

This was also true to an extent with pension business which was sought almost exclusively through established pensions brokers and consultants. Because of the advent of the State Reserve Pension Scheme a major breakthrough was made by SWIC in conjunction with Metropolitan Pensions Association, one of the leading firms of pension consultants, by the setting up of the centralised scheme concept, with particular suitability to members of the Chambers of Commerce. This allowed small companies which would normally be overlooked by the insurance industry to set up their own arrangements under the umbrella of a Chamber of Commerce scheme.

Because of SWIC's deposit administration method of pension scheme investment, a breakthrough of this nature had been possible. It also led to a satisfactory amount of conventional scheme business being written which was expected to continue to improve.

In November 1971 the general branch began to underwrite all classes of business other than motor insurance, with a good balance between marine, fire and accident, and treaty reinsurance. Because of good support from the major brokers in the London market the first full year of business produced an encouraging £1.7 million of premium income.

In 1973 business began to be transacted overseas. To enable the writing of American business an American Trust fund of £500,000 was established; this was later increased. From such a promising start it was anticipated that this side of the business would continue to develop.

As with other companies within the group, strict financial controls were in force requiring weekly cash reporting, a full monthly budget meeting, and an action minute system resulting from the twice-weekly management meetings. Mr Slater still took an active interest in the insurance company, as he did with all relatively new activities, and all new products developed required his personal approval before they were launched.

Mr Arthur Pierce, general manager of Slater Walker Insurance Company, said, discussing development;

> We are extremely careful in our relations with other members of the Group to avoid any conflict of interest. The main benefit of the Group from insurance is that it provides a further opportunity for us to use our investment expertise. In 1971 premium income was increased from £1.8 million to £4.2 million. In 1972, mainly as a result of single premium businss, the premium increased to £25.9 million and the total funds amounted to £40 million, and we expect this trend to continue.

In July 1971 SWS purchased the Pioneer Life Assurance Co. for £3.1 million in cash, and this was followed shortly after by the acquisition of Blackburn Assurance. These two companies both specialised in industrial life assurance, characterised by the use of salesmen/collectors and low premium per plan business. The two companies were subsequently integrated together, resulting in considerable operating savings, although for tax purposes separate identities were maintained.

In February 1970 SWS acquired the balance of the share capital not already held of Walker, Young and Company, an insurance broking group. Successful progress encouraged further expansion leading to a merger between Walker Young and Wigham-Richardson and Bevingtons, a specialist insurance and shipbroker, which left SWS with 43 per cent on the enlarged equity. However, the insurance industry was against brokers being directly linked to insurance companies and, in order to rationalise the group's insurance interests, Mr Slater sold the SWS broking interests in late 1972 to Anglo-Continental Investment and Finance Co. Ltd.

INVESTMENT IN PROPERTY

Despite the development of property valuation skills in conjunction with the search for asset situations, SWS did not invest specifically in property until after 1969. Then, in 1970 Mr Slater decided to embark on a programme of expansion in property investment, at first indirectly via shareholdings in quoted property companies, and later by direct investment.

Following the decision to increase the group's stake in property, the central property management team was built up and a new subsidiary, Slater Walker Properties (SWP), was subsequently formed. The group's interests were developed in four main ways: by investment in British property companies; by direct investment in office, industrial and residential property, both in the UK and in Europe; by direct investment in European property companies; and by joint ventures in which SWS generally took a stake of about 50 per cent.

The group developed shareholdings in a number of British property companies. During 1970 Slater Walker acquired large shareholdings in Cornwall Property (Holdings) Ltd, Thomas Stevens (Property) Ltd and Sterling Land Co. Ltd. These concerns with SWS assistance began to expand rapidly by acquisition, thereby reducing the SWS shareholding but basically still retaining their associate status. In 1972 Argyle Securities purchased a number of property interests from Cavenham in a complex deal arranged between Mr Slater and Mr James Goldsmith, the head of Cavenham. In exchange for shares SWS then sold a large part of its holdings in Argyle and Thomas Stevens to Anglo-Continental Investment and Finance Company, one of Mr Goldsmith's principal companies. At the same time, SWS acquired a 31 per cent interest in Charles Sprackley Industries Ltd, a quoted investment company engaged in shopfitting. This company was converted to a property company and in December 1972 acquired Associated Development (Holdings) Ltd. As a result, by the end of 1972, SWS held shares in four quoted property companies having a market value of approximately £12 million.

Direct investment in property commenced in 1971, with the acquisition of the Solicitors Law Stationery Society, a company specialising in legal publications and office supplies. The company also owned Oyez House, a substantial property, valued at about £10 million, in Central London. Oyez House was subsequently purchased by Slater Walker Properties. The principal business of Solicitors Law was then largely disposed of; 45 per cent of the issued capital was sold to the Thomson Organisation and a further 45 per cent was reissued by a public offer for sale. Later, in November 1971, the group purchased the site of the Westland Helicopters factory at Hayes in Middlesex, near Heathrow Airport, for £3.7 million. New direct purchases were made adding to the property portfolio in 1972; these included ownership of individual office blocks and buildings in London, Paris, Amsterdam and Brussels. Increasing emphasis was given to investments in European financial centres other than London. Some investment in residential properties was made via a subsidiary, Buckingham Properties, and Slater Walker Properties developed smaller interests in farmland and Mediterranean developments.

During 1972 SWS acquired a number of controlling shareholdings in European property companies as part of its expansion into Europe. These included a 53 per cent interest in Compagnie Financière Hausmann, a French quoted company, with a wide range of property interests, 67 per cent of the Belgian Compagnie Générale Foncière, a small quoted property company, and 54 per cent of Hellingman NV, a Dutch property company. Such companies, apart from their property interests, were also seen as suitable shell operations for future development as locally quoted national Slater Walker associates.

Management of Slater Walker Properties was the responsibility of Mr Roland Rowe, a main board director, and Mr John O'Donnell, who was appointed to the SWS board at the beginning of 1973. Property was managed in a similar way to the investment banking subsidiary, with five chartered surveyors, reporting to Mr O'Donnell, each with his own area and objectives within which he was encouraged to act as an entrepreneur.

In addition, there was a small central administrative and accounting function for the property company, and a project manager to oversee the developments of all building projects to ensure that they were brought in on time. Actual building was done by outside contractors, SWP being responsible for managing the letting of its completed properties. SWP also acted as a central agency for the group in reviewing all potential property developments and investigated the potential property assets in situations identified by the investment management team. This investigative activity was seen as an intrinsic part of the evaluation of asset situations. A substantial fund of information had been compiled on ownership, value and lease terms of many properties in Central London and major cities in Britain and Western Europe.

Mr O'Donnell stated that by the end of 1972 the SWS investment in property had become considerable and represented, in all forms, including shareholdings and future planned expenditure, some £80 million and was still climbing rapidly. Much of the future planning permission and return on investment was higher. Mr O'Donnell added, 'The whole of Western Europe is open to British property companies because property companies there have by and large almost a completely reversed gearing to that in the UK. In France, for example, a typical debt-equity ratio would be almost one to six, whereas in Britain the amount of debt would be much higher.' He also believed that, like merchant banking, property would in future be an area for spinning off new entrepreneurs, which would become associates as the industrial companies had done.

OVERSEAS EXPANSION

The group's first moves overseas were made by industrial subsidiaries in Australia and South Africa. These countries had a similar language, legal and financial framework to the United Kingdom, and initial investments were obtained as a result of acquisitions in the United Kingdom. The experience gained in developing interests in these countries led Mr Slater to expand the group's interests from 1969 onwards into Canada, Hong Kong, Singapore and Malaysia. Having developed in these countries, attention had turned to Western Europe in 1972 and in 1973 an initial entry was made in the United States.

Mr Slater remained flexible about the extent of his commitment to each overseas territory and his approach was essentially pragmatic. The essential questions he asked were, 'Can I achieve a significant presence in the area and can I get active and able men on the spot?' Only when the answers were positive did he go ahead. 'To try to invest otherwise overseas is mad, you might as well forget it.' Nevertheless, Mr Slater believed that expansion overseas represented a major area for long-term growth.

FUTURE PROSPECTS

In his speech to shareholders in 1973, Mr Slater advised them that 1972 had been a year of great progress for Slater Walker Securities. He went on

> Much of my statement this year is taken up with overseas activities, as these have become progressively more important to our business. As well as being of great benefit to shareholders, these activities make an increasing contribution to this country's real wealth and the long-term balance of payments position. Your company's consolidated balance sheet included overseas investments with a market value of £72 million and the overall market capitalisation of our overseas interests now exceeds £300 million. This position has been achieved mainly during the last three years from a very small base, and I am hopeful that progress overseas during the years ahead will continue on a significant scale.
>
> In addition to your company's strengthened asset position, there has been a considerable improvement in the quality of your company's earnings. An increasingly large proportion of your company's profit each year stems simply from the deployment of its continually increasing gross assets. Banking and investment advisory fees are now very substantial and are largely earned without the employment of capital. Your company's principal insurance subsidiary is still a young company and its contribution to future profits should be increasingly significant....
>
> ....Our commercial and investment banking, property and insurance interests have all been developed substantially, and we have achieved last year's prime objective of commencing operations in Europe. We now have significant investments in quoted companies in Belgium, France, Holland, Spain and West Germany.

Our prime objective in 1973 is to start operations in the United States of America, where we have been exploring investment opportunities for the last nine months.

Your directors are confident of future prospects and for this reason we have purchased in the open market, 33.4 per cent of the outstanding US dollar convertible bonds, £374,492 of the company's 8 per cent unsecured loan stock, with subscription rights attached and 139,805 of the 1973 warrants to subscribe for ordinary shares. These have been purchased and cancelled to avoid any further dilution of your company's equity capital so that existing ordinary shareholders will obtain the maximum benefit from the company's future growth.

Your company has never been in such a strong position. The long-term growth prospects of all facets of our business are excellent, our cash position is strong and our management team is young and able. Your board are, therefore, able to forecast with confidence, that, in the absence of unforeseen circumstances, there will continue to be a progressive increase in earnings and assets per share in the years ahead.

EXHIBIT 1 Slater Walker Securities Ltd.
Consolidated profit and loss statements 1968-72 (£000)
Year ended 31 December

	1968	1969	1970	1971	1972
Turnover	38,102	92,478	82,618	101,068	705
Expenses					
Depreciation	580	1,762	1,735	1,397	272
Loan stock interest	675	2,548	2,689	3,179	4,426
Short-term loan interest	765	1,001	1,098	1,557	1,342
Other interest	82	301	673	59	1,346
Directors' emoluments	52	84	93	103	183
Share of profit from associates	—	286	488	1,552	5,693
Dividend and interest received	642	1,385	1,718	1,821	1,785
Net profit before tax	4,868	10,442	12,161	16,285	17,592
Taxation					
Corporation tax	1,399	2,206	2,731	4,948	4,769
Overseas tax	469	1,641	1,215	748	698
Double tax relief	(125)	(75)	(65)	(37)	(69)
Net total tax	1,743	3,915	3,880	5,660	5,397
Minority interests	188	438	912	1,114	19
Profit attributable to parent co.	2,937	6,233	7,369	9,511	12,176
Preference dividend	70	172	193	193	213
Ordinary dividend	977	2,688	3,598	4,318	3,855
EPS (adjusted)	7.98p	10.85p	11.49p	14.02p	17.10p
Net equity assets per share (adjusted)	67.50p	69.26p	74.67p	99.25p	160.36p

Source: Annual Reports

EXHIBIT 2   **Slater Walker Securities Ltd.**

Consolidated Balance Sheets 1968-72 (£000)

Year ended 31 December

	1968	1969	1970	1971	1972
Current assets					
Stocks and work in progress	9,083	21,848	18,087	12,809	410
Debtors, loans and advances	50,290	61,596	74,313	101,063	137,458
Properties held for resale	—	—	—	7,987	14,020
Investments	19,230	10,700	7,318	27,204	22,295
(Market value of investments)	N.A.	N.A.	(8,013)	(38,651)	(41,956)
Bank balances and cash	3,599	18,117	23,192	39,177	133,231
	82,202	112,261	122,909	188,239	307,414
Fixed assets					
Freehold properties	10,956	17,898	15,365	23,493	48,708
Leasehold properties	1,434	1,880	2,595	3,282	4,137
Plant and machinery	4,416	10,228	11,251	5,835	1,343
Argentine subsidiary	—	4,803	—	—	—
Insurance companies at cost	400	420	1,052	14,284	14,494
Associates at valuation	—	—	1,371	22,343	72,616
Investments at cost	10,178	9,486	27,611	22,069	20,175
TOTAL ASSETS	109,586	156,975	182,153	279,545	468,888
Ordinary shares of 25p	7,684	11,332	11,998	13,093	17,673
Reserves	26,631	24,930	27,127	43,886	75,376
$5\tfrac{3}{4}\%$ Cumulative preference	1,763	3,362	3,364	3,364	3,364
Undistributed profit	2,533	5,600	8,642	12,325	20,317
	38,611	45,223	51,130	72,669	116,730
Unsecured loan stocks	24,634	31,187	33,347	45,130	55,130
Loan stocks of subsidiaries	749	3,432	3,541	6,132	47,730
Minority interests	1,716	4,945	7,955	11,577	5,841
Corporation tax and deferred tax	1,533	2,635	1,419	4,012	6,216
Current liabilities					
Creditors, deposits and short-term loans	34,564	56,102	71,979	124,722	216,750
Current tax	2,260	4,618	3,824	1,567	2,108
Bank overdrafts	4,828	6,708	6,799	11,118	14,468
Proposed dividend	692	2,125	2,159	2,619	3,883
	42,343	69,553	84,760	140,026	237,209
TOTAL LIABILITIES	109,586	156,975	182,153	279,545	468,888

Source: Annual Reports

Note: The 1968 figures shown here are taken from the comparative figures in the 1969 Annual Report and Accounts.

EXHIBIT 3 Slater Walker Group Organisation Chart, 1 January 1973 (simplified)

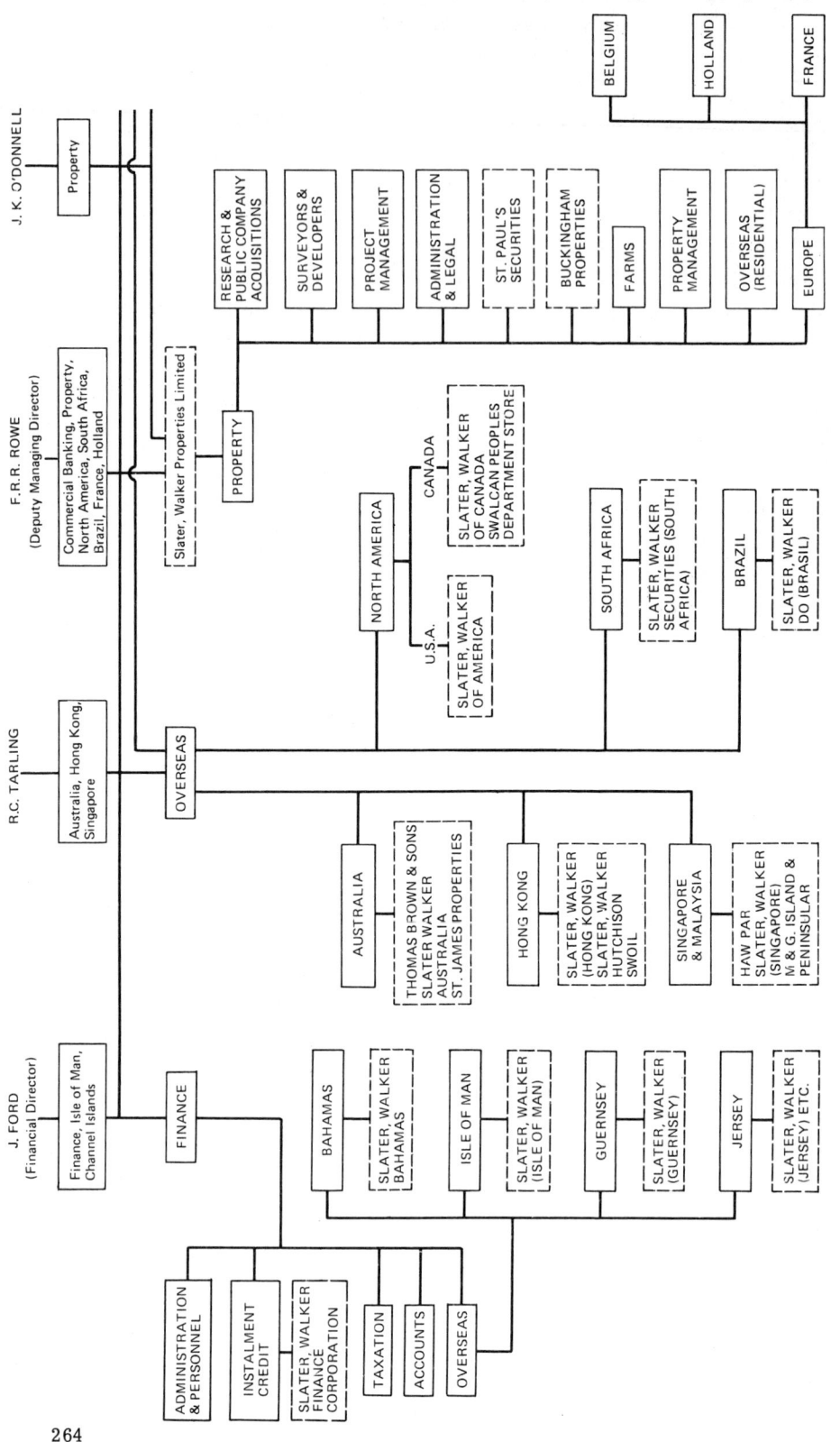

Organizational Chart

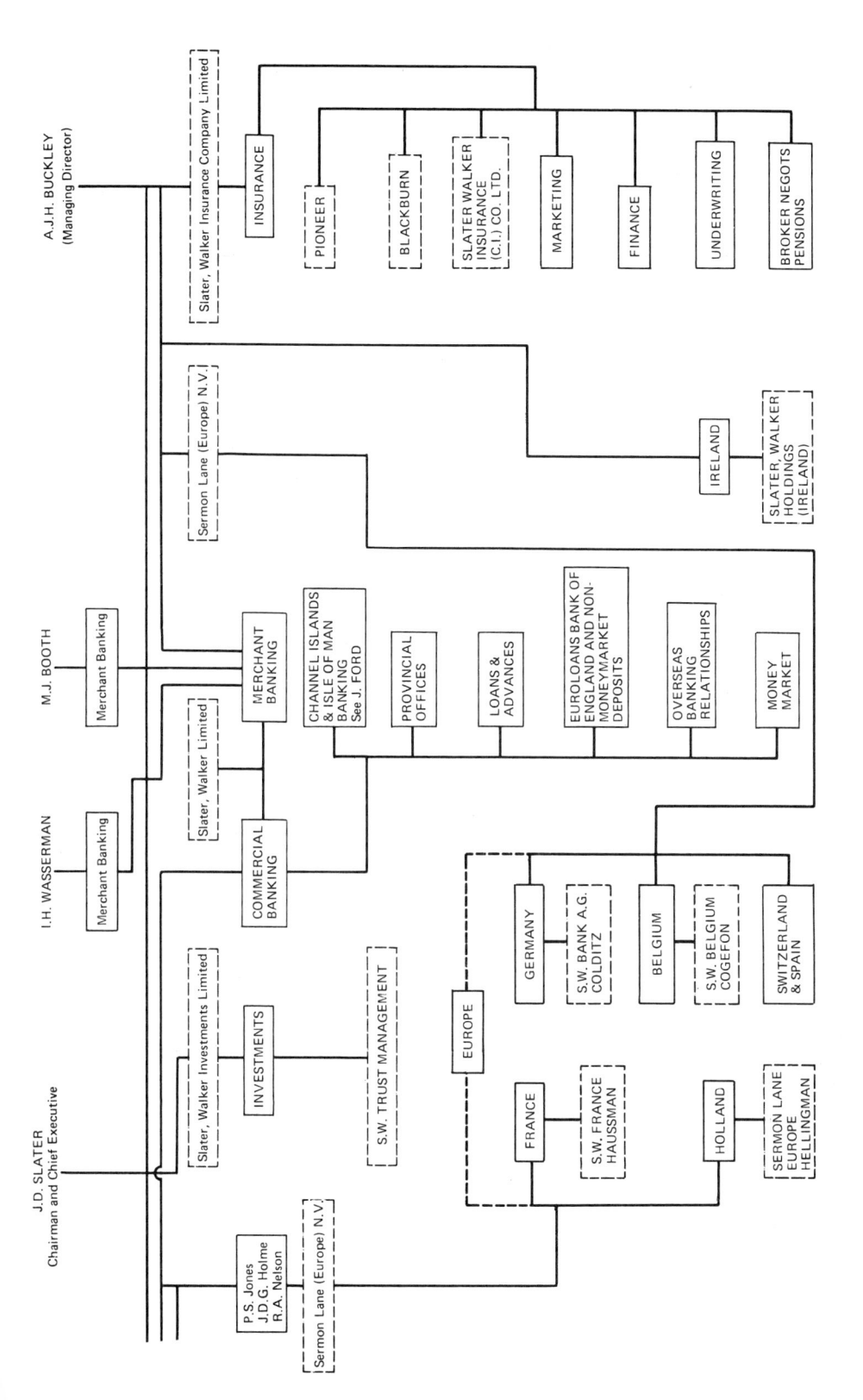

J.D. SLATER — Chairman and Chief Executive
I.H. WASSERMAN
M.J. BOOTH
A.J.H. BUCKLEY (Managing Director)

Under J.D. Slater

- P.S. Jones, J.D.G. Holme, R.A. Nelson
  - Sermon Lane (Europe) N.V.
- Slater, Walker Investments Limited
  - **INVESTMENTS**
    - S.W. Trust Management

Under I.H. Wasserman

- Merchant Banking
- Slater, Walker Limited
  - **COMMERCIAL BANKING**

Under M.J. Booth

- Merchant Banking
- **MERCHANT BANKING**
  - Channel Islands & Isle of Man Banking — See J. Ford
  - Provincial Offices
  - Loans & Advances
  - Euroloans Bank of England and Non-Moneymarket Deposits
  - Overseas Banking Relationships
  - Money Market
  - **EUROPE**
    - France
      - S.W. France Haussman
    - Germany
      - S.W. Bank A.G. Colditz
    - Belgium
      - S.W. Belgium Cogefon
    - Switzerland & Spain
    - Holland
      - Sermon Lane Europe Hellingman
  - Ireland
    - Slater, Walker Holdings (Ireland)
- Sermon Lane (Europe) N.V.

Under A.J.H. Buckley

- Slater, Walker Insurance Company Limited
  - **INSURANCE**
    - Pioneer
    - Blackburn
    - Slater Walker Insurance (C.I.) Co. Ltd.
    - Marketing
    - Finance
    - Underwriting
    - Broker Negots Pensions

265

EXHIBIT 4   Slater Walker Securities Ltd.

Analysis of turnover and profit before tax (£000)

	1972 Profits	1972 Turnover	1971 Profits	1971 Turnover	1970 Profits	1970 Turnover
Investment banking and other financial	15,604*		12,497		7,320	
Insurance	559		823		225	
Investment trusts	1,432		—		—	
Property	1,427		—		—	
Commercial and industrial activities:						
Rubber and plastics products	—	—	851	13,050	1,568	23,446
Textiles	158	—	369	9,917	425	15,122
Engineering and metal windows	1,791	—	2,629	31,107	2,101	30,708
Tanning extract	434	—	761	3,900	1,686	9,024
Optical services	—	—	112	801	689	3,485
Printing and stationery	721	—	361	3,570	—	—
Wholesale tobacconists	279	—	482	38,700	—	—
Other	387	705	(28)	23	36	783
		705		101,068		82,618
Less Expenses of holding co.	(5,200)		(2,572)		(1,889)	
	17,592		16,285		12,161	
Geographic analysis of profits:						
UK and Channel Islands	12,114		11,891		7,405	
Australia	489		650		353	
Africa	1,744		2,462		2,167	
Europe	290		—		—	
Hong Kong	2,118		—		—	
North America	837		1,280		1,481	
Other countries	—		2		755	
	17,592		16,285		12,161	

*In 1973, in a letter to shareholders, Mr Slater gave further details of the breakdown of profits from investment banking and corporate finance, as follows:

	£000
Corporate finance and investment management	5,443
Underwriting fees	1,924
Commercial banking	3,808
Investment dealing	9,205
Investment income	1,665
Instalment credit	275
Investment banking profit of associates	959
	23,279
Less overhead expenses	2,290
	20,989
Less transfer to inner reserve	5,385
	15,604

Source: Annual Reports

EXHIBIT 5 **Slater Walker Securities Ltd.**
Associated companies Dec 1972

Company	Activities	% of Ordinary share capital held by Group
Crittal-Hope Engineering Limited	Industrial holding company	47.9
Slater Walker Australia Limited (Incorporated in New South Wales)	Investment banking	34.4
Slater, Walker of Canada (Incorporated in Canada)	Investment banking	43.0
Slater, Walker Dual Trust Limited	Investment trust	49.6
Slater, Walker Investment Trust Limited	Investment trust	32.6
Slater, Walker Overseas Investments Limited (Incorporated in Hong Kong)	Investment company	35.0
Slater, Walker Securities (South Africa) Limited (Incorporated in the Republic of South Africa)	Investment banking	36.8
The Solicitor's Law Stationery Society, Limited	Printing and Stationery	25.0

Notes:

1. These were the principal associated companies, in which the Group held more than 20% of the ordinary share capital. The Directors have omitted details of other associated companies, as they consider that the list would otherwise be of excessive length.

2. Unless otherwise stated, the companies listed are all incorporated in Great Britain and registered in England.

3. The above percentages include certain holdings classified as current assets which have not been treated as associated companies for accounting purposes.

Investments in other companies

Company	Activities	%
Cranleigh Group Limited	Coach body builders and engineers	10.0
Haw Par Brothers International Limited (Incorporated in Singapore)	Investment banking	19.1
James Finlay & Company Limited (Registered in Scotland)	Trading and investment company	15.0
Marcroft & Company Limited	Rolling stock repair and general engineering	17.8
New Bridge Holdings Limited (Incorporated in the Republic of Ireland)	Investment trust	20.8
Schubert & Salzer Maschinenfabrik A.G. (Incorporated in the Federal Republic of Germany)	Textile machinery manufacturing	32.2
Southern Pacific Properties Limited (Incorporated in Hong Kong)	Pacific hotels and property development	13.0
Sterling Land Company Limited	Property investment and development	20.1
Whinsparken Investments Limited	Investment trust	25.0

Notes:

1. These were the principal companies in which the Group held 10% or more of the ordinary share capital. The Directors have omitted details of smaller investments, as they consider that the list would otherwise be of excessive length.

2. Unless otherwise stated, the companies listed are all incorporated in Great Britain and registered in England.

Source: Annual Report

EXHIBIT 6 Slater Walker Investments Ltd.   Unit trusts managed

Trust	GROWTH	CAPITAL ACCUMULATOR	HIGH INCOME	ASSETS	FINANCIAL	PROFESSIONAL	STATUS CHANGE	SLATER, WALKER GROWTH INVESTORS TRUST	SLATER, WALKER INTERNATIONAL (unadjusted)
Investment objective	L.T. capital growth	L.T. capital growth with income reinvested	Above average income with some capital growth	Investment in assets situations	Investment in UK overseas financial institutions	For large investors aiming solely for capital growth	Specialised in low P/E stocks ripe for improvements		
Commencement date	30 June 1967	24 Feb 1969	5 Aug 1969	28 Sep 1970	28 July 1971	12 June 1972	27 Nov 1972	4 April 1971	1 May 1969
Initial offer price	25p	25p	25p	25p	25p	500p	25p	113.5p	4.09 (81/9)
Capital performance (adjusted for sub-divisions)	Offer price (p) High Low	Offer price (p) High Low	Offer price (p) High Low	Offer price (p) High Low	Offer price (p) High Low	Offer price (p) High Low	Offer price (p) High Low	High Low	High Low
1967	33.9 25.0								
1968	50.4 33.9								
1969	51.5 34.2	25.0 20.8	28.5 25.0						96/- 78/6
1970	44.4 31.3	25.8 19.0	35.0 28.3	25.6 24.0					101/9 71/1
1971	54.6 36.2	32.7 21.6	53.8 33.3	43.4 25.0	29.2 25.0			184.1 113.5	5.21 3.29
1972	69.2 55.0	40.5 32.9	65.0 54.3	55.3 43.7	40.0 29.3	566.9 500.0	25.2 24.3	255.1 184.6	7.95 5.35
*1973	65.9 57.8	38.6 34.2	63.3 56.7	54.7 48.1	40.4 34.6	562.8 468.8	26.3 23.7	250.2 222.3	80.4 74.0
Estimated Gross Yield at 30.6.73	£2.40%	£2.30%	£5.26%	£2.96%	£2.00%	£2.80%	£4.00%	£1.50%	£1.40%
Offer price at 30.6.73	62.1p	36.0p	59.4p	51.6p	36.7p	479.3p	25.3p	222.3	75.7
Trust performance from launch to 30.6.73	+148.4%	+44.0%	+137.6%	+106.4%	+46.8%	-4.2%	+1.2%	+95.8%	+85.1%
F.T.—Actuaries All-Share Index from Trust launch 30.6.73	+80.6%	+15.5%	+42.3%	+38.7%	+7.0%	-9.5%	-12.8%	+34.1%	+23.3%
Management charge	Initial 3¾% Annual ½%	Initial 5% Annual 3/8%	Initial 5% Annual 3/8%	Initial 5% Annual 3/8%	Initial 5% Annual 3/8%	Initial 1% Annual ½%	Initial 5% Annual 3/8%	Initial 1% Annual 1/8% of Fund +1/8% 1% of UC*	Initial 1% Annual 1/8% of Fund +1/8% of 1% of UC*
Minimum initial investment (Units)	400	700	400	500	700	1,000	1,000	100	300

Source: Company Records

EXHIBIT 7   Slater Walker Investments Limited.   **Investment Trusts managed**

Investment Trust	Size £m. (including gearing)	Specialisation	Gearing factor	Asset value per share % rise or fall Accounting year ended in 1972	1973
SW Investment Trust	38.5	100% UK equities	33	38.5	0.9
SW Dual Trust	30	100% UK equities (split level trust)	102	—	12.6
SW Australia	6	100% Australian equities	nil	—	19.85
SW Far Eastern	6	100% Far East equities	nil	—	4.55
Whinsparken	2	Small cos with market capitalisation less than £10 m.	nil	—	(7.5)

Source: Company records